ALL THE KREMLIN'S MEN

ALL THE KREMLIN'S MEN

INSIDE THE COURT OF VLADIMIR PUTIN

MIKHAIL ZYGAR

PublicAffairs
New York

Published in the United States by PublicAffairs™, an imprint of Perseus Books, a division of PBG Publishing, LLC, a subsidiary of Hachette Book Group, Inc.

Printed in the United States of America.

PublicAffairs books are available at special discounts for bulk purchases in the U.S. by corporations, institutions, and other organizations. For more information, please contact the Special Markets Department at the Perseus Books Group, 2300 Chestnut Street, Suite 200, Philadelphia, PA 19103, call (800) 810-4145, ext. 5000, or e-mail special.markets@perseusbooks.com.

Book Design by Jeff Williams

The interpreter is Thomas Hodson and the editor of the Russian text is Karen Shainyan.

Library of Congress Cataloging-in-Publication Data

Names: Zygar, Mikhail, 1981– author, interviewer.
Title: All the Kremlin's men : inside the court of Vladimir Putin / Mikhail Zygar.
Description: New York, NY: PublicAffairs, 2016. | Includes bibliographical references and index. | Translated from Russian; no information is available about the translator.
Identifiers: LCCN 2016018443 (print) | LCCN 2016021716 (ebook) | ISBN 9781610397391 (hardback) | ISBN 9781610397407 (ebook)
Subjects: LCSH: Russia (Federation) —Politics and government—1991– | Russia (Federation) —History—1991– | Russia (Federation) —Biography—Interviews. | Putin, Vladimir Vladimirovich, 1952-
Classification: LCC DK510.763 .Z9413 2016 (print) | LCC DK510.763 (ebook) | DDC 947.086/20922—dc23
LC record available at https://lccn.loc.gov/2016018443

First Edition

10 9 8 7 6 5 4 3 2 1

CONTENTS

PART THREE: PRINCE DMITRY

PART FOUR: PUTIN THE TERRIBLE

LIST OF CHARACTERS

Abramovich, Roman. Russian business tycoon and owner of the Chelsea Football Club; made his fortune in a series of controversial oil export deals in the early 1990s when he was close to Boris Yeltsin; teamed up with the former billionaire Boris Berezovsky to take over Sibneft at a fraction of its market value; became the governor of the isolated Siberian region of Chukotka, then head of its parliament before his permanent relocation to London.

Akhmetov, Rinat. Ukrainian steel and iron ore magnate; used to be the most influential business figure in Donbass (eastern Ukraine); was the main sponsor of Viktor Yanukovych's presidential campaigns of 2004 and 2010.

Aksyonov, Sergey. Prime minister of the Republic of Crimea; organized the annexation of Crimea by Russia.

Alekperov, Vagit. One of Russia's oligarchs; owner of the oil company Lukoil.

Alexis II. Patriarch of Moscow and All Russia from 1990 until his death in 2008; alleged to have been a KGB agent.

Aven, Pyotr. Head of Alfa Banking Group, which owns Russia's largest private bank, Alfa Bank; minister of international economic relations in the early 1990s; first oligarch to make friends with Vladimir Putin and introduced him to Boris Berezovsky and many other influential figures.

Azarov, Mykola. As Ukrainian prime minister 2010–2014, suspended the preparation for negotiating Ukraine–European Union Association Agreement, which triggered civil unrest; resigned amid widespread riots and found political asylum in Russia.

Bagapsh, Sergei. President of Abkhazia from 2005 until his death in 2011; during his tenure, Russia recognized the independence of Abkhazia.

Bastrykin, Alexander. Was in Vladimir Putin's cohort at St. Petersburg State University; in 2011 named head of the Investigative Committee of Russia, which is answerable to the president of Russia and responsible for conducting investigations into local authorities and federal governmental bodies; in 2012 was alleged by anti-corruption activist Alexei Navalny of having business interests and residency in the Czech Republic.

Baturina, Yelena. The wife of Moscow's former mayor Yury Luzhkov (1992–2010); now Russia's wealthiest woman owing to the sale of her main asset, construction company Inteko, in 2011.

Belaventsev, Oleg. A close friend of Sergey Shoigu, defense minister of Russia; in charge of the operation of the annexation of Crimea; after annexation, was appointed presidential envoy of the Crimean Federal District.

Boris Berezovsky. In 1999 played a key part in promoting Vladimir Putin as Boris Yeltsin's successor and helped fund the Unity bloc; in 2000 moved from Russia to the UK and was granted political asylum in 2003; in 2012 lost the case he brought over the ownership of Sibneft against Roman Abramovich, in which he sought more than £3 billion in damages; mysteriously died in 2013 in the UK.

Borodai, Alexander. Prime minister of the self-proclaimed Donetsk People's Republic, May–August 2014; previously worked as a political adviser to Sergey Aksyonov, prime minister of the Republic of Crimea.

Bortnikov, Alexander. Director of the Federal Security Service of the Russian Federation since 2008; subject of sanctions by the EU and Canada (but not the United States) in 2014.

Chaika, Yuri. Minister of justice, 1999–2006; then effectively swapped posts with his predecessor Vladimir Ustinov and since has been prosecutor general of the Russian Federation; subject of 2015 investigation by Alexey Navalny's Anti-Corruption Foundation.

Chemezov, Sergei. CEO of Rostec, a Russian state corporation established in late 2007 to promote development, production, and export of high-tech industrial products for civil and defense sectors; old friend of Vladimir Putin's; in 2014 sanctioned by the EU and the United States.

Cherkesov, Viktor. Former KGB officer; first deputy director of the FSB under Vladimir Putin and Nikolay Patrushev; headed the Federal Service for the Control of the Circulation of Narcotic and Psychotropic Substances, 2003–2008; in 2007 publicly remarked on conflict between the Russian security agencies; in 2010 was excluded from Putin's group of high-ranking officials.

Chubais, Anatoly. Head of the Russian Nanotechnology Corporation, RUSNANO; as an influential member of Boris Yeltsin's administration in the 1990s, responsible for privatization in Russia and a key figure in introducing market economy and the principles of private ownership after the fall of the Soviet Union.

Churov, Vladimir. Chairman of the Central Election Commission of Russia, 2007–2016; known for the expression "Churov's rule #1 is 'Putin is always right'"; blamed for election fraud during the protest rallies of 2011 and 2012.

Delimkhanov, Adam. Chechen politician; close associate and cousin of the Chechen leader Ramzan Kadyrov; repeatedly accused of involvement in high-profile crimes; member of the Russian State Duma for the United Russia party since 2007.

Deripaska, Oleg. Owner of one of the largest Russian industrial groups, Basic Element, and president of En+ Group and United Company RUSAL, the largest aluminum company in the world; in 2001 married into the family of former Russian president Boris Yeltsin.

Dvorkovich, Arkady. Close aide to Dmitry Medvedev; strong supporter of liberalism; chief lobbyist for Russia's WTO accession campaign, an increase in the retirement age, and the rapid privatization of remaining state-owned assets.

Dyachenko (Yumasheva), Tatyana "Tanya" Borisovna. Younger daughter of former Russian president Boris Yeltsin; with Alexander Voloshin and Valentin Yumashev, part of a small group of his advisers known as "The Family."

Ernst, Konstantin. General director of the most popular Russian TV channel, ORT (before 2005), and then First Channel; helped to get the channel under state control in 2000; in charge of the opening and closing ceremonies at the Sochi Olympics; sanctioned by Ukraine in 2016 as one of the masterminds of Russian propaganda.

Firtash, Dmitry. Ukrainian investor and businessman; former key figure in the gas trade between Russia and Ukraine; arrested in Austria in 2014 on bribery and other charges at the request of American law enforcement agencies (actions Firtash identifies as politically motivated); supposedly connected to mafia boss Semyon Mogilevich.

Fradkov, Mikhail. Prime minister of Russia, 2004–2007; suspected of being part of "Gang of Four"; since 2007 head of Russian Foreign Intelligence Service.

Fridman, Mikhail. Russian oligarch; founder of Alfa Group; formerly co-owner of TNK-BP oil company before selling his share to state-owned Rosneft.

Fyodorov, Yevgeny. Hard-line lawmaker with the United Russia party; supporter of sanctions against Russia and an advocate of conspiracy theories; wants to redraft the Russian constitution and establish a ruling national ideology.

Gerashchenko, Viktor. Chairman of the Soviet and then Russian central bank; after Khodorkovsky's arrest in 2003, became Yukos CEO and was the last to hold that post.

Girkin, Igor (later Strelkov). Key figure in Russian occupation of Crimea and the war in Donbass; charged by the Ukrainian authorities with terrorism and sanctioned by the EU; now being sued by the families of passengers killed when Malaysia Airlines Flight 17 was shot down, allegedly by forces under his control.

Glazyev, Sergey. Russian minister of external economic relations in 1992–1993; currently adviser to Vladimir Putin on regional economic integration; in 2014 claimed the new president of Ukraine, Petro Poroshenko, was illegitimately elected; became one of the first people sanctioned by the United States.

Golodets, Olga. Deputy prime minister of the Russian Federation in charge of social affairs and policies; allegedly has a commercial connection to businessman turned politician Mikhail Prokhorov, who recommended her for the post.

Gorbenko, Alexander. Vice mayor of Moscow; since 2011 in charge of giving permits for the rallies and civil protests in Moscow.

Gref, German. One of the main liberal reformers in Vladimir Putin's government of the mid-2000s; major advocate of Russia's joining the World Trade Organization; responsible for creation of the Stabilization Fund in 2004; currently CEO of Sberbank, Russian banking and financial services company.

Gryzlov, Boris. Interior minister of Russia, 2001–2003; former leader of the United Russia party; classmate of former FSB chief Nikolay Patrushev.

Gusinsky, Vladimir "Goosy." Russian media tycoon and former owner of NTV, whose holdings were taken over by Gazprom; in 2000 was accused of money laundering and moved to Spain.

Illarionov, Andrei. Economic policy adviser to the president of Russia, 2000–2005; later became a vocal critic of Vladimir Putin and his policies.

Ivanov, Igor. Russian foreign minister, 1998–2004; played a key role in mediating the deal between Georgian president Eduard Shevardnadze and opposition parties during Georgia's 2003 Rose Revolution.

Ivanov, Sergei. Former KGB agent; longtime friend of Vladimir Putin; minister of defense, 2001–2007; considered to be one of the possible successors of Vladimir Putin in 2007 but was passed over for Dmitry Medvedev; currently Kremlin chief of staff; sanctioned by the United States.

Ivanov, Viktor. Former KGB agent; longtime friend of Vladimir Putin; headed the Federal Drug Control Service of Russia, 2008–2016; currently sanctioned by the United States.

Kadyrov, Akhmad. Chief mufti of the Chechen Republic of Ichkeria in the 1990s; at the outbreak of the Second Chechen War offered his services to the Russian government; became head of the pro-Moscow Chechen Republic administration in 2003; died in a terrorist attack in 2004.

Kadyrov, Ramzan. Son of Akhmad Kadyrov; head of the Chechen Republic since 2007; heavily criticized by international press due to alleged human rights violations, corruption, theft of public funds, and protection of criminals of Chechen origin; according to independent media investigations Kadyrov was involved in number of political assassinations, including of journalist Anna Politkovskaya and opposition leader Boris Nemtsov.

Kasyanov, Mikhail. Prime minister of Russia, 2000–2004; currently leader of the liberal People's Freedom Party, PARNAS, and one of the Kremlin's most ardent critics.

Khodorkovsky, Mikhail. CEO of Yukos, 1997–2004; in the early 2000s funded opposition parties and became an outspoken critic of the Putin regime; in 2003 was charged with fraud and tax evasion and sentenced to imprisonment; pardoned in 2013, after which he left Russia and launched the Open Russia movement to advocate democracy and human rights.

Kirill. Patriarch of Moscow and All Russia; accused of money laundering and serving as a KGB agent.

Klintsevich, Franz. Russian politician and member of United Russia Party; one of the key figures in the annexation of Crimea.

Konstantinov, Vladimir. Chairman of the Supreme Council in the Autonomous Republic of Crimea, 2010–2014; one of the organizers of the annexation of Crimea; currently sanctioned by the EU.

Kovalchuk, Yuri. Vladimir Putin's "personal banker"; largest shareholder of Rossiya Bank; one of the founders of National Media Group; owns stakes in six federal TV channels; sanctioned by the United States.

Kuchma, Leonid. Ukrainian prime minister, 1992–1993; second president of independent Ukraine, 1994–2005; presidency was surrounded by numerous corruption scandals and the lessening of media freedoms; strong ally of Vladimir Putin; selected Viktor Yanukovych as his successor but surrendered to Orange Revolution in 2004.

Kudrin, Alexei. Longtime friend of Vladimir Putin; Russian finance minister, 2000–2011; widely credited with prudent fiscal management, commitment to tax and budget reform, and championing the free market; under his tenure, Russia paid most of its substantial foreign debt; considered to be the creator of the Russian Stabilization Fund, which saved Russia from the 2008 economic crisis.

Lavrov, Sergei. Foreign minister of Russia since 2004; thought to be loyal civil servant but without any real influence on Russia's foreign policy.

Lesin, Mikhail. Media executive and adviser to Vladimir Putin, 2004–2009; minister of press, broadcasting, and mass communications of the Russian Federation, 1999–2004; co-founder of Russia Today; head of Gazprom Media, 2013–2015; laid the foundations for Kremlin's gradual takeover of independent Russian media; died mysteriously in 2015.

Lukashenko, Alexander. President of Belarus since 1994; referred to as Europe's last dictator, as he controls all branches of government and censors the press; sanctioned by European Union and the United States for alleged human rights violations.

Lukin, Vladimir. Human rights commissioner, 2004–2014; in 2014 was sent to Kiev as a mediator of talks between warring parties in Ukraine; refused to sign a peace treaty between Yanukovych and his opposition.

Luzhkov, Yuri. Mayor of Moscow, 1992–2010; dismissed by President Dmitry Medvedev for "loss of trust"; criticized for massive corruption (including giving preferential deals to the construction company of his wife, Yelena Baturina, who became a billionaire during her husband's mayorship), for bad taste in art, for traffic problems in Moscow, and for suppression of opposition protests.

Malofeev, Konstantin. Russian Orthodox billionaire; key figure linking the pro-Russia forces on the ground in Ukraine and the political establishment in Moscow during the Ukrainian crisis; closely linked to Russian separatists in eastern Ukraine and Crimea, particularly Alexander Borodai and Igor Girkin, who previously were his employees.

Mamut, Alexander. Russian billionaire entrepreneur and investor known in the late 1990s as the "Yeltsin family banker"; currently CEO of Rambler & Co.; owns the British bookstore chain Waterstone's.

Markin, Vladimir. Press secretary for the Russian Investigative Committee; known for his sensational statements and attacks on prominent figures.

Matviyenko, Valentina. Governor of St. Petersburg, 2003–2011; currently chairman of the Federation Council (the upper chamber of the Russian parliament); sanctioned by the United States, Canada, the European Union, Switzerland, and Australia.

Medvedchuk, Viktor. Ukrainian politician; chairman of the pro-Russian political organization Ukrainian Choice, which speaks against Ukraine joining the European Union; daughter Darina is Vladimir Putin's godchild.

Medvedev, Dmitry. Prime minister of Russia; handpicked as Putin's successor as president of Russia, 2008–2012.

Miller, Alexei. CEO of Gazprom; longtime colleague of Vladimir Putin.

Mironov, Sergei. Russian politician; leader of A Just Russia faction in the Parliament of Russia; chairman of the Federation Council (the upper chamber of the Russian parliament), 2001–2011; puppet quasi-opposition candidate in the 2004 and 2012 presidential elections; sanctioned because of his involvement in the 2014 Crimean crisis.

Mogilevich, Semyon. Organized crime boss, believed to be the "boss of bosses" of most Russian mafia syndicates worldwide; used to control extensive natural gas pipelines in Russia and Eastern Europe; may have a working relationship with Vladimir Putin.

Naryshkin, Sergei. Head of Kremlin administration, 2008–2011; chairman of the State Duma since 2011; sanctioned in 2014 after the annexation of Crimea.

Navalny, Alexei. Russian opposition politician; founder of the Anti-Corruption Foundation, which investigates corruption in the Russian government; gained international publicity as a critic of corruption and of Vladimir Putin; currently serving two suspended sentences following convictions on theft and embezzlement charges (considered to be retribution for his opposition activities).

Navka, Tatyana. Russian former Olympic ice skater; wife of Dmitry Peskov, the presidential press secretary; according to the Panama Papers, Navka was the registered beneficial owner of Carina Global Assets, Ltd., an offshore company in the British Virgin Islands.

Nemtsov, Boris. Prominent Russian politician and statesman and outspoken critic of Vladimir Putin; one of his last works was a report on the involvement of Russian military in the Ukrainian crisis (which the Kremlin was denying); assassinated in early 2015, allegedly by people with ties to Ramzan Kadyrov's inner circle.

Patarkatsishvili, Badri. Georgian businessman and politician; former business partner of Boris Berezovsky; made a fortune from the privatization of state-owned industries during the Yeltsin era and was the founder, together with Boris Berezovsky, of Sibneft, Rusal, Avtovaz, ORT, and many others; died in 2008.

Patrushev, Nikolai. Former director of the FSB; currently secretary of the Security Council of Russia; one of the key masterminds of Russian foreign policy; according to Robert Owen, a retired high court judge in Britain, probably approved with Putin the assassination of Alexander Litvinenko.

Pavlovsky, Gleb. Russian political scientist and spin doctor; political strategist of the election campaigns of Boris Yeltsin (1996), Vladimir Putin (2000, 2004), and United Russia (2003); an adviser to the Presidential Administration of Russia until being fired in 2011.

Peskov, Dmitry. President Vladimir Putin's spokesperson; at his wedding to Tatiana Navka (who allegedly owned the offshore company Carina Global Assets Ltd.), was photographed wearing a Swiss watch worth £400,000, almost four times his Kremlin salary.

Poltavchenko, Georgy. Longtime friend of Vladimir Putin and currently governor of St. Petersburg; in 2012 Poltavchenko signed a controversial law that prohibited advocacy of homosexual and pedophilic activities in the city.

Poroshenko, Petro. President of Ukraine since 2014; prominent oligarch who owns a confectionery company, Roshen, and a TV channel, 5 Kanal; has vast connections with Russian business and is mentioned in Panama Papers investigation.

Potanin, Vladimir. Russian billionaire entrepreneur; founder of Interros, which owns 30 percent of Russian nickel giant Norilsk Nickel, one of the sponsors of the Sochi Winter Olympics; former business partner of Mikhail Prokhorov; in 1990s was vice prime minister of Russia and allegedly invented loans-for-shares scheme.

Primakov, Yevgeny. Russian minister of foreign affairs, 1996–1998; Russian prime minister, 1998–1999; leading contender to succeed Boris Yeltsin as Russian president in 1999 but decided not to run after a huge smear campaign launched by the Kremlin.

Prokhorov, Mikhail. Russian billionaire and politician; owner of the ONEXIM Group and the Brooklyn Nets; in 2012 entered the presidential race against Vladimir Putin, gaining 7.94 percent with his own political party, but left politics the next year.

Pugachev, Sergei. Businessman, public figure, and politician; longtime friend of Vladimir Putin; accused by Kremlin of siphoning off millions of dollars from loans given by Russia's central bank in 2008 to Mezhprombank, co-founded by Pugachev in the 1990s; in 2016 sentenced in absentia to two years in prison by the high court in London; lives in France.

Putina, Lyudmila. Former wife of Vladimir Putin; after remarrying, changed her surname to Ocheretnaya.

Resin, Vladimir. Deputy of the State Duma of the Russian Federation; adviser to Patriarch Kirill of Moscow on construction; served as the first deputy mayor of Moscow under Yuri Luzhkov and acting mayor after Luzhkov's dismissal in 2010.

Roldugin, Sergey. Russian cellist and businessman; longtime friend of Vladimir Putin since the late 1970s and a godfather to his daughter Maria; according to the Panama Papers, was personally making £6.5 million a year and had almost £19 million in cash from his secret stake in Video International; five offshore companies linked to Roldugin are connected with Bank Rossiya.

Rotenberg, Arkady. Influential Russian businessman; co-owner (with his brother Boris Rotenberg) of the SGM Group and SMP Bank; in 2015 companies he controlled received numerous state contracts, including one for construction of a Siberian pipeline for Gazprom; close friend of Vladimir Putin and at one time his judo sparring partner.

Rotenberg, Boris. Influential Russian businessman; co-owner (with his brother Arkady Rotenberg) of the SGM Group and SMP Bank; awarded billions of dollars in contracts with oil and gas giant Gazprom and for the Sochi Winter Olympics by Putin; close friend of Vladimir Putin and at one time was his judo sparring partner.

Rushailo, Vladimir. Interior minister, 1999–2001; in 1999 ran military operations of federal troops against armed gangs in Chechnya and Dagestan.

Sechin, Igor. CEO of Rosneft, Russian state-owned oil giant; longtime aide of Vladimir Putin; considered to be leader of the Kremlin's *siloviki*; considered to be the second most powerful person in Russia.

Serdyukov, Anatoly. Russian politician and former defense minister; dismissed in 2012 after investigations into suspected fraud involving sale of Defense Ministry property to insiders, but was granted amnesty.

Shevkunov, Tikhon. Hierarch of Russian Orthodox Church; writer; rumored to be Vladimir Putin's personal confessor.

Shoigu, Sergei. Minister of defense since 2012; former minister of emergency situations, 1991–2012; member of Putin's inner circle; in 2014 accused by Ukraine of forming "illegal military groups" in eastern Ukraine.

Shuvalov, Igor. First deputy prime minister of Russia since 2008; one of Vladimir Putin's economic aides; currently coordinates preparations for the 2018 World Cup.

Siluanov, Anton. Finance minister of the Russian Federation since 2011; loyal to his predecessor Alexei Kudrin.

Sobchak, Anatoly. First democratically elected mayor of St. Petersburg, 1991–1996; co-author of the constitution of the Russian Federation; mentor and teacher to both Vladimir Putin and Dmitry Medvedev; active supporter of Putin during his presidential race.

Sobyanin, Sergei. Mayor of Moscow since 2010; former chief of Kremlin administration.

Strzhalkovsky, Vladimir. Former CEO of Norilsk Nickel, 2008–2012; former vice chairman of the board of directors of the Bank of Cyprus; Vladimir Putin's colleague in the St. Petersburg KGB.

Surkov, Vladislav. Russian businessman and politician of Chechen descent; personal adviser to Vladimir Putin on relationships with Abkhazia, South Ossetia, and Ukraine; considered to be the main architect of "managed democracy" and "gray cardinal" of Russian politics, 2003–2011.

Timakova, Natalya. Russian journalist and spokesperson for Russian prime minister Dmitry Medvedev.

Timchenko, Gennady. Russian billionaire; founder and owner of Volga Group, the major shareholder in the gas company Novatek; member of Putin's inner circle; co-founder of Gunvor Group (a corporation registered in Cyprus), but sold his stake a day before he was sanctioned by the United States after Russia's annexation of Crimea.

Udaltsov, Sergei. Russian political activist; leader of the Left Front movement; one of the leaders of the 2011–2013 protest movement; defendant in the Bolotnaya case and in 2014 was sentenced to four to five years in a penal camp.

Ulyukayev, Alexei. Minister of economic development of the Russian Federation since 2013; deputy chairman of Russia's central bank, 2004–2013; according to the Panama Papers, his son, Dmitry, was the head of the offshore company Ronnieville, Ltd., which later handed over power to Yulia Khryapina, believed to be Ulyukaev's wife.

Ustinov, Vladimir. Plenipotentiary envoy to the Southern Federal District; prosecutor general of Russia, 2000–2006; minister of justice, 2006–2008, during which period the highest-profile cases were criminal investigations into terrorism in the North Caucasus and into the businesses of those who showed disloyalty to the authorities.

Volodin, Vyacheslav. First deputy chief of staff of the Presidential Administration since 2011; widely considered one of the country's most influential policy architects and the person behind Vladimir Putin's presidential election campaign.

Voloshin, Alexander. Russian politician; chief of Presidential Administration, 1999–2003, and core member of Putin's team; main political strategist of Putin's first term; chairman of the board of directors of RAO (1998–2008), MMC Norilsk Nickel (2008–2010), and Uralkali (2010–2014); non-executive director of Yandex since 2010.

Warnig, Matthias. Former member of the Stasi; currently managing director of Nord Stream AG; in 2012 he was appointed chairman of the world's largest aluminum producer, Rusal; allegedly worked with Putin when the latter was at the KGB.

Yakimenko, Vasily. Russian politician and businessman; creator and leader of the pro-Putin youth movements Walking Together and Nashi.

Yakunin, Vladimir. Former president of Russian Railways, 2005–2015; founder and president of World Public Forum "Dialogue of Civilizations"; long considered part of Vladimir Putin's inner circle; sanctioned by United States following the annexation of Crimea in 2014.

Yanukovych, Alexander. Businessman and son of the former president of Ukraine, Viktor Yanukovych; during his father's presidency, became one of the richest men in the country; his businesses won nearly half of all state tenders in January 2014.

Yanukovych, Viktor. President of Ukraine, 2010–2014; removed from power during the crisis in Ukraine, partly because he had rejected a pending EU association agreement, choosing instead to pursue a Russian loan bailout and closer ties with Russia; lives in Russia.

Yevtushenkov, Vladimir. Russian billionaire; major shareholder and president of the Russian holding company Sistema; owner of the Russian company Sitronics; longtime ally of Yuri Luzhkov, then switched loyalty to Dmitry Medvedev; put under house arrest in 2014 after being accused of money laundering in connection with the acquisition of shares in oil producer Bashneft.

Yumashev, Valentin "Valya." Former journalist; chairman of the Presidential Executive Office, 1997–1998; member of Boris Yeltsin's inner circle; married Yeltsin's daughter, Tatyana Dyachenko (Yumasheva), in 2001.

Zaldostanov, Alexander. Leader of the Russian motorcycle club Night Wolves; political activist; friend of Vladimir Putin; awarded For the Return of Crimea medal by Putin.

Zhirinovsky, Vladimir. Founder and leader of the Liberal Democratic Party of Russia; ran for presidency in 1991, 1996, 2000, 2008, 2012; often seen as a showman of Russian politics and servant of the Kremlin.

Zolotov, Viktor. Commander in chief of the National Guard of Russia, created in 2016 to fight terrorism and organized crime; former bodyguard for Vladimir Putin; in the 1990s served as bodyguard for St. Petersburg mayor Anatoly Sobchak.

Zubkov, Viktor. Chairman of the board of directors of Gazprom; prime minister 2007–2008; daughter married Anatoly Serdyukov, former Russian defense minister.

Zyuganov, Gennady. First secretary of the Central Committee of the Communist Party of the Russian Federation since 1993; ran for president in 1996, 2000, 2008, 2012; currently considered to be a quasi-opposition leader, due to his loyalty to Putin; in 2014 was accused of "financing actions aimed at changing the boundaries of the territory and the state border of Ukraine" by the Ukrainian Interior Ministry.

INTRODUCTION

When I sat down to write this book, I imagined it would be a history of Russia under Vladimir Putin, detailing the changes that have taken place in the mind-set and the worldview of the man himself and his inner circle: how it all began, and where it has all led.

As the book progressed, I came to realize that the participants in the events described did not fully remember what had actually happened. People have a tendency to form memories in which they themselves are worthy, heroic, and, most important, always right. During the years of research for this book, I interviewed dozens of people from Vladimir Putin's inner circle: presidential administration staff, members of government, Duma parliamentarians, businessmen whose names were seen in the pages of *Forbes*, and a good number of foreign politicians. Almost every one of them told a story that at times had no overlap with events as portrayed by other witnesses: facts were forgotten, times and dates were jumbled up, and even their own actions and words were reinterpreted. As a rule, they asked not to be quoted. Nevertheless, because I managed to assemble such a vast array of characters, the picture that emerges is clear enough.

And in the cold light of day that picture is of a man who accidentally became king. His first thought was to cling to the throne. But, sensing that fortune was on his side, he decided to become a crusader-reformer: Vlad the Lionheart, let's call him. He wanted to go down in history. But then, seduced by the trappings of royalty, he morphed into Vlad the Magnificent. Later, tired and weary, all he wanted was to rest. But rest he could not, for he was a part of history. He was now Vlad the Terrible.

How did all these alterations take place in one man? Largely due to his entourage, the diverse retinue that played the role of kingmaker. The inner circle picked him up and carried him forward, manipulating his fears and desires along the way, to a place beyond all expectation.

History seems logical in hindsight, when the outcome is known and the events are traced back to their origins. It may even seem to have a purpose, a design, whereby what happens could not have been otherwise. Its protagonists retroactively invent grounds to justify their actions. They find cause where none existed and pluck logic out of the air.

It is logic that Putin-era Russia lacks. The chain of events that I have been able to link together reveals the absence of a clear plan or strategy on the part of Putin himself or his courtiers. Everything that happens is a tactical step, a real-time response to external stimuli devoid of an ultimate objective.

A close scrutiny of the deeds and motives of Russian politicians over the past fifteen-plus years exposes the folly of all conspiracy theories. If there is even a shred of doubt as to whether a particular event was the result of malicious intent or human error, rest assured that it is always the latter.

Did Russia's leaders in 2000 know where fifteen years of rule would lead? No. Did they know in 2014 what 2015 had in store? Again, no.

When I wrote "leaders" in the plural, it was no slip of the keyboard. It is widely assumed that decisions in Russia are made by one man and one man alone, Vladimir Putin. This is only partly true. All decisions are indeed made by Putin, but Putin is not one person. He (or it) is a huge collective mind. Tens, perhaps hundreds of people every day try to divine what decisions Vladimir Putin needs to make. Vladimir Putin himself spends his time divining what decisions he needs to make to stay popular—to be understood and approved by the vast entity that is the collective Vladimir Putin.

Over the years this collective Vladimir Putin has structured its memory so as to prove itself right in all instances, to convince itself that its actions are logical and underpinned by a strategic plan. It did not—and cannot—make mistakes. Everything done or not done was the necessary consequence of the punishing and incessant war being waged against implacable enemies.

My book is the story of this imaginary war. It is a war without end. For its end would be an admission that it was never real in the first place.

PART ONE

PUTIN I THE LIONHEART

CHAPTER 1

IN WHICH KREMLIN STRATEGIST ALEXANDER VOLOSHIN LEARNS TO TOLERATE LENIN

Alexander Voloshin looks like a model capitalist. With his gray beard and cold, piercing eyes, there is a dash of Uncle Sam in his appearance, as depicted in Soviet cartoons. All that's missing is the stars-and-stripes hat, the sack of dollars over the shoulder, and the bomb in one hand behind the back.

Voloshin's office is located in the center of Moscow near the Polyanka Metro station, a ten-minute walk from the Kremlin. The inside is austere, almost monastic. It has everything one needs and nothing else. No luxury—the secret ruler of the world does not need it.

Voloshin is no orator. He speaks in hushed tones, with a slight stutter when angry. Yet he loves to pepper his Russian speech with English and other borrowings, mainly from the world of business. "The situation in Ukraine is not very . . . ," he starts in his native tongue, ending with the word "manageable" in English. "One must always have in mind an . . . agenda." "What we have is total . . . deadlock." "The most important opinions belong to the key . . . stakeholders." It is not intentional; he just finds it easier that way. He is, after all, more businessman than politician.

Voloshin believes that he has fulfilled his primary mission: "to transfer Russia from a state of permanent revolution to a state of evolution." In other words, before he resigned from the government in October 2003, he succeeded in bringing political stability and capitalism to Russia. He says he has no regrets about his present inability to influence politics.

On the topic of politics, he prefers to speak in purely business terms: "The United States built the best economy in the world through competition. But it somehow forgot that world politics also needs competition. That's why its foreign policy is a failure." Despite subjecting America to the occasional tongue-lashing, he does so lovingly, with unexpected details: ". . . and then I bumped into Jeb Bush"; ". . . and then I spotted my old acquaintance Condoleezza Rice but decided not to say hi."

Mention Ukraine, however, and he flies into a fury; the English words at the end of his sentences are replaced by Russian expletives. For him, everything the Ukrainian government does is a crime. "What if the Canadians treated French-speakers in Quebec in that way [as Ukraine does Russian-speakers]? If they had done this, they would have ended up much worse off."

GOODBYE, LENIN

In 1999 the Kremlin had a clear plan for Lenin's overdue burial. His body was to be quietly removed from the mausoleum in Red Square and taken to St. Petersburg in the dead of night under the strictest secrecy. The country would wake up one morning to the news that Lenin no longer reposed in Red Square.

It was to be a repeat of Stalin's eviction from the same tomb, which had taken place thirty-eight years earlier, on an autumn evening in 1961. The journey to his new resting place had not been far—only to the adjacent Kremlin wall. But for Soviet leader Nikita Khrushchev, it was a symbol of de-Stalinization and the debunking of Uncle Joe's personality cult.

The reburial of Lenin was to take place "with dignity and without vulgarity," says Voloshin. A two-week cordon would have to be set up around Volkovo Cemetery in St. Petersburg (where Lenin's mother and sister are buried, and where the founder of the Soviet state himself allegedly wanted to be buried), but nothing more. Several months of protests by the Communist Party were expected, but after that, tempers would cool. The plan was to dismantle the mausoleum and erect a monument to the victims of totalitarianism on the site so that no one would have the heart to object. Coming eight years after the dissolution of the Soviet Union, it was to be a decisive blow against the remnants of Communist ideology, preventing any possibility of Soviet revanchism and a resurgence by the Communists.

As chief of staff in the Kremlin, Voloshin occupied an office just steps from Lenin's sarcophagus in the mausoleum.* "My desk stood by the window. It was no more than fifteen meters in a straight line from me to the corpse. He was lying there, I was working here. We didn't bother each other," says Voloshin wryly. In fact, Lenin did cause a great deal of bother. President Boris Yeltsin was eager to break with the past. For him, Lenin's burial would have been a symbol of the new age and the irreversible changes that had occurred, just as the burial of Stalin had been for Khrushchev. The first proposal to bury Lenin came in 1991 from St. Petersburg's first mayor, Anatoly Sobchak. But neither then nor in subsequent years could Yeltsin bring himself to do the deed—he did not want to provoke an unnecessary conflict with the Communists.

For Voloshin, however, Lenin was not so much a symbol as a specific and very active player in day-to-day policy. The struggle between Yeltsin's market-oriented reformers and the Communist Party was his primary source of daily anxiety. Lenin was an irritant but simultaneously the ace up his sleeve—a chance to deliver a sucker punch to the enemy. The Communists had become the main force in parliament and were therefore able to torpedo vital reforms. And since the 1998 Russian financial crisis they had also effectively controlled the government, which was headed by sixty-nine-year-old Yevgeny Primakov, a former candidate member of the Politburo of the Communist Party of the Soviet Union (that is, a member who participated in debates but was not eligible to vote) and former minister of foreign affairs of the Russian Federation.

---

*It is important to note that in Russia, the presidential administration and the government are two completely different organizations. The government, headed by the prime minister, works out of the House of the Government of the Russian Federation, colloquially known as the "White House." According to the Russian constitution, the government is the country's executive power. But sometimes it's far less influential than the presidential administration, which is located partly in the Kremlin and partly in Staraya Square, in the buildings once occupied by the Central Committee of the Communist Party of the USSR. And the presidential administration has almost the same importance now as the Central Committee did then. Since the late 1990s it has been the most important center of power in Russia—though this structure is not even mentioned in the constitution. It is headed by the chief of staff of the presidential administration.

Boris Yeltsin's second term as president had a little more than eighteen months left to run. Meanwhile, the Communists seemed stronger than ever. They had even launched an impeachment case against Yeltsin, indicting him on five counts: the collapse of the Soviet Union, the dispersal of parliament in 1993, the war in Chechnya, the disintegration of the army, and genocide of the Russian people. Prime Minister Primakov, for whom the Communist members of parliament had voted unanimously in September 1998, topped the polls among politicians nationwide and seemed the most likely candidate for the presidency.

Primakov was particularly renowned for making a demonstrative anti-American gesture. On March 24, 1999, Primakov was on board a plane to Washington, above the Atlantic, when he received a call from US vice president Al Gore to inform him that the United States had begun a bombing campaign against Yugoslavia to end the conflict in Kosovo. Outraged, Primakov ordered the plane to turn around and return to Moscow—a gesture that was applauded by the Russian public, whose sense of national pride had been wounded by the fall of the Soviet Union and the chaos that ensued. By contrast, the Russian press, which was both pro-Kremlin and liberal (which, in the Russian context, means pro-democracy), criticized Primakov for populism and flirting with Communist voters. *Kommersant*, Russia's top business daily, insisted that Primakov's political grandstanding had cost Russia $15 billion as a result of agreements that Washington now would not sign: "In acting in such manner, the Russian prime minister made a choice. He chose to be a Communist, a Bolshevik, oblivious to the interests of his native land and people in favor of internationalism, which is intelligible only to himself and former members of the Communist Party," railed the paper.[1]

The Atlantic U-turn was the first act of state-level anti-Americanism in 1990s Russia. It also marked the start of the decisive battle for power between the conservative anti-Westerners, under the banner of Primakov, and the liberal and pro-Western forces eager to thwart Soviet revanchism. The latter had no leader per se but did have a secret coordinator: the head of Boris Yeltsin's presidential administration, Alexander Voloshin.

The Communists had to be knocked off balance, and the reburial of Lenin might be just the thing that would do it. But under the relevant law, Lenin's body could be moved only if one of three conditions was met: (1) if the move was expressly desired by Lenin's descendants (but all were strongly against); (2) if local authorities—such as Moscow mayor Yuri Luzhkov—decreed it necessary "for sanitary and environmental reasons" (but Luzhkov had no intention of entering the power struggle on the side of the Kremlin and the liberals); or (3) if the tomb hindered public transport. It could not be moved by presidential decree alone. Violation of this law was considered a criminal offense and would have added vandalism to the Communists' list of indictments against Yeltsin. It was too risky. Therefore, the Kremlin decided to try a different tack—it would target not Lenin but Primakov.

On May 12, 1999, three days before the impeachment vote against Yeltsin in the Duma (the lower house of the Russian parliament), Primakov was sacked, with the official reason being "lack of dynamism in prosecuting reforms to solve economic issues." On May 15 the Communists failed to gain the three hundred votes they needed to commence impeachment proceedings. The presidential administration worked in close association with Duma parliamentarians, and almost all independent MPs voted against the impeachment. It was a tactical triumph for Voloshin, but it did not resolve the issue of how to prevent the Primakov-Communist alliance from securing victory the following year, when Yeltsin's second presidential term would end.

The crux of the matter was that Yeltsin's circle contained virtually no politicians with any significant approval rating. The aged Yeltsin's own approval rating was incredibly low, largely due to press and opposition (mainly Communist) allegations against his family. Journalists back then referred to Yeltsin's "Family," using a capital *F* to indicate that the president's nearest and dearest had special and at times disproportionate influence in state affairs and perhaps business as well. Yeltsin's Family included first and foremost Tatyana (Tanya) Borisovna Dyachenko, who was Yeltsin's daughter, and Valentin (Valya) Yumashev, the former head of his administration. They would later marry, tying the knot in 2001. In a broader sense, the Family also included the oligarchs closest to Tanya and Valya, Boris Berezovsky and Roman Abramovich. The last member of the Family was its "personal representative," Alexander Voloshin, head of the Yeltsin administration, who was also charged with rescuing the Kremlin from the dire situation in which it found itself.

Coming from the world of business and having worked in the 1990s for dozens of companies of varying repute, Voloshin was considered a committed statist. He upheld the interests of the state as he perceived them. A market economy seemed to him to be absolutely vital, while human rights and freedom of speech were a superfluous and at times inconvenient detail. Kremlin insiders sometimes referred to Voloshin as the "ice man" for his cold resolution in matters that seemed to him of fundamental importance.

MANAGING THE SUCCESSION

The Family was strongly opposed by Moscow mayor Yuri Luzhkov. Luzhkov had long been considered the natural successor to the Russian presidency, despite—or perhaps thanks to—his image as the antithesis of Yeltsin (much as the mayor of Paris, Jacques Chirac, had played a similar role in regard to the elderly French president François Mitterrand). Luzhkov was known across Russia neither as a liberal nor as a conservative, but simply for being a good manager.

Luzhkov wanted power for himself and rarely tried to hide his ambitions. His bid for the presidency began in 1998, when he created the "Fatherland" movement—a party that comprised a group of regional governors with a background in the Soviet bureaucracy. He had his own group of supporters inside the Kremlin, who tried to persuade Yeltsin to pick their man as his successor. But Yeltsin had never liked Luzhkov.

Luzhkov recalls that the Family sent Boris Berezovsky as its emissary with a message: Luzhkov would get the nod to succeed Yeltsin on two conditions—a guarantee of immunity for the entire Family and a guarantee of the inviolability of the results of privatization. Luzhkov refused, whereupon (in his own words) he became the target of a slander campaign.

Luzhkov was sure that the Family was in trouble, beyond salvation. According to rumors, the head of the Investigation Department of the Prosecutor General's Office had already signed warrants for the arrest of Tanya and Valya. Cynical observers asked just one question: "Will they have time to get to the airport?" Naturally, Luzhkov was reluctant to join the fight on the side of those he considered to be the losers. He wanted to associate himself with the winners.

Voloshin, the new Kremlin chief of staff, paid visits to Luzhkov and drank tea with him in an attempt to curry favor. But no amount of tea could win him over. Luzhkov smelled presidential blood and was preparing to go in for the kill. However, the vicious war of words between him and the Family had slashed his own approval rating. So the mayor of Moscow did something cunning. He supported Primakov, letting the aged patriarch of the nation take center stage, while he waited in the wings. He calculated that his turn would come four years later.

The Kremlin had no counterweight to the heavyweight Primakov. Facing defeat, the Family started casting around for a successor. It took until August 1999 to find him. His name was Vladimir Putin, director of the FSB (successor to the KGB). This young, unknown intelligence officer was the former right-hand man of Anatoly Sobchak, mayor of St. Petersburg from 1991 to 1996 and a popular first-wave democrat.

Two days before Putin's appointment as prime minister, militants from Chechnya invaded the neighboring North Caucasus republic of Dagestan. Unlike his predecessors, who had been constantly plagued by economic woes, Putin was able to score political points by taking the fight to an external enemy. A month later terrorists blew up two apartment blocks in Moscow, an event that weakened Mayor Luzhkov and slightly strengthened Putin.

Even so, it was impossible to imagine that the sorely discredited Family could actually prevail in the presidential election. Yevgeny Kiselyov, Russia's leading TV presenter and general director of the television channel NTV, declared live on air in September 1999 that Primakov was "fated to win." Primakov topped the polls and enjoyed the backing not only of Luzhkov but also of almost all of Russia's regional governors. He was financed by Russia's two largest oil companies, Lukoil and Yukos, as well as the "Russian Bill Gates," Vladimir Yevtushenkov. He was supported by the energy company Gazprom and the country's main media mogul, Vladimir Gusinsky, owner of NTV, which was Russia's most reputable TV station at the time.

But that wasn't the half of it. Three months remained until the next parliamentary elections. Since 1990 no pro-Kremlin party had ever performed well in them, and this time around the situation was worse than ever. The Kremlin didn't even have its own party. Primakov, on the other hand, had a party that was set to win the State Duma. It included almost all the country's regional governors, which meant that Primakov had administrative leverage nationwide. The Fatherland-All Russia (FAR) political bloc, formed from Luzhkov's Fatherland movement, was the firm favorite.

The dream of burying Lenin had to be postponed again. The struggle against the Communist legacy was put to one side. First and foremost, the Family and their candidate had to defeat the former Communist Yevgeny Primakov.

A NEW YEAR'S FAIRY TALE

On December 31 Alexander Voloshin, head of the Yeltsin administration, wrote an official resignation letter. One hour later his boss, President Yeltsin, resigned as well, whereupon Prime Minister Vladimir Putin was appointed acting president. It marked the successful completion of the transfer of power—what journalists described as "Operation Successor."

"What's that for?" asked Putin upon seeing Voloshin's resignation letter. The latter explained with a smile that he had been appointed Kremlin chief of staff by the former president, and Putin should name his own man. Putin returned the smile and asked Voloshin to remain in his post. The Kremlin's new lord and its old-new chief political strategist exchanged bows and went their separate ways.

Twelve days earlier, the parliamentary elections had turned out to be a triumph for Voloshin and his brainchild, the synthetic political bloc Unity. Unity had outperformed its main competitor, Fatherland-All Russia (FAR), headed by Primakov and Luzhkov—something that had seemed impossible just three months before.

The Central Election Commission had registered FAR in the elections in early September. Thirty percent of respondents to a national poll said they would support FAR, giving it a wide margin over other parties—FAR was even ten points ahead of the Communists. All seemed to be going well. It was then—three months before the election—that Alexander Voloshin began to assemble a new party to rain on Primakov's parade.

The godfather of Unity was Boris Berezovsky, whom the Russian press christened the "gray cardinal" of the Kremlin. A former mathematician and academic, Berezovsky was an erratic genius bursting with ideas, which the Kremlin exploited. He had the ear of Tanya and Valya, but Yeltsin was suspicious of him and never once granted him a private meeting. But Berezovsky compensated for this by telling stories to the press about how the Kremlin's entire policy was his work.

Berezovsky was indeed the fountainhead of Unity. He personally visited several regional governors to persuade them to abandon Luzhkov and Primakov and switch their allegiance to the Kremlin. But pretty soon Berezovsky lost interest in the routine work of party building, handing responsibility over to Voloshin's young assistant Vladislav Surkov, who would soon become deputy chief of staff. It was to be the first election campaign for Surkov, Putin's future political strategist.

The Kremlin's new project managed to attract the support of a total of thirty-nine regional governors, leaving Primakov with forty-five in the FAR camp. Next up was the identification of a leader. Putting Putin forth in that role was dangerous, since an electoral failure would make it impossible for him to succeed Yeltsin in the presidential contest. Therefore, another popular candidate was chosen as a safety net: minister of emergency situations Sergei Shoigu. "Shoigu to Save Russia" headlines appeared in pro-Kremlin newspapers even before he had agreed to run. In the end he had to be persuaded by Yeltsin himself.

Funding for Unity came primarily from Berezovsky and Abramovich, although money was also raised from some of Primakov's backers, businessmen who wanted to hedge their bets. The average check from an oligarch was for $10 million, and Unity raised a total of about $170 million.

Voloshin also courted the liberal community, explaining that FAR represented the past, Soviet revanchism, and the KGB's attempt to regain power. Primakov had indeed been appointed first deputy director of the KGB in the late perestroika years under Gorbachev, but he had never served as an intelligence officer.

All liberals, reformers, and those in favor of change should be on the side of Unity and Putin, said the Kremlin through Voloshin. In truth, Unity was full of the same kind of regional opportunists as FAR, essentially those that FAR could not accommodate. Nevertheless, Unity had made a good start. Primakov's main problem was his age, which heightened his resemblance to the ailing Yeltsin. Putin and Shoigu, on the contrary, were young and energetic. By early October only 20 percent of polled potential voters said they were planning to support FAR, down from 30 percent, and Unity's support was up from nothing to 7 percent. Asked whom they would choose in the presidential election, 15 percent of those surveyed said they would vote for Putin, while Primakov had the support of 20 percent of poll respondents.

The next two and a half months saw the dirtiest election campaign in Russian history. At the heart of it were the two political strategists who were running the election campaigns, each fighting to annihilate the other. In the Kremlin's corner was Vladislav Surkov, and in Primakov's was a young political consultant from Saratov by the name of Vyacheslav Volodin. It was the first of their many scraps. They would spend the next fifteen years fighting for influence over Putin.

On election day Surkov's Unity secured 23 percent of the parliamentary seats under the party-list proportional representation system (one percentage point behind the Communists), with Volodin's FAR receiving 13 percent. But more significant was that Putin's poll numbers had risen to 30 percent, while Primakov's remained stuck at 20 percent.

The unexpected defeat in the December 19 elections disheartened the Primakov-Luzhkov camp. However, FAR headquarters believed that since the presidential election was six months away, there was still everything to play for. Moreover, they were confident that their new Duma MPs could form a coalition with the Communists, who had the most seats, and that the Speaker of the Duma would be none other than Primakov himself, from which position he could vie with Prime Minister Putin for the presidency. Primakov's future campaign staff had even started to allocate decision-making duties among themselves. Everyone was confident that there would be no significant changes before New Year's. It was time to relax after the exertions of the past few months.

But things turned out differently. On December 31, 1999, when Boris Yeltsin announced his resignation as president and the appointment of Vladimir Putin as his successor, he ensured that the presidential election would be held in March instead of June (under the constitution new elections had to be called within three months after the resignation of a president). This meant that Primakov, Luzhkov, and other Kremlin opponents had little time to organize their opposition. They would barely have time to recover from their defeat in the parliamentary elections. It was a shady maneuver on the part of the Kremlin, but it would deliver the necessary result.

No one immediately understood that the game was over. While Primakov's camp had been busy assigning campaign roles, Kremlin chief of staff Voloshin, still accompanied day in and day out by Lenin fifteen meters away and dreaming of parting company with him, was thinking the unthinkable: an arrangement with the Communists. The main objective of the Kremlin was simple: split the alliance between the Communists and Primakov supporters. "It's more important to screw Fatherland," posited a Kremlin insider. "The party appeals to opportunists. We need to show that if they stay with Primakov and Luzhkov, they're on a siding to nothing."

On January 18, at the first session of the new Duma, it was revealed that over the New Year holidays Unity and the Communists had concluded a package deal: the Speaker of the Duma would be a Communist Party member, while the chairmanships of all committees would be shared. The other parties, including FAR, would get nothing. For Primakov's entourage it was a devastating blow. They had thought they were entering the Duma to make policy and political careers for themselves, but Voloshin made it clear that if they opposed the Kremlin, they would remain ordinary MPs in minority parties. For diehard careerists it was ruinous. Realizing that the fates had deserted Primakov, a third of FAR's up-and-coming members defected to other factions at the very first sitting. "It's a conspiracy!" shouted Primakov from the podium, and promptly left the chamber in protest.

As a result, he did not even run for president. He quit the Duma eighteen months later, handing over the reins of FAR to his protégé, the promising MP Vyacheslav Volodin. But the latter quickly swore allegiance to Putin, whereupon a merger between FAR and Unity was arranged by the end of 2001. The new ruling party was to be called United Russia, and ten years later Volodin would be the Kremlin's chief political strategist.

SOVIET SYBARITES

The amount of money that business interests gave to Putin's election campaign was embarrassingly large. Sergei Pugachev, a banker close to the Family and now friends with Putin, is said to have launched a fund-raising campaign among his peers in big business, ostensibly on behalf of Putin. But the money allegedly did not reach Putin's official campaign.

Sergei Pugachev had been welcome in the Kremlin for some time. In 1996 he was one of the main sponsors of Yeltsin's campaign. Pugachev, like many other influential businessmen, knew Putin from his St. Petersburg days, and he was quick to befriend Yeltsin's successor. Initially Putin cut a rather lonely figure in Moscow, as his personal friends had not yet moved to the capital. "There was no trace of the Yakunins, Kovalchuks, and Rotenbergs back then," says Pugachev, speaking of close friends of Putin's who would become top businessmen and billionaires within a decade.

Putin and Pugachev were neighbors in Rublyovka, the fanciest suburb of Moscow, and together they toured the dominions of the Department of Presidential Affairs to find a residence for the new prime minister. They settled on the former residence of Mikhail Gorbachev at Novo-Ogaryovo, outside Moscow. According to Pugachev, what struck Putin most of all was the fifty-meter swimming pool.*

Pugachev saw that Putin liked his new existence. On one hand, he had not sought to become president. On the other, he was enticed by the privileges of being president, especially when they increased his domestic comfort. At that time the vast majority of officials, including Putin in his role as director of the FSB, lived modestly; villas, yachts, and private jets were the unattainable preserve of the oligarchs. For Putin, the main perk of his unexpected ascension to prime minister and acting president was the upgrade in living conditions.

Pugachev remained a close friend of Putin's for a long time. They hung out with each other, drinking and going to the steam baths, and their children grew up together. However, while Pugachev did not gain political leverage from his association with the president, he still ostensibly acted on Putin's behalf to cut business deals. Perhaps it was this overexploitation of his friendship with Putin that would play a fateful role in the life of the banker ten years down the line.

THE FIRST FRIEND

On March 11, 2000, the Mariinsky Theater staged an event that was a premiere in more than one sense. In the main hall was a sumptuous production of Sergei Prokofiev's opera *War and Peace* staged by director Andron Konchalovsky, recently returned from Hollywood. And in the audience that night was the very first gathering in one space of Russia's future political elite. Theater staff stared at them with amazement—never before had they seen so many people with mobile phones.

Seated in the royal box, next to Vladimir Putin, was British prime minister Tony Blair. Putin had been acting president for one and a half months, and this was his international debut—the first time that he had received a foreign leader, and with full pomp and circumstance to boot.

Two months earlier, at a press conference at the Davos Economic Forum, US journalist Trudy Rubin had astonished the Russian delegation with a

---

*As it happens, all top Kremlin officials lived in homes once occupied by Soviet leaders. Voloshin, for instance, lived in a house that had belonged to general secretary Yuri Andropov.

direct question: "Who is Mr. Putin?" It seemed no one knew anything about Boris Yeltsin's successor. What were his chances of success, political background, degree of autonomy, motives, beliefs, hopes, fears? Did he desire reform or did he thirst for revenge? The Russian public knew no more, having been presented with a "tough guy," the polar opposite of the frail Boris Yeltsin. For Western audiences, Putin and his team opted for a "smart guy" image: a young, energetic lawyer, competent and self-confident, yet at the same time open and friendly. His role model was, in fact, Tony Blair. So it was natural that Blair was the first leader with whom Putin sought to establish amicable relations.

Memories were also still fresh of Margaret Thatcher's words upon on meeting Mikhail Gorbachev sixteen years earlier: "We can do business together." Putin did not want to be a second Gorbachev, but he counted on building the same external PR machine as the last general secretary and president of the Soviet Union had. Basically, Putin wanted to be liked. He set about paying court to Blair, as assiduously as an agent trying to recruit a target.

The British prime minister was invited to St. Petersburg, Putin's hometown, where the Russian leader could look more regal—and certainly more European—than in Moscow. First he held a meeting with Blair at Peterhof, a former tsarist summer residence outside the city. Then he gave the British prime minister a personal tour of the Hermitage. Finally, in the evening, the leaders and their wives went to the premiere at the Mariinsky.

Near the entrance to the theater a small group of demonstrators had gathered bearing signs that read "Putin means war" (i.e., the war in Chechnya).[2] The opera that the two leaders were about to see, *War and Peace*, tells the story of a bright period in the history of Anglo-Russian relations, when the two empires were allies and defeated a common enemy. Emperor Alexander I appeared on stage in act one, holding a toy poodle. Not only did Alexander slightly resemble Putin, but the Russians in the hall immediately got the reference to Putin's pet dog, Tosya.*

---

*Alexander I is one of the most enigmatic figures in Russian history. Having defeated Napoleon, he declared, "We have enough land," and did not try to increase the size of the Russian Empire. That was a first in Russian history. According to legend, in his later years he renounced the throne, faked his own death, and went to Siberia under the name of the Russian Orthodox starets Fyodor Kuzmich. In 2014, following the annexation of Crimea and the outbreak of war in Ukraine, Vladimir Putin would place a monument to Alexander I by the walls of the Kremlin.

Blair was awestruck by the truly tsarist reception at the Mariinsky Theater. Before any theatrical premiere in London, he would be forced to smile and shake hands with all and sundry. But at the Mariinsky it was different. "I noticed people fell back as he approached, not in fear or anything; but a little in awe and with reverence. It was a tsar-like moment and I thought: Hmm, their politics really isn't like ours at all," Blair marveled ten years later in his memoirs.[3] But in 2000 he chose his words more carefully: "His vision of the future is one that we would feel comfortable with," Blair said in an interview upon his return to London. "Putin has a very clear agenda of modernising Russia. When he talks of a strong Russia, he means strength not in a threatening way but in a way that means the country economically and politically is capable of standing up for itself, which is a perfectly good aim to have."[4] Putin had passed the first test, making an indelible impression on Blair. That same day Blair's press service let it be known that after his return to Downing Street the British prime minister had phoned his G7 colleagues to share his positive opinion of Putin.

Two weeks later Putin won the presidential election in Russia and appointed his own government and presidential administration. The head of the administration remained the same, Alexander Voloshin. Having overseen the smooth transfer of power from Yeltsin to Putin, he became the Kremlin's policy architect for Putin's first term and a conduit for the new president's early reforms.

Putin began his presidency convinced that he could build good relations with the West, in particular with the United States. He believed that Westerners simply did not understand the peculiarities of Russia, and so Russians would have to explain who they are, where they are, what their problems are. Putin received every Western leader and foreign minister who paid a visit to Russia—and sat with them for far longer than protocol required.

With Blair, everything seemed to be in order. The British prime minister was not overly critical of the Kremlin's military action in Chechnya, and he apparently accepted the reasons Putin carefully explained for it: that the Second Chechen War had begun when Wahhabist militants from Chechnya—under the slogan "Allah above us, goats beneath us"—invaded neighboring Dagestan. "By goats they mean us, all of us," stormed Putin.

Putin and Blair met five times in 2000. In April, elected but not yet inaugurated, he flew to London on his first foreign trip. It was in London that

Putin also gave his first post-election press conference, jointly with Blair. They called each other "Vladimir" and "Tony."

In November the British prime minister paid another visit to Russia, this time to Moscow. Putin took him to the Pivnushka restaurant. There they drank vodka (Putin had already ascertained that Blair liked hard liquor), snacked on potatoes, herring, and pickled mushrooms, and discussed how to build relations with the United States under the new administration. The US presidential elections had taken place two weeks earlier, but the outcome was still unknown. The hanging chads were still being examined in Florida, and it was unclear whether the name of the new president would be known by New Year's. Putin and Blair, both elected with their own landslide victories, poked fun at the situation in America.

THE MIRACLE OF THE CRUCIFIX

Russia played a special role in the US presidential election campaign in 2000. The Republicans accused outgoing president Bill Clinton and his vice president, Al Gore, who was now the Democratic candidate, of "losing Russia." The elections coincided with the publication of a special report entitled *Russia's Road to Corruption: How the Clinton Administration Exported Government Instead of Free Enterprise and Failed the Russian People*, which claimed that the Clinton administration had failed terribly on Russia.[5] The report compared 1945 and 1991, the respective ends of the Second World War and the Cold War. The United States was the victor in both these wars, but in the first case the Truman administration had managed to avoid revanchist sentiment in Europe by implementing the Marshall Plan, which resuscitated Europe's (particularly Germany's) economy and put the continent back on the road to normalcy, making allies of European countries in the process, while in the second the Clinton administration did the opposite. International Monetary Fund (IMF) money earmarked for the restoration of the Russian economy was stolen with the alleged connivance of the US government, there was no de-Sovietization in Russia (unlike the de-Nazification of Germany after World War II), and by the turn of the new millennium Russian anti-Americanism was reaching new heights—a stunning contrast to the mood in the early nineties. At the time of the collapse of the Soviet Union, the United States had enjoyed great popularity among Russians. Ten years later it had all fizzled out. The Russian public, the report stated, now blamed America for the poverty and corruption sweeping the country. The Clinton administration had squandered a historic opportunity to help Russia become a democratic state because it had trusted too narrow a circle of leaders: President Boris Yeltsin, Prime Minister Viktor Chernomyrdin, and Vice Prime Minister Anatoly Chubais, architect of the pro-democracy reforms. The blame for all this, according to the report, lay with three people who had been personally involved in Russian matters: Vice President Al Gore, Deputy Treasury Secretary Larry Summers, and Deputy Secretary of State Strobe Talbott. There is no doubt that the report was a typical preelection ploy to discredit Gore—the group that authored the report was headed by Republican congressman Christopher Cox. Incidentally, the final part of the report asserted that not all was lost: the new Russian president, Vladimir Putin, was trying to carry out necessary reforms and it was vital to assist him. It would be the last chance for both Russia and America. The report did not explicitly say so, but the implication was that such an important task could not be entrusted to a Gore administration.

Putin, and especially his right-hand man Voloshin (who spoke excellent English), were potentially desirable partners for Washington. According to transcripts of telephone conversations between Clinton and Blair, released in 2015, the president of the United States thought that "Putin has enormous potential. He's very smart and thoughtful. We can do a lot of good with him." And later he added: "His intentions are generally honorable and straightforward, but he just hasn't made up his mind yet. He could get squishy on democracy."[6]

Alexander Voloshin got on well with Larry Summers and even better with Strobe Talbott, and he knew how to build relations with a potential Gore administration. Much less was known about the Republican candidate, George W. Bush. Therefore, Voloshin decided to send a large delegation from Unity to attend the Republican National Convention in August 2000, where Bush would receive the Republication presidential nomination. Voloshin explained to the delegation that the Republicans were more pragmatic and constructive politicians, not as "ideologized" and less concerned about human rights, and noted that relations between Russia and the United States had always been much easier under Republican presidents. A meeting was arranged between the Americans and the Unity group, and both Bush and his foreign policy adviser, Condoleezza Rice, made a very good impression on Putin and Voloshin's envoys. In January 2001 the victorious Bush invited Unity representatives to attend his inauguration.

In getting to know Bush, Putin's approach was just as meticulous as it had been with Blair. Before their first meeting in the Slovenian capital, Ljubljana, Putin studied an in-depth dossier on Bush, full of personal details. Above all, he noted that Bush had been fond of alcohol in his youth, but at the age of forty he had quit drinking and become deeply religious. So during the initial small talk at the meeting in Ljubljana, Putin told Bush a story about himself. He had once had a dacha outside St. Petersburg, which a few years earlier had burned to the ground—fortunately none of his family had been hurt. Miraculously, the only object to survive the fire was a crucifix given to him by his mother. The incident convinced him that miracles do happen, Putin concluded. The God-fearing Bush was deeply affected. "I looked the man in the eye. I found him to be very straightforward and trustworthy and we had a very good dialogue. I was able to get a sense of his soul," he would say after that memorable first meeting.[7]

The new US president also believed that he had to engage with Putin for the sake of good future relations. Bush initially thought that Russia could become a typical European country like Germany—not a superpower like the United States or China, but a normal prosperous nation.

In the summer of 2000 Putin made the decision to close all military bases overseas that Russia had inherited from the Soviet Union, including ones in Vietnam and Cuba. Military and intelligence officials were shocked, but he patiently explained to them that the bases had been obsolete for many years. Russian foreign minister Igor Ivanov expounded the Kremlin's reasoning: "For ten years our navy has not set sail in the Indian Ocean or used naval bases in the region."[8] Nor had the hugely costly Lourdes radar station in Cuba nor the Cam Ranh naval base in Vietnam ever been used. Far more could be achieved through surveillance from space than through maintaining old Soviet bases, it was argued. As usual, patriots in the armed forces cursed the political leadership for its betrayal of national interests. But they went along with the decision.*

---

*In 2013 Putin would reconsider that decision, renewing the agreement with Vietnam on the use of the naval base at Cam Ranh.

THE "FAT DECADE"

Putin's team really did start to carry out systemic reforms without delay. Even before his inauguration Putin ordered a number of his old acquaintances from St. Petersburg—liberal economists working under the city's first democratic mayor, Anatoly Sobchak—to draw up a reform plan for the new government. Presiding over this creative group were German Gref and Alexei Kudrin. After Putin's election they received ministerial portfolios: economic development and finance, respectively.

As they set about making plans for the future, they realized that they were in luck: In 1999, just when Putin was appointed prime minister, global oil prices had begun to rise. And so in 2000, for the first time since perestroika, Russia's finance ministry, under Kudrin, was able to achieve a budget surplus. Now it was necessary to take advantage of this windfall. The St. Petersburg economists set their sights high.

The government set the income tax rate at a flat 13 percent. The number of different types of taxes was reduced by two-thirds, with the remaining tax burden shifted to the oil sector. Revenues rose because more companies preferred to pay taxes rather than to avoid them with shady schemes. A new land code was drawn up, and for the first time since the 1917 revolution the purchase and sale of agricultural land was permitted.

These startling reforms were approved by the Duma. Whereas under Yeltsin the parliament had refused to pass any law that came from the government, under Putin everything went smoothly thanks to the new coalition: Primakov's former supporters had merged with Unity, giving the new pro-Putin party United Russia a majority. It voted for all the Kremlin-sponsored bills.

Oil prices continued to rise at a pace that enabled the government to pay off foreign debts ahead of schedule. The population became richer—it was a Putin-inspired economic miracle. After the lean nineties, Russia welcomed the fat decade that began the twenty-first century.

Alongside the Gref-Kudrin economic reforms, Putin and Voloshin implemented some radical political changes. For example, Voloshin came up with the idea for a new-look Federation Council, the upper house of the Russian parliament. Previously home to just regional governors, it would now house professional senators, who would represent the regions. Somewhere along the line political scientists dubbed the new policy "managed democracy"—since under Yeltsin everything had been "unmanaged." The first step in improving manageability was better control over the regions. Preventing regional leaders and business lobbyists from hindering the reforms was the sole objective.

The shake-up was very unpopular with the governors themselves, who were expelled from parliament and hence deprived of the right to vote at the federal level. Especially unhappy were those who had sworn allegiance to Putin and supported Unity during the election campaign. Why was Putin punishing his allies? The governors asked Boris Berezovsky to convey their general mood of disquiet to the president; after all, he had persuaded them to support Putin in the first place. The president received Berezovsky but did not listen to him.

Despite some grumbling, the reforms were supported by a majority of the parliament. Even Primakov's former underlings voted for them. In order to prove their loyalty to the new government, ex-members of FAR were willing to vote for anything. It was then that Voloshin and his deputy Surkov decided to wrap up the process of merging Unity and FAR into the pro-Putin party United Russia. At the same time all positions in the Duma would be redistributed, since the previous package deal with the Communists was no longer required. Indeed, after this defeat the Communists never fully recovered; they ceased to be a political force and became quite harmless. Voloshin, no longer threatened by the specter of Communism, dropped the idea of moving Lenin.

Instead, at the end of 2000 the Kremlin had the idea of putting the symbolism back into Russia's state symbols. No one had sung the national anthem for a decade, for the simple reason that it had no words: in November 1990 the Supreme Soviet of the Russian Soviet Federative Socialist Republic (RSFSR) had adopted a melody by the great nineteenth-century Russian composer Mikhail Glinka as the national anthem, but it was purely instrumental. Voloshin did not like it, and neither did Putin—it was too bland, they thought. They drew up a long list of alternative anthems, mostly old military marches. At the last minute, however, Putin tore them up. He decided to restore the old Stalinist anthem, but with new lyrics. What's more, the task of composing the new words would be entrusted to the author of the previous version, the old Soviet poet Sergei Mikhalkov, father of Andron Konchalovsky (who had directed *War and Peace* at the Mariinsky) and Nikita Mikhalkov, also a film director.

The Communist-hating Voloshin was not amused. The Family foresaw what a blow it would be to Boris Yeltsin, now retired, because of his hatred of Communism and Soviet symbols. But Putin convinced his advisers that the new anthem would assist the reform process. Since painful economic reforms (such as the planned cancellation of the vast array of Soviet-style privileges and concessions for retirees) were unavoidable, it was better not to vex the people over a trifle. Let the old folks rejoice, and let the Kremlin save its energy for liberal reforms and deregulation, exhorted Putin. Voloshin acquiesced. For the sake of the reform program, Russia would sing the Soviet anthem.

CHAPTER 2

IN WHICH POLITICAL ÉMIGRÉ BORIS BEREZOVSKY IS NOT INVITED TO THE ROYAL WEDDING

I never met Boris Berezovsky, despite the fact that I worked nearly a decade for Kommersant, *which he owned back in the 2000s.*

Writing a book about Gazprom in 2007, I felt obliged to interview him, yet I intentionally didn't do so. It seemed to me that Berezovsky could have somehow discredited the book, since his reputation at that time was dubious, to say the least. Besides, I was convinced that Berezovsky was an inveterate liar. What's the point of interviewing someone you can't trust?

A year before his death, he gave a long interview to my colleagues at TV Rain. Shortly afterward, he eloquently expounded his version of events from the late 1990s and early 2000s during a lawsuit he brought against former oil oligarch Roman Abramovich (now owner of the Chelsea soccer club) in London. But the London Commercial Court, agreeing with my assessment of the man, found Berezovsky to be an "inherently unreliable" witness and ruled against him.

However, Boris Berezovsky had one feature that sharply distinguished him from all the other characters in this book: he repeatedly admitted that he had made mistakes. At the end of his life (not before), he often regretted his actions. Some say that he was genuinely sorry. Others are not so sure.

GET GOOSY

"Yesterday I felt like Berezovsky," Roman Abramovich likes to joke. "I set up meetings with different people all at the same time." People who knew Berezovsky often remember him as an erratic mathematical genius, full of ideas but unable to keep track of them all.

An oft-told Berezovsky tale relates how he once invited a trio of business colleagues to meet with him at the same time: NTV's Vladimir Gusinsky, Yukos head Mikhail Khodorkovsky, and Vladimir Potanin, the head of the conglomerate Interros. It's said they were put in different rooms to keep them apart. But then a pal of Berezovsky's turned up for a prearranged sauna session. Berezovsky went to the sauna (which was in his house) and promptly forgot about his guests. An hour later, now strolling around the house, his guests bumped into each other. They adjourned to the living room, where a bathrobe-clad Berezovsky was surprised to discover them a short while later. What happened to Berezovsky in the 2000s came as a far greater surprise, although that too was a muddle of his own making.

Berezovsky first met Putin in the early 1990s, and he introduced the future president to Boris Yeltsin's inner circle. It was Berezovsky who in the summer of 1999 had first toyed with the idea of Putin as Yeltsin's successor. By late 1999, however, the idea had taken on a life of its own and was out of Berezovsky's hands. The more it spun out of control, the more it haunted him.

Berezovsky could not see the writing on the wall. What he failed to understand was that it was not Putin who was out of control but Berezovsky himself who was out of favor. As early as autumn 1999 the Family is said to have spoken unanimously: "It's time to ditch Borya [Boris]." Berezovsky's political vanities—and especially his never-ending interviews and sweeping comments—were beginning to irk Tanya, Valya, Voloshin, and Abramovich, who decided that he was doing more harm than good. Once the threat of losing their power and freedom had receded, they gradually began to sideline their former friend.

Berezovsky was deeply resentful of their lack of appreciation for his role in securing Putin's victory and dispatching the Family's foes. In 1996, when Berezovsky and Gusinsky had urged big business to support Yeltsin, they had been rewarded. Gusinsky's NTV became a national channel, and Berezovsky was appointed deputy secretary of the Security Council. But during the 1999–2000 campaign, when Berezovsky and Gusinsky fought on opposite sides and the latter, together with Primakov, Luzhkov, and dozens of governors, were vanquished, there was no special reward for the winners or any particular retaliation against the losers. Luzhkov remained in his post as mayor of Moscow. Primakov was appointed to the sinecure role of head of the Chamber of Commerce and Industry. Their former supporters dissolved into the ranks of the Putin-affiliated Unity Party. The only one to be punished was Vladimir Gusinsky, for having waged an information war against Putin.

What had really stuck in the Kremlin's craw was NTV's *Kukli* (a Russian satirical puppet show), in which Putin had been portrayed as Zaches the Dwarf from *The Tales of Hoffman*. "Nothing personal, just business," Voloshin reportedly said at the time. Gusinsky's holding company, Media Most, was indebted to state-owned companies to the tune of more than $1 billion. But whenever a creditor demanded repayment, Gusinsky used NTV to launch an attack on the lender, which immediately backed down and extended the loan on preferential terms. It was easy to live on debt.

A month after Putin's inauguration, however, the Prosecutor General's Office opened a criminal case against Gusinsky, who was promptly arrested and placed in Moscow's notorious Butyrka detention center. "That was perhaps unnecessary," admit Kremlin staff. But the rules of the game were now being set by the new president's entourage, which included many high-ranking officials from the military and the security services, known as the *siloviki*. Berezovsky was satisfied. The day of Gusinsky's arrest he gleefully exclaimed, "They've got Goosy!" Elsewhere, big business was in shock. The oligarchs wrote a joint letter demanding Gusinsky's release. The only one who didn't sign was Berezovsky.

At the time of Gusinsky's arrest, Putin was on an official visit to Spain. In response to journalists' questions about Gusinsky, he replied that he knew nothing since he was unable to "get through to the prosecutor general." Gusinsky spent three days behind bars, during which time he was visited in his cell by press minister Mikhail Lesin and they signed an agreement under which the oligarch was to be released in exchange for handing over control of NTV.* Upon his release, Gusinsky immediately left Russia—and revealed

*Four years later, Lesin would resign from the ministry, but the company he founded, Video International, would have a monopoly on Russia's TV advertising market. Eventually he would be forced to leave the company by its new owner, Putin's friend Yuri Kovalchuk. Lesin would be found dead in the Dupont Circle Hotel in Washington, DC, in November 2015.

details of the agreement that he had signed under duress. It was a blow to the international image of Putin, who had just returned from a promotional tour around Europe. Gusinsky went into negative PR mode, openly criticizing the new Russian president. Putin was vexed not by the crudeness of the operation against Gusinsky (he punished none of the ringleaders) but by the scandal. Therefore, he instructed his subordinates not to amputate Gusinsky's TV station until passions had subsided.

Gusinsky's arrest had a domino effect. Almost all the oligarchs were subjected to investigations, searches, and seizures. It was not a planned operation; the *siloviki* around Putin simply understood the leadership's signals that it was time to restore order.

In the later Yeltsin years the Prosecutor General's Office had launched many high-profile criminal cases, with the apogee of the "oligarchic wars" arriving at the end of the 1990s. But the style of the new onslaught was different and a sign of the times. *Kommersant* published headline after headline beginning with the phrase "They came for . . ."—a clear allusion to Stalin's purges and the 3:00 a.m. knocks on the door. However, if each case is considered in isolation, it is clear that 2000 was no return to Stalinism. Every instance of "They came for . . ." turned out to involve a case of commonplace racketeering. The very first in *Kommersant*'s infamous series of headlines was "They came for [Vagit] Alekperov," CEO of Lukoil, which at the time was Russia's largest oil company—and which had financed the Primakov-Luzhkov alliance in the Duma elections. And while the company was being investigated, in fact it was not about politics at all. All the MPs who previously had been paid by Lukoil and had spent their time in parliament lobbying for the interests of the company had already jumped ship, having refused to join the FAR faction in the Duma. They had formed their own group and voted in solidarity with Unity before being swallowed up by the new United Russia.

The investigation of Lukoil was rumored to have been initiated by a well-known banker. Before the Duma elections in 1999 he approached Lukoil's management saying that he was collecting money on behalf of the Kremlin—and because of his longtime friendship with Putin, he pocketed $50 million. To prevent Lukoil from asking for the money back after the election, the enterprising banker went to the Prosecutor General's Office, with which he had close ties, and "ordered a hit" on the company. A brief investigation followed, after which Alekperov decided not to go after his $50 million.

THE *KURSK* TRAGEDY

Berezovsky's lack of control over the new government annoyed him so much that he decided to go to extremes to get Putin's ear. Having exhausted all verbal, "diplomatic" means, he opted for what he knew best—adventurism.

A week after *Kommersant* had begun to shape the image of Putin's Russia with its "They came for . . ." headlines, Berezovsky announced his intention to leave the Duma seat he had been elected to in 1999. At the time no one understood the reason for his decision. Publicly Berezovsky stated that he planned to throw himself into creating a real opposition force. Shortly thereafter, he came into serious conflict with the powers that be.

The first major test for Putin was the *Kursk* nuclear submarine disaster. On August 12, 2000, the ninety-seventh day of his presidency, the vessel sank in the Barents Sea. Putin thought nothing of it at first, as the military reported that everything was under control and would soon be put right, and so he departed for his vacation in Sochi. A rescue operation began only the following day, when it became clear that the 118 crew members on board were trapped at a depth of 108 meters. Still, it took Putin another five days to interrupt his holiday and return to Moscow, for which he was slaughtered in the press.

On August 22, when news broke that all 118 sailors had perished, Putin went to meet relatives of the victims in the coastal village of Vidjaevo, in the northern region of Murmansk. The meeting did not go well. The hysterical relatives accused Putin of inaction and the military of time-wasting and incompetence for not seeking assistance from abroad. In response, Putin attacked the TV coverage of the incident, asserting three times that the public had been "lied to" by reporters and media owners. He began by saying, "There are people on TV today who shout and scream, yet over the past decade they're the ones who've destroyed the army and navy in which people are now dying. Today they're lining up to defend the armed forces, but tomorrow they'll try to ruin them even more! They've stolen everything and have everyone in their pockets! They legalized theft!" In the middle of the meeting, he returned to this theme: "They stole money, bought up the media, and now manipulate public opinion." And in conclusion: "Their logic is very simple. Target the mass audience to show the military and political leadership that we need them, that they have us on a hook and that we should be afraid of them, listen to them and accept that they will continue to rob the country, the army, and the navy. That is their true purpose. We cannot simply tell them to stop. That would be the right thing to do, but it has to be done more subtly. We need to implement our own information policy. But that requires effort, money, and right-minded people."[1]

Recording devices were banned at the meeting, but a transcript appeared a week later in *Kommersant-Vlast*, a sister publication of Berezovsky's *Kommersant*. A couple of days after that, the TV channel ORT (Russian Public Television, also controlled by Berezovsky) aired a prime-time news show, *Vremya*, hosted by Sergei Dorenko, who a year earlier had helped Putin to become president. Dorenko analyzed Putin's statements on the *Kursk* tragedy and accused him of lying. Among other things, he aired part of a recording of the meeting with relatives of the victims. It would be his last broadcast. Legend has it that after Dorenko's notorious broadcast, ORT received a telephone call from Vladimir Putin himself. He felt that the station had betrayed him. And he never forgave Berezovsky.

Taking ORT from Berezovsky did not require much effort. According to Voloshin's testimony in the Berezovsky-Abramovich case in London, Voloshin simply called the station's general director, Konstantin Ernst, and told him to ignore Berezovsky, saying something like, "Kostya [Konstantin], don't listen to Berezovsky. Don't do what he says. Otherwise we'll take action." It was perfectly legitimate, since Berezovsky owned 49 percent of the channel, while the government had 51 percent; the major shareholder simply decided to reassert its rights and took control of the channel. "The party's over," Voloshin told Berezovsky, according to his statement in the London court. That meant that Berezovsky could no longer give the channel instructions or influence its editorial policy. The only ORT employee to protest was Dorenko, who was immediately fired.

In late August Voloshin informed Putin that Berezovsky was seeking a personal meeting. Putin agreed, but it was not so much a meeting as a dressing-down. Not mincing words, Putin told Berezovsky that he no longer controlled ORT and that he could sell or keep his stake as he pleased; it would make no difference.

It was another shock for Berezovsky. He had always expected that Putin would eventually lose his nerve and give in. In early September 2000 he wrote him an open letter that he published in his own paper, *Kommersant*: "Mr. President, please stop before it's too late! Don't let the genie out of the bottle. The genie of the unlimited power. He ravaged our country for more than seventy years. You are not equal to the task. Both you and Russia will be destroyed."[2] In the letter he promised to transfer his stake in the company to a team of journalists and intellectuals. However, that plan was never carried out, and a month later, in October 2000, he sold his shares to his old friend Roman Abramovich.

Twelve years later, when Berezovsky sued Abramovich for allegedly underpaying him for his stake in ORT and other companies, among them the major oil company Sibneft, the details of that deal would become known. The London court published a transcript of a wiretapped conversation between Berezovsky, Abramovich, and Badri Patarkatsishvili in Le Bourget, France, in which the three oligarchs discussed the sale of ORT and the personal involvement of Russian Central Bank head Viktor Gerashchenko in transferring the money from Abramovich's account to Berezovsky's. Abramovich told the court that Putin and Voloshin had instructed him to buy ORT from Berezovsky, and he asserted that Berezovsky had owned no shares in his companies and that the regular payments made to him later had been purely for "political protection."

It was the *Kursk* tragedy that kick-started the struggle between Putin and the "manipulators of public opinion"—that is, non-state-controlled media. It was not a premeditated strategy, but a spontaneous reaction to external stimuli. But it soon gathered a momentum of its own, since silent critics are always preferable to vocal ones. It was a necessary by-product of the ongoing reforms, Voloshin told his colleagues at the time.

THE NEW ANDROPOV

Another concern for Boris Berezovsky, which few others shared, was that Vladimir Putin was a KGB alumnus. Berezovsky did not trust the intelligence services. Putin's past life did not unduly bother Berezovsky at first, but as he gradually lost influence he became increasingly inclined to see the mark of the KGB in Putin's behavior, and it troubled him.

Putin was indeed close to the FSB, the KGB's successor, and relied on its support. In December 1999, one and a half weeks before Yeltsin appointed him as acting president, Putin went to the organization's headquarters at Lubyanka Square in Moscow to celebrate Chekist's Day, which marks the anniversary of the founding of the secret service. Speaking at the reception, he joked that "the government's undercover FSB team has coped admirably with the first stage of the task."[3] The audience burst into applause. Outsiders who saw a recording of the event afterward shuddered.

In 1999 Putin sanctioned a widespread celebration to mark the eighty-fifth anniversary of the birth of the late Yuri Andropov, who became secretary general of the Communist Party of the Soviet Union (CPSU) in 1982, after more than twenty years as head of the KGB. He is still revered in the Russian secret service as the wisest leader the Soviet Union has ever had. In December 1999 the memorial plaque in honor of Andropov that had been torn down in 1991, after the collapse of the Soviet Union, was restored to the KGB/FSB building in Lubyanka Square.

Five years later, on the occasion of the ninetieth anniversary of his birth, numerous books and articles appeared about how Andropov could and should have saved the Soviet Union from disintegration. His untimely death in 1984, after barely eighteen months in power, derailed plans for reforms that would have taken the Soviet Union down the Chinese route and avoided perestroika and the collapse of the country. Veterans of the intelligence services saw Putin as the reincarnation of Andropov, the man to restore the greatness of the Soviet Union from the ashes of the lost empire.

Although Putin did not consider himself the successor to Andropov, neither was he particularly enamored of the KGB's legendary chairman. By contrast, the new director of the FSB, Putin's former deputy Nikolai Patrushev, saw Andropov as a role model. As a young man Andropov had lived in Karelia, in northern Russia. That was where Patrushev had worked in the early 1990s, rising to the post of Karelian minister of security.

In 2004 Patrushev wrote an article in the pro-government newspaper *Rossiyskaya Gazeta* to mark the ninetieth anniversary of Andropov's birth. "For senior officers and young employees alike," wrote Patrushev, "Andropov is a true statesman and a representative of the country's strategic elite, who put national interests above all else. . . . Time cannot diminish the glory of those who sincerely and honestly served and continue to serve the Motherland."[4] Back in 2004, pride in the Soviet past—never mind in the tools of Soviet repression—was out of fashion. Ten years down the line, however, it would become a core element of Putin's rhetoric. And in 2014 Patrushev, now head of the Security Council, would become one of the main architects of Russia's new isolationism in the wake of the Ukraine crisis.

PAYBACK TIME

Putin's economic team understood that there was little time to push through "breakthrough" (i.e., painful) reforms, since in the run-up to the next election the reform program would have to ease up. They did what they could to exploit rising oil prices and the president's popularity to implement almost revolutionary changes. The oligarchs and schemers whose influence had waned after Yeltsin's resignation were repugnant to the young liberals serving as Putin's economic advisers, who secretly rejoiced that those former power brokers no longer had the keys to the Kremlin. Life was simpler without them. They also stoically put up with the howls of indignation in the press about the side effects of the reforms, thinking that such complaints were inevitable.

What Putin's liberal government did not expect, however, was obstacles from the West, which not long before had applauded the "brilliant team" put together by the new Russian president. The Russian government was up to its eyeballs in debt to both the Paris Club of public lenders (which had generously lent money to the Soviet Union and then Russia in the 1990s) and the London Club of private investors, commercial banks, and corporations (which had also allowed the Russian government to borrow heavily). The payments to service the debts were set to rise year on year, peaking in 2003. Economists spoke with horror of "the 2003 problem" and saw it as the year when the Russian economy would collapse under the debt burden.

Putin's newly appointed prime minister was Mikhail Kasyanov, who had served as Russia's finance minister before Putin entered the government in 1999. Kasyanov's area of expertise lay in negotiating with international lending institutions. Although Kasyanov had been Putin's first deputy prime minister, he was not an obvious favorite for the post of prime minister, as he had not been involved in developing the economic reforms. That was the task of the Center for Strategic Research, headed by German Gref. Moreover, Gref and Alexei Kudrin had known Putin in St. Petersburg. So either one of them would have seemed a more natural choice to head the government. But Putin opted for Kasyanov, partly because he was closer to the Family, and partly because Russia's external debt was such a crucial issue. Kudrin landed the post of finance minister, while Gref got an entirely new department, the Ministry of Economic Development.

Ironically, it was far simpler to secure an agreement with the private banks than with the public lenders. Mikhail Kasyanov arranged for more than a third of the debt owed to the London Club to be written off, but the Paris Club demanded payment in full, despite the fact that its heavyweight members included Putin's new friends George W. Bush and Tony Blair. Business is business—nothing personal.

By the end of 2001 the situation had become so critical that Putin did not let anyone from his economic team to leave Moscow for the New Year holiday. On January 3, 2002, they all gathered at the Kremlin to decide how to extricate the country from its pile of debt. Putin, Kasyanov, Voloshin, Kudrin, and Gref were there, as well as Andrei Illarionov, who was Putin's economic adviser, Russia's G8 sherpa, and the Kremlin's new enfant terrible, and who was also known for his extreme radical libertarianism and monstrous character.

The meeting devolved into a terrible row between Kasyanov and Illarionov. The prime minister said that the Paris Club had to be cajoled to forgive some of the debt, since any attempt to repay it in full would bleed the Russian economy to death. Illarionov shouted that everything had to be paid back, because Russia had to justify the honor of G8 membership and not go begging for debt postponement and restructuring. The irate Kasyanov retorted that there was nothing humiliating about debt restructuring. Voloshin clearly preferred Illarionov's radical position: the chief of staff was in favor of paying up with head held high, despite Finance Minister Kudrin's assertion that the money wasn't there. Putin decided to wait awhile. He sent his creditors a letter saying that Russia was prepared to pay interest on the outstanding Soviet debt but was seeking a deferment on the principal sum.

But the Paris Club had other ideas. Despite Moscow's request, it continued to insist that Russia pay up in full, since the economic situation was favorable and oil prices were rising. In mid-January the German Ministry of Finance issued a press release stating that if Russia did not start paying back its debts, Berlin would oppose Russia's full membership in the G8. At that time German chancellor Gerhard Schroeder was not one of Putin's closest foreign allies, and it was clear that he was speaking on behalf of the other members of the organization as well. For the Kremlin, it was a blow. Russia's accession to the G7 in 1997 was perhaps the only positive legacy that Boris Yeltsin had bequeathed Putin. Now Putin and his government were on the verge of losing the opportunity to become a full-fledged member of the prestigious club.

Putin was so enraged by Schroeder's statement that he immediately changed his mind and stopped the discussion between Kasyanov and Illarionov. The G8 sherpa's argument won the day: *We are strong, and the strong must pay up.* Kudrin was ordered to find the money. Kasyanov was furious. All the years of painstaking effort had crumbled to dust, and Putin no longer wanted to listen to him. To top it all off, without consulting anyone, Illarionov held a press conference at which he announced that Russia would pay up—and quickly at that. He knew that he had Putin's support, and he was eager to publicly humiliate Kasyanov. Before that moment Kasyanov had been considered a powerful, highly influential figure, but now he was reeling. Kudrin was also in an awkward position, because he had no clear plan for raising the money. As a result, the entire liberal camp inside the Russian government was at loggerheads for several weeks, and harbored ill feeling toward the West for having forced them into a corner.

The fears turned out to be completely unfounded. The price of oil remained steady the whole year at around $27 per barrel (the previous decade it had been nearly half that), which meant that suddenly the money was there to pay off not only the Paris Club but also the IMF. In 2001 Russia posted a budget surplus and ceased to coordinate its economic policy with the IMF. However, the enmity between the economic insiders continued; in February 2004 Kasyanov was dismissed, and Illarionov resigned in December 2005.* Neither Kudrin nor Gref ever thought of interceding on their behalf to keep them in power.

THE RUSSIAN AND US "WARS ON TERROR"

In contrast to the sunken *Kursk*, the military operation in Chechnya (the Second Chechen War) was no problem for Putin. In fact, it was a triumph. His presidential rating soared on the back of the intervention. The only cause for concern were the numerous questions from Western colleagues. To the West, the operation in Chechnya appeared to be a war against the Chechen people,

---

*Ironically, the two adversaries Kasyanov and Illarionov would both later become opponents of Vladimir Putin.

involving systematic violations of human rights, crimes against civilians, and widespread torture, which Russia had also been accused of during the First Chechen War (1994–1996). However, there was a major difference between the two campaigns in Chechnya.

During the first war, the warring parties were divided into "us" (the Chechens) and "them" (the Russians). But in 2000 Putin bet on Akhmad Kadyrov, the chief mufti of the Chechen Republic and a former warlord, who agreed to switch his allegiance to Russia. Hence, the us-them divide was now between supporters of Kadyrov and supporters of the underground movement.

It meant that Putin could lay all the blame on the "terrorists," some of whom were affiliated with al-Qaeda, including the Jordanian-born Omar Ibn al Khattab. Putin also asserted that the war had started when Wahhabis invaded Dagestan in August 1999. However, Boris Berezovsky and Vladimir Gusinsky, now political émigrés, attacked Putin's version. Gusinsky gave numerous interviews about human rights abuses in Chechnya, while Berezovsky alleged that the second Chechen operation had been organized by Putin's entourage as part of his election campaign.

When Putin told Western colleagues about his war on terror, they listened attentively, nodded, and said they would do what they could to assist. In reality things turned out differently. Kremlin intelligence indicated that US embassy employees in Azerbaijan were issuing fake documents to Chechen rebel groups. The evidence was immediately presented to the US ambassador in Moscow. The Americans apologized and assured Moscow that the guilty party, most likely an errant individual, would be recalled from the diplomatic mission forthwith.

However, it soon became clear that the United States was in no hurry to help Russia in its fight against terrorism—failing, for instance, to shut down Islamic organizations accused by Moscow of funding the Chechen underground. "We've carried out checks. These organizations are engaged in purely humanitarian activity," Washington said in a statement, according to a Kremlin official. Incidentally, after 9/11 the organizations were all immediately shut down. The Kremlin resented Washington's insistence that the funds had been earmarked for purely humanitarian purposes. The lives of Russian soldiers did not matter, but when US citizens were targeted, measures were taken.

Nevertheless, 9/11 offered a rare moment of unity between Russia and the United States. Vladimir Putin was the first world leader to call President

Bush to offer his support. From that moment on, it was easier for Putin to explain whom and what Russia was fighting in Chechnya.

The Kremlin backed Washington's next move: the invasion of Afghanistan. The Taliban regime in Afghanistan had always been extremely hostile to Russia. First of all, the Taliban were the ideological heirs of the mujahedeen, who had repulsed the Soviet Union in the 1980s. Second, they had destabilized the situation in Tajikistan and Uzbekistan, increasing the chances of a full-scale war on Russia's southern borders. The Americans had in fact tacitly supported the Taliban throughout the 1990s, so their decision to overthrow the regime was very much welcomed by Moscow.

Just before the bombing started in Afghanistan, Washington sought Moscow's approval for a temporary air base in Kyrgyzstan to support the forthcoming operation—only for the duration of the military campaign, one year at the most, it was said. US national security adviser Condoleezza Rice initially phoned Alexander Voloshin, after which Bush spoke to Putin directly. Moscow's consent was needed because the supply lines would go through Russia; there was also the fact that Kyrgyzstan would not agree without Moscow's backing. The fight against the Taliban was entirely in Russia's interests, Putin and Voloshin reasoned, and so they told the Kyrgyz president and the Americans that they had no objection.

The military operation in Afghanistan was a lightning strike. After just one week the Taliban had seemingly dissolved, leaving power to the pro-US government of Hamid Karzai. A couple of years later, of course, the Taliban would start to reemerge from the caves and mountains, waging an exhausting guerrilla war against NATO troops. But back in early 2002 it looked like a crushing victory for the newly united civilized world against a stone-age enemy.

In late 2002 Voloshin inquired of Condoleezza Rice as to when the United States was planning to leave Kyrgyzstan, since the military operation was, after all, complete. "You know what? It turns out we really need this base, like, permanently," was the alleged response.

Putin was furious. The Americans seemed to be double-crossing him at every turn. Moreover, they never took responsibility for their mistakes, while all the time lecturing the Kremlin about how to behave.

The real turning point was the war in Iraq. George W. Bush, urged on by oil lobbyists and military hawks on one hand and his own neoconservative ideology on the other, decided to overthrow Saddam Hussein. The decision was made in April 2002—immediately after the end of the operation against the Taliban in Afghanistan. But over the next few months US government representatives, headed by Rice, discussed the matter with the Kremlin as if the decision had not already been made, speaking eloquently about the horrors of Saddam Hussein's regime, its links to al-Qaeda, and its stockpiles of chemical and biological weapons. British prime minister Tony Blair was also in on the game.

Rice did not know, however, that her lurid reports of Saddam Hussein's atrocities were greeted with skepticism in Moscow. Russian diplomats knew Saddam far better than their US counterparts did. Former prime minister and onetime Putin adversary Yevgeny Primakov was a Middle East expert, spoke fluent Arabic, and was practically a pal of Hussein's, while the pseudo-oppositionist Communist leader Gennady Zyuganov and populist Vladimir Zhirinovsky were frequent guests in Baghdad. The Russian companies Lukoil and Zarubezhneft produced oil in Iraq, and other Russian companies were involved in the UN's Oil-for-Food program. And while the formal links between Russia and Iraq were extensive, the informal links were even more so. The Monday flight from Moscow to Baghdad, for instance, always had prostitutes on board for the sons of Saddam Hussein and their entourage.

A couple of years later a UN investigative commission led by former US Federal Reserve chairman Paul Volcker would accuse several dozen Russian companies, as well as the Russian Ministry of Emergency Situations and even the Russian Orthodox Church, of receiving oil allocations as compensation for political support and of paying huge kickbacks to the Iraqi government.[5] Volcker would also accuse several Russian politicians of bribery. All denied the charges, but only Alexander Voloshin would prove to the UN inquiry that his signature on a number of documents uncovered during the inquiry was forged.

In any event, Moscow's knowledge of the inner workings of Iraq was far deeper than Washington's. The Kremlin had no desire whatsoever to overthrow the predictable and controllable Saddam Hussein, whom it knew to be surrounded by corruption but not weapons of mass destruction. Russia had business interests in Iraq, which it would lose in the event of war. But these arguments went unheard by Condoleezza Rice. So instead the Russians made a case for a diplomatic solution, to prevent civilian suffering. But that too made no impression on the Americans.

The year 2002 was dominated by the Iraq debate. Bush and Blair continued to lie to Putin about the dangers of Baghdad's supposed chemical and biological weapons. Putin found it far easier to deal with Gerhard Schroeder and Jacques Chirac. They too advocated a nonviolent approach, although cynical self-interest was not far from the surface. French companies had contracts in Iraq and allegedly had received bribes, which may have prompted Chirac's anti-war stance. Schroeder's pacifism also had an ulterior motive: Germans were due to go to the polls in October 2002, and, faced with the imminent defeat of his social-democratic SPD, Schroeder staked his party's future on voters' anti-war sentiment, knowing that opposition to America's invasion plans would go down well. The more "pacifist" the chancellor became, the higher his approval rating soared. In the end he achieved the impossible: reelection. Putin joined Schroeder and Chirac in an anti-war coalition against the pro-war alliance of the United States, Britain, and Spain.

Putin, Schroeder, and Chirac were united not only by cynical calculation but also by heartfelt irritation. All three were incensed that Bush had made the decision to go to war without even bothering to ask their opinion. The leaders of Russia, Germany, and France (and, incidentally, those of Britain and Spain) were not privy to the proceedings of the virtual "board of directors of the world" at which US vice president Dick Cheney, the heads of the oil companies and defense contractors under his patronage, US defense secretary Donald Rumsfeld, his deputy Paul Wolfowitz, and other influential neocons talked shop. Their opinions counted for more than those of Washington's G8 colleagues.

According to Kremlin aides, the war in Iraq permanently changed Putin's attitude toward the United States. He was particularly offended by his friend Tony Blair's acquiescence, articulating his indignation at every subsequent meeting they had, even during press conferences. The British press was disconcerted: here was Putin publicly haranguing the prime minister, who just stood there grinning inanely, saying nothing. Remarkably, it was not the end of their friendship.

No chemical or biological weapons were ever found in Iraq. A few years later retired US Secretary of State Colin Powell would publicly apologize for his role in having mistakenly misinformed the world community.

A UNIQUE TEAM OF JOURNALISTS

The "fight for peace" greatly increased Vladimir Putin's appeal abroad. In June 2003 the Pew Research Center published a poll indicating that the Russian leader was the world's most popular politician, followed by Chirac in second place and Schroeder in third. However, all three leaders had marred their relations with the United States.

According to US media, the administration had different solutions for each of the "rebel" leaders: France should be punished, Germany ignored, and Russia forgiven. For a while Putin was described in the American press as "Saddam's friend," though he had never actually met the Iraqi leader in real life, unlike, say, George H. W. Bush. However, the label stuck.

Putin suffered far greater reputational damage overseas at the hands of his former friends Boris Berezovsky and Vladimir Gusinsky. Back in November 2000, when the scandal around the *Kursk* submarine had died down, the Russian *siloviki* remembered about the two men and went after them with renewed vigor. The Prosecutor General's Office announced that Vladimir Gusinsky once again was facing detention, while Berezovsky was simply summoned for questioning. The statements were just threats, however, since by that time both had long left Russia. Gusinsky was living at his villa in Spain, while Berezovsky had relocated to his mansion in London. Both stated that they had no plans to return to Russia.

On December 6, 2000, an international arrest warrant for Gusinsky was issued through Interpol, and a week later the Spanish police took him into custody. Gusinsky's case was handed to renowned judge Baltasar Garzón, who had investigated the case of former Chilean president Augusto Pinochet. Gusinsky spent eleven days in a Spanish jail, after which Garzón released him on $5.5 million bail, though Gusinsky's passport was taken away and he remained under house arrest.

The case was thoroughly investigated by the Spanish authorities. In April 2001 Garzón ruled that the charges against Gusinsky were politically motivated and that he could not be extradited. Garzón's decision was aided by events in Moscow: during Gusinsky's trial in Spain, his main asset, NTV, had been systematically dismantled. The Russian gas monopoly Gazprom, which had lent heavily to Gusinsky and bought shares from him, decided to seize the TV company in lieu of unpaid debts.

The assault on NTV was a major domestic political scandal in the winter of 2001. Russia was divided into two camps: those who declared the raid to be an attack on free speech, and those who said that NTV served the private business interests of Gusinsky and the matter had nothing to do with freedom of speech. Both points of view were partially true. It was particularly ironic, however, that the role of NTV-killer belonged to the prominent liberal Alfred Koch, general director of Gazprom-Media and a friend of Anatoly Chubais, the architect of Yeltsin's economic reforms. Thirteen years later Koch himself would turn dissident and leave Russia to avoid criminal charges, never to return.*

Today, the pillaging of NTV is seen as a dark harbinger of the clampdown on press freedom that was to come. However, at the time many people were unconcerned by it. Rallies in support of NTV were attended only by aging intellectuals. Meanwhile, the young and prosperous middle classes were indifferent to the fate of the channel, and many liberal leaders (who in those days even had their own faction in the Duma) sided with Gazprom, since they could not forgive Gusinsky and NTV for having supported the Primakov-Luzhkov alliance in the 1999 parliamentary election.

The methods employed were unscrupulous. The Prosecutor General's Office questioned NTV's top news anchor, the bold and fiery journalist Tatyana Mitkova, about how she had received a loan to buy an apartment. In response, her colleague Svetlana Sorokina, a talk show host, issued an appeal to Putin to save the TV channel from being shut down. A couple of minutes after her emotional speech on the air, the president called the station and invited the journalists to the Kremlin for talks. But the discussion did not produce a solution.

Gusinsky tried and failed to get help from abroad. He was keen to sell his stake to CNN founder Ted Turner but could not close the deal.

On the night of April 13–14, 2001, Gazprom replaced the security guards outside the NTV studio and stopped all journalists, including general director Yevgeny Kiselyov, from entering the building.† Those loyal to Gusinsky were taken off the air, but a few days later they were given shelter by Boris Berezovsky, who, despite having sold ORT, still owned another major

---

*Few people remember that Gusinsky's and NTV's lawyer, the young Pavel Astakhov, was once an ardent defender of free speech. Ten years down the line he would become not only a government mouthpiece but also a champion of populist anti-Americanism. As commissioner for children's rights in Russia, he advocated the infamous "anti-adoption" law, which initially prohibited just US citizens from adopting Russian children, but was then extended to cover all countries in which same-sex marriage was legal.

† Some employees (including the recently interrogated Tatyana Mitkova) decided to stay with the channel and work under Gazprom management. Ten years later Mitkova would become a symbol of state propaganda.

channel, TV-6. He fired his entire journalistic staff and invited the NTV team to come and work for him. But the debt-ridden TV-6 was closed a year later in similar circumstances, although this time the creditor was not the state gas company, Gazprom, but the private oil firm Lukoil.

To dampen the scandal, Voloshin decided to give NTV's "unique team of journalists," headed by Yevgeny Kiselyov, another chance. Ten oligarchs chipped in to create a new high-quality channel from the rubble of NTV and TV-6. It would not belong to Berezovsky, Gusinsky, or any other single individual. Voloshin appointed Yevgeny Primakov to head the channel's supervisory board. His logic was that the journalists had wanted Primakov to be president, so now he would preside over them personally. But TVS, as the channel was called, lasted only a year, from 2002 to 2003. The co-owners quarreled and began to buy up each other's shares, after which the presidential administration decided to pull the plug. In any event, it never won many viewers.

Berezovsky was not yet a wanted man when he stuck up for NTV's journalists. But his close friend Nikolai Glushkov was arrested on charges of embezzling funds from the Russian national airline, Aeroflot (in which Berezovsky was a shareholder). Later Berezovsky claimed that Glushkov was simply used to put pressure on him. But by autumn 2001 (just after the NTV team had relocated to his TV-6), he too was in trouble.

In September 2001 the Prosecutor General's Office charged Berezovsky in absentia with aiding and abetting fraud and money laundering. A month later he applied for political asylum in the United Kingdom. However, the British government was in no hurry to respond, as in the aftermath of 9/11 Russia and Britain were allies in the fight against international terrorism.

But the fugitive oligarch continued his struggle. In early 2002 he financed the publication of a book entitled *Blowing Up Russia*, followed by a documentary film version called *Assassination of Russia*. Both were authored by Berezovsky's closest associates (one was former FSB officer Alexander Litvinenko), and both put forward the conspiracy theory that the bombings in Moscow and elsewhere in autumn 1999 were the work not of Chechen terrorists but of Russia's own intelligence services. The authors and Berezovsky claimed that the attacks were carried out to promote the newly appointed prime minister, Putin, as a people's champion in the fight against terrorism.

After these accusations against the FSB, the attacks on Berezovsky intensified. TV-6 was shut down even before the book and film were released. That was followed in August 2002 by new charges against him, and in October that same year an international warrant was issued for Berezovsky's arrest. Russian officials had every confidence that Britain would extradite their man. The Iraq debate had damaged the political and ideological affinity between Moscow and London, but Tony Blair and his government did not want to spoil relations with their old friend even more. On April 2, 2003, the day before the Iraq War began, the UK Home Office denied Berezovsky political asylum. The question of extradition would now be for the courts to decide. After the hearing, the eccentric Berezovsky posed for photographers wearing a Putin mask, saying, "Call me Vladimir."

In August 2003, while Berezovsky was fighting for the right to stay in London, there was good news for the Russian Prosecutor General's Office from Greece: Vladimir Gusinsky had been arrested at Athens International Airport. After he had been released by the Spanish court, Russia had filed new charges against him and placed him once again on the international wanted list through Interpol. Greek police arrested the former media mogul and took him to a city jail. The chances of extradition to Russia from Greece were thought to be much higher than from Spain.

NORD-OST

Without doubt, one of the blackest days of Vladimir Putin's presidency to date is October 23, 2002. That evening a group of terrorists seized a theater in Moscow during a performance of the musical *Nord-Ost*. About 850 people were taken hostage. For Putin, it was a catastrophe. Not only was the war he had promised to end three years earlier not over, but it had come to the capital.

According to the memoirs of members of his inner circle, Putin was convinced that his political career was finished. One source compares his state of mind to that of Stalin in June 1941. On hearing that Germany had invaded the Soviet Union and already taken Minsk, Stalin was in shock. He went to his dacha and did not emerge for several days. When Politburo members came to ask him to head the newly formed war committee, Stalin (according to the memoir of Anastas Mikoyan) "was huddled up in a chair" as if waiting to be arrested.

Putin, of course, did not go anywhere. But he was sure that society would never forgive him for such a terrorist attack on Moscow. FSB director Nikolai

Patrushev managed to stay calmer, even though the free passage of armed Chechens to Moscow had been the result of a failure by his agency.

As it turned out, there were no political implications. Three days after the seizure, the FSB pumped knockout gas into the hall and then stormed the theater. Reports vary, but between 130 (official version) and 175 (human rights organizations' version) people died, most from adverse reactions to the gas and lack of medical assistance. The unconscious hostages were piled into buses; some did not actually die from the gas but choked on their own vomit or were crushed. All the terrorists were killed during the rescue attempt, so there was no one to interrogate during the subsequent investigation. How it was masterminded remains a mystery.

Six months later journalist Anna Politkovskaya published an interview with a man who claimed to be a member of the group of terrorists that had seized the theater.[6] He said that he was Chechen and that he had been recruited by the Russian security services. In the interview he stated that Russian security officials knew in advance about the attack in Moscow. The veracity of his version of events is difficult to prove; the interviewee was killed in a car crash shortly afterward, and Anna Politkovskaya herself was assassinated in 2006.

The security chiefs who organized the operation to free the hostages received state awards, and FSB director Patrushev's first deputy was decorated with the Hero of Russia medal. The only ones punished for the terrorist attack on the theater were reporters. The new-look NTV was forced to undergo another change of management when the general director, Boris Jordan, an American of Russian descent, was dismissed, having spent the previous eighteen months helping to wrest the channel from Gusinsky. Putin accused him of wanting to "make money from the blood of his fellow citizens—if he considers them to be his fellow citizens, that is."[7] The purported reason was that NTV had shown a live broadcast of the storming of the theater (although NTV officials say there was no such broadcast).

The chemical composition of the gas used during the rescue attempt remains classified. Former hostages have sued the Russian government in various courts, including the European Court of Human Rights in Strasbourg, France. But the Kremlin still refuses to say what the gas actually was. The disclosure of that information is still needed in order to adequately treat former hostages.

THE ROYAL WEDDING

On June 24, 2003, Vladimir Putin arrived at London's Heathrow with his wife, Lyudmila. At the airport he was met by Prince Charles. Together they made their way to Horse Guards Parade, where the Queen was waiting for them. This was not just a visit, but a state visit complete with an official welcoming ceremony, a sumptuous reception, and all the associated pomp and circumstance. "Never have relations between our two countries been so good," Tony Blair told Russian journalists.[8] Indeed, it was the first state visit to the United Kingdom by a Russian head of state since 1896, when the last Russian tsar, Nicholas II, visited Queen Victoria.

But come the appointed hour Putin was not there. He and Prince Charles were stuck in traffic. The Queen had to wait fourteen minutes, which under other circumstances might have caused an unprecedented diplomatic scandal. But the Queen forgave Putin's unintentional tardiness, and after that everything went off without a hitch. Putin and the Queen rode in the lead carriage to Buckingham Palace. Behind followed Lyudmila Putin and the Duke of Edinburgh in the second carriage, with the heir to the throne, Prince Charles, and Russian finance minister Alexei Kudrin (no one's heir) in the third.

Later that evening the Queen gave a state banquet in honor of the Putins, who were staying at Buckingham Palace. Russia's ruling couple were shown around Westminster Abbey and the Tower of London. The president met the leaders of Britain's three largest political parties and flew to Edinburgh for a day trip, where he addressed an audience of scientific, academic, and business leaders.

"Russia is undoubtedly part of Europe," Putin told the gathering of Scottish intellectuals, to applause.

> Europe continues to the east of the Urals Mountains, because if we take the people who live in the Far East they are little different from the Russian citizens who live in the European part of the country.
>
> That is a very good potential for the future development of Europe, but today we must be realistic about the goals we set ourselves. We should make sure that no new dividing lines appear in Europe, that people are able to communicate with one another, that the rules of the Schengen zone

> are not perceived as something similar to the Berlin Wall, which divided Europe until a few years ago.
>
> We must do everything to enable Russia and Europe help each other to develop in a harmonious and stable way. We have a mutual interest in each other because even the structures of the Russian and European economies mutually complement each other.[9]

Not for nothing did Putin mention economics. He and Blair held an energy conference, which produced several momentous statements. First, in the presence of the two leaders, BP CEO Lord John Browne and Tyumen Oil Company (TNK) owner Mikhail Fridman signed an agreement to establish the joint Anglo-Russian company TNK-BP. The British oil giant bought 50 percent of the Russian company, making it the second-largest oil company in the world, overtaking its bitter rival Royal Dutch Shell. News of the forthcoming deal had first broken in February 2003, and the preparations, overseen personally by Vladimir Putin, went smoothly. TNK-BP was registered in Russia, but its CEO, Robert Dudley, had come from BP and was American. It was a remarkable breakthrough. The British company was now producing Siberian oil. British journalists joked that Putin had repeated the achievement of Alexander II, who had paid a state visit to London in 1874 with the intention of marrying off his daughter to Prince Alfred, the Duke of Edinburgh. Putin had come to marry off his "daughter company" to Lord Browne of BP.

It was a symbolic moment. Among those applauding in the hall were not only Putin and Blair but also the head of Gazprom, Alexei Miller, and Mikhail Khodorkovsky, the owner of Yukos, which by that point had surpassed Lukoil as Russia's largest oil company. Khodorkovsky's business partner Platon Lebedev would be arrested in Russia just a week later as part of what would come to be known as the "Yukos affair." And a decade later Fridman would sell his stake in TNK-BP, removing most of his assets from Russia and relocating his family to London. In the end the "marriage" was short-lived, and its offspring chose to live outside Russia.

The merger of TNK and BP was not the only achievement of that historic visit. Putin and Blair announced another ambitious project—the construction of the North European Gas Pipeline (later renamed Nord Stream). Costing $5.7 billion, the pipeline would connect Russia and Britain. The two governments signed a memorandum of understanding, which meant that the proposed co-investors, Gazprom and Royal Dutch Shell, could go ahead with signing the necessary agreements. As Tony Blair proudly stated, thanks to these deals and Royal Dutch Shell's prior investments in the Sakhalin-2 project in the Russian Far East, Britain was now the largest foreign investor in the Russian energy sector.

Throughout Putin's stay in London, the presence of Boris Berezovsky in the same city was not too much of an issue, despite the fact that just a few blocks from Buckingham Palace a human rights film festival was taking place, at which *Assassination of Russia* was premiered. The organizers printed a giant ticket for Putin and Blair and happily showed it to the media.

The state visit lasted four days and was perhaps the zenith of Russian relations with the Western world. Afterward, it didn't take long for cracks in the relationship to appear. On September 9 the UK Home Office revised its original decision and granted Berezovsky political asylum. The next day a London court refused to extradite him to Russia.

On October 14, a Greek court refused to extradite Gusinsky. Immediately afterward, before the Russian Prosecutor General's Office had time to appeal, he flew to Israel.

In November a different London court ruled on the case of Akhmed Zakayev, another of Putin's bugbears. The Russian authorities considered him to be a Chechen terrorist leader, but again their request for extradition was denied.

The Putin-Blair friendship had survived Iraq, but it could not withstand Berezovsky's and Zakayev's political asylum. The Russian president felt betrayed. Blair assured Putin that it was out of his hands, since he had no influence over Britain's independent legal system. For Putin, though, the Home Office document granting Berezovsky political asylum carried a strong whiff of political involvement.

For his part, Putin would forget about the idea of running a gas pipeline under the Baltic Sea to Europe—though he would remember it three years later, albeit with a new partner in the shape of Gerhard Schroeder. And in 2006 Royal Dutch Shell would be stripped of its Sakhalin deposits as the temperature of Anglo-Russian relations dipped to Cold War levels.

CHAPTER 3

IN WHICH RUSSIA'S RICHEST MAN, MIKHAIL KHODORKOVSKY, LOSES HIS BUSINESS AND FREEDOM, AND THE FAMILY DISAPPEARS

I met Mikhail Khodorkovsky on December 22, 2013, a day after his release from prison, at the Hotel Adlon in Berlin. Khodorkovsky came across as a modest and shy intellectual—a far cry from descriptions of him before his incarceration as a tough, commanding, purposeful leader. He said he had no plans to enter politics, but it seemed that he spent almost every waking moment talking to the press.

He answered all questions precisely and without hesitation, as if he'd rehearsed his replies. And when the cameras stopped rolling, he started asking questions himself, mainly about the power balance in the Kremlin. Khodorkovsky was trying to figure out the lay of the land—how things had changed, who was now in charge. Most of all, he was interested in his longtime foe, Igor Sechin, who at that time was the CEO of Rosneft, the oil company. "Do you think Sechin will become prime minister?" he asked.

A year after his release, Khodorkovsky had toughened up. He had revived his Open Russia Foundation and hired an insane number of journalists, who were not very clear about what Khodorkovsky wanted from them.

He readily agreed to be interviewed for this book, but set a very limited time frame, and the whole interview was conducted via FaceTime. A fan of technology, Khodorkovsky was clearly pleased that he had been able to use the latest gadgets even when in jail.

Speaking about the Yukos affair, for some reason he employed military metaphors, not business terminology: "Putin was behaving like a classic military commander. When I served as an army officer, we were taught not to yell at solders standing to attention. So when he noticed broad disaffection among big business, Putin located the command center [that is, he found the key person] and smashed it. After that, no one dared step out of line."

Putin could not have said it better himself.

BARBECUE SAUCE

In summer 2001 Vladimir Putin gathered together a dozen of Russia's top business leaders for a barbecue at his summer residence in Novo-Ogaryovo. The gathering would go down in history as the "barbecue meeting." He explained the new rules of the game to the oligarchs, so that they could avoid the fate that had befallen Gusinsky and Berezovsky. The number one rule was simple: *don't meddle in politics.* Mikhail Khodorkovsky recalls that the advice was mainly directed at media moguls. But every major business leader had the levers to exert political pressure on the authorities.

"Yukos was the exclusive supplier of oil products in forty-two regions of Russia. If I'd stopped supplying petroleum products, the country would have ground to a halt. The regions would have revolted. Ambulances, fire engines, and all essential services would have stopped running after just three days," says Khodorkovsky.

If the oligarchs complied with Putin's request not to exploit their power, they would have no problems with the law enforcement agencies. Everyone breathed a collective sigh of relief and gladly accepted the president's terms.

But Putin's words were not as clear as they could have been. Some (Prime Minister Mikhail Kasyanov, for instance) assert that they contained a warning not to finance opposition parties. Others disagree, saying that in those days sponsorship of political parties was commonplace. The Duma was home to an entire faction, Regions of Russia, wholly funded by Lukoil. Yukos did not have a faction of its own, but one of its co-owners, Vladimir Dubov, a Duma MP, was reputed to be the oil industry's chief lobbyist in parliament.

The early 2000s were a good time for Mikhail Khodorkovsky, who succeeded in turning Yukos into Russia's largest public company. The company's operations became more transparent and thus attractive to foreign investors. The head of Britain's BP, Lord Browne, wrote in his memoir that in 2002, when planning how to gain access to Russian oil, he had considered three investment options: Yukos, Rosneft, and TNK, in that order.

"17 February 2002: Several black armoured cars pulled up outside the house, and numerous burly bodyguards emerged," writes Browne, describing a meeting with Khodorkovsky in his memoir *Beyond Business*. "Khodorkovsky, like many of the oligarchs, lived in a gated compound with high walls and security lights, outside Moscow, and was paranoid about security. My house was much less grand, less protected, but nevertheless secure."

According to BP's then CEO, over lunch he and Khodorkovsky discussed the purchase of a 25 percent stake plus one share in Yukos. Browne felt that it was not enough. But when he hinted that he'd like more, Khodorkovsky replied: "You can take 25 per cent, no more and no control. If you come along with me, you will be taken care of."

"Bespectacled, soft-spoken Khodorkovsky could be at first glance be mistaken as unassuming," recalls Browne. "But as the conversation progressed, I felt increasingly nervous. He began to talk about getting people elected to the Duma, about how he could make sure oil companies did not pay much tax, and about how he had many influential people under his control. For me, he seemed too powerful. It is easy to say this with hindsight, but there was something untoward about his approach."[1]

Mikhail Khodorkovsky, who had seemed "too powerful" to the head of BP, was at that moment dizzy with success. Not only had he turned his company into the largest in Russia, becoming the country's richest man, he was also the darling of the whole Russian liberal intelligentsia. He financed the Open Russia Foundation, which sponsored a good half of all Russia's nongovernmental organizations, donated money to cultural and educational projects, and provided Internet access for remote rural schools. Khodorkovsky himself gave lectures and speeches, demonstrating that despite not being a politician he was ready to lead.

Putin, of course, could not ban the oligarchs from being popular with the people, but in many ways that was what he had meant at the "barbecue meeting."

A PARLIAMENTARY REPUBLIC

Khodorkovsky quickly became the unofficial leader of the entire Russian oil industry. In 2002, when the government introduced a tax on mineral extraction, it was Yukos that led the fight against it. The new tax sought to increase the tax burden on oil companies. The day before the amendments to the Russian tax code were due to be considered, Minister of Economic Development German Gref, who had proposed the tax reforms, received a visit from Vasily Shakhnovsky, the president of the Yukos subsidiary Yukos Moskva. He confidently told the minister that the law would be rejected because it was "contrary to the interests of Yukos," and if the government insisted, then oil producers would write a joint letter demanding the resignation of Gref and Kudrin for being "unprofessional." He instructed the government to postpone the discussion of the bill in the Duma and wait for Yukos to draft a set of counterproposals.

Gref and Kudrin were furious. The next morning the two of them went to the Duma to defend their proposed tax. They still believed that the Duma, in which pro-Kremlin factions had a majority, would not reject a bill introduced by the government. However, their attempt to get the bill through failed miserably. It was unanimously voted down by the Communists as well as members of many other factions, including ones loyal to the Kremlin.

For the government liberals it was a bitter lesson. Now they had to reckon with another rising force in the shape of Mikhail Khodorkovsky. Neither Kudrin nor Gref relished the prospect. It took them a whole year to finally push through a tax on mineral extraction.

Khodorkovsky used his influence to lobby for laws that benefited others too, not just the oil industry. Today he recalls how in early 2003 he and members of United Russia discussed the possibility of changing the constitution to introduce a "French-style presidential-parliamentary republic": "They all knew that Yeltsin's 1993 constitution had overcooked the presidential powers, but attempts to persuade the government could only be made after 2004." That would be after the next presidential election. People close to Khodorkovsky say that he saw himself as a future prime minister inside a new government.

In the 2004 presidential election Vladimir Putin was due to stand for re-election to a second term. Before that, however, were the Duma elections in December 2003. To make the necessary amendments to the constitution and reduce the president's powers, Khodorkovsky needed a pliant, even docile parliament. Therefore, the year before the election Yukos began to fund almost all the existing opposition political parties, including Yabloko, the Union of Right Forces, and the Communists.

Voloshin, Putin's chief of staff, was kept informed of Khodorkovsky's growing political ambitions. On several occasions Khodorkovsky had discussed with Voloshin the idea of switching to a different model of government. Now the Kremlin saw that Yukos was serious about the idea, seeking to gain control of the relevant Duma committees and constantly talking about a parliamentary republic.

Though Voloshin still despised the Communist Party, he was happy for Yukos to sponsor it: the more money they took from capitalists, the more they would surrender their "moral authority" and the more they would decompose on the inside and cease to be Communists, he reasoned. Everyone understood that the Communist electorate did not vote in exchange for money, so increased party funding would not improve their results. And if half the Communists' party list was made up of businessmen, it would push them toward social democracy, thought Voloshin.

THE NEW ELITE

While influential liberal ministers such as Alexei Kudrin and German Gref were irritated by Khodorkovsky's growing influence, Alexander Voloshin and Mikhail Kasyanov were far more concerned about someone else, an unexpected opponent they had not seen coming. His name was Igor Sechin, and he worked under the very noses of Voloshin and his staff.

The first couple of years they did not even notice Sechin, assuming that he was a minor functionary who carried Putin's briefcase, met the president every day by the elevator, arranged his meetings, and took care of his correspondence. However, by the middle of Putin's (and Sechin's) first term in the Kremlin, they realized that they had greatly underestimated the president's secretary. It turned out that this ideal apparatchik, who always stood to attention when in the presence of the head of state, was greatly respected by the FSB. He successfully lobbied for some unexpected staff appointments, and he was the focus of the informal group of old friends who had served with Putin in the KGB and known him back in St. Petersburg, the *siloviki*. In addition to Sechin, this group included prosecutor general Vladimir Ustinov (he and Sechin were in-laws through their children's marriage), FSB head Nikolai

Patrushev, Voloshin's assistant Viktor Ivanov, and a handful of oligarchs, including Rosneft head Sergey Bogdanchikov and banker Sergei Pugachev.*

Voloshin and Kasyanov had seriously underestimated Sechin's proximity to the president. In fact, he had been Putin's private secretary for much of the 1990s at the St. Petersburg mayor's office. He had also been quite visible, since Putin had been the only member of the mayoral administration to have a male secretary. When Putin resigned, Sechin asked to go to Moscow with him, and Putin agreed. Sechin had the complete trust of the future president.

According to Stanislav Belkovsky, who headed the National Strategy Council, an informal union of Russia's most influential political scientists, liberals in the presidential administration saw Sechin as another Alexander Korzhakov, Boris Yeltsin's all-powerful bodyguard, who had also struggled with young reformers only to be toppled by them during the 1996 presidential election. The new batch of liberals hoped to push Sechin aside in a similar manner.

Khodorkovsky says that everyone could feel the impending conflict: "Sechin's followers had their own agenda, while we wanted to move toward a more transparent economy." He continues, "Everyone sensed that very soon Putin would have to make a choice: the *siloviki* or the liberals."

However, both "*siloviki*" and "liberals" are little more than convenient labels. Belkovsky claims that the standoff between them was not ideological and that the two opposing camps represented the old and the new elites. On one side of the conflict were the Family and its associates, who held all the levers of power; on the other side were the young careerists, still short of political and financial clout. The old elite sought to defend their position, while the new wanted to take as much as they could from the former.

To combat Sechin, says Belkovsky, Voloshin decided to bring in the head of Yukos. Voloshin had no desire to expose himself to risk, so he came up with the idea of using Khodorkovsky to topple Sechin, who at the time was head of the board of directors of Rosneft, besides his position in the Kremlin. They thought it would be quite simple. The attack was scheduled for February 19, 2003, the day the Kremlin was due to host a meeting between Putin and

---

*Today Pugachev says that he had no special relationship with the intelligence forces, and for him Sechin was always "the man who carried Putin's briefcase." At the same time, Pugachev describes Patrushev as a lifelong friend and Khodorkovsky as someone he did not get along with.

members of the Russian Union of Industrialists and Entrepreneurs (RUIE), a group of the most influential oligarchs.

THE GHOST OF LOANS-FOR-SHARES

Khodorkovsky says that a few days before that memorable encounter, the RUIE members had a meeting with the presidential administration to discuss the upcoming session. Alexander Voloshin was not present, so the meeting was chaired by his first deputy, Dmitry Medvedev. The participants agreed on everything, including the need to discuss corruption and ways to deal with it. Initially Alexander Mamut, a businessman close to the Family and a long-time friend of Roman Abramovich, was scheduled to speak about this matter. But Mamut pulled out, so Khodorkovsky stepped in. He had prepared a speech criticizing Rosneft for allegedly buying the small company Northern Oil for three times the market price.

On the day of the meeting with Putin, Khodorkovsky decided to show the text of the speech to Voloshin to make sure it wasn't too pointed and could be safely delivered in front of the media. "I'll just go and ask the president," said Voloshin. He soon returned, saying: "Yes, it's okay. The president says it can all be filmed."

A dramatic scene then played out in full view of the cameras. After Khodorkovsky delivered the prepared speech, Putin answered him personally. He defended the Northern Oil deal, saying that Rosneft simply lacked reserves and there was nothing wrong with trying to increase them. But Yukos, continued Putin, had "super-reserves," and there were questions as to how the company had gotten them. "It's highly relevant to the matter at hand," Putin asserted, referring to the discussion they were having about how to tackle corruption. Moreover, the president reminded Khodorkovsky that Yukos had had problems with nonpayment of taxes. "How did these problems arise? Come and take your ball back," concluded Putin, the implication being that Khodorkovsky should be more careful where he aimed his aspersions.

After the meeting, Pugachev says, Putin drew him aside and asked him indignantly who this Khodorkovsky was.

"The president of Yukos," replied Pugachev.

"And where did he get this Yukos, eh? After everything they've had a hand in, he accuses me of taking bribes? He's got some nerve, preaching to me in front of everyone."

As Belkovsky interprets it, Putin was in essence saying, "Either we recognize that everything was stolen and we respect the code of silence, or we start making accusations. If you're charging me with Northern Oil, then, boy, I'll find something to charge you with."

To understand Putin's irritation, it is worth recalling the infamous loans-for-shares auctions, which is how the oligarchs became oligarchs in the first place. In 1995 the Russian government came up with a plan to ensure the reelection of Boris Yeltsin in 1996. The plan envisaged that all major state-owned enterprises, including those involved in petroleum and other natural resources, would be privatized by the largest banking groups. The banks lent the government money and received company shares as collateral. Everyone knew the government would never repay the loans, which meant that the enterprises would become the property of the creditor banks.

There were a couple of additional details, including, for instance, the fact that the banks lent the government the government's own money. Before each deal the Russian Ministry of Finance opened an account with each bank and deposited funds there—and that account was the source of the bank's loan to the government.

However, the collusion did not end there. Formally, each auction involved several bidders. But in fact the result of each auction was a foregone conclusion. During the Berezovsky versus Abramovich lawsuit in London in 2011, Abramovich admitted that the auction for the sale of Sibneft was a sham, as it had been known in advance that a structure linked to Abramovich and Berezovsky would win. One rival bidder was pressured into withdrawing, while another was a front company linked to Khodorkovsky, who was in league with Berezovsky.

Russia's largest natural resource deposits and companies were sold under this prearranged scheme, including Yukos (bought by Khodorkovsky), Sibneft, Surgutneftegaz, Sidanko (later TNK), Lukoil, Norilsk Nickel, Mechel, and Novolipetsk Steel. Curiously, a number of the largest banks, such as Inkombank and Alfa Bank, either were excluded from this distribution of state property or lost every bid. Their subsequent attempts to challenge the results of the auctions also failed. But those who got lucky did so in a big way, above all Boris Berezovsky, Mikhail Khodorkovsky, and Vladimir Potanin. Incidentally, Potanin, who was first deputy prime minister in 1996–1997, is generally considered to be the original architect of the loans-for-shares auctions.

All the auctions were conducted in two stages. The first part, in which the state companies were pawned, occurred before the 1996 presidential election. The second part, when the ownership rights were transferred, happened afterward. That way the government could be sure that all the bankers would keep to the arrangement.

In this way, back in 1995, Khodorkovsky's Menatep Bank bought a 45 percent stake in Yukos for $159 million. By 1997, shortly after Yukos shares began trading publicly, the company's market capitalization had reached $9 billion. And by 2003, thanks to good management and a policy of total transparency, its capitalization was close to $15 billion.

The person behind the drive toward Russian privatization, Anatoly Chubais, who served as first deputy prime minister between 1994 and 1996, later told the *Financial Times* that the government "did not have a choice between an 'honest' privatisation and a 'dishonest' one, because an honest privatisation means clear rules imposed by a strong state that can enforce its laws. . . . We had no choice. If we did not have the loans-for-shares privatisation, the communists would have won the 1996 elections and this would have been the last election Russia ever had, because these guys do not give up power easily."[2]

In 2014, in an interview with the newspaper *Vedomosti*, Khodorkovsky had this to say about the auctions:

> In what way was it a collusion? There was a long list of enterprises to be privatized, around eight hundred, and everyone stated which of them they'd be able to handle. The problem at the time was not the money to be paid to the government, but the availability of personnel. I could have taken a lot more; there were no restrictions. The government went ahead with the auctions because it somehow had to resolve the situation with the 'red directors' [those who favored a planned economy], who on the eve of the election stopped paying people's salaries, not to mention taxes. They [the red directors] were forever creating stress points. It was a political issue. I knew full well from my bit of managerial experience that my team had enough resources to cope with no more than one enterprise.[3]

However, he admitted that in the early 2000s he had felt pangs of conscience over the unfair privatization and had even suggested that a law be passed on compensation payments: "We looked at the British experience [of privatization], prepared a note, and sent it to Putin through Prime Minister

Kasyanov. We suggested paying into the pension fund to cover its inevitable future deficit. Kasyanov said, publicly and privately, that he had conveyed the note to Putin, but the latter had said: 'Now is not the time.'"

In any event, Putin took Khodorkovsky's rebuke over alleged violations related to the sale of Northern Oil almost as a challenge to a duel. He knew that Russia's business leaders had all gotten their assets from the state practically as a gift. According to this logic, any infringements under the Northern Oil deal were small matters compared with the loans-for-shares auctions. Khodorkovsky simply did not have the moral right to publicly lecture the president about the harm of corruption.

THE CHOICE IS MADE

Mikhail Kasyanov, who sat next to Putin during the meeting with RUIE, recalls that after the encounter Putin amazed him with his remarkably accurate knowledge of the details of the Northern Oil deal. The president began rattling off figures that even the prime minister himself did not know. Kasyanov realized that there had been more to the deal than he had imagined.

"We could not guess that the decision had already been taken, the choice had already been made," says Khodorkovsky now. He believes that Rosneft's acquisition of Northern Oil was carried out under Putin's personal supervision and that the kickbacks were used to finance the election campaigns of 2003 and 2004.

However, only with hindsight does the meeting of February 19, 2003, seem like a watershed moment. Back then none of the key players thought much of it. Khodorkovsky went about his business as if nothing had happened, cutting deals and making bold statements.

First, he actively campaigned in favor of the imminent military operation in Iraq, calling on Russia to support the Americans against Saddam Hussein to ensure that Russian oil companies got a fair slice in the postwar distribution of the country's natural resources.

Second, he held merger talks with Roman Abramovich, even suggesting that part of the combined Yukos-Sibneft company could be sold to a US giant, such as ExxonMobil or Chevron. In short, Khodorkovsky was two steps away from co-owning the largest oil company in the world. Of course, he knew that without Putin's consent none of these plans could be realized. The government could have easily blocked the deal through the Federal Anti-monopoly

Service. But the Kremlin issued no negative signals, and on April 22, 2003, the heads of Yukos and Sibneft officially announced the merger.

"We understood that no US giant would spend $20 billion without the Russian president's approval," says Khodorkovsky. Therefore, he and Abramovich worked to get the deal rubber-stamped by the authorities. The head of Sibneft, a close friend of Putin's, sought the president's backing, while the head of Yukos set about coordinating it with Kasyanov's office.

A couple of weeks after the RUIE scandal, recalls Kasyanov, Khodorkovsky came to him with a draft law seeking to set the privatizations of the 1990s in stone and make them impossible to undo. Under the proposal, the owners of enterprises that had been privatized in the 1990s for a song (and which by the early 2000s were worth billions of dollars) would pay compensation to the state in return for a solid guarantee of their inalienable property rights, which would in turn hike the capitalization of their assets. Khodorkovsky took the proposal to the prime minister on behalf of the oligarchs. The initiative would benefit everyone: the treasury would get a tax windfall, while the oligarchs would increase the investment appeal of their companies. Such a law was of particular interest to Khodorkovsky and Abramovich, who wanted to sell a share of their future company to the Americans at the highest possible price.

Kasyanov says that the law could have contributed $15 billion to $20 billion to the budget. He liked Khodorkovsky's idea and presented the ready-made bill to Putin. But the president was unmoved. Kasyanov took the two pages of text away with him, and the matter was never raised again.[4]

OPERATION ENERGY

Meanwhile, the *siloviki* had not been idle. Today Khodorkovsky says that they were busy with an operation involving the collection of compromising material on the heads of all energy companies. Khodorkovsky asserts that the original target of the operation was not Yukos but Alfa Group. But Vladimir Putin did not sanction an assault on the latter, since he had known Alfa's head, Pyotr Aven, since the early 1990s and was even indebted to Aven for having brought him into the Kremlin elite and introduced him to Boris Berezovsky, among others. Second, Alfa Group, with Putin's blessing, was preparing for the merger between its subsidiary TNK and Britain's BP. Putin was not about to risk that momentous deal or his friendship with Tony Blair.

So the *siloviki* shifted the focus onto Yukos. Today Mikhail Khodorkovsky cannot even remember at what point he realized that his company was in serious trouble. "We felt the tension in the spring of that year, 2003, but never thought there was a threat to the company itself," he says. Even the arrest of a member of Yukos's security division, Alexei Pichugin, did not portend what was about to happen. Khodorkovsky just thought it was a private matter between Pichugin and the authorities. After Pichugin's arrest he had a final meeting with Putin at which he and Abramovich told the president about the forthcoming merger. Kasyanov recalls that Putin made many caustic remarks that day. "Why are you telling me all this?" Putin sneered. "Even if I don't like it, you'll still go ahead, right?" Yet Putin knew full well that without his consent the deal would collapse.

The final straw was the arrest of Platon Lebedev, Khodorkovsky's partner and the vice president of Yukos. He was taken to a cell from a hospital bed, after which it became clear that the campaign against Yukos had begun in earnest.

The media linked the start of the operation to the publication of a mysterious report entitled "State and Oligarchy" by the National Strategy Council, headed by Stanislav Belkovsky, who authored the document himself. Although from a credible source, the report read like a denunciation:

> Russia is on the verge of a creeping oligarchic coup.
>
> Having completed the privatization of the national economy's main assets, the oligarchs are now trying to privatize the political space of Russia. In this regard, the institution of the presidency as the basis of the political system of post-Soviet Russia is being transformed from being the guarantor of stability at the top (as in the period 1992–2002) into a potential obstacle to total monopolization and a possible threat to the logic of oligarchic modernization.
>
> In view of the above, it should be noted that the oligarchic model of Russia resembles the Venetian Republic in the Middle Ages [according to this analogy, the oligarchs are the Council of Ten, and their de facto elected president is the Doge].
>
> It should also be noted that the families of most of the oligarchs live permanently outside Russia; their descendants are studying abroad. Many highlight the fact that the oligarchy does not link personal and familial strategic interests with Russia as a geopolitical and ethno-cultural entity.

> The continued large-scale export of capital from Russia is due not only to the peculiarities of the country's investment climate, but the oligarchs' basic understanding of personal/familial strategy. This strategy is usually linked with the West and almost never with Russia. The oligarchic system of values is based upon:
>
> - Hedonism
> - The cult of money as an instrument of power
> - Deliberate disregard for people outside their oligarchic corporations.[5]

Further into the report, Belkovsky gets more specific, naming the owners of Russian Aluminum (Rusal) in cooperation with the leaders of Yukos and Alfa Group—the four richest men in the country—as potential conspirators: Roman Abramovich, Oleg Deripaska, Mikhail Khodorkovsky, and Mikhail Fridman. The author writes that they "rely on exclusive political and administrative resources, including, but not limited to, special influence on Prime Minister Mikhail Kasyanov and Chief of Staff Alexander Voloshin."

In conclusion, the report cites Mikhail Khodorkovsky as the leader of the conspirators: "By combining the administrative resources of Sibneft's shareholders, who are known for their lobbying capability and informal control over various government agencies, Mikhail Khodorkovsky is able to pursue ambitious long-term objectives. Many observers agree that Khodorkovsky has his sights set on a political career. Indirect evidence of that is Yukos funding for parties trying to enter the State Duma."

The end of the report is clearly intended to scare the president:

> Since the institution of president, from the standpoint of the ruling class, has fulfilled its historic mission and is therefore no longer needed (and is potentially dangerous), the decision has been taken to limit the powers of the president of the Russian Federation and transform Russia from a presidential into a presidential-parliamentary republic (a quasi-French model). The main ideologist of this transformation is the head of Yukos (Yukos Sibneft), Mikhail Khodorkovsky. He is explicitly and implicitly supported by other key figures of the oligarchic pool (R. Abramovich, O. Deripaska, M. Fridman). As early as 2004, Russia could have a new government, controlled by and accountable to parliament. The leading candidate for prime minister of such government, formed in accordance with the new constitution, is Mikhail Khodorkovsky.

The report was published in May 2003 and, according to the media, soon ended up on Vladimir Putin's desk, put there by presidential aide and *siloviki* leader Igor Sechin. Moreover, independent media in 2003 alleged that the report itself had been commissioned by Rosneft head Sergey Bogdanchikov (who was believed to hold the *siloviki*'s purse strings at that time).

Today Belkovsky claims that no one ordered the report. He acknowledges that the tone was provocative but holds that the report itself was veracious. Belkovsky asserts that Yukos executives themselves created the hype around the report, in particular Khodorkovsky's second-in-command, Leonid Nevzlin. "Yukos itself publicized the report and drew attention to it. They were sure they'd got hold of God by the beard—if they pretended to be 'political,' they thought they'd be untouchable," says Belkovsky.

According to Belkovsky, what most struck Putin was not the report about the "oligarchic coup" but wiretaps of Khodorkovsky's telephone conversations that Sechin also presented: "They didn't realize everything was being listened to. In conversation with democrats who idolized him, Khodorkovsky frequently described Putin as a nonentity, without knowing that Putin would find out about it."

In addition to talking about changing the constitution and the prospects of heading the government (which Khodorkovsky confirms), it is rumored that Sechin made one other accusation against Khodorkovsky that Putin could not ignore. In regard to the pending deal with Chevron or Exxon-Mobil, Khodorkovsky allegedly spoke to Condoleezza Rice and promised that, as president, he would rid Russia of its nuclear arsenal. Khodorkovsky insists that he said no such thing. However, what matters is that Putin apparently believed that he had.

MISSION COMPLETE

The arrest of Platon Lebedev was a clear hint that Mikhail Khodorkovsky should follow Boris Berezovsky and Vladimir Gusinsky abroad. However, Khodorkovsky did not go anywhere; on the contrary, he set off on a tour of Russia. He was arrested in October 2003 at Novosibirsk Airport.

Stanislav Belkovsky believes that Khodorkovsky was sure that he would not go to prison, since he had the support of Voloshin and Kasyanov. But Voloshin was unable to help because he had no idea that Khodorkovsky was about to be imprisoned. "Voloshin thought that Putin would at least call to ask for his advice before taking action," says Belkovsky. "Voloshin thought that Khodorkovsky would not be jailed because it would be overkill. But for Putin there was nothing wrong with overkill."

Khodorkovsky's arrest came as a shock to many in the Kremlin, who only learned about it in the news. On that day, the libertarian presidential aide Andrei Illarionov met presidential aide Vladislav Surkov, who had started out as Khodorkovsky's bodyguard, becoming his spin doctor before leaving Menatep for the Kremlin. "Slava [Vladislav]! What do we do now?" asked a shocked Illarionov. "What are *you* going to do?"

"You know what, Andryusha [Andrei]?" said Surkov with a smile. "There are no limits to human flexibility."

Nevertheless, his boss Alexander Voloshin did find that his flexibility was limited. He submitted his resignation on October 30, 2003, five days after Khodorkovsky's arrest. Shortly thereafter, it was Surkov who would become the Kremlin's chief political strategist.

"Voloshin could have stayed, since Putin did not demand his resignation. But that would have indicated that Voloshin and Abramovich had rigged everything to take Yukos away from Khodorkovsky," says Belkovsky.

Incidentally, in December 2003 Belkovsky was no longer the head of the National Strategy Council; instead he worked as an adviser to Boris Berezovsky. Later he worked as an adviser to Mikhail Khodorkovsky too, and did so until the newly released Khodorkovsky moved to Switzerland. Evidently the head of Yukos had no ill feelings over the "Russia Prepares Oligarchic Coup" report.

Voloshin prefers to talk about his resignation more philosophically. "We felt we'd lost our drive. In the first years in power we did a lot of good: the flat rate tax, private ownership of land, and other reforms. Everything was progressing steadily. I dedicated my life to it. I thought I was pushing the country forward. In all other aspects, life in the Kremlin is a waste. You never see your children. You never have time to read a book. It's not life in fact. You have to be mentally ill to enjoy it. Or you need to be able to cut yourself into parts. There are people who can do that. I could not, I remained a whole person."

Today Voloshin says that he fulfilled his historic mission of rescuing Russia "from permanent revolution" in the 1990s and helping it advance toward "evolutionary development." "The 1990s were a time of opportunity for the intellectual and creative classes, but for people in general they were very hard. The rules of the game were constantly changing. The main objective for all was simply to survive. People suffered. The transition to the evolutionary period changed everything: white became black, black became white. Freedom and the market economy in Russia are far from perfect, but today they do exist. We now have a critical mass of participants. The intellectual and creative classes have had to make sacrifices, but life is better on the whole. On the face of it, the political and economic situation is more stable."

In 2005 Khodorkovsky was sentenced to eight years in prison. In 2010 he was tried again, and his sentence was extended to fourteen years. However, in 2014 he was pardoned and released.

THE FAMILY DISAPPEARS

The Yukos case was an earthquake that completely changed the balance of power in Russian politics. The so-called Family departed from the scene. The last person close to both the Family and Vladimir Putin, Roman Abramovich, bought the Chelsea soccer club and moved to England. The deal to merge Sibneft with Yukos had been derailed, but Abramovich never publicly expressed regret about it. Two years later he would sell Sibneft to Gazprom at a price one and a half times its estimated market value. Before that, he would sell almost all his remaining assets in Russia: his stakes in Aeroflot, Rusal, Irkutskenergo, Krasnoyarsk HPP, and RusPromAvto.

As soon as the plan to use Yukos in the fight against the *siloviki* failed, the Family, Russia's most important political clan, which had ruled the country during the previous decades, immediately capitulated. The only pocket of resistance came in the form of an article published in *Novaya Gazeta* and reproduced online: "The Negative Consequences of the Oppositionist Minority's 'Summer Offensive' Against the President's Policy," by renowned political strategist Gleb Pavlovsky.[6]

The "minority" group was the *siloviki* (the report mentioned Igor Sechin, prosecutor general Vladimir Ustinov, FSB insider Viktor Ivanov, and businessmen Sergey Pugachev and Sergey Bogdanchikov). Pavlovsky asserted that this group was none other than "the new systemic opposition, which has effectively created a parallel center of power and is attempting to correct the policies of the president from within, backed by the law enforcement agencies under the guise of supporting and strengthening the 'weak' president."

The report was of little relevance to the *siloviki*, who remained omnipotent for at least the next three years. But it had unpleasant consequences for the author: he was sued for libel by Sergey Pugachev for $1 million and lost.

However, one part of the report can be considered prophetic. Here is how Pavlovsky described the objectives that the "power group" set itself in 2003:

> First: create a new type of business in the wake of the "Yukos affair," completely loyal to the new rulers who define economic policy; disobedience will be suppressed by force; business itself can be private, but the state must have a prominent role in its management.
>
> Second: create strong state monopolies or holding companies with state participation in the most attractive sectors of the economy.
>
> Third: promote economic growth through the redistribution of resources and property in fuel, raw materials and other sectors of the economy, as well as through the introduction of a "resource rent," the creation of state monopolies (including re-monopolization of alcohol production), and tighter control over business.
>
> Fourth: sharply increase the strong-arm component of government by turning the *siloviki* into the president's main and effectively only recourse; the *siloviki* will be involved in all areas of the political sphere, from elections to citizens' private lives.
>
> Fifth: form a new "leftist-populist" ideological platform of power based on a simplified and ideologized orthodoxy, focused on the mass public sector and "anti-oligarchic" medium and small business.

It took a long time (the fifth element, the formation of a new leftist-populist platform, took ten years), but the prophecy was ultimately borne out.

THE LAST MEMBER OF THE FAMILY

The tectonic shifts in the Kremlin could not fail to have an impact on public policy—all the more so given that the next Duma elections were scheduled for December 2003. For the first time in Russian history, the ruling party (in 2003 this was United Russia, formed from the merger of Unity and Fatherland) was the favorite. The Communist Party, which had topped the party-list elections in Russia for almost ten years, was set to lose because before his resignation the Communist-hating Voloshin had created a Kremlin-friendly synthetic party called Rodina (Motherland) specifically designed to take votes away from the Communists.

Finally, the pro-democracy parties Yabloko and Union of Rightist Forces (URF) were completely demoralized and not ready for the elections. They had lost funding from Yukos just as the election campaign got under way, and they had no clear message for voters, since they had not risked publicly standing up for Khodorkovsky. National TV channels had portrayed the Yukos affair as a struggle between Putin and the oligarchs who had plundered the country, and this view was quite widespread. Going against public opinion and defending the interests of business, or at least expressing the concern of small entrepreneurs, was a step too far for the pro-democracy parties.

The disappearance of the liberal group inside the Kremlin went hand in hand with the departure of the pro-democracy parties from the Duma: Yabloko and UFR did not break the 5 percent threshold and so were excluded from the Russian parliament. The Kremlin did not even put obstacles in their way; it simply concentrated on ensuring victory for United Russia.

The Family was no more, but of its remnants, one person remained in power who was not a protégé of Putin but more of a rival: the prime minister, Mikhail Kasyanov.

Over the New Year holiday the prime minister went skiing in Austria. He was invited to the home of Austrian chancellor Wolfgang Schüssel, where they were joined for one day by the leader of the losing party URF, Boris Nemtsov, who had flown over specially. He urged Kasyanov to become the new leader of his party. Kasyanov thought about it but declined.

While Kasyanov was away, new dispatches landed on Putin's desk, testifying that Kasyanov was a key figure in a plot to overthrow Putin—they claimed that he was in fact "discussing the details right now with Chancellor Schüssel."

The outline of the supposed plot was as follows. The next presidential election was scheduled for March 2004. If turnout was lower than 50 percent, it would be invalid. How could such a low turnout be achieved? By convincing all the candidates to withdraw. Among the reports presented to Putin, says Kasyanov, were fake transcripts of supposed conversations with Nemtsov. Kasyanov and Nemtsov had allegedly discussed how, if all Putin's opponents withdrew from the race, only Putin and his puppet, Federation Council Speaker Sergei Mironov, would be left. People would lose interest and "vote with their feet." New elections would then be set for June, by which time Putin's mandate would have expired (on May 6). Under the constitution, the prime minister, Mikhail Kasyanov, would serve as acting president until the June election, putting the levers of power in his hands for one month.

There was in fact no such conspiracy, but the presidential administration was already taking steps to crush it. The Kremlin called in sixty-six-year-old Viktor Gerashchenko, a former long-term chairman of the Central Bank often called the "Russian Alan Greenspan," a charismatic elderly gentleman who had just been elected to the Duma on the party list of the populist bloc Rodina. "Viktor, we would like to ask you to run for president," said the Kremlin apparatchiks. He tried his best to refuse, saying it would be too time-consuming, but was told, "Viktor, you don't understand. We are *asking* you to run for president." So Gerashchenko announced his candidacy, perhaps not fully suspecting that he was being used to make the elections more interesting and, hence, less likely to fail.

When Kasyanov returned from vacation, he did not immediately realize what had happened. He recalls that at a reception to mark Russian Army Day on February 23, Putin behaved very oddly, spending the whole evening whispering in the corner with FSB director Nikolai Patrushev.

The next day Putin summoned Kasyanov to the Kremlin and announced that he had decided to use his constitutional right to dismiss the prime minister. Kasyanov, who remembers that Putin looked nervous and confused, promptly corrected him: "You can't dismiss the prime minister. You can only dismiss the entire government."

Putin told Kasyanov that everyone knew about the alleged plot, at which Kasyanov expressed genuine surprise. Then Putin offered the now former prime minister the post of secretary of the Security Council, an offer Kasyanov refused.

Kasyanov resigned quietly without making any statements, and remained silent for several years. All that time the authorities left him alone, as was true for all the other protégés of the Family.* Only in the run-up to the 2008 presidential election did Kasyanov attempt to return to politics—and failed. Or rather, he was annihilated. All the national media made a point of bringing up an old story, first peddled by Gusinsky, that in his capacity as prime

---

*Patrushev, incidentally, was not punished for spreading rumors and went from strength to strength.

minister Kasyanov had taken a 2 percent cut of deals he endorsed, earning him the nickname "Misha Two Percent." Kasyanov was not allowed to register as a candidate, and in any case he never polled more than that same 2 percent.

Pummeling Kasyanov and not allowing him to run for president was less about defeating the remnants of the Family than about combating Vladimir Putin's main phobia. The debacle of the Orange Revolution in Ukraine was still fresh in his mind. Mikhail Kasyanov could not be allowed to become a Russian Viktor Yushchenko.

PART TWO

PUTIN II THE MAGNIFICENT

CHAPTER 4

IN WHICH KREMLIN CHIEF OF STAFF DMITRY MEDVEDEV CREATES A NEW RUSSIAN CLASS

Dmitry Medvedev comes across as something unusual for a politician: he seems like a good person. His lack of self-confidence is evident from the way he tries to create the impression of self-confidence. At the same time, he knows how to listen, and even likes to seek advice. For example, he might ask a journalist before a TV interview what color tie he should wear—or maybe it'd be better if he didn't wear a tie at all?

Dmitry Medvedev began his career as a teacher. At times his manner is still that of a rookie teacher unsure of what reaction he will get on entering the classroom for the first time, so he tries to be more mature and more serious than necessary. Or he can go too far the other way and awkwardly adopt youth slang. Medvedev seems accustomed to be being a fish out of water.

At other times Medvedev resembles a diligent student. When duty requires him to say things he doesn't agree with, he recites the words as if he had to learn them by heart for an exam. He can even expand on a topic he finds deeply unpleasant.

Of course, Dmitry Medvedev never planned to become a politician. He entered politics by accident, maybe even against his will. He was indeed a diligent student, which is partly why he doesn't quite fit in. Yet he seems to believe that patience can conquer all.

DIMA

Having accepted the resignation of Alexander Voloshin, Putin appointed Voloshin's deputy, Dmitry (Dima) Medvedev, as the new head of the presidential administration. Completely unknown to the public, Medvedev too was from St. Petersburg. In 2000, in Moscow, he had headed Putin's campaign office.* After that he became head of board of directors of Gazprom.

Medvedev inherited a powerful legacy, as the presidential administration had been a major power center since 1999. As the new chief of staff, Dmitry Medvedev was now the most powerful civil servant in all of Russia. Perhaps it is because Medvedev held two key positions, as chief of staff and as head of Gazprom, that he was able to fly under the radar for several years: he remained balanced between the two posts and never tried to throw his political weight around—at least, not until Putin made his next move.

Putin announced that Medvedev was Voloshin's "official successor" even before he became president. He talked about it in March 2000 in *First Person*, an official biography, published just before the election, that consisted of interviews given by Putin to three journalists from Berezovsky's *Kommersant*: Natalya Timakova, Natalia Gevorkyan, and Andrei Kolesnikov. Shortly after the book was released the journalists went their separate ways: Timakova went to work in the Kremlin, and later became Medvedev's spokesperson and right hand; Gevorkyan went to live in Paris, and fifteen years later became Mikhail Khodorkovsky's media adviser; Kolesnikov remained at *Kommersant* and stayed faithful to Putin, becoming his daily biographer and "assigned correspondent."

In this short excerpt from their book, Putin lists his closest and most trusted advisers:

Q: Whose proposals do you listen to, and who do you trust? You said your goal in the first year is to formulate a team. Who is on your team?
A: Trust? Sergei Ivanov, Secretary of the Security Council.
Q: Have you known each other for a long time?

---

*Everyone knew that the campaign office was only a formality and did not actually do anything (since Putin did not do traditional campaigns with debates and outdoor billboards). Putin's real election campaign in 2000 was coordinated by Voloshin, who gave orders to national TV channels and organized Putin's road show around the country.

A: I've known him for a long time, but not very well. We began working together in the Leningrad Directorate of the KGB. At that time I only knew that he existed. Then he went to Moscow, and did several long stints abroad. We had many friends in common. I heard stuff about him from all different people, and it was positive. He knows several languages: English, Swedish, and Finnish, I think. And I think that he is in the right job. He recently returned from the States, where things went very well. He met Clinton, [Madeleine] Albright, and [Samuel] Berger. I'm happy with his work.

Q: But there isn't anyone you've spent a lot of time with?

A: Of course, it is always better to have had the benefit of direct experience working together. But let's agree that there is such a thing as comradeship. I get that feeling with Ivanov and with Nikolai Patrushev and also with Dima Medvedev.

Q: Medvedev is heading your election campaign. Is he also from [St.] Petersburg?

A: He taught civil law at Leningrad University. He has a doctoral degree in jurisprudence and is a fine expert. I needed some people when I worked with Sobchak in the mayor's office. I went to the law faculty for help, and they suggested Dima. When I was deputy mayor, Dima was my adviser, and he worked with me for about a year and a half. Then, after our unsuccessful elections, he left the mayor's office and went back to the university.

Q: You recently invited him to Moscow?

A: Just this year. Actually, I had originally planned for Dima to head up the Federal Securities Commission. He is a specialist in the securities market. He seems to like working on our team, but we haven't yet decided specifically where to use him.

Q: Who else?

A: I trust Alexei Kudrin. He is now first deputy minister of finances. I think that he's a decent and professional guy. We both worked for Sobchak and we were both his deputies. In years of working together, you can learn a lot about a person.

Q: And where did Igor Sechin come from?

A: Sechin also worked with us in [St.] Petersburg, in the protocol department. He is a philologist by training. He knows Portuguese, French, and Spanish. He worked abroad, in Mozambique and Angola.

Q: Was he in combat?

A: Yes. Then he landed on the executive committee of the Leningrad City Council. When I became deputy mayor and was choosing my staff, I considered a lot of people, and I liked Sechin. I suggested that he come to work for me. This was in 1992–1993. And when I went to work in Moscow, he asked to come along, so I brought him with me.

Q: Now what will happen with the old guard in the Kremlin? Everyone says, just wait, Putin will win the elections and he'll be free of them. In the best case, he'll fire them.

A: You know, that kind of logic is characteristic of people with totalitarian mentalities. That's how they expect a person to behave if he wants to remain in his post the rest of his life. But I don't want that.

Q: But there are some figures that the public has a uniformly negative reaction to, such as Pavel Borodin [head of the Presidential Property Management Department]. Then there's also the chief of the presidential administration, Alexander Voloshin. He's not beloved by the public.

A: Voloshin is not well liked by the public, or by a part of the establishment. As groups and clans fought among themselves, a negative feeling emerged. Voloshin was not immune to it. And those clans fought dirty. I don't think that's a basis for firing someone. Voloshin suits me just fine for today. The work he is doing rather particular. We discussed who could be put in his place, and we considered Dima Medvedev. Voloshin himself said, "Let Dima work as my deputy, and then, when he grows into the job, let him be considered as my replacement." There's no sense in second-guessing it now.[1]

Putin seemed to know back in 1999 that Medvedev would grow into Voloshin's role. When it finally happened, journalists were right to say that Putin's "St. Petersburg set" was delighted when Family member Voloshin finally resigned. "Byzantium has fallen!" declared finance minister Alexei Kudrin, commenting to *Kommersant* on the news of the resignation.[2]

The new head of the presidential administration was the polar opposite of his predecessor, and was certainly not Byzantine in any way. Indeed, he resembled a humble clerk from the pages of Gogol. A few months after his appointment, he proposed a new administrative structure, although the changes were cosmetic: the only things that changed were people's job titles, not the people themselves. For example, the title of "first deputy head of the administration," of which there had been two (Sechin and Surkov), was no more. All other deputies were renamed "presidential aides."

Medvedev told journalists (perhaps in jest) that the reorganization had been undertaken so that foreigners would have a clearer idea about who did what in the administration. "It's better that way. When I travel abroad, which happens occasionally, no one knows what 'deputy head of the administration' means. They don't realize it's an important job. They understand the word 'aide,' especially in America, where chief of staff Andrew Card is Washington's top presidential aide."[3]

But Medvedev's main achievement in his new position was the adoption of the Law on the State Civil Service, which he himself wrote. This law was essentially a repeat of the administrative reforms undertaken by Peter the Great in the early eighteenth century, introducing a table of ranks for civil servants. Medvedev re-created this table, but instead of "privy councilors" and "state councilors" there were "acting governmental advisers" of the first, second, and third classes. Moreover, Medvedev, as Russia's top civil servant, often said that the state apparatus was not bloated and did not need to be cut. On the contrary, compared with other countries, there was even a lack of professional civil servants, he thought.

The next decade was a golden time for the Russian civil service, whose numbers nearly quadrupled over that period. We can only guess at how individual civil servants prospered. In 2003 Russian officials were still unsophisticated and not overly corrupt. True, they could show favor to businessmen in return for a small courtesy. The most common form of bribery, for instance, was a family holiday abroad. Businesses arranged vacations for civil servants and their families (costing several thousand dollars at most) in return for contracts worth millions. It was not even considered a conflict of interest for officials and businessmen to be so close. For example, everyone knew that the deputy mayor of Moscow, Vladimir Resin, who was in charge of construction, spent time with his family at developer Shalva Chigirinsky's luxurious pad in Monaco. No one minded.

Within five years, officials would develop a real taste for luxury and start to realize their own worth—after all, why take handouts from billionaires if you can become a billionaire yourself? But at the beginning of the 2000s such a revolutionary idea had not yet occurred to them.

THE IDEAL CANDIDATE

Medvedev's priority as head of Putin's administration was to get the president reelected for a second term. While in 2000 he had been the head of the nominal campaign office, now, in 2004, he was in charge of the real campaign office—the Kremlin. The top campaign spin doctor, however, was not Medvedev but Vladislav Surkov, still in his Voloshin-era role as first presidential aide.

At first glance, the election was a formality: Putin was set to win easily. The intrigue lay elsewhere. As the first term (and the Yukos affair) drew to a close, Yeltsin's old guard finally gave way to Putin's puppies. The "Petersburgers" (as the Russian press called them) acquired real power and finally emerged from the shadows after four years of what was, in effect, probation.

"Thank you for showing us how to run the country. Now we can do it ourselves" is a phrase allegedly uttered by Putin's aide Igor Sechin. Mikhail Kasyanov asserts that Sechin escorted him out of the White House, the Russian parliamentary building, with those very words after the former prime minister's "unexpected resignation."

The top contenders for Kasyanov's job were finance minister Alexei Kudrin, defense minister Sergei Ivanov, and the new head of Putin's campaign office, Dmitry Kozak. But Putin made a strange choice, bypassing the Petersburgers in favor of an unknown entity: Mikhail Fradkov.

Seemingly a faceless bureaucrat who had come out of nowhere, Fradkov in fact had extensive experience in the apparatus of government. He had served in various government bodies (although his official biography does not mention them), had been the minister of foreign economic relations and trade in several governments under Yeltsin, had headed the tax inspectorate in Putin's early years, and in 2003 was Russia's ambassador to Brussels when he was summoned to the Kremlin, to the general astonishment of the entire political elite. His main advantage was that he posed absolutely no threat to Putin.

They had known each other since the early 1990s, when Fradkov had effectively been Putin's boss. At that time Putin headed the external relations committee of the St. Petersburg mayor's office, while Fradkov was Russia's deputy minister of foreign economic relations. However, that was not the main reason for the appointment, as Putin later told reporters.

In early 2003 the Kremlin reorganized the security services and decided to abolish three powerful agencies in one fell swoop: the Federal Agency of

Government Communications and Information (FAGCI), the Federal Border Service, and the tax police. The duties of the first two were assigned to the FSB, while tax issues fell within the remit of the Ministry of Internal Affairs. The heads of the agencies being eliminated reacted differently to the news of their dismissal (even though all were given new appointments), with some even trying to argue with Putin. Only Fradkov's reaction pleased the president.

"Mikhail Yefimovich [Fradkov], forget that you're an agency head, and tell me what you think is in the best interests of the state. Do you think your functions can be transferred to the Interior Ministry? Just be honest with me," the president asked, according to a Kremlin source. Fradkov answered that it would be much more efficient that way, adding that he hoped his "people would not suffer from any decision taken." Fradkov's willingness to sacrifice himself was noted by Putin, who rewarded him with the EU ambassadorship in Brussels. But more than that, Putin remembered him as a man of exceptional loyalty.

"I can easily imagine Putin's thought processes in selecting Fradkov for prime minister," says a former Kremlin senior aide. "He had a few pluses and no minuses. He had experience in all areas: the tax police, the economy, the ministry of foreign economic relations—and internationally as ambassador in Brussels. And he never got above himself."

In the prime minister's chair, Fradkov set about duplicating the reforms that Dmitry Medvedev had carried out as chief of staff, reducing the number of managers while increasing the overall number of staff. Six deputy prime ministers were whittled down to one, and twenty-three ministers became fourteen, but each ministry had several federal agencies added to it.

The more the state apparatus grew, the less productive it became. Both Voloshin and Kasyanov say that at the end of their respective stays in power the reforms had effectively stopped. Fradkov's arrival caused a flurry of spurious activity, but little else. But the new prime minister was aware that he had been appointed for that very purpose. His mission was not to show ambition and not to steal a march on anyone.

Paradoxically, the official economic policy proclaimed by Putin ahead of his reelection was highly ambitious. The president demanded a doubling of GDP by 2010. German Gref, the minister of economic development and the architect of Putin's reforms, meekly argued that 2010 was too soon, though 2015 might be possible, but eventually gave in and assured Putin that it could be done. Insiders had an explanation for Fradkov's apparent nonchalance: "No one gets fired for poor performance—they get fired for disloyalty." So Fradkov was not afraid that he might fail to execute the president's instructions. Besides, he had not succeeded in any of his previous posts; almost all the departments in which had he worked had been declared superfluous and disbanded. That was how he had made it to the prime ministership.

DOUBLING GDP

The 2004 presidential election itself went off almost without a hitch, with Putin receiving 71 percent of the vote. However, just as the votes were being counted, the building opposite the Kremlin, the historic Manezh Exhibition Center, in the very heart of Moscow, caught fire. Two firefighters died in the blaze.* The exact cause remains unclear. Government officials quietly speculated that the accidental beneficiary of the conflagration would be Moscow Mayor Yuri Luzhkov, who could use it to settle a "conflict of interests" with investors. Luzhkov himself arrived at the scene of the fire just minutes after it broke out and almost immediately insisted to the press that arson had been ruled out.

Journalists talked quietly of a bad omen. But Putin is said not to have been angry in the slightest. The election had been won; everything else was a trifle. He did not punish Yuri Luzhkov, his former enemy, for (allegedly) ruining his celebration. Luzhkov had delivered a decent result for Putin in Moscow—69 percent of the vote. That was the main thing.

Putin's best result was in Chechnya. The new Chechen leader, Akhmad Kadyrov, the former chief mufti of the republic (who had declared a jihad against the Russians in the 1990s before switching allegiance to Putin in 1999), served up 92.4 percent of the vote. It symbolized Putin's first term: the war in Chechnya, which had led him to the Kremlin four years previously, was over.

On May 9, 2004, the day after Putin's inauguration, a bomb exploded during the Victory Day celebrations in the Chechen capital, Grozny. It had been planted in the VIP section, where the Chechen president was seated.

*The building had been put up in 1817 by decree of Tsar Alexander I in honor of the fifth anniversary of Russia's victory over Napoleon. Now, five years into Vladimir Putin's rule, it had burned down. Together with reporters, Putin ascended one of the Kremlin towers to observe the scene.

Kadyrov died on the way to the hospital. That same day Putin summoned the assassinated president's younger son to the Kremlin. Ramzan Kadyrov was wearing a track suit and barely holding back his tears. The only phrase he said on camera was "The Chechen people have made their choice, and that choice is final." The meeting with Ramzan Kadyrov meant that Putin had also made a final choice: the next head of the Chechen Republic would be Ramzan Kadyrov—who, incidentally, had not yet turned thirty and therefore could not legally become president of the republic, though he began preparing for office all the same. First he led the Chechen security forces in the capacity of deputy prime minister; then he took over as prime minister. Three years later he became lord and master of his native land.

A GLAMOROUS SUMMER

The summer of 2004 was perhaps the calmest and most lackadaisical in the history of Putin's Russia. All state activity effectively ceased, and the Russian capital de facto moved to Sochi, where all the country's leaders combined work with vacation.

Putin spent almost the whole of August there. He received visits from various foreign leaders, including Serbian prime minister Vojislav Kostunica, Belarusian president Alexander Lukashenko, Armenian president Robert Kocharian, Ukrainian president Leonid Kuchma, and Kuchma's heir, Viktor Yanukovych.

The calmest summer in living memory came to an abrupt end, however, with an episode of déjà vu. Four years previously, in late August, Putin's holiday had been interrupted by the *Kursk* tragedy. This time two planes were blown up shortly after taking off from Moscow's Domodedovo Airport by female Chechen suicide bombers, called "black widows." So as not to repeat his previous mistakes, Putin immediately went to Moscow for a meeting in the Kremlin—and then returned to Sochi.

The attacks happened a few days before the upcoming presidential elections in Chechnya (to replace the assassinated Akhmad Kadyrov). The elections were required to demonstrate that the republic's new pro-Putin regime was absolutely legitimate, and so they went ahead. Many journalists who went to Chechnya reported that polling stations were almost empty—voters were simply afraid to go outside. Despite that, the official turnout was listed as 85 percent.

The day after the election, Jacques Chirac and Gerhard Schroeder paid a visit to Putin's dacha. They stated that they had no doubts about the legitimacy of the Chechen elections. The war in Chechnya, the motif with which Putin's presidency had begun, was now history. No one was interested in what was happening there. At the luxurious residence in Sochi, the French president and the German chancellor assured Putin that they had no complaints.

This triumph, and the end of the calm summer, was again marred the very next day, September 1, 2004, the start of the new academic year across Russia. Barely had Chirac and Schroeder had time to leave Sochi before a group of terrorists seized a school in Beslan, 100 kilometers from Grozny, in the Russian republic of North Ossetia; 1,128 people were taken hostage, including many children. For some, it was their very first day at school. It was the worst terror attack in Russian history (worse even than the attack during the performance of *Nord-Ost*) and undeniable evidence that the war in Chechnya was far from over.

Putin once again interrupted his vacation and flew to Moscow. But this time the authorities somehow contrived to commit even worse mistakes than during the *Kursk* incident. Official television reports underestimated the number of hostages, claiming there were between two hundred and five hundred. That was followed by reports that the terrorists did not want to negotiate, although surviving witnesses say that the terrorists handed over several videotapes with recordings of their demands. Finally, according to the official version, the storming of the school that took place on September 3 was triggered by the explosion of an improvised explosive device inside the building. But according to an independent investigation conducted by Duma MP Yuri Saveliev, most of the 333 deaths were caused by external gunfire from special forces as they burst into the building.[4]

On the day the victims were buried, many state leaders arrived in Beslan, including Fradkov, Medvedev, Moscow mayor Luzhkov, the speakers of both chambers of parliament, and the prosecutor general. They did not go to the cemetery. Instead, they held a televised memorial gathering on the central square. It poured rain the whole day, and the officials from Moscow stood the whole time on a podium in front of the cameras holding black umbrellas. None of the locals who had lost children in the school came to meet them.

The causes of the terror attack were never properly investigated, and the worst Russian crime of the 2000s remains unsolved.

The day after the assault, Putin delivered a wordy, philosophical speech, very similar to George W. Bush's after 9/11. However, in contrast to the terror attacks in the United States, there was not a single foreigner among the victims in Beslan: they were all Ingush, Chechen, and Russian. Because there were no foreign victims, Putin's speech was far less internationalist than Bush's. He began with memories of the Soviet Union:

> Today, we live in a time that follows the collapse of a vast and great state, a state that, unfortunately, proved unable to survive in a rapidly changing world. But despite all the difficulties, we were able to preserve the core of what was once the vast Soviet Union, and we named this new country the Russian Federation. We all hoped for change, change for the better. But many of the changes that took place in our lives found us unprepared.

Then he began blaming external enemies:

> Our country, formerly protected by the most powerful defence system along the length of its external frontiers, overnight found itself defenceless both from the east and the west.
>
> It will take many years and billions of rubles to create new, modern, and genuinely protected borders.
>
> But even so, we could have been more effective if we had acted professionally and at the right moment.
>
> In general, we need to admit that we did not fully understand the complexity and the dangers of the processes at work in our own country and in the world. In any case, we proved unable to react adequately. We showed ourselves to be weak. And the weak get beaten.
>
> Some would like to tear from us a "juicy piece of pie." Others help them. They help, reasoning that Russia still remains one of the world's major nuclear powers, and as such still represents a threat to them. And so they reason that this threat should be removed.

It was all very vague. Putin went on to explain that changes would be made to the political system because of the "wartime situation":

> This is not a challenge to the President, parliament or government. It is a challenge to all of Russia, to our entire people. Our country is under attack.

> Dear fellow citizens, those who sent these bandits to carry out this dreadful crime made it their aim to set our peoples against each other, put fear into the hearts of Russian citizens and unleash bloody interethnic strife in the North Caucasus. In this connection I have the following words to say.
>
> First, a series of measures aimed at strengthening our country's unity will soon be prepared.[5]

By "strengthening unity" Putin meant the abolition of regional gubernatorial elections. Henceforth, governors would be handpicked by the president and rubber-stamped by the regional parliaments.

Mikhail Kasyanov, who by this time had already been relieved of his prime ministerial duties, was sure that the abolition of gubernatorial elections had already been planned before the Beslan massacre occurred. He believes that Putin simply needed a pretext to announce the decision, and the hostage crisis provided it.

Presidential administration staff do not corroborate this theory. On the contrary, they say, the mood before Beslan was relaxed. There was no such plan. The decision to scrap gubernatorial elections was made out of exasperation and despair.

The terror attack in Beslan ended what might have been a peaceful and serene summer for Putin. Remarkably, the disproportionate response to the attack—a response that effectively turned Russia into a unitary state—left society generally unmoved. For most people, it had indeed been a serene summer. The public was satiated by the constant inflow of petrodollar revenues, which lasted for another four years, until the crisis of 2008.

Russia was in the midst of the strangest period in its history, when the focus of everyone's attention switched to consumption. For the first time ever, in terms of wealth and comfort Russian society was not trailing behind the rest of the world but leading the way. Ordinary Russian citizens snapped up the very latest iPhones, iPads, plasma TVs, cars, washing machines, juice extractors, and vacuum cleaners. In every major city in Russia there appeared hypermarkets, multiplex cinemas, bowling alleys, restaurants, and nightclubs. People became accustomed to traveling abroad. Russia was clumsily learning how to be a rich country.

The political and business elite were, of course, used to luxury. Now they took over the French Riviera and the best Alpine ski resorts, where Moscow socialites flew in private jets for one night just to have a drink and take a stroll. Not having one's own jet was considered downright shameful, and so there developed a waiting list for Falcon jets among the Moscow business elite—the manufacturer could not keep up with the demand from wealthy Russians. A new moneymaking scheme appeared: less well-off entrepreneurs signed up for a business jet and then sold their place on the waiting list to billionaires who were later in line. The oligarchs were forever trying to outdo each other: Roman Abramovich had the most expensive yacht, while Mikhail Prokhorov had the loudest parties, replete with models.

The symbol of Moscow's high society was the restaurant Mario. The entire *Forbes* list of Russian billionaires dined there, as did even Putin himself on occasion—the entire second floor was cordoned off whenever he was there. The young lord of Chechnya, Ramzan Kadyrov, preferred the Italian restaurant Antinori; when he chose to dine there, the restaurant was closed completely.

Nightclubs in Moscow were built and opened in just three or four months, only to shut down soon afterward because the jaded audience wanted something new. Reserving a table at one of these clubs cost a fortune, but still it was impossible to get one, says Ksenia Sobchak, one of Russia's "it girls" and daughter of Anatoly Sobchak, the late mayor of St. Petersburg and Vladimir Putin's former boss. Government officials generally did not frequent such clubs, but businessmen did: Roman Abramovich, Mikhail Prokhorov, Vladimir Potanin, Oleg Deripaska, and so on.

The country rode through the first decade of the twenty-first century in a state of semi-oblivion. There was scarcely any politics, no public life, just solid hedonism. During this period Moscow's oligarchs and their crowd were, of course, far wealthier and lived in far grander style than the army of state officials. Ministers and governors, though not poor, viewed the insane luxury from a distance. They had not tasted Cristal champagne or gone skiing at Courchevel. While the Muscovites played, the Petersburgers worked, busily taking hold of power. Five years later they would have acquired real wealth themselves, but by then the party would be over.

CHAPTER 5

IN WHICH UKRAINIAN PRESIDENTIAL CHIEF OF STAFF VIKTOR MEDVEDCHUK IS THE LAST UKRAINIAN TO ENJOY PUTIN'S TRUST

At the beginning of the 2000s Viktor Medvedchuk was like an extraterrestrial compared to other Ukrainian politicians: totally European, intelligent, educated, and highly effective. That is how Medvedchuk is described by Moscow political consultants Marat Gelman and Gleb Pavlovsky, who worked with him during that time.

Today Medvedchuk makes quite a different impression. Nowadays he prefers to avoid journalists, and if he does say anything, he uses so many words that any sense is lost in the flow of verbiage. He is a master at disguising his true feelings and never saying what he really thinks.

Viktor Medvedchuk is surrounded by a huge entourage. To talk to him, you need to pass a dozen cordons, answer hundreds of questions, and push your way through countless aides and advisers. They're a diverse crew: gorilla-like bodyguards, accountant types, women who look like models, other women who look like schoolteachers. When you peel away these layers and finally reach the most influential man in Ukraine, you discover almost nothing. You find yourself face-to-face with a mirror. He has the ability to reflect the views of whomever he is talking to, and at times he reflects nothing at all.

But Medvedchuk is true to himself. He really does want to lead Ukraine down the path that he believes is European and offers salvation. But he is convinced that Ukraine can only develop together with Russia—like in the days when the mighty Soviet Union was "ruled by Ukrainians." That, in his opinion, is the road to the future. It was the Soviet Union, ironically, that made him a European and made modern Ukraine a developed country with huge potential, he believes. While his opponents tout their own "European path," he considers that theirs is provincial, leading only to the "wayside" of Europe, to poverty and misery. Perhaps that is why Medvedchuk likes having a diverse retinue—to dispel any sense of provincialness.

A CRIMEAN FRIEND

While the Russian oligarchs were tasting true luxury, Vladimir Putin spent his vacations at his residence near Sochi. Although opulent, it is still very Soviet. His main alternative destination was Crimea, particularly since his friend Viktor Medvedchuk, the head of the Ukrainian presidential administration, owned a dacha there.

Medvedchuk was born in the Tyumen region of Russia, grew up speaking almost no Ukrainian, and, although a citizen of Ukraine, shared some of the "Ukrainophobia" of Moscow officialdom. In his youth he is said to have collaborated with the KGB. In the 1970s and 1980s he worked as a lawyer in Kiev, where he "defended" Ukrainian dissidents Yuri Lytvyn and Vasyl Stus. Both received the maximum sentence, and both died in the camps. In his last plea Lytvyn accused his lawyer Medvedchuk of excessive passivity due to orders from above. As a result, Ukrainian dissident circles labeled Medvedchuk a KGB agent. But his background was not a problem for Putin.

Medvedchuk got on well with Putin and his closest aides, first Voloshin and then Medvedev. In 2004 Medvedchuk even went to St. Petersburg to have his newborn daughter Dasha baptized there. The godparents at the ceremony, which took place in Kazan Cathedral, were Putin himself and his chief of staff's wife, Svetlana Medvedev. Medvedchuk was to become the Kremlin's main source of information about what was happening in Ukraine. In fact, he even replaced his Moscow counterpart Dmitry Medvedev as the Kremlin's real shaper of policy toward Ukraine.

Former Kremlin officials say that Putin was obsessed with Ukraine almost from day one of his presidency. "We must do something, or we'll lose it," he said over and over again.

LENINGRADERS AND UKRAINIANS

After the collapse of the Soviet Union, it became the custom for the Russian Ministry of Foreign Affairs to deal only with *foreign* countries, that is, countries outside the Commonwealth of Independent States (CIS), which was made up of all the former Soviet republics except the Baltic countries. CIS countries were handled by the presidential administration. In fact, it was a continuation of the old Soviet model, whereby the Soviet republics were subordinate to the Central Committee of the Communist Party of the Soviet Union (CC CPSU). Since the presidential administration was located in the very same building as the CC CPSU on Moscow's Staraya Square, the tradition continued despite the fact that the Soviet Union no longer existed. Ukraine, the second-largest post-Soviet republic and Russia's closest partner, was personally overseen by the head of the administration: first Voloshin and then Medvedev.

Ukraine was always a special case for Staraya Square. The "Ukrainian clans" inside the CC CPSU itself were traditionally the most powerful. They can be said to have ruled the Soviet Union for decades. If one looks at the membership of the Politburo, it is clear that it was dominated by Ukrainians and those with strong Ukrainian connections. The most prominent of these were Nikita Khrushchev and Leonid Brezhnev. Khrushchev led Ukraine (as first secretary and chairman of the Council of Ministers) from 1938 to 1949, while Brezhnev headed the Zaporozhye and Dnepropetrovsk regions of Ukraine from 1946 to 1950. In addition, the Ukrainian clan in the 1950s–1980s included Nikolai Podgorny, head of the Presidium of the Supreme Soviet (i.e., the formal head of state); Nikolai Tikhonov, head of the Council of Ministers; Alexei Kirichenko and Andrei Kirilenko, second secretaries of the Central Committee (i.e., heads of the administration); Politburo members Vladimir Shcherbytsky, Pyotr Shelest, and Dmitry Polyansky; and interior minister Nikolai Shchelokov.

Dnepropetrovsk, a powerful industrial center in the east of Ukraine, was Leonid Brezhnev's primary source of personnel for the state apparatus.

Tellingly, years after Brezhnev's death the "Dnepropetrovsk clan" was still formidable. Another of its natives, Leonid Kuchma, became president of Ukraine in 1994.

The second-largest group in the Soviet leadership consisted of Leningrad natives. In 1949, under Stalin, they were purged. Accused of wanting to create a Russian Communist Party as a counterweight to the CPSU and to move the capital from Moscow to Leningrad, twenty-three were executed by firing squad, including Stalin's first deputy in the government (and, according to rumors, potential successor), Nikolay Voznesensky; secretary of the CC CPSU, Alexey Kuznetsov; chairman of the Council of Ministers of Russia, Rodionov; and the regional leaders of Leningrad, Pyotr Popkov and Yakov Kapustin. Five years later, after Stalin's death, the "Leningrad affair" was proven to have been fabricated, and all those executed were rehabilitated. Despite the purge, Leningraders still held important positions, including the head of the Presidium of the Supreme Soviet and the head of the Council of Ministers of the USSR (Nikolay Shvernik and Alexei Kosygin, respectively). Party leaders from Leningrad (first Frol Kozlov, then Grigoriy Romanov and Lev Zaikov) were almost always guaranteed a place in the Politburo. Such privilege was granted to only one other regional leader: the first secretary of the Communist Party of Ukraine.

During the twentieth century the Ukrainians and Leningraders were the two major forces in the Soviet government. They alternately fought and collaborated with each other. At the start of the 2000s, when the Petersburgers came to power and Ukraine was led by the Dnipropetrovsk clan, it was not difficult to find common ground.

However, even Kuchma, a typical Soviet "red director," and his team, who could not have been more congenial, annoyed Kremlin officials. It was not the fact that the Ukrainians were a generation older and hence less liberal and reformist than the Moscow political elite. The problem was their Ukrainianness.

One former senior government official recalls that when he visited Kiev he was put up in an official residence on Bankova Street, in a building adjacent to the presidential administration. He didn't have to go far for the talks. Kuchma himself phoned and said that he would look in on his visitor from Moscow. When the Ukrainian president turned up, he immediately asked the staff to "lay the table." Although it was eleven in the morning, vodka was still compulsory. The cordial negotiations dragged on until the evening. All the Russian official's scheduled meetings had to be canceled, since he couldn't refuse the president. But what troubled the official during their conversation was Kuchma's attitude toward Ukrainian nationalists. "They are more Ukrainian than we are, of course. The future belongs to them. We have to keep learning from them," Kuchma's guest recalls the president as saying.

This attitude had always exasperated Moscow. Even minor things, such as "translating" first names from Russian into Ukrainian, were irksome: Nikolai became Mykola, Dmitry became Dmytro, Alexander became Oleksander, Vladimir became Volodymyr, and so on.

"Ukrainization" irritated the Soviet Politburo, too. Debates about whether Ukrainian is a language or just "incorrect Russian" and protests about violations of Russian-speaking Ukrainians' rights can be found even in the minutes of the meetings of the Central Committee. The most prominent Ukrainophobes were KGB chairman Alexandr Shelepin (under Khrushchev) and Mikhail Solomentsev, chairman of the Council of Ministers of the RSFSR (under Brezhnev). But in Soviet times Ukraine and the Ukrainian language always had robust defenders at the very top. Under Putin, however, the idea of Ukrainian national statehood was discouraged.

Dmitry Medvedev, the new man in charge of Russian policy on Ukraine, did not have a particular personal opinion on the matter. He took his lead from Putin and Voloshin.

PROBING FOR WEAKNESS

In 2005 Kuchma's second term as president was due to expire, and he could not decide whether to run for a third or appoint a pliable successor and become prime minister, thereby retaining de facto power. His potential successors took turns traveling to Moscow to be assessed, exactly as Central Committee candidates had done twenty years previously. Most of Kuchma's potential successors were Medvedchuk's predecessors—former heads of the president's administration, trusted people. The current head of the presidential administration, Medvedchuk, was keen to run himself (and Putin would have considered his candidacy), but Kuchma warned that Medvedchuk was "unelectable." His preferred choice was Donetsk governor Viktor Yanukovych.

Putin did not like Yanukovych. But Kuchma's observance of the old Soviet rules about gaining approval of a successor was purely ceremonial. In fact, he was not planning to give Putin a choice. He handpicked Yanukovych, explaining with utmost sincerity that no one else was suitable. Only Yanukovych would be able to fund his own election campaign. "Are you going to pay for someone else's campaign?" was the argument Kuchma used to quash dissent. "Does Moscow want to spend all that money on its own candidate? If not, then let it be Yanukovych."

The Kremlin, however, suspected that this argument concealed two unpleasant facts. First, Yanukovych had won Kuchma's "tender" by offering the largest amount. Second, the governor of Donetsk, though not one of Kuchma's clan, was clearly a close and manageable ally. Being a sly politician, Kuchma saw that through the weak Yanukovych he could effectively remain in power, which would not be possible under a Kremlin-friendly apparatchik. Moreover, Moscow genuinely believed that Kuchma was not planning to go anywhere. In its view, he was merely testing the waters to see if he could run for a third term. By choosing a bad successor, Kuchma wanted to promote himself as the better option. So Yanukovych was duly appointed prime minister.

Six months remained till the presidential elections in Ukraine, and Kuchma was still unsure whether to vacate his seat, and if he did, whether he would officially nominate Yanukovych to replace him. Opposition leader and former prime minister Viktor Yushchenko had already begun an election campaign. Yanukovych had established a campaign office, but he was waiting for the go-ahead from Kuchma before doing anything. Kuchma was still scheming, however. The Ukrainian constitution allowed the president only two terms, but there might be a loophole. If the next presidential election failed to take place, for whatever reason, he might be able to arrange an extraordinary ballot in which he could participate.

Kuchma made several trips to the Kremlin. Putin advised him not to derail the elections: the government should act according to the law, and power should be handed to a successor. The election was scheduled for the end of October 2004. Only in April did Kuchma finally decide not to run, whereupon Yanukovych officially announced his candidacy.

AUTUMN CARNIVAL

In the autumn a great number of Russian political strategists headed for Ukraine. Some had signed contracts ahead of time, knowing that the upcoming presidential elections in Ukraine would be a bonanza. Others jumped on the bandwagon at the last minute, realizing that the abolition of gubernatorial elections in Russia meant that they would have to start earning on the side.

In the 1990s and the first half of the 2000s, these political strategists were a special caste. Their numbers mushroomed. Regional election campaigns were big business in Russia, and every candidate (especially the incumbent) employed a large team of specialists skilled in black PR. They generally used methods that were not only unethical but also illegal.

In autumn 2004 nearly every Russian "political technologist" (as these spin doctors are called in Russia) was in Ukraine. Not only that, but there was a detachment of Russian special forces and a group of advisers from Putin's administration. Kiev became home to the so-called Russian club—a permanent team of Russian political consultants holding endless (and aimless) roundtable meetings.

Although Yanukovych was Moscow's officially backed candidate, Russian political consultants also worked for the opposing camp of Viktor Yushchenko, whose election campaign was funded by London exile Boris Berezovsky. It was he who assigned Stanislav Belkovsky to the "orange camp" as a political adviser.

Moscow's preference for Viktor Yanukovych was blatant. Putin met with him once every couple of months or so, and did not hesitate to voice his support. Yanukovych twice visited Putin in Sochi and three times went to Putin's residence outside Moscow. The Russian president even phoned to congratulate Yanukovych on his birthday and visited him in Crimea (although Putin stayed with Medvedchuk). Three weeks before the election Viktor Yanukovych repaid the compliment by attending Putin's birthday celebration.

A lot was invested in securing victory for Yanukovych. Russia eased the restrictions on Ukrainian migrant workers (allowing them to stay in Russia without registration for ninety days, at a time when even Russian citizens moving from one city to another inside Russia had just three days to register), reduced energy prices, and abolished the VAT on exports of oil and gas to CIS countries (a gift worth $800 million).

The closer the elections drew, the more comical Putin's support for Yanukovych became. On October 28, 2004, three days before the election, a parade was held on Khreshchatyk Street, Kiev's main thoroughfare, to mark the sixtieth anniversary of Kiev's liberation from the Nazis. In fact, Kiev had been liberated on November 6, 1944, but the Ukrainian authorities shamelessly held the event a week early, turning it into a powerful preelection show in support of Viktor Yanukovych. A victory banner representing the red flag hoisted above the German Reichstag on May 9, 1945, was brought in from Moscow specially. The parade on Khreshchatyk Street was more like a carnival procession, featuring hundreds of performers dressed in Second World War uniforms marching in front of the guests of honor. On the VIP platform were Ukrainian president Leonid Kuchma; his chosen successor, Viktor Yanukovych; Vladimir Putin; Putin's chief of staff (and future successor) Dmitry Medvedev; and, for some unknown reason, Azerbaijani president Ilham Aliev (who had inherited the presidential chair from his deceased father, Heydar Aliev). The event was unprecedented: the Russian president was personally involved in an election campaign in a foreign country.

The main theme of this patriotic carnival—that Russian and Ukrainians had fought together against the Nazis—was not the key campaign message for Yanukovych. At the suggestion of Russian spin doctors, a negative PR war was waged against Yushchenko, who was dubbed "anti-Russian," "nationalist," and even "pro-fascist." In hindsight, the campaign in 2004 seems like a rehearsal for the information war of 2014.*

The most mysterious episode of the campaign was a dinner Viktor Yushchenko had with heads of the Ukrainian special services. Afterward Yushchenko fell ill, and a few days later was hospitalized with severe poisoning. Austrian doctors saved his life, and the once handsome Yushchenko returned to Kiev in the midst of the election campaign with a severely disfigured face. It was a blow to his campaign, but on the other hand, it was also proof positive that his enemies would stop at nothing and that Yushchenko was ready to sacrifice himself for his own people. No one believed in his sacred mission more than Yushchenko himself.

The circumstances of the poisoning have yet to be properly investigated to this day. Yushchenko says he knows who masterminded the attack on him, but he cannot talk about it publicly.

Russian political analyst Gleb Pavlovsky, who at the time was the Kremlin's "enforcer" inside the Yanukovych camp, says the poisoning of Yushchenko

* What would turn into a tragedy ten years later began humorously. YouTube back then was still in its infancy, but there was one video that was a hit with the Russian-speaking community in Ukraine. On the podium during the parade, Yanukovych offers a sweet to Medvedev, who happily pops it into his mouth. Yanukovych then offers one to Putin, who declines, clearly unimpressed by such triviality.

effectively altered the course of the entire campaign. The carnival atmosphere was replaced by fear. Henceforth it was no longer about political games, but a matter of life and death.

Yushchenko's main rival in the elections was not Yanukovych, in fact, but Putin, who carried on as if it were his own personal campaign. (Incidentally, Putin's approval rating in Ukraine was very high—far higher than that of Kuchma, Yanukovych, or Yushchenko. The tragedy in Beslan and fear of Chechen terrorism had dented it slightly, but not much.) Ahead of the first round of voting, the Russian president gave an interview with Ukraine's top three TV channels. Belkovsky, who was working for Yushchenko, says that the orange camp was disheartened by the spectacle. Putin's calm, confident, persuasive performance dashed the hopes of Yushchenko's supporters, most of whom had until that point thought their man had a great chance of winning.

"You cannot fight the inevitable," said Yanukovych aide Gleb Pavlovsky in a TV debate with Yushchenko aide Stansilav Belkovsky. (These, of course, were the two Moscow political scientists who a year before had staged the battle of the reports during the Yukos affair.) Belkovsky also behaved as if he thought a Yanukovych victory was inevitable, describing Yanukovych's supporters as "vampires" and "werewolves."

Surprisingly, the first round of the election was almost a dead heat, with Yushchenko ahead of Yanukovych by half a percentage point (39.87 percent to 39.32 percent). The Kremlin was not alarmed: they still had no doubt their man Yanukovych would win. Everything was under control, it seemed. The historic events that followed were the first—and worst—defeat of Vladimir Putin's first decade in office.

ORANGE NIGHTMARE

On November 12, 2004, Putin sailed to the Crimea for the official opening of a new ferry service. With him on board was Leonid Kuchma. Yanukovych met them at the Crimean port Kerch, together with Ukrainian transport minister Georgy Kirpa, who had just signed a package of agreements with his Russian counterpart on the construction of a new port in Kerch for container transport. These preelection promotional contracts would never be implemented. And six weeks later, on the night of the second ballot, Kirpa would shoot himself upon learning of Yanukovych's defeat.

The second round of voting was held on November 21, while Putin was on an official visit to Brazil. When the polling stations closed in Kiev, it was 4:00 p.m. in Rio de Janeiro. Putin telephoned Kuchma, who said that exit polls pointed to a Yanukovych victory. Putin called Yanukovych to congratulate the new president, which was immediately reported by news agencies. By the morning of November 24, the Ukrainian electoral commission had declared Yanukovych the winner, and the next day Putin sent his official congratulations.

On the night of the vote, November 21–22, tens of thousands of Yushchenko supporters gathered on Maidan Nezalezhnosti (Independence Square). They pitched tents and remained there under orange banners for a nearly a month in the bitter cold, calling for the results of the "rigged" election to be annulled. One of the leaders of the Maidan protest, Yuri Lutsenko, said that Putin's blatant support would prove to be Yanukovych's eventual downfall: voters were outraged that the Russian president had so shamelessly tried to impose his will on them.

Yanukovych's Moscow adviser, Gleb Pavlovsky, says that he had serious misgivings about leaving his hotel, which was not far from Maidan. To pass through the crowds of people in the city center, he had to don an orange scarf. Having arrived safely back in Moscow, he discovered that the Kremlin was completely out of touch, with everyone drinking champagne and congratulating him on a successful campaign. They all thought the job was done: Yanukovych was president, and the Maidan crowd could be ignored.

But the crowd stayed put.

The authorities decided not to disperse the thousands of protesters, as Kuchma was afraid of taking responsibility for what could have been a bloodbath. Moreover, he was retiring soon, and he was loath to risk his own future for the sake of his successor, Yanukovych. He had been advised by US senator Richard Lugar, who was in Kiev as the head of a delegation of election observers, that any action that resulted in violence meant he could face the same fate as Slobodan Milosevic.

Moscow, meanwhile, was calling on Kuchma to act fast and decisively. Kuchma went to his country residence to consider his options. Yanukovych was perplexed and unable to do anything. The presidential administration building in Kiev was almost totally empty. The only person who continued his duties in the face of the protests that were engulfing Kiev was Viktor Medvedchuk. He remained in constant direct communication with Moscow and flew there regularly to consult with Putin. In Kiev it was said that he had his own private plane and airstrip for this purpose. It was Medvedchuk who in the end got Ukraine's Central Election Commission to announce the official results of the second round and declare Yanukovych president.

But it was too late. What seemed like the whole of Kiev was out in the main square wearing orange scarves. Ukrainian TV stations began to side with the opposition. On November 26, Polish president Aleksander Kwasniewski, Lithuanian president Valdas Adamkus, and former NATO secretary general Javier Solana arrived in Kiev and seated Yushchenko, Yanukovych, and Kuchma around the negotiating table. Moscow also sent a representative to Kiev—Duma Speaker Boris Gryzlov, who is credited with the phrase "Parliament is not a place for discussion." He was in Kiev not to parley but to disrupt the negotiations.

During the first round of talks Yushchenko issued his main demand: annul the results of the second round of voting and hold the election anew. The next day the Ukrainian parliament demanded that the second-round results be declared null and void. It was now up to the Supreme Court to decide.

Putin was maddened by what was happening in Kiev. He could not understand why Kuchma did not disperse the Maidan protesters, since Yanukovych was not yet president. Kuchma replied that he could not do that, since he was under severe pressure from Washington. Putin did not try to hide his irritation. Returning from Brazil, he stopped over in Portugal, where he yelled at journalists asking about Ukraine. He accused the international community of bias, since it had recognized the recent elections in Afghanistan, Kosovo, and Iraq (all of which were undemocratic in his view) but for some reason refused to recognize the results of Ukraine's runoff ballot.

On November 25 Putin went to The Hague for a meeting with European Union leaders. At the final press conference he raged and railed, openly accusing the United States of interfering in Ukraine's internal affairs, implying that Senator Richard Lugar had been orchestrating Yushchenko's campaign from the start.

Russian media coverage was one-sided, its point being that the West had organized an anti-Russian coup in Ukraine. All of a sudden, the separatism card was played. On November 26, members of the Lugansk Regional Council voted in favor of the creation of a southeastern republic in Ukraine and appealed to Vladimir Putin for support. Just two days later, on November 28, the city of Severodonetsk in Ukraine held a "congress of deputies of all levels"—a gathering of opponents of the Orange Revolution from fifteen Ukrainian oblasts (regions). The tone was set by the governor of the Kharkov region and the head of the Donetsk Regional Council, who suggested holding a referendum on the creation of a "southeastern federative state with its capital in Kharkov." Putin's special representative at the congress was Moscow mayor Yuri Luzhkov, a seasoned populist who back in the 1990s had positioned himself as a defender of the rights of the Russian-speaking population of Ukraine, especially in Crimea. However, he gave no specifics at the meeting, clearly lacking authority from the Kremlin; all he said was, "There are two diametrically opposed forces at work in Ukraine. One is crude external interference in Ukraine's domestic affairs; the other is Russia, which fully respects the country's sovereignty. As the mayor of Moscow, I take my hat off to Viktor Yanukovych."[1]

Yanukovych himself, who still hoped to become president of Ukraine and wanted to use the congress as a trump card in the political game, was even less to the point: "Things are on the verge of collapse. Let us try to find a solution without resorting to drastic measures. If one drop of blood is spilled, it will turn into a stream. Our goal is to protect the law and people's rights. Let us please make a decision that will ensure the country's integrity and statehood."[2]

The participants talked, then went their separate ways. The idea of autonomy would be completely forgotten for ten years.

Leonid Kuchma, meanwhile, suddenly remembered that six months previously he had wanted this exact outcome: failed elections and the chance to run for a third term. On December 2 he, along with Medvedchuk, went to Moscow to discuss the plan with Putin. He tried to convince the Russian president of the value of his idea, but Putin no longer trusted Kuchma. The only person in Ukraine he trusted was his godchild's father, Medvedchuk. But even Medvedchuk could not convince Kuchma to declare a state of emergency.

Following the talks, the presidents of Russia and Ukraine issued a statement in which they proposed to annul the results of both rounds of elections and hold another ballot "without foreign interference." In actual fact, no one disputed the results of the first round, which had been essentially a draw. But both sides contested the second; countering the Yushchenko camp's assertion of vote rigging in Yanukovych's favor, Yanukovych's supporters said that there had been rigging in favor of Yushchenko in Kiev and in western Ukraine. As a result, the Supreme Court overturned only the second round and scheduled a third round (or, rather, a rerun of the second) for December 26.

On December 8, after much debate, the Verkhovna Rada (the Ukrainian parliament) adopted several compromise laws. At Yushchenko's request, it amended the election law and introduced rules to make falsification much more difficult. In addition, on the eve of the December 26 ballot it reshuffled the Central Election Commission. Moreover, at Kuchma's suggestion, changes were made to the constitution: the president lost a significant part of his mandate, which passed to the government, which was formed from the parliamentary majority. Kuchma's calculation was simple: the parliamentary majority at the time was on his and Yanukovych's side. He still hoped to remain afloat and become prime minister. But Kuchma was not to know that following Yanukovych's defeat on December 26 most of his supporters would switch allegiances.

The results of the December 26 balloting (51.99 percent for Yushchenko, 44.20 percent for Yanukovych) came as a shock to Moscow. Until the very last minute the Kremlin's crack team of political scientists, political consultants, and Duma MPs had been reporting that the situation was under control, that Ukrainians would "reject the orange plague," and that "the pro-Western candidate had no chance." Once the results of the vote were revealed, Yanukovych's political consultants from Moscow could not take responsibility for the failure. To admit that the money paid to them had been wasted and that they had messed up would be suicide. All they could do was report back to say they had done all they could—and blame the West. Putin could not admit even to himself that he had acted clumsily, misread the true intentions of Kuchma and Yanukovych, and relied too heavily on his friend Medvedchuk.

The defeat was particularly painful because the Kremlin did not understand its causes. How could Russia's backbreaking efforts have failed to produce the desired result? Only if the enemy—that is, the West—had tried even harder, they concluded.

Three months before the Maidan debacle, Vladimir Putin had been caught off guard by the terror attack in Beslan and had instinctively laid the blame at the door of Russia's conniving enemies. The defeat in Ukraine left him in no doubt that his instincts had been right.

CHAPTER 6

IN WHICH DEPUTY CHIEF OF STAFF VLADISLAV SURKOV DEFENDS THE BESIEGED KREMLIN

Vladislav Surkov resembles a romantic hero from a nineteenth-century novel. He can give the impression of a solitary, pensive recluse even when walking along the red carpet in the Grand Kremlin Palace. He looks like a philosopher even when having a drink in the small hours in downtown Moscow's Cafe Pushkin, a favorite haunt of rich foreign tourists and Russian pop stars. He always looks like a man who knows much more than he says, who has everything worked out in advance, and so treats all questions with undisguised sarcasm. Even so, he can easily charm his interlocutors. He can say wonderfully cynical things, but always looks sincere and wise.

To many Surkov seems like an evil genius. He talks in a charming manner about terrible things: murder, war, death. "Who said that war is not a twenty-first-century tool? This century humanity possesses the deadliest weapons in its history, and this century will see the deadliest wars," says the sophisticated intellectual with a smile.

Even long after midnight, talking about contemporary art and drinking in the company of stars (for example, rock singer Zemfira and cult actress Renata Litvinova), he remains a statist, loyal to Vladimir Putin.

Of course, he does not consider himself an ordinary civil servant. He sees himself as a kind of samurai, who gives himself entirely to the service of the emperor. He is unlike the others. Vladislav Surkov himself is fully convinced of that fact.

RENTED APARTMENT

On February 17, 2005, a large rented apartment in central St. Petersburg hosted a secret meeting, almost like a gathering of underground revolutionaries. The Orange Revolution had just claimed victory in Ukraine, and the young people entering the apartment talked about nothing else. More than that, they were discussing the possibility of a similar "color revolution" happening in Russia.

One of the last to arrive was a little older, forty, and was accompanied by a bodyguard. This was Vladislav Surkov, deputy head of the presidential administration, the Kremlin's chief political strategist, and he shocked the St. Petersburg youth with his free and even oppositionist views. For example, he cursed all of Russia's political parties, including the ruling United Russia. (The fact that Surkov had effectively created the party and was in charge of it at that moment was not mentioned.)[1]

Surkov fervently denounced the venality of politicians, explaining to his young audience that the next generation of politicians should be driven by ideology and commitment and that all those gathered in the apartment had the potential to shape the politics of the future—and maybe even form the backbone of the future government.

The meeting, of course, was not a circle of rebels. Quite the contrary. It was a gathering of what would become the pro-government youth organization Nashi, or "Ours." Surkov artfully copied the external trappings of rebellious youth organizations to turn the movement into a powerful state structure. The coup in Ukraine, along with those in Georgia and Serbia, had resulted in "foreign control," which could not be allowed in Russia, explained Surkov and his aide Vasily Yakimenko, the future leader of Nashi, to the young people assembled. Moreover, they said, a branch of the Ukrainian youth movement Pora!, or "It's Time!," had already been set up in Moscow. Nashi would act as a counterweight to such puppet organizations.[2]

Ten days later Nashi's first congress was held at a sanatorium outside Moscow owned by the presidential administration. There were pro-Kremlin activists from previous groups, student activists from Moscow's universities, and representatives from associations of soccer fans. They were to form the basis of the "youth law and order detachments," which, if necessary, could forcefully resist the impending revolution in Russia.

All organizational meetings were held in the strictest secrecy, as if it were a clandestine society aimed at regime change rather than a security measure. *Kommersant* journalist Oleg Kashin, who tried to infiltrate the first congress, was told that there was no such thing as Nashi and was immediately expelled from the sanatorium.[3]

On May 15 Nashi finally came out of the closet by holding a somewhat belated Victory Day celebration in Moscow. Around sixty thousand people were bused into the capital from neighboring regions to commemorate Germany's surrender to the Soviet Union at the end of World War II (known in Russia as the Great Patriotic War), an event normally commemorated on May 9. Leninsky Prospekt, a major thoroughfare that leads to Vnukovo Airport, was blocked off. Orators at the rally declared that the event was the "real Russian Maidan."

In early July Nashi organized a summer camp at Lake Seliger in the Tver region. The two-week jamboree brought together three thousand young people from forty-five regions. For two weeks the participants played sports and listened to concerts by trendy musicians (the aforementioned Zemfira, the most popular rock singer in the country, made an appearance).

Political analyst Gleb Pavlovsky, who the year before had overseen Yanukovych's campaign in Kiev, turned his Foundation for Effective Politics into the most important pro-government think tank and delivered lectures to members of the organization. "Your main problem," he said, "is overconfidence in your own existence. It is not guaranteed, I assure you. European civilization is built on the need for a constant enemy, especially during periods of relative calm. At the turn of the previous century that enemy was the Jews; today it is the Russians. For the West, Russians are outcasts no matter what they do or how good they are. Russians are the Jews of the twenty-first century. You must be aware of that. You have to be tougher, learn how to handle a rifle and meet your opponents with force. I believe that Nashi is the fist that society must show to the neo-Nazis. It must become more active."[4]

In the autumn Pavlovsky would go even further. He would become the chief propagandist of Surkov's staff, hosting *Realpolitik*, a weekly analytical program broadcast on NTV during prime time on Sunday. Pavlovsky now regrets it: "That's when we started to waste time. Back then what we were doing seemed important. But in fact the government had devised all sorts of illusory goals and was energetically fulfilling them. It was all pointless. But we were focused inward and didn't realize it."

On July 26, the day after the camp ended, the most prominent Nashi activists paid a visit to President Putin, who said: "Your organization is a shining example of civil society. . . . I hope very much that Nashi will be able to influence the situation in the country."[5]

Nashi turned into a permanent structure and perhaps Russia's only full-fledged political organization that had other functions apart from mass rallies or conventions. Activists were given study or work placements, as well as free training and vacations. It used the network marketing principle: the more friends an activist invited to join, the higher his or her status became.

Surkov was aware that at the heart of any revolution lies a negative agenda—it is much easier to mobilize the masses to fight *against* something than to fight *for* something. Of course the thousands gathered in Kiev's Independence Square wanted democracy and freedom. But they were driven more by the struggle against the corruption of Leonid Kuchma's regime. And the primary motivation was to be rid of the influence of Russia and Putin. Fear of an external enemy, especially an age-old one, is always the best mobilizing agent. Surkov took all that into account in formulating Nashi's message. In fact, Surkov acted as if he were preparing a revolution. He selected the most active and enterprising young people and then loaded them with ideology—the idea of uprising and rebellion against external enemies, which in this case were the United States and the global conspiracy against Russia.

Nashi was Surkov's most eye-catching project, but not the only one. After the Orange Revolution, he was commissioned to draw up the Kremlin's strategy for preventing a similar revolution in Russia. The deputy head of the presidential administration analyzed all the major driving forces that had helped make the revolution in Kiev—the youth organization Pora!, Ukrainian pop musicians playing in Maidan, nongovernmental organizations involved in monitoring the elections, and independent media (above all Channel Five, owned by chocolate tycoon Petro Poroshenko)—and began targeting their Russian equivalents.

In April, in a Moscow hotel, Surkov held a secret meeting to recruit Russia's most popular musicians, which went well. All Russian state TV channels were issued with stop lists of people whose names could not be mentioned, as well as a list of people who could not be criticized.

Back in autumn 2003 the Russian Public Opinion Research Centre (VTsIOM), the country's largest polling agency, had been effectively seized; its director, Yuri Levada, and his entire team had left the organization, replaced by a group of individuals who had been handpicked by Surkov but who had no particular expertise in the field.

In December 2005 the State Duma adopted a set of amendments to the law on NGOs. The main aim was to stop the financing of political activities from abroad. Surkov repeatedly stated that the law was needed to thwart the West's attempts to orchestrate a color revolution in Russia. "Everyone knows that Freedom House's [chairman] James Woolsey once headed the CIA," argued Surkov on May 16 (the day after Nashi's rally on Leninsky Prospekt) at a closed meeting with business leaders, referring to a US-government-supported NGO that characterizes its mission as "the expansion of freedom and democracy around the world." "Only an idiot would believe that the organization's mission is purely humanitarian."[6] By October Human Rights Watch, Amnesty International, and Doctors Without Borders had been forced to temporarily suspend their activities due to "incorrectly filed documents."

Moscow Helsinki Group, the oldest human rights organization in the country, faced more unpleasantness. A few days after the adoption of the amendments to the law on NGOs, the state TV channel Rossiya showed the documentary film *Spies*, which told about a fake stone in a park in central Moscow that British diplomats had used as a drop to transmit secret information. The film showed real footage and named specific individuals, including the UK embassy's second secretary, Mark Doe. It was also claimed that Doe had funded Russian human rights groups, such as Moscow Helsinki Group, then headed by seventy-eight-year-old Lyudmila Alexeyeva, who had been nominated for the Nobel Peace Prize on several occasions. Alexeyeva herself was shocked by the allegations, saying that she had never heard of Doe and had only ever received one grant from the British authorities.*

Putin, Surkov, and comrades were gripped by more than just paranoia. They were being fed daily reports about Western partners carrying out intelligence

---

*Interestingly, few people actually believed Rossiya's claims—*Spies* looked too much like a crude piece of Soviet-era propaganda. However, six years later Jonathan Powell, a former chief of staff under Tony Blair, admitted in an interview that the "spy stone" really had existed, and that many of the facts in the documentary were true.

work on Russian soil, which against the backdrop of the Ukrainian revolution led them to some very frightening conclusions.

BESIEGED FORTRESS

The new ideological doctrine developed by Surkov was called "sovereign democracy." It essentially replaced the "managed democracy" of Alexander Voloshin, who, as the Kremlin's policy architect during Putin's first term, had believed in the need for economic and political reform—democracy would not simply grow by itself, but needed external assistance. Surkov's concept was that the problem would not be solved through simple internal adjustment, since Russia's problems were not only internal, and possibly not internal at all. Rather, Russia was hampered by an external enemy forever encroaching on its sovereignty. Therefore, Russian democracy had to be unique, and ready to defend itself against external threats.

Back in early 2005 the Kremlin really did feel like a besieged fortress. The reasons were many, above all the humiliation by the Orange Revolution in Kiev. Panic was beginning to set in.

At about the same time as the events in Ukraine, presidential elections were taking place in Abkhazia, a small self-proclaimed breakaway republic that had split from Georgia in the early 1990s and bordered Sochi (meaning that it was located just a few dozen kilometers from Putin's favorite residence). Russian bureaucrats liked to visit Abkhazia when they got bored of the officious atmosphere of the presidential resort, and in essence the Kremlin treated Abkhazia like a utility room of the president's summer residence.* Therefore, its choice of candidate for the presidential elections was based on one simple criterion: Whom did Putin prefer? But Putin did not have time (or any particular desire) to filter the candidates, so he randomly opted for the head of the local KGB, Raul Khajimba.

Once the choice was made, Khajimba was given all the trappings befitting Putin's chosen one—roughly the same as for Yanukovych, but scaled down,

---

*One day a Kremlin official relaxing on the beach in Sukhumi, the coastal capital of Abkhazia, was approached by a local resident, who said that he could not take his son abroad for medical treatment since no country in the world recognized Abkhazian passports. The official told Putin about it and suggested (supposedly for altruistic purposes) that Abkhazians be given Russian passports. No sooner said than done.

given the size of Abkhazia. While vacationing in August in Sochi, Putin appeared in front of the cameras with Khajimba, also accompanied by Yanukovych. Sukhumi was also paid a visit by Russian "experts" (mostly from the FSB), who said live on air that Abkhazians should "thank Russia for its support"—that is, vote for Russia's choice. But on October 3, 2004—one month before the first round of the Ukrainian elections—the opposition leader, Sergei Bagapsh, gave Putin's chosen candidate a thrashing at the ballot box.

Abkhazia might have been forgiven were it not for the unfolding horror of Ukraine. And the voter mutiny might have been suppressed had the citizens of the unrecognized republic and Bagapsh himself—a former local Communist Party secretary and director of a local energy company—not been so hard-nosed.

When the newly elected Bagapsh and his team visited Russian officials in Sochi, they were received by Vladislav Surkov.* No sooner had they crossed the threshold than he began rebuking them. Bagapsh and his comrades were so offended that they returned to Sukhumi forthwith.

The president-elect did not yield to the pressure of the FSB until Russia decided to cut off Abkhazia's oxygen supply—its exports to Russia of mandarin oranges, the revenue from which fed the entire republic. Under siege, Bagapsh agreed to a compromise—new elections and the promise to appoint Putin's losing protégé vice president if Bagapsh won again. He was duly reelected president on January 12, 2005. A day later Viktor Yushchenko was recognized as Ukraine's new head of state.

On top of the Ukrainian and Abkhaz revolutions, the Kremlin still remembered the Rose Revolution, which had occurred the year before in Georgia. The driving force of that movement, which had removed Eduard Shevardnadze as president, was the revolutionary youth group Kmara, or "Enough," which was actively supported by US nongovernmental organizations.

But the 2003 revolution in Georgia had gone strangely unheeded by the Kremlin at the time. First, Russia was fed up with Shevardnadze, a Georgian who had been the Soviet minister of foreign affairs and Mikhail Gorbachev's right-hand man. Old-timers in Moscow spoke of how Shevardnadze was personally to blame for the breakup of the Soviet Union, since during his

---

*Surkov was actually responsible for internal policy inside the presidential administration, but Russia never considered Abkhazia a foreign land, even though de jure it was part of Georgia.

tenure as foreign minister he had deliberately signed agreements that damaged Russia's interests and accelerated the collapse of its empire.

In the 1990s Shevardnadze's policy had been condemned by Moscow as anti-Russian. For instance, he was one of the main supporters of the Baku-Tbilisi-Ceyhan oil pipeline, the first route to bypass Russia in delivering oil from the Caspian Sea to the West.

Putin and Shevardnadze were the best of enemies. The latter was accused of supporting Chechen terrorists, and Russian warplanes had repeatedly bombed the Pankisi Gorge, in northern Georgia, where Chechen militants were said to be hiding. Eduard Shevardnadze's Georgia was the first country against which Putin imposed sanctions—visa requirements were introduced for Georgian citizens entering Russia, although citizens of all other countries in the Commonwealth of Independent States (the successor to the Soviet Union) enjoyed visa-free travel.

So Shevardnadze's overthrow during the Rose Revolution in 2003 had not provoked any tears in Moscow. Ironically, on November 22, 2003, members of the Russian Security Council, after their traditional weekly meeting, went to the Georgian restaurant Genatsvale, located on Ostozhenka Street in the most expensive area of Moscow, not far from the Kremlin. As described by British journalist Angus Roxburgh, right in the middle of dinner Putin got a call from Eduard Shevardnadze, who wanted to talk to him over a secure phone line about the public unrest that had bubbled up in Tbilisi.[7]

According to exit polls, the parliamentary elections held on November 2 had been won by the opposition party, led by Mikheil Saakashvili. But the authorities proclaimed victory for themselves. By November 22 the anti-government demonstrations had reached their apogee, and protesters had broken into the parliament building. Shevardnadze had no other option but to seek help from his sworn enemy, Vladimir Putin.

In spite of the hostility toward Shevardnadze, the Security Council trusted the Georgian opposition even less, and did not welcome the prospect of a people's revolution in a neighboring country. So it was that Russian foreign minister Igor Ivanov left the Genatsvale restaurant for the airport and flew immediately to Tbilisi. For one thing, he himself had been born in Georgia, and for another, he had worked with Shevardnadze back in the Soviet Foreign Ministry. It was a reconnaissance mission more than anything else, since Putin did not really understand what was going on in Georgia and why. He issued no precise instructions to Ivanov, but the latter understood that his task was to prevent bloodshed and revolution. Faced with the unknown, the Kremlin always prefers the status quo.

Upon arrival in Tbilisi, Ivanov went to the square in front of the parliament building to speak with the opposition leaders, including Mikheil Saakashvili. He met with his friends in Tbilisi and in the morning went to Shevardnadze's summer residence. By now he was convinced that Shevardnadze had lost all authority and influence. Ivanov would probably have tried to stop the impending revolution if Putin had explicitly demanded it. But instead the Russian foreign minister simply told Shevardnadze that he had no faith in the latter's political future and recommended that he start negotiations as a matter of urgency. A few hours later Ivanov seated Shevardnadze and the three leaders of the opposition (led by Saakashvili) around the same table, patted them all on the shoulder, and said, "President Putin asked me to help you find a political solution. That's up to you now—to hold talks and avoid bloodshed. So I will leave you now."[8]

Ivanov then flew to Batumi, on Georgia's Black Sea coast, where he learned that Shevardnadze had resigned. The former president had been expecting words of support from Ivanov, and when they did not come he interpreted it as a demand to surrender to the electoral victors.

On January 4, 2004, a presidential election was held in Georgia. It was won by Mikheil Saakashvili, who a month later went to Moscow on his first foreign visit as president. At a meeting in the Kremlin Saakashvili enthusiastically expressed admiration for Putin, saying that he would like to emulate the Russian leader.* Saakashvili also assured Putin that he would try to correct the numerous mistakes committed by Shevardnadze.

Saakashvili recalls how, in response, Putin delivered a short lecture about relations with the United States. He told a story about how in 2003 he had been due to fly to Moldova to sign an agreement on the Moldovan-Transdniestrian settlement. The lead plane had already taken off when he received a call from Moldovan president Vladimir Voronin, who reportedly said that the signing would not take place because the "second secretary of the US embassy has forbidden it." Then he told another story about how the Lithuanian president had asked him for an oil discount, but Putin had refused because the Lithuanians had "misbehaved." "The moral was

*Indeed, over the next few months he began to build a top-down power structure in Georgia based on the Russian model.

simple," Saakashvili says. "Don't behave badly, and don't be friends with the Americans."

Despite everything, Putin and Saakashvili parted on good terms: the Georgian president was charmed by his senior comrade, and the Russian leader was convinced that he had set his younger counterpart on the right path.

Putin's attitude toward Georgia and Saakashvili changed dramatically after the latter backed the Orange Revolution in Ukraine, and the Kremlin began to rethink its attitude toward the events in Georgia. The involuntary initiator of the Georgian revolution, Igor Ivanov, could not argue, since by that time he had been dismissed. As the curtain came down on Vladimir Putin's first term, the Russian Foreign Ministry was handed to Sergei Lavrov.

Only in autumn 2004 did the Kremlin's conspiracy theorists suddenly realize that they had underestimated the enemy. The revolutions on Russia's borders in Georgia, Ukraine, and even Abkhazia were the result of an anti-Russian plot, they thought. Moreover, it was obvious that the next target of the overseas patrons of the color revolutions would be Russia itself—something that had to be avoided at all costs.

In 2005 the panic intensified. In April there was another revolution in Kyrgyzstan, a small country in Central Asia and one of the poorest republics of the former Soviet Union. Protesters overthrew President Askar Akayev and ransacked his residence. Akayev himself fled to Moscow, assuring his hosts that he had fallen afoul of a US conspiracy—certainly not that he had been overthrown by shopkeepers tired of constant extortion.

US officials claimed that they had had no hand in the revolution in Kyrgyzstan. On the contrary, Akayev suited them, since back in 2001 he had allowed Washington (with Putin's consent) to site a military base at the airport outside the capital, Bishkek. However, President George W. Bush welcomed the Kyrgyz people's desire for democracy, which the Kremlin took as an open confession of the US role in Akayev's overthrow.

The Kyrgyz revolution very nearly spread to neighboring Uzbekistan, the most populous of the Central Asian republics. The eastern part of the country, located in the Fergana Valley, is effectively cut off from the rest of Uzbekistan by a mountain range. Only a small pass connects the two halves. The outskirts of the Fergana Valley belong to Kyrgyzstan, and from there the taste of revolutionary victory spread to areas inside Uzbekistan, where protests soon followed. Initially they were not directed against the central authorities: in the city of Andizhan, inside the Fergana Valley, a number of business leaders had been jailed and their companies unlawfully seized, and family members had simply gathered in the main square to demand the return of their breadwinners.

Soon the entire city joined in the demonstration. The jailed business leaders were broken out of prison by the protesters, and the local authorities fled the city. On the night of May 13, 2005, police fired on the protesters. The shooting started in the main square, which was the focal point of the rally. Residents of Andijan fled in fear to the border with Kyrgyzstan, about 15–20 kilometers from the city. But army divisions stationed along the way fired at the fleeing people. Many were killed, but several thousand managed to cross the border into Kyrgyzstan. The Uzbek authorities demanded their extradition as terrorists, but instead Kyrgyzstan sent them to EU countries as refugees.

As the first leader to put down a color revolution, Uzbek president Islam Karimov became a hero to Vladimir Putin. Five months after the Andijan massacre, Russia and Uzbekistan signed a treaty ensuring that if a threat to Karimov's regime ever arose again, Russia would provide military aid.

"The post-Ukraine neurosis spread to internal politics," says Gleb Pavlovsky today of that period, when he was an adviser to the presidential administration. "We all felt unprepared for a color revolution in Russia. I was no exception."

So it was that Vladimir Putin's Russia entered a new historical stage. Integration with the West, friendship with European leaders, and talk about European values were all put on hold. Moscow's medieval Kremlin, which no invading force had captured for centuries, felt like a besieged fortress. The panic forced Putin to demand that Vladislav Surkov take immediate action.

A MILITARY EMPEROR

The next US presidential elections were held on November 2, 2004, just three days after the first round of voting in Ukraine and twenty days before the second, which marked the start of the Maidan protests. The US ambassador to Moscow, Alexander Vershbow, held a reception at his official residence, Spaso House, that evening. A monitor on the wall showed a live CNN broadcast, and guests happily took pictures of themselves with the cardboard cutouts of George W. Bush and John Kerry in the hall. At that time US embassy receptions were attended by most of Moscow's high society, including State

Duma members and government media journalists. Ten years later it would become bad form, and at the entrance correspondents from those very same media would pester guests with the question "How much are the Americans paying you?"

But on November 2 Spaso House hosted the political beau monde, including those Russian advisers of Yanukovych who had just arrived from Kiev. They proudly walked around the room, radiating confidence that Yanukovych's campaign under their guidance was going brilliantly and victory was certain. Political scientist Vyacheslav Nikonov, who was the grandson of Stalin's foreign minister Vyacheslav Molotov and who a few years hence would set up the Kremlin-backed Russky Mir (Russian World) Foundation and become a Duma MP, was casually sipping whisky and joking about America's "political instability," since no one knew who would win the US election, Bush or Kerry. In Ukraine there was no such problem, of course. Everyone knew that Yanukovych would triumph.

Soon came the news that George W. Bush had won, with 51 percent of the vote to Kerry's 48 percent. Bush's victory made a huge impression on the Kremlin, as he was reelected for a second term and his party gained full control over both houses of Congress. He seemed to be absolute master of the world—a "military emperor," as they called him in the Kremlin. For a long time George W. Bush was Putin's model of the ideal president, says Gleb Pavlovsky: "a strong leader, forever breaking the rules." Putin looked at Bush with envy, respect, and fear.

In January 2005, in his second inaugural address, Bush stated: "It is the policy of the United States to seek and support the growth of democratic movements and institutions in every nation and culture, with the ultimate goal of ending tyranny in our world."[9] Called the "Bush Doctrine," it represented a new approach to US foreign policy, in which the United States assumed the role of global policeman, backed up by language about the struggle for democracy and human rights.

"The Kremlin thought that Bush would soon set his sights on Russia," says Pavlovsky. "The panic stemmed from overestimating his role and importance. We had a feeling that Bush was here to stay. He'd been elected for a second term, which meant forever. That was the prevailing atmosphere in the world back then, so it wasn't surprising we thought so too. We were convinced we had to close ranks and defend ourselves."

Even so, Putin was still hoping to restore relations with Bush. He liked the "military emperor" and wanted to establish a fair, equal partnership with him, though he was offended that Bush apparently did not consider him an equal. In bilateral meetings the US president always reassured Putin that everything between them was fine. But as soon as the presidents parted company, something went wrong, be it the revolution in Ukraine, Iran's nuclear program, the mess in Iraq, the presence of US intelligence officers in the Caucasus, or US plans to deploy a missile shield in Europe. Therefore, Putin drew up a list of grievances he had against Bush. At their next meeting he took the list out of his pocket and put each point to Bush.

Putin's arguments essentially boiled down to the fact that in international relations Russia was always treated as inferior. Putin had been the first to support Bush in his "war on terror" in 2001, the same year that Russia closed its overseas bases in Vietnam and Cuba. Russia bit its lip when the United States withdrew from the ABM Treaty and embarked on a second wave of NATO expansion in Eastern Europe in 2004, when the inclusion of three former Soviet republics, Estonia, Latvia, and Lithuania, meant that the alliance now bordered the Russian Federation.

Putin expected respect and mutual concessions in exchange, but there were none. The United States did not even abolish the Jackson-Vanik amendment to the Trade Act of 1974, which restricted commercial ties with the Soviet Union in response to Moscow's refusal to allow the emigration of Jews to Israel (the so-called refuseniks). The Soviet Union no longer existed and all the Jews who wished to emigrate had long gone (many had in fact returned), yet the amendment was still there.

Other bones of contention were Bush's reluctance to ratify the Treaty on Conventional Armed Forces in Europe, the desire to deploy a missile defense system in Europe (allegedly against Iran), and the prospect of NATO membership for more former Soviet republics—this time Georgia and Ukraine. Instead of gratitude for his cooperation, all Putin heard were reproaches about freedom of speech, the Yukos affair, Chechnya, and so on.

Bush listened patiently to all Putin's accusations, but his aides were indignant. They were adamant that Putin had no right to interfere in the affairs of other states, such as Ukraine or Georgia, and would be better advised to put his own house in order. Bush's entourage did not share their president's liking for Putin.

SIXTY YEARS WITHOUT WAR

Gleb Pavlovsky relates that until about 2005 the Kremlin was warm to the idea of joining NATO and actively discussed the preconditions for accepting an invitation, should one be made.

Even before being elected president, Putin asked NATO secretary general George Robertson at their first meeting, in February 2000, when Russia would be able to join the alliance. Robertson was not prepared for the question and answered routinely that every country that wanted to join should apply according to established procedure. Putin was irked. He was convinced that Russia should not have to wait in line like other countries; on the contrary, it should be invited to join.

The NATO-Russia Council was set up in 2002, on the initiative of Italian prime minister Silvio Berlusconi, as an intermediate stage with a view to Russia's full membership in the North Atlantic Alliance. Berlusconi even arranged a luxurious summit in Rome to celebrate his idea, and Russia's permanent representative to NATO was given a place at the table alongside the member countries. Behind closed doors the group discussed in depth the question of how to admit Russia as painlessly as possible, and in such a way that made Russia feel respected and valued.

The accession to NATO of the East European countries, including the Baltic republics (of which Putin was informed after the fact), was the first serious challenge. The color revolutions were the second. Then, in 2005, the proclamation of the "Bush Doctrine" and the transformation of the Kremlin into a besieged fortress put an end to such hopes once and for all.

In April 2005 Putin delivered his annual address to the Federal Assembly, Russia's bicameral parliament. Its most striking phrase, one that was subsequently quoted by all the world's media, came at the very beginning: "The collapse of the Soviet Union was the greatest geopolitical catastrophe of the twentieth century." However, the speech was not about revanchism or nostalgia. On the contrary, Putin (reading the words of the Kremlin's policy chief, Vladislav Surkov, who had prepared the speech) said that Russia was a European country, that European values were Russia's "reference point," and that for 300 years Russia had "walked hand in hand with European nations," including in the struggle for human rights. Moreover, Putin told his despondent audience of officials and lawmakers that "we do not plan to hand over the country to a corrupt, ineffective bureaucracy" and that "it is politically expedient to hold a dialogue with society."

"For modern Russia the values of democracy are no less important than the pursuit of economic success and social well-being," he explained, adding that "our values also define our commitment to strengthening Russian statehood and sovereignty." The audience broke into applause after that statement.

Putin finished his message with a reference to the Great Patriotic War:

> Victory was achieved not only by the force of arms, but by the fortitude of all the nations that made up the Soviet Union. Russia, which is linked to the former Soviet republics, now independent states, through a common historical fate, the Russian language and a great culture, cannot remain detached from the general desire for freedom.
>
> In asserting Russia's foreign policy interests, we aim to achieve economic development, strengthen the international authority of our neighbor countries, and synchronize the pace and parameters of the reform process in Russia and the CIS states. We are willing to adopt the best practices of our neighbors and share with them our ideas and results.[10]

Strangely, neither Putin nor Vladislav Surkov thought to evoke the pathos of the Great Patriotic War and draw analogies with contemporary Russia.

The sixtieth anniversary of Victory Day, coming up on May 9, was an important test for Putin. In post-Soviet Russia, Victory Day was the only Soviet holiday that was still relevant (Labor Day and Revolution Day were no more), and it had acquired "holy" status. The occasion symbolized the decisive role of the Soviet Union in the victory over fascism, for which the world ought to be eternally grateful to Russia. (Ten years later state propaganda even invented a slogan for this holiday: "The world remembers that it was saved.") For Putin, it was especially timely. He needed Russia's foreign partners to show the utmost respect both for him and for Russia.

He remembered the example of Boris Yeltsin. In 1995 Russia was going through hard times, yet the fiftieth anniversary of Victory Day was celebrated with great pomp and circumstance. A new memorial, Poklonnaya Hill, was built specially in Moscow's Victory Park, where the main military celebrations on that day were held, including a parade of military hardware. The traditional parade site, Red Square, hosted only the first "historical" part of the parade: a column of veterans (who in 1995 were still quite numerous). The guests of honor at the 1995 commemoration included all the heads of the CIS countries and almost all the G7 leaders, among them Bill Clinton from the United States and Britain's John Major, plus Chinese president Jiang Zemin and UN secretary general Boutros Boutros-Ghali.

For the sixtieth anniversary, Putin decided not to build anything new, but rather to concentrate on the solemnities and ceremonies in Red Square. There was no modern military equipment at all. Twenty-five hundred veterans rode across the square on 1940s military trucks, while others watched from the grandstand.

As for high-ranking guests, the goal to outdo 1995 was achieved. Moscow hosted more than fifty current and former presidents, prime ministers, and chancellors, plus the UN secretary general and the UNESCO director general. Nearly all the invitees came, including all the heads of the now G8, with one exception: Tony Blair, who was busy with his election campaign.

Bush behaved exactly as Putin wanted, taking a seat next to the Russian president on the podium, standing for the Russian national anthem, wiping away tears at the sight of the veterans, and saying heartfelt things about the contribution of the Russian people to the victory over Germany. But the effect was inevitably spoiled—and not because on the eve of May 9 a group of US congressmen introduced a bill to exclude Russia from the G8 for systematic violations of human rights (the Kremlin was by now accustomed to ignoring such provocations). No, it was "our friend George" himself who put a damper on everything.

On the way to Moscow he had contrived to stop over in Riga, Latvia, for two days, and even stated there in a TV interview that he was planning to raise with Putin the question of whether Russia would formally acknowledge that the Soviet presence in the Baltic countries, which had begun just before World War II, had been an occupation. Immediately after the event in Moscow (missing a gala dinner at the Kremlin), Bush flew to Tbilisi, where he was met with a truly historic reception. On the main square of the Georgian capital 150,000 people waving American flags had gathered to welcome the US president. Addressing the crowd, he described the Rose Revolution as a triumph for democracy and lauded Georgia as a "beacon of liberty" in the former Soviet Union and throughout the world. At the end of the visit Georgian president Mikheil Saakashvili renamed the street along which Bush had traveled from the airport in honor of the American president.

It all confirmed Putin's eternal suspicions of the Americans as inveterate hypocrites. The mask was finally dropped a year later, in May 2006, when US vice president Dick Cheney arrived in Vilnius to deliver a keynote speech about democracy, freedom, and the rejection of Russian authoritarianism. From there Cheney flew to Kazakhstan for oil talks with President Nursultan Nazarbayev, who had run his country as an autocracy for sixteen years. Putin was both angered and amused: "Comrade Wolf knows whom to eat. He eats and listens to no one," he said opaquely about his former American allies a week later, citing a Russian aphorism about backstabbing friends.

SOVEREIGN DEMOCRACY

In their struggle against an imaginary color revolution, Surkov and his team had in mind a specific year when it might happen: 2008, when Vladimir Putin's second presidential term was due to come to an end.

"In 2008 we will either preserve our sovereignty or be ruled externally," Surkov told a party meeting in Krasnoyarsk at the end of November 2005, alarming his listeners. "We will be with the United Russia Party, and we ask you to join us, because it will be a struggle even harder than in 1993." In 1993 there had been a genuine civil war in Moscow, and Yeltsin had ordered tanks to shell the parliament building. The audience did not really understand Surkov's anxiety, but sensed that the situation was serious.

Under the constitution Putin did not have the right to run for a third term, which complicated matters. First of all, he had to decide if it was worth trying to stay in office for a third term, as so many of his colleagues from other CIS countries had done.

For instance, the president of Belarus, Alexander Lukashenko, had been elected in 1994 for the first time and then changed the constitution in 1996, allowing him to start his "first" five-year term from scratch. In 2001 he was reelected for a second term. Then in 2004 he held (and won) a referendum to abolish the limit on the number of presidential terms. In 2006 he was reelected for a third term; in 2010 (when he held the election a year early) he was reelected for a fourth, and in 2015 for a fifth.

The presidents of Kazakhstan and Uzbekistan, Nursultan Nazarbayev and Islam Karimov, respectively, went down a similar route: Nazarbayev made regular constitutional amendments to extend his term, while in the mid-2000s

Karimov simply started ignoring the constitutional limitations and did not even bother to explain why his mandate was forever being prolonged.

Despite such precedents, Putin had no intention of becoming another "last dictator in Europe," as the press had dubbed Lukashenko. It was important for Putin the lawyer to be seen to act within the law. Although his inner circle advised him to consider a third consecutive term, his mind was made up.

In the time remaining before the election, Putin had to decide how to handle the transfer of power. Some possible scenarios were developed by Surkov, who presented them to his boss. Putin analyzed them all, but put off making a final decision.

A vital prerequisite for the peaceful transfer of power was a docile parliament that under no circumstances would support a color revolution. For this, Surkov needed to overhaul the electoral system and create a "party of power" capable of fixing the "2008 problem," which was what Kremlin called the upcoming presidential election.

The most important element of Russia's "sovereign democracy" was the ability to tinker with the electoral system. First there was a sharp reduction in the number of parties and a tightening of the registration rules, essentially allowing only puppet parties approved by the presidential administration to participate in the election. Second, the mixed system of parliamentary elections (under which half the State Duma was elected according to party lists and the other half from single-member districts) would be scrapped in favor of party lists only. In other words, independent candidates who did not belong to a registered political party would no longer be able to stand for parliament. This eliminated candidates that were not approved by the Kremlin.

The new electoral system suited United Russia, the ruling party that Surkov had cobbled together from two former sworn enemies: the pro-Putin Unity and the Primakov-Luzhkov alliance Fatherland-All Russia. As early as April 2005 Surkov began to prepare for the 2008 election. But the task of transforming United Russia from a herd of unprincipled bureaucrats into something more meaningful proved to be far more challenging than building a counterrevolutionary youth organization such as Nashi.

Surkov decided that the party had to attract more outstanding personalities; moreover, there should be more intra-party debate. The idea was to internalize the political process, so that the polemics would take place within the ruling party, not between parties—along the lines of Japanese politics, where decades-long battles had been waged within the country's Liberal Democratic Party.

To this end, Surkov created two wings inside the party: one liberal, the other conservative. There was also a large-scale purge of the party leadership. Old and inefficient "Putinites" from the security services were expelled and replaced with specially selected careerists. They were to make the party more manageable—for Surkov, of course. The key position of secretary general of the Presidium of the General Council went to Vyacheslav Volodin, then the Vice Speaker of the Duma and the former leader of Primakov's FAR party faction.

On assuming office as the new party head, Volodin outlined several key principles, including "United Russia's support for European values," "liberalization of party life," "development of party discussion," "outreach to the population," and "tough action against opponents who brainwash the public." The manifesto was pure Surkov.

Ironically, six years later Volodin would ditch his patron, and only one of the above principles would remain relevant: tough action against opponents. He had a creative approach to the ideological methodology inherited from Surkov: the war against the external enemy (as an effective and highly popular way to consolidate power) would become total, and the green shoots of intra-party debate would be uprooted forever.

CHAPTER 7

IN WHICH DEPUTY PRIME MINISTER IGOR SHUVALOV COMES UP WITH A PLAN TO MAKE RUSSIA AN EMPIRE ONCE MORE

Igor Shuvalov is something of an aristocrat, like his namesake Count Shuvalov, who served in the Russian government in the eighteenth century. Among Putin's officials, Shuvalov stands apart—he seems to be slightly above and apart from the rest, yet remains extremely loyal to his boss. He gives the impression of being a man on a mission. He seems to sense that he is an organic part of the power structure: he could hold office today, a hundred years ago, or a hundred years hence, and it would make no difference. For Shuvalov, there is no moral dilemma regarding the regime's actions and his own convictions. He did not choose to be Putin's field marshal; fate decided for him.

Casually mentioning Catherine II and Alexander II in conversation, Igor Ivanovich makes it sound as if they are his colleagues. And he strongly objects to being called a civil servant: "I'm not a civil servant. I am a statesman."

Journalists quip that he and Igor Sechin—another Igor Ivanovich, for they share the same first name and patronymic—represent an angel-demon pair sitting on Putin's shoulders: Shuvalov gives good advice, Sechin bad. It's also said jokingly that Putin once asked his secretary to put him through to Igor Ivanovich. "Shuvalov?" asked the secretary. "No, the real one," said Putin.

ENERGY SUPERPOWER

In August 2005 Vladimir Putin received a visit at his Sochi residence from his new friend Silvio Berlusconi. After the Russian president introduced the Italian prime minister to his pets, Koni the Labrador retriever and Vadik the pony, the two leaders spoke at length about Italian business in Russia before turning to Russia's support for Italy's aspiration to become a permanent member of the UN Security Council. Since this was unlikely, they agreed that Russia would at least try to stop Germany from acquiring such status.

Putin liked to chat with Berlusconi ever since he had become disillusioned with Bush. The Italian prime minister was now his role model. Berlusconi had used his business empire to win elections and then used politics to further enrich his business. That made Berlusconi a natural ally of Putin's. Neither man ever criticized or found fault with the other.

At the end of the conversation in Sochi, Putin told his friend Silvio about the upcoming G8 summit in St. Petersburg. As the host country, Russia had the privilege of setting the agenda, and the main topic was going to be energy security. Berlusconi nodded approvingly, since he always found common ground with Russia on energy issues. Shortly after the meeting with Putin, he agreed that Gazprom would supply gas to Italy's ENI at a reduced price in exchange for friendship and political support.

It was Igor Shuvalov's idea to make energy security the leitmotif of the G8 summit. Putin's new chief economic aide, a corporate lawyer with vast experience, had worked with virtually all the Russian oligarchs, had become a millionaire, and was probably the richest member of the presidential administration. In January 2005 Putin appointed him as his sherpa to the G8 and entrusted him with the task of organizing this, the first-ever G8 summit on Russian soil. At the same time Shuvalov began to develop Russia's new foreign policy approach. While Vladislav Surkov was building his concept of "sovereign democracy" and preparing to defend Russia against "color revolutionaries," Shuvalov suggested that Putin adopt a more assertive position in matters of foreign policy.

The new strategy was given the title "energy superpower." At the upcoming summit Russia planned to offer European countries a pact: Moscow would take care of ensuring a flow of fuel sufficient to supply every house in Europe, and in return Europe would show friendship, understanding, and loyalty, as Silvio Berlusconi had. The concept appealed very much to Putin. It allowed him to demonstrate a new, more pragmatic approach to relations with Europe. He did not want to talk to European leaders about human rights, freedom of speech, or Chechnya. He was tired of hearing only criticism. The only way to silence the liberals was to steer the conversation toward business matters.

Putin appointed Shuvalov as his chief economic negotiator, whereupon the latter began to represent Russia in the G8, in the WTO, at Davos, and in talks with the European Union. His strategic aim was essentially to convert Russian oil and gas into political influence and make Putin the energy emperor of Europe.

THE PUTIN-SCHROEDER PACT

A week after the meeting with Berlusconi in Sochi, the Russian president flew to Berlin. His other friend, German chancellor Gerhard Schroeder, had serious problems ahead of Germany's parliamentary elections. His Social Democrats were way behind the Christian Democratic Union/Christian Social Union alliance in the polls. Putin had a history of rescuing Schroeder. Three years previously the German leader had been heading toward doom in the elections but had miraculously survived by joining Russia and France in opposition to the 2003 invasion of Iraq. This time around Putin came bearing gifts: Gazprom, the Germany power company E.ON, and the German-based chemical company BASF struck an agreement to build a gas pipeline under the Baltic Sea. In early September, ten days before the elections in Germany, the three companies' CEOs put pen to paper in the presence of Putin and Schroeder. The deal was good for German business, but it did not save Schroeder—he lost, albeit by a slim margin, to opposition leader Angela Merkel.

In Europe the reaction to the Russian-German deal was mixed. Poland, the Baltic countries, Ukraine, and Belarus were indignant. Polish president Aleksander Kwasniewski called the contract "the Putin-Schroeder Pact," alluding to the Molotov-Ribbentrop Pact of 1938.[1] Belarusian president Alexander Lukashenko described it as "Russia's most idiotic project to date."[2] The heads of Lithuania, Latvia, and Estonia asserted that the pipeline would cause an environmental disaster in the Baltic Sea. Such reactions were not surprising, since the new pipeline was set to bypass all these countries, depriving them of transit revenue. Lukashenko and Kwasniewski hoped instead that Russia would build a second branch of the Yamal-Europe pipeline, which ran through Belarus and Poland. But Putin had no such intention. He remembered only too well that Kwasniewski and Lithuanian president Valdas Adamkus had mediated the negotiations between Yushchenko, Yanukovych, and Kuchma in the midst of the Orange Revolution in Ukraine and had done everything possible to secure victory for Viktor Yushchenko.

But Western Europe eyed the pipeline agreement quite differently. After the signing in Berlin, Putin went to London for a scheduled Russia-EU summit. The European press applauded him. When Putin spoke about energy security and Russia's willingness to provide Europe with fuel, his audience listened approvingly. Putin took delight in rubbing the Russian-German agreement in Tony Blair's face, since four years previously the pipeline had been proposed as a Russian-British project. But Putin wanted nothing more to do with London, preferring to work with Berlin instead.

There was so much hullabaloo surrounding the project because at that time Europe was expected to run out of gas by 2010. North Sea reserves were drying up, and British and Norwegian production was falling. The European Commission approved the project immediately, with Belgium, Britain, and the Netherlands all expressing interest. European governments declared their readiness to allow Gazprom to distribute gas in their countries. The Dutch company Gasunie proposed that the pipeline be extended from Germany to the Netherlands and later to Britain. Gazprom agreed to build a major gas storage facility in Belgium. Spur pipelines to Sweden and Finland were also considered. It all meant that Gazprom was set to own the largest gas transmission system in Western and Northern Europe within five years.

CYNICAL POLITICS

After the parliamentary elections in Germany, without even waiting for the formation of a coalition government, Gerhard Schroeder went to St. Petersburg for Putin's birthday celebration. "A visit from the German chancellor is the best present I can have," Putin gushingly told reporters.[3] However, it turned out that Schroeder had come not just for a slice of birthday cake but to look for a new job. When the talks on Germany's new government finished and it was clear that Schroeder would play no part, it was announced that he had been appointed the head of the shareholder committee of the North European Gas Pipeline Company (NEGPC), the operating company of the future Nord Stream pipeline.

The news shocked many German voters, but their criticism of him did not bother Schroeder. He had always been a frequent visitor in St. Petersburg. For instance, in 2004 the German chancellor and his wife, Doris, had adopted a three-year-old girl from an orphanage in St. Petersburg. Once he retired from politics, he practically emigrated to Russia.

Mikheil Saakashvili, then president of Georgia, said that Vladimir Putin looked on Schroeder as a trophy. Once, during a CIS summit, Putin was showing his guests, the leaders of the former Soviet republics, around his residence near St. Petersburg, Constantine Palace. Putin took them to the wine cellar, where, as if by chance, they stumbled upon Gerhard Schroeder. Putin beckoned to the former German leader, asked him to propose a toast, and then let him go, says Saakashvili. "Imagine my surprise when one year later Schroeder popped up in exactly the same place and repeated his performance. This time, however, Putin was trying to impress guests of the St. Petersburg Economic Forum."

Schroeder's successor, Angela Merkel, did not get on as well with Putin. They tried to get along during her first year in office, but by 2007 the Russian president stopped hiding his irritation with the overly principled Merkel. Knowing that she was afraid of dogs, he deliberately brought his huge black Labrador to meetings with her in Sochi. They made an interesting threesome, even delivering a press conference together—the Russian, the German, and the dog. Merkel was said to be practically semiconscious with fear, not to mention furious at being treated in such a manner.

Schroeder and Berlusconi were firmly ensconced as Putin's new friends after the fallout with Bush and Blair. Putin found it so much easier to deal with these two European cynics, and the feeling was mutual. However, whereas Schroeder was to some extent dependent on Putin, Berlusconi became a true friend and partner. According to WikiLeaks, the Italian prime minister was the only foreign leader allowed to stay at the Kremlin. Diplomats say that Putin spoke to Berlusconi more than any other foreign leader, and vice versa.

They visited each other's homes, their families becoming friends in the process. Putin and his daughters vacationed at Berlusconi's villa in Sardinia. His daughters, Katya and Masha, were friends with the Italian prime minister's daughter Barbara. When Berlusconi came to Moscow, Putin invited him to dine with his family. And during Berlusconi's trial in 2009 (on charges of paying for sex with an underage prostitute), it was revealed that the most luxurious four-poster bed inside Palazzo Grazioli, the Italian prime minister's residence in Rome, was known playfully as "Putin's bed."

Transcripts from WikiLeaks reported that US diplomats were convinced that Berlusconi and Putin were in business together. Valentino Valentini, the Italian prime minister's Russian-speaking aide, flew to Moscow on business several times a month.

Moreover, the Italian oil and gas company ENI enjoyed a privileged relationship with Gazprom. For instance, in 2005 the two companies signed a package agreement covering direct supplies of gas to consumers in Italy. That same year an Italian parliamentary investigation revealed that a close friend of Silvio Berlusconi's, Bruno Mentasti-Granelli, had a substantial interest in a company that would play a major role in distribution of the gas. As a result of the scandal, the deal was put on ice. But other projects between ENI and Russia were developing rapidly. The Italian company, for example, was the only foreign firm allowed to buy a piece of the shattered Yukos empire.

But Putin and Berlusconi's number one pet project was the South Stream gas pipeline, the sister of Nord Stream. Thus Putin's friends Schroeder and Berlusconi were set to become the guarantors of Europe's energy security, thereby implementing Russia's new foreign policy strategy as devised by Igor Shuvalov.

Gazprom's South Stream partner was, of course, supposed to be ENI. Under the original plan, the pipeline would pass through Bulgaria, Greece, and Serbia to Italy, and finally terminate in France. In 2009 Vladimir Putin was on the lookout for another retired European leader, similar to Schroeder, to head the project. He tried to woo former French president Jacques Chirac and former Italian prime minister and European Commission head Romano Prodi. Both refused. By 2009 times had changed and European politicians, even retired ones, knew that collaboration with Putin was reputational suicide.

Back in 2005, Putin had made another attempt to turn Russia into an energy superpower through informal friendly relations, this time with the United States. In December 2005, at a time when Europe was still bewitched by Russian-style energy security, former US secretary of commerce Donald Evans paid a visit to Moscow. Evans was a close childhood friend and onetime drinking buddy of George W. Bush's. Both had reportedly stopped drinking upon turning forty; what's more, Evans had allegedly given Bush a Bible divided into 365 sections for daily reading. And it was Evans who had chaired Bush's presidential campaign in 2000. Putin made Evans a generous offer: the post of chairman of the board of Russian state oil giant Rosneft. Evans was tempted but ultimately refused.

If more world politicians had accepted Putin's offer of friendship and money, à la Schroeder and Berlusconi, then perhaps the new Cold War would not have happened. Vladimir Putin would have forgotten about the "color revolutions" and been reassured that Western leaders were all equally unscrupulous and pliable. Indeed, perhaps Russia would have become an energy superpower, or at least have cobbled together its own cartel of powerful top managers.

But none of this happened. And the reason was again Ukraine.

MANAGING UKRAINE

For a couple of months after conceding defeat in the Orange Revolution, the Kremlin had no idea how to approach Ukraine. It had to rebuild its strategy to gain influence over the new Ukrainian authorities, since the previous tactic of relying solely on the country's head of state had failed miserably. By spring 2005, however, the Kremlin found that all key positions in Ukraine's new government were held by familiar faces. The prime minister, for example, was now Yulia Tymoshenko, who for many years had represented Ukraine in gas talks with Gazprom. The new secretary of the National Security and Defense Council was chocolate tycoon Petro Poroshenko, who was well known to the Russian presidential administration; during the Orange Revolution, he had even flown to Moscow on a diplomatic bridge-building mission. However, President Viktor Yushchenko seemed less amenable—mainly, it should be said, because he was seriously ill. Having been poisoned during the election campaign, he spent the whole of 2005 fighting for his life, top aides recall. His personal physician had to hold his arm while he signed documents.

Moscow, meanwhile, decided that relying on Ukrainian politicians was too dangerous—they were irresponsible and changed too frequently. Moreover, Putin trusted only one person in Kiev, his friend Viktor Medvedchuk. But after the Orange Revolution the latter was no longer head of the Ukrainian presidential administration and no longer had any influence in the government. But he retained his influence over Putin. It was Medvedchuk who devised a new system of relations with Ukraine. Henceforth the dialogue would be conducted not through the president but through business.

"Ukraine does not do politics; it does business" is a catchphrase attributed to Medvedchuk. And given the weakness of the new government, it was clear that business was free to dictate the rules. In fact, an informal committee of Ukraine's top oligarchs was set up to "manage" Ukrainian policy. Its head was Medvedchuk, who acted as an intermediary between the Ukrainian oligarchs and Putin.

The most influential group in the shareholder committee of "Ukraine Inc." were those with links to the gas trade. Ever since the early 1990s the supply of Russian gas through Ukraine to Western Europe had been a highly opaque business. The trading scheme had not changed since; only the names of the profiteers were different. The most recent gas agreement, which was intended to put an end to the shenanigans and replace them with a new structure (at least superficially), had been signed three months before the Orange Revolution. Russia and Ukraine had agreed that they would use an intermediary company to be called RosUkrEnergo (RUE). This company was to replace the previous mediator, the murky Hungarian-registered Eural TransGas (ETG), which was alleged to have links with Russian crime boss Semyon Mogilevich. The new go-between looked respectable: 50 percent of the entity belonged to Gazprom and 50 percent to Austria's Raiffeisenbank, at least according to the initial press releases. Later it turned out that the second 50 percent of the stock was merely managed by Raiffeisen Investment on behalf of a company called Centragas, whose real owners were as yet unknown. The suspense grew, as did the company: Gazprom assigned it the right not only to supply gas to Ukraine but also to export 17 billion cubic meters of Russian gas to Western Europe.

Only in April 2006 did the owners of Centragas announce themselves: they turned out to be Ukrainian businessmen Dmitry Firtash, who owned 90 percent of the company, and Ivan Fursin, who owned 10 percent. Moreover, Firtash admitted that he had also owned ETG. Why did Gazprom and the Russian government hand Firtash the opportunity to earn several billion dollars a year? Who was behind Firtash and this colossal corruption scheme? To this day no one knows for sure.

The head of the Ukrainian security service, Alexander Turchinov, appointed by Viktor Yushchenko, claimed in 2005 that Semyon Mogilevich was behind RUE. There were indeed many links between Firtash and Mogilevich: Mogilevich's ex-wife worked for Firtash's offshore company Highrock Holdings, and Mogilevich's partner Igor Fisherman was a financial director at another of Firtash's companies, Highrock Properties. For many years Mogilevich and Fisherman were second and third on the FBI's most-wanted list, behind only Osama bin Laden.

The question is, how did Mogilevich get Russia and Ukraine to hand over control of their most important trade? And did this mafia boss really nip Russia-Europe cooperation in the bud?

THE FIRST GAS

At his first meeting with Vladimir Putin, on January 24, 2005, Viktor Yushchenko proposed a new gas trading scheme that entailed giving up barter methods and switching to cash payments based on the European model—an offer that made Gazprom very happy. Just as the two men were about to face the media after their meeting, Yushchenko suddenly felt even more ill than usual. Putin noticed and whispered to him, "Lean on my shoulder." Yushchenko remembers this moment fondly.

Moscow could see that Ukraine's "orange" government was descending into chaos. The champions of Maidan had spent their first year in power in a state of constant bickering and internal conflict. In September 2005 Viktor Yushchenko took a dramatic step, simultaneously dismissing his two most hostile "allies": prime minister Yulia Tymoshenko and National Security and Defense Council secretary Petro Poroshenko.

Tymoshenko had extensive experience with gas negotiations and was a staunch opponent of RUE. Throughout her entire premiership she sought to remove the company from the trading scheme. Gazprom insiders claim that she was trying to get a piece of the pie. Her dismissal meant that RUE no longer had any opponents in the Ukrainian government.

After Tymoshenko's dismissal, Ukraine's new team of negotiators flew to Moscow to agree on the parameters of the new agreement. In Moscow they were received by Putin himself, since he had a firm grip on Gazprom. The Ukrainians were amazed by how involved he was in the matter and the ease with which he sketched out a new gas price formula on a piece of paper; they were far less well versed in the subject. Realizing that the negotiators were incompetent, Putin began to scoff at them, saying in a pompous speech that he would not allow the "orange revolutionaries" to rob the Russian people. He demanded that they accept Gazprom's demands, otherwise tomorrow the price would be very different.

Gazprom's offer was $90 per thousand cubic meters starting early in 2006, rising to $230 per thousand cubic meters over the next three years. Ukrainian gas companies were horrified by the price and refused to accept it. The very next day, as promised, Vladimir Putin appeared on television and stated that Gazprom's new "offer" was $230 per thousand cubic meters as of January 2006. Even Gazprom itself was shocked by this exorbitant demand.

Russian state television began reporting that Gazprom could turn off the taps to Ukraine at the end of 2005. The company's European partners, meanwhile, were sent letters warning them that they could face gas shortages starting New Year's Eve, since Russia was preparing to cut supplies by the exact amount of Ukraine's consumption, and so Kiev would most likely siphon off some of the gas bound for Europe.

For Putin the move seemed a step in the right direction. It clearly demonstrated to the Europeans that their dependence on unreliable transit countries such as Ukraine posed a risk to their energy security. The logical solution, in his opinion, was to build new pipelines circumventing Ukraine—that is, Nord Stream and South Stream.

Gazprom had not been bluffing, and on January 1, 2006, the pressure in the pipes dropped. On January 2 gas deliveries to Austria fell by a third; Slovakia and Hungary saw a 40 percent reduction. On January 3 another negotiating team flew from Kiev to Moscow. They were taken, appropriately, to the Hotel Ukraine in central Moscow, where they talked into the early hours.* The Russian side proposed a compromise: the price of $230 would be cut if the sale was conducted through RUE. Dmitry Firtash immediately joined the talks and confirmed his company's readiness to intercede.

As a result, late that night a remarkable deal was struck: Gazprom would sell gas to RUE for $230 per thousand cubic meters, as Putin had announced, but Ukraine would buy it from RUE for $95 (close to the initial price offered by Gazprom). RUE's losses would be covered by Gazprom, and the Russian monopoly would give RUE the exclusive right to sell gas to Europe at market prices.

Even after the deal was announced, Vladimir Putin publicly stated that he did not know who was really behind the "Ukrainian" half of RUE. "RosUkrEnergo with its non-transparent Ukrainian 50-percent stake is nothing compared to the various manipulations that were going on in the gas sector over

*The hotel was rumored to house the office of Semyon Mogilevich.

these last 15 years," he said.[4] Only in 2011 did it become known that Dmitry Firtash was linked to the Rotenberg brothers, Boris and Arkady, childhood friends of Vladimir Putin—back in the 1960s all three had gone to the same judo club.

The New Year gas war was headline news in Europe. The scales fell from European eyes, and Putin's hypnotizing words about "energy security" were suddenly seen in a very different light. If anyone posed a threat to Europe, it was Gazprom. European officials and politicians, returning from their Christmas holidays in January 2006, were now saying that the continent was overly dependent on Russian energy. Viewed on the map, Gazprom's Nord and South Stream projects suddenly looked like a pair of giant pincers with which Russia would squeeze Europe.

The G8 summit in St. Petersburg, which Shuvalov had organized in his capacity as Russia's sherpa, did indeed discuss energy security. "We insisted that energy security was about ensuring stability for producers, transit countries, and consumers," says Shuvalov. "We told the other countries: 'Look, we're more dependent on you than you are on us!' But they wouldn't listen. They said, 'No, we want two or three suppliers.'"

That effectively spelled the end of the South Stream project. From the outset, the pipeline was said to be political, with no real economic justification. The Europeans had already proposed their own variant: the Nabucco pipeline, which would run from Azerbaijan to Europe, bypassing Russia. This project too was purely political and uneconomical, and so it was abandoned even earlier. Vladimir Putin continued to cherish the idea of South Stream right up until 2014, when he suddenly announced that Russia would not implement the project after all, mainly to spite Europe.

The first gas war sacrificed the long game for the sake of a few peanuts. Shuvalov's "energy superpower" concept was dead in the water.

CHAPTER 8

IN WHICH DEPUTY PRIME MINISTER SERGEI IVANOV IS CONVINCED THAT HE IS THE HEIR TO THE THRONE

Sergei Ivanov is the Soviet James Bond. The real thing, that is, without embellishment or exaggeration, without cinematic romanticism or Hollywood gloss.

He is the ideal Soviet spy, indistinguishable from the crowd. A sort of Agent Smith from The Matrix, *both by name (Ivanov is a very common Russian surname) and by appearance. In the 1990s Russia's two intelligence services—the FSB (internal affairs) and the SVR (foreign affairs)—tried to recruit him. In the end, it was the FSB, headed by none other than Vladimir Putin, that managed to get him; Putin seems to have tricked SVR director Vyacheslav Trubnikov into letting him "borrow" Ivanov without ever returning him.*

Sergei Ivanov is also the ideal Soviet man: an intellectual with a degree in philology, fluent in English and Swedish, an aficionado of ballet and basketball. He reads the Western press every morning and resents the way it distorts Soviet reality.

I was unable to speak to Sergei Ivanov personally, so I had to make do with his public speeches, interviews he had done with other journalists, and conversations with his companions. They all say that Ivanov is a very honest man and above corruption. Such words are rare. But Ivanov is, after all, a model Soviet officer.

Ivanov believes wholeheartedly in what he says. This, however, is very common among officers of a defunct empire. They remain ever faithful to its lost cause.

OPERATION SUCCESSOR

In autumn 2005 Vladimir Putin decided to start preparing for the 2008 elections and even outlined an election campaign. Oil prices were high, and most of the profits from oil sales (at the insistence of finance minister Alexei Kudrin) were deposited in Russia's stabilization fund. However, Putin decided that some of the surplus needed to be spent on the transfer of power to his chosen successor. Certain "priority national projects" were earmarked, and the government started allocating additional money (150–200 billion rubles a year, about $6–8 billion) to health, education, housing, and agriculture. To make sure that voters associated the oil windfall with a specific person and accepted Putin's successor as their benefactor, Putin had to appoint someone to be in charge of distributing the money. Russian citizens always have a special sense of gratitude and affection for an official who gives them money—even if the money is rightfully theirs to begin with.

Putin assigned the role of cash dispenser to Dmitry Medvedev. To make him more recognizable to voters, he needed to be moved to a more prominent position—for instance, to the government. But Medvedev was not keen, since he understood that his closeness to Putin inside the presidential administration was his most valuable asset. Putin joked that he was going to appoint Igor Sechin, Medvedev's worst enemy, as his new chief of staff. "Well, in that case, I'm not going anywhere. I'll stay in the Kremlin," said Medvedev stubbornly. "Why do I need to be in the government? I'll be an open target, and Sechin will start plotting against me."

Putin liked Medvedev's lack of ambition. "Okay, we'll see," said Putin evasively.

On November 14, 2005, Vladimir Putin announced a major new reshuffle of officials, the third of his presidency. Perhaps to enhance the effect, Putin never replaces just one official, but changes many, from disparate areas of government. The first such staff makeover was in 2003, when he replaced several members of the *siloviki*, disbanded Mikhail Fradkov's tax inspectorate, and created the Federal Service for Drug Control, headed by his old friend Viktor Cherkesov. The second came in 2004, when he replaced Kasyanov with Fradkov and removed all of Kasyanov's team. Now a third historic moment had arrived.

Putin gave little explanation for the reasons behind the permutations, announcing only that the head of the presidential administration, Dmitry

Medvedev, was now first deputy prime minister, and that defense minister Sergei Ivanov was also a deputy prime minister. Putin said that Medvedev's move was due to his new responsibility for national projects, but he did not explain Ivanov's promotion at all. However, officials understood that it was to make the government more "balanced." The new chief of staff was not Sechin but the relatively unknown (among the Moscow elite) Sergei Sobyanin, governor of the Tyumen region.

Putin has never been one for clarity and predictability, so he did not simply declare that Medvedev was his choice to succeed him as president. The parallel elevation of two close associates was intended to demonstrate that everything was still up in the air. But that was only for the sake of appearances, say Putin's former aides. In autumn 2005 Putin was already grooming Medvedev as his successor. Ivanov's promotion was simply to cover up the operation and keep everyone guessing. He was also trying to protect Medvedev to some extent, for if Putin had announced him as his chosen successor at such an early stage, all Medvedev's enemies would have united against him and quite possibly eaten him alive long before the presidential election.

But with time Putin's attitude began to change. Ivanov, brought in to be Medvedev's sparring partner, caught Putin's eye as a potential champion boxer. Moreover, everyone was so keenly discussing the two "candidates" that Putin himself started to believe there really was a contest. He decided to wait and see how Medvedev and Ivanov would cope with their duties.

Sergei Ivanov was one of Putin's oldest and most trusted friends. They had met back in the late 1970s, when both worked at the KGB in Leningrad (now St. Petersburg). However, Ivanov had been far more successful as an intelligence officer than Putin was. Ivanov was stationed at the Soviet *rezidenturas* in Finland and Kenya, while Putin toiled away in East Germany. A position in a capitalist country, or even in the Third World, was considered much more prestigious than one in a socialist neighbor. But even if Putin envied his more successful comrade, he did not show it in 1998, when Yeltsin appointed Putin head of the FSB. On the advice of his deputies, Nikolai Patrushev and Viktor Cherkesov, he brought in Ivanov too. Moreover, he lured him from the SVR, to which Ivanov had transferred and where he had been promoted to the rank of general.

When Putin became prime minister in 1999, it was Ivanov who landed the key post of secretary of the Security Council; later, as president, Putin entrusted the Ministry of Defense to his former KGB colleague, at a time when war had again broken out in Chechnya.

Ivanov performed one other important function: he established links with Washington. In 2001, when Putin became acquainted with George W. Bush, the two presidents agreed that in order to facilitate communication they should assign representatives to maintain permanent contact with each other so that they could resolve issues promptly. Bush appointed Condoleezza Rice, while Putin chose Sergei Ivanov.

In contrast to Medvedev, who until 2005 was unknown to the public, Ivanov was recognizable. He carried out reforms of the army, beginning the transition from conscription to a contract system. What's more, he managed to do it without picking a fight with the top brass from the Ministry of Defense. On the contrary, wherever he went he was surrounded by a throng of satisfied, potbellied generals.

Everyone inside the Kremlin perceived Ivanov and Medvedev's elevation as the start of the election race, and many saw it as a challenge, primarily those officials who had their own alternative view of the "2008 problem." They included deputy chief of staff Igor Sechin and prosecutor general Vladimir Ustinov, who immediately began to wage their own private war against Ivanov, who they believed was the stronger candidate—and the one they feared more.

A LOW BLOW

On New Year's Eve 2006, at Chelyabinsk Tank Academy, a tragedy occurred: a drunken sergeant began to bully one of the soldiers. There are different accounts of what happened exactly, but it is known that Private Andrei Sychev was forced to remain squatting for at least three hours. As a result, gangrene set in, and two weeks later he underwent an operation to amputate his legs and genitals.

It was a shocking incident, but not unique. According to the Prosecutor General's Office, in the six months from January to June 2006, seventeen people died from "army hazing" in peacetime Russia. For the Ministry of Defense that was a good result, since in the same period the year before there had been twice as many. The figures did not even account for soldier suicides—in 2005 there were 276.

Nevertheless, it was the case of Private Sychev that had an impact. He was taken to a civilian hospital, not a military one, and the doctors reported the incident to the Committee of Soldiers' Mothers, as well as relatives and journalists. The Military Prosecutor's Office took charge of the investigation on the personal orders of Prosecutor General Ustinov. Thus began a war between the Prosecutor General's Office and the Ministry of Defense.

The Prosecutor General's Office made sure that the Chelyabinsk tragedy became known to everyone. National media began covering the incident after a detailed account of the investigation appeared on the official website of the Prosecutor General's Office on January 25, 2006.

When, on January 26, journalists asked defense minister Sergei Ivanov to comment, news of the tragedy had already spread throughout the media. Ivanov, who was at the time on a trip to Armenia, said: "I have spent the past few days far from Russian territory, high up in the mountains, and have not heard about the incident in Chelyabinsk. I don't think it's anything serious, otherwise I would know about it." The minister's words did not go down well, as it indicated that he (or, rather, his aides) did not consider the amputation of a soldier's legs and genitals to be "anything serious."

The scandal continued to unfold. A month later there was a protest rally in front of the Defense Ministry in Moscow at which protesters carried a banner reading "Ivanov's legs should be amputated." An appeal from a group of human rights defenders calling for the minister's dismissal was presented to Putin. Meanwhile, a survey by the radio station Echo of Moscow found that 95 percent of students believed that Ivanov should resign immediately. The media also recalled how a year earlier a car driven by Ivanov's son, an employee of VTB Bank, had run over and killed an elderly woman. Not only had he escaped punishment, but charges had been brought against the son-in-law of the deceased woman for allegedly assaulting the minister's son. No one in the Kremlin, least of all Ivanov himself, was in any doubt that he was being hunted by the prosecutor general.

Putin had never intended for public opinion or his entourage to decide who his successor would be; that was his job, and his alone. Moreover, Ivanov was not the only one complaining about Sechin and Ustinov's underhanded tactics; so was Medvedev. So Putin decided to nip the political intrigues in the bud.

THE GANG OF FOUR

Back on April 13, 2005, at the suggestion of Vladimir Putin, the upper house of the Russian parliament, the Federation Council, had met to approve Vladimir Ustinov for a new term as prosecutor general. Ustinov was by now an almost legendary figure, perhaps the most powerful *silovik* in the country. Moreover, the Prosecutor General's Office had become a model of political arbitrariness—it implemented the will of the Kremlin with little regard for legal niceties.

The presidential administration always assigned its most important tasks to Ustinov. For instance, on the eve of any regional election the authorities unfailingly brought charges against any unwanted candidates and barred them from running.

Ustinov's main accomplishment in Putin's eyes was, of course, the show trial of Mikhail Khodorkovsky and Platon Lebedev. Each was sentenced initially to eight years in prison. Putin once told the press that during a private conversation in October 2003 it was Ustinov who had insisted on Khodorkovsky's immediate arrest.

Ustinov personally led the investigation into the *Kursk* submarine accident, concluding that it was a result of technical problems in the torpedo battery, absolving the military from blame.

Ustinov also investigated the terrorist act in Beslan. The case was the apotheosis of official high-handedness. The investigators dispatched from Moscow persistently ignored the victims' accounts, as if the conclusion had already been decided in advance, which it most likely had.

Under Ustinov, the Prosecutor General's Office turned into a well-oiled repressive mechanism. The department demonstrated that no one was safe from its attention. Anyone involved in business could suddenly be accused of fraud or economic crime, and with Ustinov at the helm such accusations would certainly be made if the target had political aspirations.

Ustinov liked to interfere in areas that had never before been within the purview of the Prosecutor General's Office, such as housing. "Everything is our business," he said. Moreover, the prosecutor general was seemingly concerned about morality and ethics. In his public appearances he waxed indignant about the decline of spirituality and how his department could help turn the tide. The Russian Orthodox Church often cropped up in his speeches.

Ustinov regularly attended various church-related "patriotic" events where he would be regularly lauded as Russia's "man of the year."

Despite the prosecutor general's somewhat controversial reputation, political expediency won the day. One hundred forty-nine members of the Federation Council voted to extend Ustinov's term in office, one abstained, and the rest were absent.

A year later, on June 2, 2006, the chairman of the Federation Council, Sergei Mironov, suddenly announced that the president was going to relieve the prosecutor general of his position. The senators in the upper chamber of parliament were in shock. If the most powerful official in the country had fallen from grace, that meant revolution, they surmised.

Members of the relevant committees (security and defense, and legal matters) were informed a few minutes before the parliamentary session. They approved Putin's request to accept Ustinov's "resignation" unanimously, without asking a single question. When one single senator, a former governor of the Kaluga region named Valery Sudarenkov, asked about the reason for Ustinov's departure, it caused confusion. "The statement does not specify a motive," snapped Mironov. "We did not consider the motive. We considered only the prosecutor general's resignation statement," echoed the chairman of the relevant committee, clearly bewildered by it all.

One hundred senators voted to accept Ustinov's resignation, two abstained, and another thirty-six were at a loss and took no part in the vote, not even officially abstaining. When reporters asked the head of the Defense and Security Committee why the senators had not asked about the reason for the prosecutor general's resignation, he replied: "Once, a while back, the Federation Council showed too much interest in the prosecutor general's departure, after which it was reformed," he replied, referring to 1999, when the Federation Council refused to grant the request of Alexander Voloshin, head of Yeltsin's administration, to dismiss the prosecutor general at the time, Yuri Skuratov.[1] A year later Voloshin, now head of President Putin's administration, took his revenge by changing the procedure by which senators were appointed to the Federation Council. All the former senators were replaced with obedient newcomers.

The operation against Ustinov bore the hallmark of the security services: the enemy had to be caught off guard and given no time to react. It was classic Putin. To this day he loves to dish out unexpected appointments and resignations. Generally (such as in the case of Mikhail Kasyanov's departure) he announces the reshuffle himself, or at least makes a comment. But on this occasion Putin was silent. A day passed, two days, and still no word. Officials and MPs were perplexed: was Putin so afraid of Ustinov that he had to get rid of him in such a secretive and precautionary manner?

In fact, according to a Putin insider, the president's goal was simply to demonstrate his power. The true target of Putin's strike was not Ustinov personally, but the inner circle in general.

The fact is that by 2006 a close-knit group of kindred souls was beginning to establish an independent existence in the corridors of power. Back in November 2003 Prosecutor General Ustinov's son Dmitry had married presidential aide Igor Sechin's daughter Inga (the wedding was held just a month after another major event uniting Sechin and Ustinov, the arrest of Mikhail Khodorkovsky). The two top officials began to see each other very often. They had a great deal in common: a rather conservative outlook on the political system, distrust of the West, and an interest in Slavophile philosophy and the Orthodox Church. Over time the circle widened to include prime minister Mikhail Fradkov and Moscow mayor Yuri Luzhkov. This peculiar foursome began to meet regularly in private to discuss Russia's future.

Such a clique of top-level officials could not fail to arouse suspicions. In terms of membership, it was impressive: the president's closest aide, the most powerful *silovik* in the country, the veteran and still popular mayor of Moscow, and the prime minister, who despite being weak and timid would nevertheless take control of the country were anything to happen to Putin.

In the run-up to the presidential election of March 2004, Putin had taken Sechin's warnings about the disloyalty of Mikhail Kasyanov to heart and gotten rid of the prime minister. The situation now was similar, but this time Sechin himself was the target.

The next presidential election was fast approaching, and for Putin it would be the toughest yet, since he was about to hand over power to a successor. He needed everything to go smoothly and painlessly. He was still not entirely sure whom he would choose, Sergei Ivanov or Dmitry Medvedev, but he knew for a fact that both were already uneasy about the Sechin-Ustinov-Luzhkov-Fradkov fraternity.

Putin was well aware that Sechin hated both Ivanov and Medvedev. Sechin had even used the case of Private Sychev to attack Ivanov. But it was one thing for Sechin to keep Ivanov in check, and another thing entirely to jeopardize the entire transfer of power.

There was plenty of bad blood among the Gang of Four. Luzhkov was an enemy of the Family from way back, while Sechin was a more recent foe, having put Khodorkovsky behind bars and ejected Kasyanov from the prime minister's chair. Second, going even further back to Putin's St. Petersburg days, Sechin considered himself to be the president's right-hand man and always tried hard to sideline other potential friends, including Ivanov and Medvedev. Sechin's jealousy irritated others who were necessarily in close proximity to the president, such as Putin's chief bodyguard, Viktor Zolotov, and Viktor Cherkesov, who had been Putin's deputy at the FSB. Zolotov and Sechin were deeply hostile to each other, but Zolotov had to keep it to himself. Then, all of a sudden, an opportunity arose. Putin began to take an interest in what the Gang of Four talked about when left alone. Zolotov and Cherkesov gladly supplied him with transcripts of bugged conversations.

Those transcripts confirmed Putin's suspicions: a plot was slowly maturing. The four discussed, among other things, Mikhail Fradkov's potential to be a great president, since he was already an excellent prime minister, they said. Putin, however, had never even considered Fradkov as a successor or even thought to discuss the prospect with the four of them.

In fact, Sechin and company were just letting off steam. Their ambitious talk was, ultimately, just talk. All Sechin needed was a dressing-down, while Luzhkov could be left alone, since he would be scared stiff as it was. By contrast, Putin decided that Ustinov had become inordinately influential. That is how a former Putin aide interprets the president's train of thought back then. As for Fradkov, Putin did not even consider him—he was clearly the junior partner and was simply being used as a tool.

For five days after the news of Ustinov's departure broke, everyone wondered what would become of the overly presumptuous prosecutor general and who would replace him. Putin's decision surprised everyone: he simply castled his pieces. The post of prosecutor general went to the more modest (and allegedly Family-connected) justice minister, Yuri Chaika, and in turn Vladimir Ustinov became Russia's new minister of justice. Within a few months Chaika had fired almost all of Ustinov's deputies (who went with their boss to the Ministry of Justice). Likewise, Chaika's team transferred to the Prosecutor General's Office. Kremlin insiders joked that it would have been much easier and cheaper simply to change the signs outside the respective buildings.

Joking aside, the exact same thing happened a few years later when Medvedev and Putin swapped seats, taking with them their armies of assistants and lackeys.

THE EMPIRE STRIKES BACK

At the end of August 2005 an event occurred that unexpectedly transformed the entire gamut of Russian politics, both internal and external. At first glance, it had nothing whatsoever to do with Russia—but appearances are deceptive. On August 29, the Gulf Coast of the United States was hit by Hurricane Katrina. Louisiana, Mississippi, Florida, Alabama, and (the other) Georgia turned into disaster zones. The US authorities failed to evacuate the residents of New Orleans in advance and did not foresee that the levees would not withstand the storm surge. For a few days New Orleans was at the mercy of criminals and looters, which even delayed the rescue operation. President George W. Bush came under a barrage of criticism for failing to cut short his vacation in Texas on learning of the tragedy—that is, he repeated the exact same mistake that Putin had made five years earlier when the *Kursk* sank.

The Russian Ministry of Emergency Situations offered assistance in the form of two rescue aircraft. The US authorities initially refused but changed their minds a few days later and asked that the planes be sent. Putin, defense minister Sergei Ivanov, and emergency situations minister Sergei Shoigu were amazed by such chaos in the world's biggest economy. But most shocking of all, at least for Putin, was what happened in the immediate aftermath: Bush's approval rating fell through the floor.

Vladimir Putin (especially in the first years of his presidency) never relied on polling data. Nor did he ever accept his aides' assurances that his approval rating was high. "It could collapse at any moment," he would say. Remembering how television and the second war in Chechnya had made him the most popular politician in the country in a matter of months, he believed that the reverse could happen just as quickly. After every tragedy in Russia, be it the *Kursk* submarine, the attack during the *Nord-Ost* performance, or Beslan, Putin expected his rating to plummet and the public to hold him personally responsible. But it never happened. However, now Putin's nightmare was coming true, only not for him but for a man whom he considered to be even more powerful: the "military emperor of the world," George W. Bush.

The most surprising thing was that Bush did not respond. He was unable to counter the charges of inefficiency, shift the blame onto someone else, change the agenda, or distract the public's attention with some other event. Bush, whom Putin believed to be a far stronger leader than himself, turned out to be a weakling. This gave Putin huge confidence and radically changed the tone of Russia's negotiations with the United States. He realized that he was dealing not with a military emperor but with a lame duck.

In October 2006, as described by Angus Roxburgh, Putin taunted Condoleezza Rice, making her wait several hours in a hotel lobby until he agreed to receive her; during that time he was busy drinking with friends at Barvikha, outside Moscow. After a meeting of the Security Council, some members had decided to stay on and celebrate the recent birthdays of deputy prime minister Dmitry Medvedev and Security Council secretary Igor Ivanov. Putin saw nothing wrong with making the US secretary of state wait until the evening. When evening came, he decided that instead of interrupting the party it would be better to invite Rice to the table and let her talk directly with the entire Security Council. US national security adviser Stephen Hadley recalls that he was dumbfounded when they arrived at Meyendorf Castle on Rublyovka Highway and found a dozen of Russia's most powerful people seated around a table with snacks and drinks. "Condi, come and join us. We've got some top-secret materials for you," quipped Sergei Ivanov, pointing at the bottles of Georgian wine. But Rice was not in the least put out. She icily asked Putin for a brief private conversation. He agreed, taking with him his go-between for US relations, the selfsame Sergei Ivanov, and foreign minister Sergei Lavrov as an interpreter.

The conversation ended in acrimony, with Rice and Putin fighting over the situation in Georgia. The US secretary of state insisted that all countries neighboring Russia had the right to decide their own destiny, while Putin answered that Russia would not tolerate a Georgian military intervention in the frozen conflicts in Abkhazia and South Ossetia. The conversation was heated, completely unlike the idyll of four years earlier.

Back then Sergei Ivanov and Condoleezza Rice had enjoyed a cordial relationship. In May 2002 George W. Bush, with his wife and entourage, visited

Putin in St. Petersburg. Putin took his US counterpart to the Mariinsky Theater to see *The Nutcracker*. On the way there, Ivanov and Rice discovered a mutual passion for ballet, and also realized that they didn't actually want to see *The Nutcracker* for the hundredth time. As soon as the lights went down in the hall, Ivanov (then defense minister) suggested to Rice (then national security adviser) that they go find something more interesting. She agreed, and Ivanov took her to the rehearsal studio of Boris Eifman to watch some Russian avant-garde ballet. Security Council secretary Vladimir Rushailo (Condoleezza Rice's Russian counterpart) was sent to keep an eye on the fugitives. He was extremely displeased by the violation of protocol. But Ivanov and Rice were delighted.

By October 2006 that was a distant memory. Condoleezza Rice, having ruined the congenial get-together, looked down on Putin and Ivanov from her vantage point atop her high heels, almost screaming. They answered her with the same fury and contempt.

Two weeks later the Republicans suffered a crushing defeat in the US midterm elections, losing the Senate and the House of Representatives, which they had controlled for two years. For Putin it was a clear sign that Bush was a loser, even within his own administration. It was time to play hardball.

In 2007, in an effort to avert the deployment of a US missile defense shield in Europe, Putin made an unexpected proposal: a joint US-Russian system. Instead of the United States installing a new radar station in the Czech Republic, the existing Gabala facility in Azerbaijan could be used instead. The Americans were shocked. Neither Bush nor Rice had expected Putin to display such openness and willingness to cooperate. But a month later Pentagon experts arrived in Azerbaijan to inspect the Gabala radar station and were not impressed. They reported to the White House that the radar equipment was outdated and did not meet US requirements. Bush, having verbally agreed to Putin's breakthrough offer, started backtracking.

A long-distance showdown occurred in February 2007. Vladimir Putin and Sergei Ivanov arrived at the Munich Security Conference to give Bush a dressing-down. Putin had prepared a speech that was intended both to demonstrate his attitude toward the dethroned "emperor of the world" and to call upon the entire world community to engage in a new dialogue. Putin began by attacking the United States and the "Bush doctrine":

> The unipolar world that had been proposed after the Cold War did not take place either.
>
> The history of humanity certainly has gone through unipolar periods and seen aspirations to world supremacy. And what hasn't happened in world history?
>
> However, what is a unipolar world? However one might embellish this term, at the end of the day it refers to one type of situation, namely one centre of authority, one centre of force, one centre of decision-making.
>
> It is world in which there is one master, one sovereign. And at the end of the day this is pernicious not only for all those within this system, but also for the sovereign itself because it destroys itself from within.
>
> And this certainly has nothing in common with democracy. Because, as you know, democracy is the power of the majority in light of the interests and opinions of the minority. . . .
>
> Today we are witnessing an almost uncontained hyper use of force—military force—in international relations, force that is plunging the world into an abyss of permanent conflicts. As a result we do not have sufficient strength to find a comprehensive solution to any one of these conflicts. Finding a political settlement also becomes impossible.
>
> We are seeing a greater and greater disdain for the basic principles of international law. And independent legal norms are, as a matter of fact, coming increasingly closer to one state's legal system. One state and, of course, first and foremost the United States, has overstepped its national borders in every way. This is visible in the economic, political, cultural and educational policies it imposes on other nations. Well, who likes this? Who is happy about this?[2]

The most explicitly anti-American part of the speech provoked such a reaction that the second and third parts of speech were forgotten. The second part was also ambitious, but far more peaceful: Putin proposed to develop a new "architecture of global security" in which NATO should heed the opinion of Russia and the other BRIC countries before acting. The third part contained a list of traditional Putin grievances: the refusal of Europe and the United States to ratify the Treaty on Conventional Armed Forces in Europe, NATO's eastward expansion, barriers to Russian investment in Europe, the endless talks around Russia's accession to the World Trade Organization, and so on.

Such international populism went down very well in some quarters, and Putin's proposal for a world that would no longer be dominated by the United States brought dividends. He was even declared *Time* magazine's "Man of the Year," though not for his achievements—after all, in 2007 his main task had been to coordinate Operation Successor and ensure a transfer of power that suited him. No, recognition came thanks to his new rhetoric, which began flowing as soon as he realized that he no longer had to try to please Bush or anyone else. In an interview in June 2007, on the eve of the G8 summit, he said cryptically: "After the death of Mahatma Gandhi there's nobody to talk to."[3] Having parted company with George W. Bush, Putin was left alone with himself, fully confident that he was now the strongman of world politics.

WAR EVERY DAY

The nearer his second term came to its end, the more neurotic Putin, and hence Russian foreign policy, became. He was not sure that Operation Successor would succeed after all: he was still undecided as to whom to choose, and he did not know whether there might be unforeseen difficulties.

The second source of irritation was relations with the United States. The pent-up resentment had to be vented on someone, so Russia spent the whole of 2006 and 2007 picking fights with its smaller neighbors.

In spring 2006 Russia decided to punish Georgia and Moldova for their new pro-Western policies. Imports of Georgian and Moldovan wines to Russia were banned, as well as imports of Georgian mineral water.

The Georgian authorities announced the disclosure of a Russian spy ring, in response to which Russia launched a full-scale anti-Georgian campaign. Within a week all migrant workers from Georgia had been expelled, and to expedite the process police officers went around to all the schools and drew up lists of children with Georgian-sounding names. Air links with Tbilisi were suspended.

In Poland thugs beat up the children of Russian embassy employees. Putin saw this as a deliberate provocation to humiliate Russia. He recalled that Polish president Aleksander Kwasniewski, a former Communist, had wormed his way into his confidence, but then had become the main mediator in the talks after the Orange Revolution in Ukraine. It was essentially Kwasniewski who had facilitated the rise to power of Viktor Yushchenko. Russia launched an anti-Polish campaign, on top of the Georgian one, banning Polish imports.

Lastly, in spring 2007 Russia set its sights on Estonia. Under the influence of local nationalists, the Estonian authorities decided to move a Red Army monument and the remains of Soviet soldiers from one of Tallinn's central squares to a military cemetery. The Russian-speaking population of Estonia started a protest, which Vladislav Surkov's Nashi immediately co-opted, dispatching its "troops" to Tallinn. At the same time, the Estonian embassy in Moscow came under siege as Surkov's propaganda machine kicked in. Russian state television started calling Estonia's leaders the heirs of the Nazis and began to draw parallels between the events of 2007 and the Second World War, as if the struggle between "Russians" and "fascists" were alive and well. This metaphor was adopted by President Putin himself, speaking at the Victory Day parade on May 9: "These new threats, just as under the Third Reich, show the same contempt for human life and the same aspiration to establish an exclusive dictate over the world," he said, referring to the United States, essentially comparing it to Nazi Germany.[4] Five months later he condemned the EU for "making heroes of the Nazis and their henchmen"—and by "henchmen" he was referring to the governments of Estonia and Latvia.* This was Putin's first and, for a long time, only such analogy. The next attempt to frame Russia's political present in the past and revive the ghosts of World War II would come seven years later, in 2014.

Sergei Ivanov, being not just a potential successor but Putin's commissioner for relations with the United States, began making tough foreign policy statements. Following the anti-Estonian campaign, he met with activists from Nashi (as well as their supervisors, Vladislav Surkov and Gleb Pavlovsky) and thanked them for their assistance. Although the siege of the Estonian embassy in Moscow was in violation of the Vienna Convention and the authorities officially declared that they had nothing to do with it, the defense minister said that he was "in favor of patriotic sentiment" and "grateful for it."[5]

In 2007 Sergei Ivanov was effectively the second most important international face of Russia. His rather bellicose statements made the news, which

---

*The Russian government had trouble with both Baltic countries mainly because it blamed them for violations of the rights of Russian-speaking minorities in those countries. After the collapse of the Soviet Union these Russian-speakers, known as "the occupants," were not granted citizenship; instead they got only "aliens' passports." Also outraging Moscow were marches in those countries by veterans who had fought on the side of Nazi Germany during World War II.

naturally raised his approval rating. Meanwhile, both potential successors tirelessly traversed the country, supposedly supervising regional matters, though in fact it was plain electioneering. Medvedev opened new hospitals and universities, handed out free housing, and visited new agricultural enterprises. Ivanov, in his role as supervisor of the defense industry, attended the opening of new factories and promised to build Russian aircraft and computers. All these visits were covered on television. Every evening news bulletin had reports on Putin, Ivanov, and Medvedev. Both candidates had their own staffs and, more important, their own informal headquarters from which to mount an election campaign.

By summer 2007 it was clear that Ivanov was in the lead. His patriotic talk clearly had greater resonance with viewers. Although there was no direct order from above, more and more news items about him were appearing on state TV. Ivanov's approval rating was far higher than Medvedev's. Not only that, Ivanov was more to the liking of the Kremlin's chief policy strategist, Vladislav Surkov. Ivanov liked the latter's youth movements, and he readily adopted Surkov's rhetoric about nipping the "color revolution" in the bud.

According to Kremlin and government insiders, it was Ivanov who made the first mistake. He believed he had a very good chance of winning. He could not help notice that he was ahead of his rival in all respects. In June 2007, for instance, Ivanov was unexpectedly given the honor of opening the St. Petersburg Economic Forum. President Putin spoke on the second day, while the first day went to Deputy Prime Minister Ivanov, who was not even responsible for the economy.

Where exactly Ivanov came unstuck is not clear, but one episode stands out. During a visit to Asia, Putin and Ivanov discussed air defense systems with potential buyers. Ivanov, the defense minister, was more up to speed on the topic and at one point started to answer questions without even looking at Putin. The president turned to him and said in a low voice: "Are you already answering instead of me?"

THE THIRD UNKNOWN

In September 2007, six months before the presidential election and three months before the parliamentary elections, Putin suddenly gave his entourage a surprise. Everyone was expecting the succession issue to be cleared up soon, but Putin, for no apparent reason, muddied the waters even further by sacking the government of Mikhail Fradkov. Moreover, he humiliated the prime minister even more than he had his friend Ustinov a year earlier. Putin had dismissed Ustinov by telling him to feign his resignation (though, as he bid his staff farewell, Ustinov let slip that his departure was not voluntary). But Fradkov was forced to resign publicly in front of the television cameras. The spectacle was extremely unconvincing. The prime minister mumbled something, trying to explain why he was resigning, although he was clearly perplexed by the news of his own retirement.

The main reason behind Fradkov's dismissal was, of course, private ambitions. The longer Putin delayed naming his heir to the throne, the more Fradkov believed that he too was in the running. This hope was also nurtured by his longtime friend Igor Sechin. Although they had escaped punishment for their involvement in the Gang of Four, they had nevertheless moderated their activity. However, Fradkov, an experienced bureaucrat, was fond of throwing various monkey wrenches into the works of both successors, who were officially his deputies. There is no doubt that both Ivanov and Medvedev informed Putin of this "sabotage." So when the time to transfer power arrived, Putin decided to get rid of any unnecessary layer of authority that could inadvertently upset his plan.

In 2004, after Fradkov's appointment, Putin had praised his new prime minister, recalling how in 2001 Fradkov had courageously and uncompromisingly advocated the dismantling of his own department (the tax inspectorate) in the interests of the state. But in 2007 Putin's eyes and ears on the ground told him that Fradkov's oft-told version of events was quite different. His tax police had allegedly ruffled the oligarchs' feathers, and the billionaires had gone running to the president with a pack of lies about Fradkov's methods, simply to get rid of his highly efficient department. Putin apparently believed the fat cats' slander and, unwisely, disbanded the tax police. It was only in 2004, after the Yukos affair, that Putin realized his mistake and reinstated Fradkov.

On hearing that the quiet prime minister had started telling stories, Putin, according to witnesses, laughed out loud before drawing his own conclusions.

Fradkov was replaced by the no less mysterious Viktor Zubkov, Putin's old friend from the foreign relations committee of the St. Petersburg mayor's office in the early 1990s, who had spent the previous year in the modest post of head of the financial intelligence unit. As a civil servant, he was average; as a politician, he was downright weak. Only once, in 1999, had Zubkov run for anything—the governorship of the St. Petersburg region. He had finished a disappointing fourth, despite having the patronage of Putin, who at the time was prime minister.

Putin, it seems, did not explain to Zubkov why he was offering him the premiership. He simply said (according to a presidential aide) that "the motherland needs your experience" and "we will work as a team." Most likely Putin was embarrassed to say that he needed a placeholder with no personal ambition to keep the position for six months. But Zubkov did not get the memo. Just two weeks after his appointment he told reporters that he was not ruling out his own nomination for the presidency. Moreover, the unknown Zubkov began behaving extravagantly. For instance, during his first few days in office he gave the governor of Penza a public scolding, threatening to assign him to a children's choir if he didn't immediately raise the salaries of kindergarten teachers.

A week later Putin reprimanded Zubkov, telling him to forget any ideas about launching an electoral campaign. This time the message got through, and Zubkov was not seen again until the following May, when he conceded the post of prime minister to Vladimir Putin himself.

Having dismissed Fradkov's government, Putin finally chose his successor. The change of government was a symbolic gesture that marked the end of the behind-the-scenes tussle and the start of the chosen one's election campaign. By September 2007 the entire inner circle knew that the choice had been made: Dmitry Medvedev.

Putin and Medvedev spent the vital months before the election working out in detail the mechanisms for transferring power. "We've got it all covered," boasted Putin in conversation with his closest associates. To avoid potential miscommunication, the head of the presidential administration, Sergei Sobyanin, took charge of the government staff, while the head of the government staff, Sergei Naryshkin, moved over to the Kremlin. They knew each other's duties well and kept the communication channels between the "tandem" (as Putin and Medvedev were known) in working order. "Who would have thought that six months later Sobyanin and Naryshkin would not be talking to each other, and that the Kremlin and the government would be on the verge of chucking grenades at each other?" says a party to the above conversation.

PART THREE

PRINCE DMITRY

CHAPTER 9

IN WHICH GEORGIAN PRESIDENT MIKHEIL SAAKASHVILI RETAINS POWER—AND SOMETHING FAR MORE VALUABLE

Mikheil Saakashvili loves life, even more than he loves power. All the time he was president of Georgia, he was forever being compared with Putin. In some ways they mirrored each other: both tried to look like strong, macho, militant leaders able to fly a plane and drive a Formula One race car. Saakashvili, of course, imitated Putin (although he asserts that it was the other way round). But when it came to the crucial choice between la dolce vita *and power, he, unlike Putin, chose the former.*

As president of Georgia he was full of surprises, able to spend half a day in a restaurant with journalists sipping Moët & Chandon or fly by helicopter to a nightclub on the coast and be back in the capital the following morning. His seemingly relaxed way of life did not jibe with the image of a reformist president willing to sacrifice himself for the sake of his country. Nor was it in step with the image of a dictator who values power more than life itself.

Unexpectedly, Saakashvili really did give up power to the opposition—an unprecedented act in the former Soviet Union. I met up with him in Kiev inside the Ukrainian presidential administration building on Bankova Street, where he was preparing to return to power—only this time not in his native land but as governor of Odessa in southern Ukraine.

Mikheil Saakashvili carried out perhaps the most impressive economic reforms in the whole of the Commonwealth of Independent States. The mastermind behind many of the transformations is believed to have been the late Georgian politician and businessman Kakha Bendukidze, while the architect of the celebrated police reform was former prime minister Vano Merabishvili (now, ironically, in prison). But the fact remains that no other post-Soviet country saw such quick and effective reforms. True, they could have gone further, but great progress was made in the first couple of years, before stagnation set in.

Saakashvili lived in grand style and often flew on business of questionable importance in the company of young female assistants. Although he was not an ascetic by any means, no one has ever accused him of personal enrichment. All the charges later brought against him in Georgia relate to abuse of office and squandering of public funds, not embezzlement. With Saakashvili you are never short of questions. Perhaps the most interesting is why he became Putin's enemy number one. He himself is sure it is because he altered Georgia's foreign policy vector and became a successful reformer.

Saakashvili's recollections of events are full of factual inaccuracies. He sometimes mixes up locations in a way that even uninitiated listeners notice. But maybe that's not important. And maybe Putin's enmity is not about reforms or politics at all. Maybe it's the fact that Saakashvili was able to fulfill Putin's dream of living the good life without having to fight for power. That will probably remain forever beyond Putin's grasp.

HEREDITARY ENEMIES

Dmitry Medvedev inherited Vladimir Putin's enemies list, headed by Georgia and its president, Mikheil Saakashvili. Even when the "anti-Georgian campaign" of 2006 came to an end, Saakashvili retained his status. Kremlin insiders loved to chew the fat about how Putin hated "Mishiko" (the nickname of the tall, corpulent Georgian president). In a conversation with Belarusian president Alexander Lukashenko, Saakashvili had once allegedly referred to the Russian leader as a "Lilliputian," after which Lukashenko had, the story goes, immediately conveyed the information to Putin.

To some extent that story rings true, as retelling the content of confidential conversations is very much in the nature of Alexander Lukashenko. He always tells his interlocutors what people say about them behind their backs, and his brutal honesty is sometimes appreciated. However, Saakashvili himself says that the story is a Kremlin-invented myth. Either way, it goes some way to explaining Putin's hostility.

According to Saakashvili, Putin from the outset tried to demonstrate his power. For instance, during Saakashvili's first overseas tour as president of Georgia, one of the countries he visited was Germany. At his first meeting with Chancellor Schroeder, Saakashvili was still amicably disposed toward Putin (the acrimony was yet to come), but he told Schroeder about the problems in Russian-Georgian relations. A few days later, when the Georgian president had returned to Tbilisi, he was visited by the Russian ambassador with a transcript of that private meeting with Schroeder. "I wish to draw your attention to the points in your conversation with the German chancellor that we did not like," said the ambassador.

"Back then I believed Schroeder to be a major Western leader. So I was shocked that he had given Putin the full transcript of our conversation," says Saakashvili.

The closer Putin came to the end of his first term as president, the clearer it became that friendly relations with Georgia were unattainable. On April 4, 2008, NATO held a summit in Bucharest, at which Georgia and Ukraine were due to receive candidate member status. Under the so-called Membership Action Plan, accession to NATO seemed a done deal. Only a few loose ends needed to be tied up.

It is symbolic that of all the CIS countries, only Georgia and Ukraine tried to join NATO and break free of Moscow's influence. Both countries had had a special position in the Russian Empire and its successor, the Soviet Union. Georgia had only been incorporated into the Russian Empire in 1801, yet by 1812 a descendant of the Georgian royal dynasty, Pyotr Bagration, had become one of the outstanding heroes of the Napoleonic Wars, dying in the Battle of Borodino.

During the first years of the Soviet Union, there were many influential people of Georgian extraction. The Politburo in the 1930–1950s contained three: general secretary of the Communist Party Joseph Stalin, commissar of Soviet heavy industry Sergo Ordzhonikidze (who opposed the Stalinist purges and committed suicide in 1937), and the orchestrator of the purges, the head of the NKVD and the Gulag, and the "father of the Soviet atomic bomb," Lavrentiy Beria.

Joseph Stalin, who was born in the Georgian town of Gori, to this day remains a polarizing figure for both Russia and Georgia. When Khrushchev denounced Stalin's personality cult at the Twentieth Party Congress in 1956, unrest broke out in Tbilisi and people died during its suppression. But Stalin's popularity lived on, particularly among the Georgian political elite. Vasily Mzhavanadze, first secretary of the Georgian Communist Party between the 1950s and the 1970s, was part of the conspiracy against Khrushchev and managed to preserve the Stalin Museum in Gori. And Gori's monument to Stalin was not demolished after the debunking of his personality cult or even after the collapse of the Soviet Union.

Nevertheless, Georgia in the late Soviet years was a center of de-Stalinization and even de-Sovietization. Georgian art, cinema, music, and theater were an important part of Soviet culture. Tengiz Abuladze's pre-perestroika film *Repentance*, filmed in the Georgian language in 1984, became perhaps the main symbol of the onset of glasnost, and in 1987 it received the Grand Prix at the Cannes Film Festival. The film tells the story of a local Georgian tyrant cursed by his descendants. The deceased tyrant's face is reminiscent of both Beria and Mzhavanadze. At the end of the film the dead dictator's own son digs up his father's corpse from its resting place and throws it off a cliff.

One of the last Communist leaders of Georgia, Eduard Shevardnadze, had become Soviet foreign minister in 1985, and along with Gorbachev was one of the architects of the new Soviet foreign policy, which led to the end of the Cold War and the fall of the Berlin Wall.

According to Saakashvili, Putin was forever talking about Stalin in private, especially the fact that he occupied Stalin's former office in the Kremlin. "What did I care? I don't give a damn about Stalin," says Saakashvili.

It's hard to say how much of a damn Putin gave. In public he rarely mentioned Stalin, yet he liked to use the dictator's former dacha at Volynskoe in Moscow for important negotiations.

In any event, it was the presidents of Georgia and Ukraine, Mikheil Saakashvili and Viktor Yushchenko, who were the main supporters of Euro-Atlantic integration in the former Soviet Union. And George W. Bush, in the last year of his presidency, was convinced that the two post-Soviet republics should be granted NATO candidate member status. Saakashvili recalls that a few weeks before the Bucharest summit he was in Washington. Before a morning meeting with Bush, he received a call from Angela Merkel. "Whatever Bush says, I will not allow a NATO track for Georgia and Ukraine," she warned. Saakashvili told Bush, who replied: "You take care of your own business. Leave that woman to me."

But there was no avoiding a brawl at the summit in Bucharest. Merkel was up for a fight, supported by French president Nicolas Sarkozy. Their argument was that Ukraine and Georgia were not ready to join the alliance. As for Ukraine, most of its population strongly opposed NATO. As for Georgia, Merkel and Sarkozy said that, first, Mikheil Saakashvili did not resemble a true democrat (since in November 2007 he had closed down the largest opposition television station and violently dispersed a rally protesting against his government) and, second, Georgia had two unresolved border conflicts with Russia. Would NATO countries be prepared to send troops into Abkhazia and South Ossetia on Russia's southern border if the "frozen" conflicts there suddenly warmed up?

France and Germany's position caused outrage in Eastern Europe. At the general meeting of heads of state, Merkel and Sarkozy were effectively accused of being pro-Russian and drunk on Russian gas. Moreover, German foreign minister Frank-Walter Steinmeier was lectured that, given its history, Germany had no moral right to block Eastern European countries' path to freedom. Steinmeier was deeply insulted.

The dinner on the opening day of the summit turned into a bickerfest. Even after coffee had been served, the US and German delegations carried on arguing. The "talks" continued into the next morning. According to eyewitnesses, the most curious dispute was between Angela Merkel and Condoleezza Rice, the only two women in a roomful of men. Standing apart, they talked loudly and heatedly to each other in Russian, which they both spoke well. It was during that morning's conversation that Merkel proposed a compromise: the Membership Action Plan (MAP) would not be offered to Georgia or Ukraine, but the final statement would say that both countries would one day certainly "be members of NATO"—without specifying when, of course.

This compromise, which was eventually adopted by all member countries of the North Atlantic Treaty Organization, did not suit Georgia, Ukraine, or Russia. Saakashvili was indignant. But even more indignant was Vladimir Putin, who arrived in Bucharest on the last day of the summit, when the decision not to extend the MAP had already been made. All the same, he was furious that NATO was still keeping Georgia and Ukraine hanging on by approving the prospect of future membership.

According to witnesses, at a meeting behind closed doors Putin flew into a rage on the topic of Ukraine. "Ukraine is not even a country," he told

Bush. "Part of it lies in Eastern Europe, and the other, more significant part was given by us as a gift!" He finished his short speech with these words: "If Ukraine joins NATO, it will do so without Crimea and the eastern regions. It will simply fall apart."

Few paid attention to Putin's warning, since all were focused on the smoldering tensions between Moscow and Tbilisi. The idea of conflict breaking out between Russia and Ukraine seemed preposterous. Besides, Putin only had a month left in his term. The inauguration of the new president, Dmitry Medvedev, was scheduled for May 7.

THINGS CAN ONLY GET WORSE

Medvedev started out by trying to reset relations with Saakashvili. During their first meeting, according to Saakashvili, Medvedev said that it was not he and Saakashvili who had started the conflict; rather, they had inherited it and should now lay it to rest. He proposed that they chat more often. However, when Saakashvili subsequently phoned Moscow to talk with his new colleague, he was put through to Putin. "What's Medvedev got to do with anything?" Putin, who was now prime minister, told Saakashvili. "You need to talk with me, Mikheil. I'm in charge of relations with Georgia."

Immediately after the Bucharest summit, storm clouds began gathering over Georgia. There was a strong feeling that war could break out at any moment. Georgia dispatched troops to the border with South Ossetia, while Russia upped its peacekeeping contingent, which had first been sent there in 1992 in accordance with a UN resolution. Georgia sent drones over the two unrecognized republics of Abkhazia and South Ossetia; they were shot down. Russia set up consular services in the two regions. Georgia called that an "annexation" and demanded that Russian peacekeepers in the "conflict zone" be replaced by NATO forces.

In late May 2008 Russia sent its Railway Troops into Abkhazia. The US State Department, the Organization for Security and Co-operation in Europe, and the European Union all fiercely condemned the action. Saakashvili says that he immediately tried once more to contact Medvedev, but was again put through to Putin.

"Yes," Saakashvili paraphrases Putin, "we've read the statements from the West. They used a lot of ink and paper. You know what you can do? Tell your friends to take their statements and shove them up their ass." There was a pause. "That's right, up the ass."

A month later Saakashvili and Medvedev finally met for a second time. Both presidents were in Kazakhstan to celebrate the tenth anniversary of the relocation of the capital to Astana. Saakashvili says that he had to chase Medvedev down for a head-to-head meeting, which the latter was conspicuously trying to avoid. Only in the evening, at a Kazakh nightclub of all places, was he able to catch up with his Russian counterpart. When asked why they had not spoken for such a long time, Medvedev is reported to have said, "We belong to the same generation, we like the same music, we come from the same profession. But Moscow has its own inner logic. If we meet officially, Russian-Georgian relations will get even worse."

"How could they be worse?" asked Saakashvili.

"You'll see. Things could get much worse."

Medvedev described the meeting very differently in a television interview in 2011: "Saakashvili's difficult to avoid. He's very sticky. Several times during that trip he came over to talk to me. . . . Once we talked over a cup of tea and a glass of wine in the evening. He can say what he likes."[1]

According to Saakashvili, the Russian authorities planned the coming war in advance. The facts, however, suggest that the Georgian president himself did what he could to ensure a military denouement. Medvedev recalls that Saakashvili went quiet a month before the war, and in July stopped all communication. Russia was adamant that he sign agreements with Abkhazia and South Ossetia on the non-use of force, but the Georgian president responded that he would sign an agreement only with Russia, not with its puppets.

According to Saakashvili, in summer 2008 the Americans assured him that nothing would happen. *Russia does not want a war, and you will not provoke one or be provoked,* was the message.

Condoleezza Rice says otherwise. She writes in her memoirs that she and Bush repeatedly told Saakashvili: "You can't use force, and so the threat to do so doesn't do you any good."[2]

She visited Georgia on July 10. Saakashvili took her to dinner at the Kopala restaurant, overlooking the Kura River. She recalls that she urged him to sign an agreement on the non-use of force. "How can I do that when Putin is doing the things he's doing!" shouted Saakashvili in response. Rice insisted: "Don't let the Russians provoke you. And don't engage with Russian military forces. No one will come to your aid, and you will lose."[3] That is how Rice remembers the meeting. However, at the final press conference she said publicly that the United States supported the territorial integrity of Georgia and would be ready to stand up for it.

Throughout July there were skirmishes and clashes between Georgia and South Ossetia. At the start of the month Georgian troops took the strategic heights over Tskhinvali, the administrative center of South Ossetia. Soon afterward Russian fighter jets appeared in the sky above Georgia—at the exact moment when Condoleezza Rice arrived in Tbilisi. Georgia promised to shoot them down. Next came the joint US-Georgian military exercise codenamed Immediate Response 2008. That was followed by Russia's exercise Caucasus 2008, in which 8,000 service personnel and 700 pieces of military equipment drilled combat scenarios in Abkhazia and South Ossetia.

Saakashvili says that in early August he was on vacation at the Italian spa town of Merano, a favorite haunt of wealthy Russians. There in his hotel room he learned from Russian news that Russian military correspondents were already in South Ossetia. Russia's Channel One reported that Georgia was planning to violate the Olympic Charter by starting a war against South Ossetia on August 8, the opening day of the Beijing Olympics. Saakashvili immediately interrupted his vacation and returned home, where, it seems, he began to fulfill Channel One's prophecy.

"BETWEEN YOU AND ME"

Since the start of August 2008 there had been skirmishes along the border between South Ossetia and Georgia, with fatalities on both sides. On August 7 Mikheil Saakashvili announced a unilateral cease-fire. But later that night he gave the order to start storming the South Ossetian capital, Tskhinvali. According to Georgian intelligence, a column of the Russian 58th Army had already passed through the Roki Tunnel, which links South Ossetia to the Russian region of North Ossetia. A full-scale war had indeed broken out on the opening day of the Beijing Olympics.

Saakashvili says that Putin planned to overthrow the Georgian government, so he had to be proactive to prevent the coup from taking place.

"Russian armored columns were already in Georgia. We tried to reach Tskhinvali to block them, but it was too late. They wanted it to look as though rebels had entered Tbilisi and that the Russian military was on its way simply to keep the peace and stop the bloodshed. We had to prevent that scenario from unfolding," says Saakashvili.

On one point he is clearly overstating his case: the armored columns passed through the Roki Tunnel on August 8, one day later than he claims. If Russian tanks had been in South Ossetia on August 7, Saakashvili certainly would not have declared a "unilateral cease-fire."

At three o'clock in the afternoon on August 8, Russian television broadcast an address to the nation by President Medvedev, who announced the start of an operation to "enforce peace." He did not call it a war, so the approval of the Federation Council, the upper chamber of the Russian parliament, was not needed (although if he had asked for it, he would have received it unanimously). It was Medvedev's presidential debut. The decision to commence the operation was his, and he took it without even consulting Putin in advance, he says. Apparently he spoke with Putin only the day after.

At that precise moment Vladimir Putin was in Beijing for the opening of the Olympic Games. There he talked to George W. Bush, but the conversation they had was inconclusive. Bush demanded that Georgia's territorial integrity be respected, but his tone must not have been sufficiently threatening, since Russian tanks continued their advance toward the Georgian capital.

French president Nicolas Sarkozy attempted to assume the role of mediator. At first he tried to talk with Putin at the opening of the Olympic Games in Beijing, asking the Russian prime minister not to start a war with Georgia, but to give him, the current EU chairman, forty-eight hours—or twenty-four, or at least twelve—to try diplomacy. Putin said no three times, and then flew from China to North Ossetia and then on to Sochi, where he met with Medvedev.

Condoleezza Rice was also on vacation. Despite knowing that war was imminent, she decided not to cancel her trip to Greenbrier in West Virginia. Sergei Lavrov called her there on August 10. She describes the conversation in detail in her memoirs:

> "We have three demands," [Lavrov] said.
>
> "What are they?" [Rice] asked.
>
> "The first two are that the Georgians sign the no-use-of-force pledge and that their troops return to barracks."
>
> "Done," [Rice] answered. . . .
>
> "The other demand is just between us. Misha Saakashvili has to go." . . .

> "Sergei, the secretary of state of the United States does not have a conversation with the Russian foreign minister about overthrowing a democratically elected president," [Rice] said. "The third condition has just become public because I'm going to call everyone I can and tell them that Russia is demanding the overthrow of the Georgian president."
>
> "I said it was between us," he repeated.
>
> "No, it's not between us. Everyone is going to know."[4]

And she hung up. She did indeed phone the British and French foreign ministers, and a few hours later the US ambassador to the United Nations, Zalmay Khalilzad, outlined the content of the conversation at a meeting of the UN Security Council.

"I felt I had no choice. If the Georgians wanted to punish Saakashvili for the war, they would have a chance to do it through their own constitutional processes. But the Russians had no right to insist on his removal. The whole thing had an air of the Soviet period, when Moscow had controlled the fate of leaders throughout Eastern Europe. I was certainly not going to be a party to a return to those days," writes Rice in her book.[5]

Putin did not remain silent: "It is not the cynicism itself that is surprising, but the scale of the cynicism. The ability to present white as black and black as white. The artful ability to portray the aggressor as the victim of aggression and to ascribe blame to the true victim," he said of Washington's position. He recalled that Franklin D. Roosevelt was supposed to have said of the Nicaraguan strongman, Anastasio "Somoza may be a bastard, but he's our bastard." Saakashvili was the new Somoza, in Putin's eyes. Moreover, Putin compared the Georgian president with Saddam Hussein: "Hussein was rightly hanged for destroying Shia villages. But Georgia's leaders, who have wiped out ten Ossetian villages in no time at all, are somehow worthy of protection."[6]

By August 11, Russian tanks had taken Gori, the birthplace of Stalin, and were nearing the capital, Tbilisi. Saakashvili's office was in panic. Officials were busy packing, burning documents, and taking down pictures from the walls. Saakashvili called Bush and said, "Take a look at your watch and remember the time when the Soviet Union returned."

Rice cut short her vacation, while Bush returned from Beijing and US defense secretary Robert Gates came back from Germany. However, Washington took no concrete action. As described by Condoleezza Rice, during a meeting of the Bush administration the chest-thumping calls for the United States to do something were interrupted by a question from national security adviser Stephen Hadley: "Are we prepared to go to war with Russia over Georgia?"[7]

That the Kremlin's main objective had indeed been regime change in Georgia was later confirmed by Medvedev. "Saakashvili should actually be thankful to me for halting our troops at some point. If they had marched into Tbilisi, Georgia would most likely have a different president by now," Medvedev said in an interview three years later. Asked why the tanks were not ordered to enter Tbilisi, Medvedev immediately replied: "Our only objective was to halt the invasion that Saakashvili had unleashed. Besides, I'm neither a judge nor an executioner. I'd like to stress once again that it is up to the people of Georgia to assess Saakashvili and decide his fate through a democratic vote or other means, the way it sometimes happens in history."[8]

THE WAR THAT WASN'T

All this time French president Nicolas Sarkozy had been pursuing his diplomatic mission. He was due to fly from Paris to Moscow on August 12, 2008, and then on to Tbilisi. Shuttle talks were arranged. The French president's plane was already airborne when Dmitry Medvedev announced live on Russian state television that the "peace-enforcing" operation had achieved its goals and was over. Sarkozy touched down in Moscow feeling like an idiot: the goal of his visit had been achieved without him.

But that was not the end of the antics. His scheduled meeting with President Medvedev was interrupted after forty minutes by Vladimir Putin, who immediately announced that he was going to "hang Saakashvili by the balls." Sarkozy said later that during those talks Putin had come up to him, grabbed his tie, and shaken him to demonstrate the seriousness of his intentions.

Sarkozy flew from Moscow to Tbilisi with a six-point plan that he had developed in Moscow with Medvedev and Putin. Saakashvili agreed with the first five points but flatly refused the sixth, which stated that negotiations would begin in Geneva on the status of South Ossetia and Abkhazia, and that during the negotiations Russian peacekeepers would remain in both regions. Georgia could not accept that, and Sarkozy flew back to Moscow. This time he had a condition of his own: the talks would continue between him and Medvedev without Putin.

At this point the Bush administration also decided to take action. "Russia has invaded a sovereign neighboring state and threatens a democratic government elected by its people. Such an action is unacceptable in the twenty-first century," said Bush on the White House lawn.[9] Two days later, on August 13, he announced the start of a humanitarian operation: sixteen transport aircraft flew to Georgia, and the US Sixth Fleet sailed through the Bosphorus Strait. This formidable display of force was what caused Putin to halt the tanks, says Saakashvili. However, chronologically it does not add up, as Medvedev had announced the end of the operation several days before.

The most amazing thing about the "Five-Day War," as it became known, was its transience. The sides hurled horrific accusations at each other, yet a year later everything was practically forgotten. Georgian foreign minister Grigol Vashadze, who had taken Georgian citizenship only a year before the war stated, having lived and worked in Moscow at the Russian Foreign Ministry until 2005, lamented in the midst of the hostilities: "Russia will never wash the blood off its hands. It has not yet atoned for the sins of its predecessor, the Soviet Union. Prague, Budapest, now us. Russian foreign policy prepared this nightmare. What next? They won a small war. People died in the tragedy. Moscow will not be allowed to forget 'Georgia 2008' for decades to come."[10]

But the outcome couldn't have been more different. Everything was forgotten.

Russia had accused Georgia of "genocide" against the Ossetian population. Russia's UN representative talked about thousands, even tens of thousands, of victims. (A few years later, however, Russia's Investigative Committee estimated that just 162 people had died in South Ossetia.) During the first hours of the war 40,000 Russian troops entered Georgian territory. Russian planes bombed Gori and Poti, after which South Ossetian forces, with Russian cover, seized and ransacked Gori. Over five days 397 people in Georgia lost their lives. Yet just eighteen months later Russia and Georgia restored air links. And two years later Georgia unilaterally abolished all visa requirements for Russian citizens entering the country.

The last act of the short war came on August 26, 2008. President Medvedev announced that Russia had recognized the independence of Abkhazia and South Ossetia. It was expected that Russia would annex them, but that did not happen. Perhaps that is why Russia, and Medvedev personally, did not face any nasty consequences. The label "the man who began his presidency with a war in Georgia" did not stick—maybe because nobody in the world believed that it was his war anyway.

In autumn that same year, 2008, Russian state television broadcast a program during which viewers would vote for the most popular historical figure in the country's history. The preliminary online vote saw Joseph Stalin win hands down. That was too much for the Kremlin to stomach, so the result had to be falsified. Stalin slipped to third place, behind Alexander Nevsky, a thirteenth-century hero, and the great reformer of the early twentieth century, Pyotr Stolypin.

In Georgia, meanwhile, a decision was made to demolish the monument to Stalin in Gori, which had been put up during his lifetime and survived all the successive waves of de-Stalinization. The deed was finally done two years later, in 2010, under the cover of night, so as not to provoke excessive public outcry.

WORLD WAR

Saakashvili recalls that when the Russian tanks halted their advance outside Tbilisi, Vladimir Putin disappeared. For almost a month he was absent from the news before popping up on August 31, when state television showed him tranquilizing an Ussuri tiger at a reserve in the Russian Far East. The purpose was to attach a GPS transmitter to the tiger's collar and then track its movements through the forest. The footage was impressive. In it, Putin aims the tranquilizer gun at the tiger and fires a shot before bravely approaching the slumbering beast and fastening a collar around its neck. However, zoologists later admitted that it had all been staged. The tiger had in fact been borrowed from the local zoo and was not about to be released into the wild. For the prime minister's safety, the animal had been pumped full of tranquilizers in advance. In fact, Putin's shot apparently caused an overdose that killed her. This was not announced publicly, and for a long time afterward Putin's official website contained a banner inviting visitors to follow the movements of the "very same tiger," which was allegedly bounding around in the forest.

But in late August Ussuri tigers, and even the war in Georgia, were on the back burner. There were more serious goings-on in the world. On September 15 one of the largest investment banks in the world, Lehman Brothers, filed for bankruptcy. The next day Russia saw the first omen of things to come, when the bank KIT Finance also declared itself insolvent. All trading on the stock exchange was suspended the following day by order of the Russian regulator.

The Russian stock market had in fact been falling since May. In summer the downward trend intensified due to two factors: the war in Georgia, and the "doctor" incident. In late July Prime Minister Putin held a meeting with representatives of the iron and steel industry, at which he was deeply angered by the absence (for medical reasons) of Igor Zyuzin, the owner of Mechel, one of Russia's largest mining and metals companies. "He may be ill, but Mr. Zyuzin would be advised to get better more quickly," flared Putin. "Otherwise we'll send a 'doctor' to sort him out."[11] Putin's menacing tone scared investors. Mechel's shares collapsed, causing its value to drop by $5 billion. A week later President Medvedev called upon those in power to stop "spooking business." However, he failed to resuscitate the investment climate. Everyone was talking about Putin's "doctor."

In August the war in Georgia had been on everyone's mind, but by September the collapse of the financial market had taken over. On September 17 Russia's top economists were invited to a meeting with First Deputy Prime Minister Igor Shuvalov at the behest of German Gref, who had been behind Putin's reforms. Now, however, he was acting on the other side of the barricades. In 2007 Gref had left the government and managed to get Putin to appoint him as head of Russia's largest state bank, Sberbank. Gref feared that without state support the financial market would collapse, and he wanted to talk his colleagues into allocating funds to state-owned banks. The meeting was attended by finance minister Alexei Kudrin, minister of economic development Elvira Nabiullina (Gref's successor), Central Bank head Sergei Ignatyev, and various leaders of public financial institutions.

The situation was compared to 1998, when Russia had defaulted and hundreds of banks gone bust. Then Kudrin stepped in. The ever frugal finance minister proposed allocating 500 billion rubles (nearly $21 billion) from the state budget to the country's largest banks. This unprecedented largesse was doubled by First Deputy Prime Minister Shuvalov, who proposed an additional 500 billion rubles from the National Welfare Fund for the purchase of corporate securities. The next day a meeting was held with President Medvedev. The latter proposed allocating a slightly less generous 250 billion rubles from the budget and 250 billion from the National Welfare Fund.

"Alexei Leonidovich [Kudrin], don't announce the news. I'll do it," said Medvedev, not wishing to let Kudrin have the kudos. The sole benefactor of positive PR should always be the president.

Liberal economists in the government were delighted that the state was not leaving the business world to grapple with the crisis alone. Kremlin and government circles began to say that Russia was an "island of stability," a place that the global crisis would pass by, thanks to the foresight of the government and, in particular, Alexei Kudrin, who had saved up the petrodollars for a rainy day. In 2008 many people in Russia believed that the world was doomed but that Russia would be okay—even those who understood that Russia could never be an "island of stability," since its economy was too dependent on world oil prices.

Insiders say that Vladimir Putin, having assumed the prime minister's chair for the second time, now acquired a number of new traits, above all the belief that he was an expert in absolutely everything. He immersed himself in all matters that landed on his desk. He began to demonstrate arcane knowledge and deliver lectures to all and sundry, including his own ministers. Occasionally he listened to the economic advice of Alexei Kudrin, whom he considered to be an expert, but gradually he came to the conclusion that his own expertise surpassed anyone else's. Not only that, but he had greater experience, a broader outlook, and more information at his fingertips. "You simply don't know what I know," was Putin's response to members of the government who dared to offer their own opinion.

Putin was quick to distill the essence of the financial crisis as he saw it: it had been triggered by US domestic issues and was solely the fault of the United States. America had infected the entire whole, and the thought irritated him. He questioned how Washington dared to reproach other countries when its own blunders had caused such global misery. The Americans should put their own house in order before preaching to others, he mused. "Go and teach your wife how to cook soup" is how Putin encapsulated this sentiment, responding to international observers' criticism of the presidential elections in Russia in 2008.

THE UKRAINIAN FRONT

Despite the cessation of hostilities in the Caucasus, the Georgian war continued, oddly enough, in Kiev. From the first, Ukraine's "orange" government had been a loyal ally to Mikheil Saakashvili. President Viktor Yushchenko had flown to Tbilisi during the war in August 2008 to show support. That September the Ukrainian parliament had voted on a special resolution condemning Russian aggression, although not enough MPs were in favor for it to pass. The government's resolution was opposed not only by Viktor Yanukovych's Party of the Regions but also by Yushchenko's ally in the ruling coalition, Yulia Tymoshenko.

This unlikely alliance of enemies, Yulia Tymoshenko and Viktor Yanukovych, had taken root back on September 8, 2005, before the first gas war, when Yushchenko had fired Tymoshenko from the post of prime minister. Late that evening Tymoshenko held talks with Yanukovych. She did not leave his office for four hours. The receptionists were getting agitated. And when she finally left, Yanukovych sat there, lost in thought. When he at last came round, his press secretary asked, "Well, what do you think of Yulia?" Yanukovych breathed in the scent of the perfume his guest had left behind, and said: "She's so vile. Even if I'd wanted to, I couldn't have fucked her."

Two years later, in autumn 2007, Ukraine held snap parliamentary elections, in which Tymoshenko did well: second place, with 31 percent of the vote. Although she was behind Yanukovych's Party of the Regions, the "oranges" were again able to cobble together a coalition, and Tymoshenko became prime minister once more.

However, a year later relations between Yushchenko and Tymoshenko broke down completely, and by September 2008 the president was sure that his prime minister was in secret negotiations with Moscow to win its backing in the next presidential election. That was why, thought Yushchenko, she had not voted for the resolution in support of Georgia—because she was trying to please Putin. Moreover, Tymoshenko and Yanukovych this time around unexpectedly joined forces and voted together for a set of laws that greatly reduced the president's powers. The betrayal was evident.

In early October 2008 Prime Minister Tymoshenko did indeed go to Moscow for gas talks, since Ukraine had to settle a debt of $2 billion. Yushchenko tried some unusual methods to prevent her from going, even commandeering the plane on which the prime ministerial delegation usually flew to Moscow. But Tymoshenko went anyway, chartering an eight-seat private plane. She arrived at the talks in Novo-Ogaryovo, outside Moscow, with her trademark braid and perfect makeup (before even the most urgent talks in any country she always went first to the Ukrainian embassy, where her stylist would be waiting). Tymoshenko knew that her feminine charm and powers of persuasion were her main weapon. Even as prime minister, she studied three days a week with a private teacher to improve her oratory and elocution.

However, most of the talks with Putin were not about gas but about Georgia. Right on the eve of her visit the Russian newspaper *Izvestia* alleged that the Ukrainian authorities had sent arms and military experts to Georgia during the August war. Tymoshenko made a point of expressing shock at the revelation.

"A few months ago no one could have imagined that Russians and Ukrainians would ever fight against each other," said Putin histrionically. "But it happened, and those responsible made a huge mistake."

"I know that Georgia is a complex affair, but we want a peaceful settlement of this conflict and for peace to reign supreme," added a pompous Tymoshenko.[12]

Despite their mutual understanding, there was no agreement on a new gas price for Ukraine. Tymoshenko wanted to eliminate RUE as the intermediary between the two countries. Gazprom said it could be done, but first the debt had to be repaid. What's more, Dmitry Medvedev stated soon afterward that if Ukraine did not pay, Gazprom would appeal to the Stockholm Court of Arbitration. Gazprom threatened to raise the price from $179.50 to $400 per thousand cubic meters. Yushchenko also went on the offensive, threatening to review the agreement on the stationing of Russia's Black Sea Fleet in Crimea. Putin took it to mean that Yushchenko was spoiling for a fight.

At this point the Kremlin formulated a plan to try to get Tymoshenko and Yanukovych on the same side. The idea was for them to create a ruling coalition in the Verkhovna Rada (the Ukrainian parliament), impeach Yushchenko over the alleged illegal shipment of arms to Georgia, and then share the posts of president and prime minister between them. December 4 was the date chosen for announcing the new union. But at the last minute Yushchenko's faction derailed the plan by agreeing to all Tymoshenko's terms. The gas war continued unabated.

On December 26, as previously detailed, Gazprom warned European consumers that supplies through Ukraine could be disrupted. Yushchenko's associates remember the events as follows. On December 31 the head of the Ukrainian state gas company Naftogaz, Oleg Dubina, who was Kiev's chief negotiator, returned from talks in Moscow in a relaxed frame of mind. He requested a meeting with Yushchenko "behind Yulia's back" and told the president that Gazprom CEO Alexei Miller had promised him gas at $250 per thousand cubic meters "if Putin agrees." Yushchenko opined that the price was high but acknowledged that there was no alternative. Ukraine's leaders calmly departed for the New Year holidays. Those who believe this version of events say that Gazprom's position was a ruse, since Miller knew that Putin would not agree to the price and was simply playing for time.

The Russian version, as told by Vladimir Putin on numerous occasions, is almost the exact opposite. Dubina refused the price of $250, and on December 31 Yushchenko recalled the Ukrainian delegation from the negotiations. This version is reiterated by Tymoshenko, who lays the blame for the gas crisis squarely with Yushchenko.

Viktor Yushchenko says that he recalled no one. If he had, he insists, he certainly would have remained in Kiev over the New Year break instead of going to the Carpathian Mountains. In any event, on New Year's Eve Gazprom reduced the gas supply by the exact amount of Ukraine's domestic consumption. By January 7, 2009, transit through Ukraine had stopped completely, leaving Austria, Romania, Slovakia, and Poland without gas. For nearly three weeks Europe was in a state of panic.

Vladimir Putin blames Viktor Yushchenko, saying that the latter tore up the agreement because he wanted to preserve RosUkrEnergo as an intermediary: "We are observing Ukraine's political disintegration. That indicates a high level of corruption inside the relevant government structures, which are fighting not over the price of gas, but to save their intermediaries."[13]

The gas war continued until January 17, when Yulia Tymoshenko went to Moscow to see Vladimir Putin. Remarkably, the media spent less time reporting on the talks than on Tymoshenko's black dress with a large zipper down the back—making the dress able to be removed in a single motion, they joked. To be fair to the press, the two prime ministers did not disclose the details of the agreements they signed, so there was nothing else for journalists to write about.

The Ukrainian presidential administration spent that day trying to figure out what price Tymoshenko had agreed on, but she just replied, "It's okay," without naming a figure. A whole week later Kiev finally received a fax from Gazprom in which the Ukrainian authorities learned the details. The ten-year contract stipulated that in the first quarter of 2009 Ukraine would buy gas at a price of $360 per thousand cubic meters (with a slight discount later in the year). Not only that, there were no intermediaries. Tymoshenko had fulfilled her long-standing promise to get rid of RUE.

The agreement between Putin and Tymoshenko was indeed impressive. A week later the "godfather" of the gas mafia, Semyon Mogilevich, whom Tymoshenko described as RUE's "underground supervisor," was arrested in Moscow. At the same time the nominal co-owner of RosUkrEnergo, Dmitry Firtash, was put on Russia's federal wanted list. The secret patrons of the gas mafia, without whom the company could not have operated so long and so successfully, most likely turned them in, preferring to deal with Tymoshenko.

However, Dmitry Firtash's business did not suffer too much. He remained the owner of a network of regional gas and chemical companies and, according to Yushchenko's former energy adviser Bogdan Sokolovsky, continued to receive gas directly from Russia, bypassing Naftogaz and formal arrangements. He was able to resell part of the gas in Europe by declaring that it had been produced in Ukraine.

Yulia Tymoshenko claimed the agreement with Putin as a personal victory, while Yushchenko called it state treason because of the exorbitant price and onerous conditions. Relations between Tymoshenko and Yushchenko were ruined forever. Instead, she continued to negotiate with the eternal enemy, Viktor Yanukovych, on the establishment of a so-called broad coalition, encouraged by Vladimir Putin, who was eager for Yushchenko's opponents to unite against him and impeach the Ukrainian president.

This time the arrangements for a "broad coalition" were carefully spelled out. Yanukovych and Tymoshenko were to make amendments to the constitution to ensure that the president would be elected by parliament rather than by popular vote. Thereafter, Yanukovych and Tymoshenko would assume the offices of president and prime minister, and alternate in the roles until 2029.

A close eye was kept on the deal by Viktor Medvedchuk, who was now effectively Putin's special representative in Ukraine. He understood how badly the Russian president needed "Spotty" (as the Kremlin called Viktor Yushchenko because of his now pockmarked face) to be overthrown.

However, the plan failed—for the third time. On June 7, 2009, Trinity Sunday, Viktor Yanukovych went to pray at the Kiev-Pechersk Monastery. Afterward he told reporters who had gathered outside that he would not join a "broad coalition." The Kremlin was sure that Yanukovych had been persuaded by Yushchenko that he could become the popularly elected president all on his own without having to depend on Tymoshenko. Tymoshenko's camp, meanwhile, was certain that Yanukovych had been swayed by her sworn enemy Firtash.

Yushchenko was rescued, albeit briefly. He saw his constitutional term through to the end before being routed in the next election. But the failed "broad coalition" was another defeat for Putin in Ukraine and his second unsuccessful attempt to overthrow an enemy. In 2008 he had been unable to string Saakashvili up "by the balls," and one year later Yushchenko too had escaped from the Kremlin's clutches.

CHAPTER 10

IN WHICH BARACK OBAMA BECOMES THE KREMLIN'S BEST FRIEND AND WORST ENEMY

When Barack Obama gave his first speech in Russia, his listeners were openly falling asleep. Perhaps the great orator was tired after a long election campaign, or maybe his eloquence and charm just had no effect on the Russian audience. The speech was delivered in 2009 at a graduation ceremony at the New Economic School in Moscow. It lasted about an hour and the students were nodding off despite the fact that Obamamania was at its peak everywhere in the world, including Russia.

Vladimir Putin did not like the new American president from the start. For him, Barack Obama was both soft and intractable. He was too ideological and wholly unpragmatic. It was ever thus. Since the days of the Soviet Union, Moscow has always found common ground with the Republicans, but not with the Democrats.

Obama's highfalutin words about the international community's desire to see a strong and free Russia, about the essential value of human rights, and about the United States not wanting to impose its policies on other countries provoked a wry smile among Putin's entourage. Even the young economics students, fluent in English, did not really believe it either.

For Putin, it was blatant hypocrisy. George W. Bush had openly stated that the United States intended to impose its will on others. His frankness had earned Putin's respect, while Obama's rhetoric aroused suspicion.

Paradoxically, Obama, the most idealistic and peace-loving US president in living memory, became a symbol of war in Russia, a target for Russian state propaganda and racist jokes, and a hate figure for millions of patriotic Russians. He was caricatured as an ill-fated enemy doomed to be defeated by Vladimir Putin. Obama might be surprised to learn what they say about him in Russia, a lot of which is pure hokum. But he probably wouldn't be too bothered, since Russia has never been a priority for him.

Introducing the US president to the students in Moscow, the master of ceremonies recalled that Obama's parents had met at the University of Hawaii during a Russian language lesson. Although Obama quoted Pushkin in his speech, he never really made an effort to understand what made his Russian partners tick. Putin and his team could not forgive such indifference.

OUT OF THE SHADOWS

For the first two years of his presidency Dmitry Medvedev's main task was simply to be seen. The world's media referred to him as Putin's "handpicked successor" and no one took him seriously. Even when he sent troops into Georgia, everyone said it was Putin's war, as though Medvedev himself did not exist.

In early June 2008 Medvedev proposed a new treaty on European security. Though the proposal largely fell on deaf ears around the world, for the Kremlin it was a vital issue, one that an enraged Putin had addressed during his Munich speech in 2007. Irritated by NATO's expansion, Russia began to demand that its interests be taken into account. By 2007 it had become an obsession for Putin, and in 2008 Dmitry Medvedev chimed in, but with a very different, conciliatory tone. They were playing good cop, bad cop. But no one was listening to Medvedev's proposals back then, at a time when war with Georgia was imminent. The military hostilities undid years of good relations between Europe and Russia. Trust in Putin plummeted, while confidence in Medvedev had yet to take root.

After the war Medvedev's team had to grapple with two completely conflicting goals. Domestically it was important to show that Medvedev was strong and independent, and that he had declared war without consulting Putin. Yet internationally it was more expedient to pin the war on Putin and portray Medvedev as a qualitatively new type of politician.

The task of shaping Medvedev's new image fell to two people: Vladislav Surkov, the Kremlin's chief policy architect, and Natalya Timakova, Medvedev's spokesperson, who acted more like an adviser. As the closest and most influential policy strategist in Medvedev's circle, she co-opted many of Surkov's powers, causing conflict between them.

November 4, 2008, was election day in the United States. Chicago spent the entire night celebrating the victory of its senator from Illinois, Barack Obama. After eight years of the warmongering Bush, Obama's election campaign had come as a breath of fresh air. The winning candidate spoke not about God and America's historic mission but about ordinary folk. He too was an ordinary person, he said, and all ordinary people have the capacity to change their lives and the world around them. "Yes we can," replied his voters, using the words that had become the Obama campaign's slogan. The old warhorse John McCain was blitzed by this young lawyer and social media adept (most of Obama's campaign money was raised online).

Moscow's reaction to Obama's election was rather peculiar. On November 5, after the election results had been announced in the United States, Medvedev delivered his first address to the parliament. The main tidbit was his promise to place Iskander missiles in the Kaliningrad region, a Russian exclave surrounded by EU countries. The dovish Obama had been given a Cold War welcome, and not from the hawkish Putin but from the smiling Medvedev.

If one reads the text of Medvedev's speech, it seems even more paradoxical today than it did at the time. For a start, it had multiple authors. The key passages were written (some jointly, some separately) by Dmitry Medvedev, Vladimir Putin, Vladislav Surkov, and Natalya Timakova.

Overall, Medvedev's first keynote speech was imbued with an age-old Surkovian principle: usurp your opponents' slogans. The speech was surprisingly anti-regime in content. There in front of Russia's top paper-pushers, he attacked the bureaucracy with more force and fury than any oppositionist: "Bureaucracy scares business into toeing the line. It takes control of the media so that everyone remains silent. It interferes in the electoral process so that no outsider comes to power. It pressures the courts to deliver selective justice." Medvedev was not to blame for much of that, but as head of state, he was now responsible for the sins of state control over the media and the lack of free elections. Medvedev was essentially denouncing himself. However, that was one of Surkov's favored methods. By highlighting the problem and expressing disgust, Medvedev effectively detached himself from it.

Medvedev criticized the state apparatus as if he had nothing to do with it. But most ironic of all were the proposals to liberalize Russia's electoral legislation. Medvedev did not try to change anything, but he harshly criticized the status quo. When one considers that Surkov worked on the speech, it seems clear that the Kremlin strategist was instructed by the new president to expose the flaws of his own electoral law, which Surkov had devised in 2005 to combat the "color revolution" threat.

Having paid homage to civil society and free elections, Medvedev made one final proposal: to increase the president's term from four to six years and the term of members of parliament from four to five years. The constitutional change was initiated not by Medvedev, of course, but by Vladimir Putin. He himself had not touched Yeltsin's 1993 constitution and had even bowed to it by not running for a third consecutive term. However, he made sure that his successor amended the text as soon as possible.

The proposal to change the constitution was cynically timed to coincide with the document's fifteenth anniversary. Despite stating that "the reformist itch should not be allowed to affect the constitution," the new president took to rewriting part of it.

THE RUSSIAN OBAMA

As the search for the president's new image continued, it became apparent that the best role model was none other than Barack Obama. Medvedev was a block of wood from which the "Russian Obama" could be gradually sculpted. Moreover, the Russian president himself liked his US counterpart. Although he never said so, not even to those close to him, he clearly wanted to emulate Obama. Hampered by a lack of charisma, Medvedev was nevertheless assured by Natalya Timakova that he would grow into the role. She set up a video blog for him, plus Twitter and Facebook accounts, and bought him an iPhone and iPad. Medvedev loved gadgets and did not need to pretend to enjoy using them. His boyish enthusiasm at times made him more like a hipster than a president, but that was no bad thing, his image-makers believed.

Although Medvedev had fallen under Obama's spell, the new US administration eyed the Russian with skepticism. Vice president Joe Biden and secretary of state Hillary Clinton did, however, try to offer assurances that the mutual resentment of the Bush era was history. Speaking in February 2009 at the Munich conference, Biden said that Russia and the United States should press the "reset button on their relationship." That was how the now infamous "reset" was born. A month later Sergei Lavrov and Hillary Clinton met in Geneva, where the US secretary of state gave her colleague a symbolic button they were to press together. Printed on the button was the word "reset" in both English and Russian. Unfortunately, the Russian version was misspelled, and instead of "reset" (*perezagruzka*) it said "overload" (*peregruzka*). Lavrov explained the mistake to his embarrassed colleague but still agreed to press it, joking that he would "try to prevent system overload in Russian-US relations." The Freudian slip was more symbolic than the trivial act of pressing the button. The United States and Russia still did not understand each other, did not speak the same language (literally and figuratively), and despite both sides mouthing that bygones were bygones, absolutely nothing had changed. Medvedev and Putin did not want a reset. They did in fact want the overload that Clinton had inadvertently offered, combined with greater clout for Russia in world affairs, more respect, a sense of partnership, and proof that their opinion mattered. The Obama administration was ready to renounce the role of global policeman and other excesses of the Bush era, but all the old prejudices against Russia remained.

Barack Obama first came to Moscow in July 2009. He met with Medvedev at the Kremlin, while Putin received him at Novo-Ogaryovo, where a sumptuous breakfast with caviar was laid out. Trying to make conversation, Obama began by asking rhetorically, "How did we get into this mess [in US-Russian relations]?" In response, Putin gave him an hour-long lecture as to how precisely it had happened. Obama listened without interrupting.

As it happens, Obama liked neither Putin nor Medvedev, despite all Medvedev's attempts to be friends with his US counterpart, as Putin and Bush had once been for a time. A new agreement on the reduction of strategic offensive arms was meant to symbolize the reset. Medvedev desperately wanted to sign it, but diplomats could not settle the details. The White House's open disdain for the new Russian leader did not help: senior US officials mocked Medvedev's gadget-mania in front of reporters, saying, "Maybe we won't sign a deal. Maybe we'll just send him a text message."

In the end, an agreement was finally signed, but it was an empty shell—more an opportunity for a photo shoot in front of Prague Castle in the Czech capital, where the signing took place, than a real document. Russia wanted to bind the new agreement to a US commitment not to deploy a missile defense shield in Europe. The Americans flatly refused. As a result, Moscow added and unilaterally signed an addendum to its side of the bargain, reserving the right to withdraw from the treaty if Washington went ahead with installing a shield in Europe.

An equally striking demonstration of the lack of friendship between Medvedev and Obama occurred during the Russian president's visit to the United States in June 2010. First of all, Obama took Medvedev to his favorite eatery—Ray's Hell Burger in Arlington, just outside Washington. Medvedev ordered a burger with cheddar, jalapeños, onions, and mushrooms, plus a Coca-Cola to wash it down, and Obama got one with cheddar, onions, lettuce, tomato, and pickles, plus iced tea; the two presidents split an order of fries. In the photos they looked very chummy.

But the meeting did not go as amicably as the White House had planned. In the checkout line Obama was unexpectedly greeted by a soldier recently returned from Iraq. Turning his back to Medvedev, Obama began an animated conversation with the veteran. The Russian president stood patiently, tray in hand, waiting to be noticed again.

Three days later, at the G8 summit in Toronto, it became known that the Americans had arrested a group of ten Russian spies. Obama did not even mention it to Medvedev. There were no more illusions about friendship between the two presidents.

THE ANTI-PUTIN

Meanwhile, back home in Russia, the struggle to present Medvedev as something other than a Putin clone (or "Mini-Me," as he was sometimes portrayed in the West) was raging. The first interview Medvedev gave with Russian print media was for *Novaya Gazeta*, which Putin had barely ever spoken to and which had employed the investigative journalist Anna Politkovskaya, whose murder "caused more harm than her activities," to use Putin's words. And in 2009 Medvedev wrote a landmark article entitled "Russia, Forward!" It was published in its entirety by Gazeta.ru, the best online media resource at the time.

However, this flirtation with liberal society did not bring the desired results. Having waxed lyrical about democracy and then amended the constitution to extend the president's term in office, Medvedev was seen by many as Putin in sheep's clothing. For the first three of Medvedev's four years in office, Moscow intellectuals fiercely debated the question of whether Medvedev could be trusted. Some, such as human rights veteran activist Lyudmila Alexeyeva, said that he should be supported: "The worst thing that can happen is that we are wrong. It may turn out that he's no better than Putin. But if we do nothing, we'll just end up with Putin anyway." But most, including poet Dmitry Bykov, believed that Medvedev was "Putin's shadow" and that it was naive to waste time on false illusions. They poked fun at Medvedev's love of gadgets and Natalya Timakova's attempts to impart an aura of rebelliousness to the Russian president. Timakova was hurt by the ridicule but says that Medvedev did not mind. Others close to Medvedev, however, say that not only was he offended, he also made a mental note of all those who had mocked him.

The culmination of Medvedev's fling with the liberals came in the summer of 2010. The focus of protest activity had moved to Khimki Forest—a small piece of land near Moscow, through which a highway was due to run from the capital to St. Petersburg. For some reason (probably a dispute between the two main contractors), the future highway was national news: local environmentalists protested against the felling of the forest and were joined by opposition politicians and civil society activists. The campaign to preserve the forest was backed by Russian musician Yuri Shevchuk and even U2's Bono. When the struggle for Khimki Forest reached near-cosmic proportions, Dmitry Medvedev made a surprise move, announcing that he had listened to the protesters and decided to cancel (or rather "reconsider") the construction project. Vladimir Putin never would have done that. He believed that giving in to protesters was a sign of weakness, comparable to negotiating with terrorists.

The fact that the road was built anyway makes the whole episode rather surreal and a bit of a sham. Six months after the peak of the protests the regional authorities decided that the environmental concerns were not justified and the road would not cause any harm. No one protested. Five years later, when the highway was finished, many liberal activists agreed that the road was good and the journey to Sheremetyevo Airport was now much easier.

What passed under the radar was that Arkady Rotenberg, a childhood friend and judo partner of Vladimir Putin, was a co-owner of one of the companies that built the road.

CHAPTER 11

IN WHICH DEPUTY PRIME MINISTER IGOR SECHIN TURNS INTO A RUSSIAN CHE GUEVARA

Igor Sechin loves orange juice and considers the humble minibus to be the most convenient mode of transport. Everywhere he goes, wherever he flies, he is always met on the ground by a minibus, which sets off the moment Sechin takes a seat. All others have to jump in on the move.

Insiders say that Sechin is like a cyborg. He can go without sleep for days on end and works standing up; it's even said that he cured himself of cancer. Maybe it's the orange juice.

He arouses fear and knows it. He can hold a meeting and smash everyone to smithereens, leaving his subordinates loosening their ties and reaching for the brandy when he departs. Then he'll suddenly come back into the room, pretending to have forgotten something, and finish them off.

Sechin speaks very softly, which is wholly incongruous with his demonic ways and brutal appearance. But such contrast works to his advantage. This once humble executive officer, who has attained real power, knows how to teach his subordinates the value of discipline. In Sechin's reception room no one is allowed to read magazines; that results in immediate expulsion. You have to sit on the edge of your chair and tremble. It's a ritual—because that is how Sechin himself behaves before meeting with his superiors.

OUR MAN IN HAVANA

In early August 2008, just days before the start of the war in Georgia, a large delegation flew from Russia to Cuba. It consisted of three ministers (energy, communications, education), the heads of Rosneft and Surgutneftegaz (both major oil companies), the head of Gazprom, Security Council secretary (and former FSB head) Nikolai Patrushev, and the delegation head himself, Igor Sechin.

Sechin worked for many years in St. Petersburg as Putin's private secretary. When his patron moved to the government, Sechin was appointed deputy prime minister in charge of energy and head of the government commission for relations with Latin America, since Sechin spoke Spanish and Portuguese. He had started his career as a military interpreter in Angola and Mozambique, where he worked alongside Cuban military experts. Sechin has fond memories of his Havana comrades. Back in his student days he had been enamored of Latin American revolutionaries, and not only Che Guevara.

But Sechin had not taken a third of the Russian government to Cuba to reminisce about the good old days. In summer 2008 the outgoing Bush administration was finalizing plans for the deployment of a missile shield in Europe. US secretary of state Condoleezza Rice was due to sign agreements on the siting of a radar station in the Czech Republic and missiles in Poland, a stone's throw from the Russian border.

Russia had to respond, but how? For starters, the newspaper *Izvestia* wrote that Russia was preparing to reopen its military bases at Lourdes in Cuba and Cam Ranh in Vietnam, which Vladimir Putin had closed in 2001. Moreover, the paper advised the Russian government to place strategic bombers in Cuba. For some reason the publication caught the eye of US Air Force chief of staff Norton Schwartz, who said that in doing so Russia would "cross a red line." It was only then that Moscow realized that it had completely forgotten to discuss the subject with the Castro brothers.

Russian-Cuban relations after the collapse of the Soviet Union were tricky, to say the least. The Cubans were offended and convinced that Moscow had betrayed them. Sechin wanted to renew the old friendship and reestablish ties with Cuba, not least so that the Americans would finally "get their comeuppance," as Nikita Khrushchev had told Richard Nixon back in 1959.

But Russia's landing force in August 2008 achieved nothing—Fidel Castro did not even receive the delegation. Sechin, however, was persistent and continued to visit Latin America about once a month. On the second occasion he crisscrossed Cuba, Venezuela, and Nicaragua, peddling Russian arms and the services of Russian oil companies, primarily Rosneft, of which he was the chairman of the board of directors.

Thanks to Sechin's powers of persuasion over Daniel Ortega and Hugo Chávez, first Nicaragua and then Venezuela recognized the independence of Abkhazia and South Ossetia. No one had asked Sechin to do it. He simply figured that, in contrast to the long and arduous process of signing oil contracts, securing recognition of the two breakaway republics would be a quick and effective way to demonstrate to Putin his ability and loyalty.

Sechin got on much better with Chávez than with the Castro brothers. At their first meeting the Venezuelan president clasped the Russian deputy prime minister and said: "At last! Now we are not alone in the battle against the American empire! Now we have Russia on our side!"[1] Russia paid generously for Venezuela's recognition of Abkhazia and South Ossetia, providing a loan of $1 billion for the supply of weapons. An oil consortium was also set up for the joint development of Venezuelan oil fields, although Russian oil companies have yet to profit from it.

Sechin's policy was essentially the logical continuation of Igor Shuvalov's "energy superpower" concept. But whereas Shuvalov had tried to apply it to the obstinate Europeans, Sechin applied it to the compliant Latin Americans. It was pure politics and made no economic sense, but it gave Latin American leaders a sense of newfound importance. Putin was pleased with his longtime assistant, while Sechin's subordinates were ever more shocked by his endurance, saying that after the hours-long flight from Moscow to Caracas he went straight to the gym, after which he held marathon talks with Chávez—and never once dozed off.

Sechin gradually became the antithesis of Medvedev. The president was Russia's public face in dealing with the West, while the anti-Western Sechin was reserved for countries not aligned to the United States.

CAPTAIN HOOK

Sechin's transformation into a public politician was a surprise for everyone, since his strength stemmed from his proximity to the president and ability to play administrative games. During Putin's first term Sechin had been the president's personal secretary and the first person to greet him each morning.

It was Sechin who energized the president, looked after his schedule, and wrapped up the daily business. Moreover, Sechin's power was doubled by the fact that he followed almost medieval rituals of loyalty to his boss, which drew him close and made him invulnerable. No one else in the presidential administration, for instance, took the time to accompany the president to the airport and meet him there on his return, but Sechin did.

After Putin moved to the government, Sechin did everything possible to become head of the government staff and remain close to his mentor. However, he was stymied by Dmitry Medvedev, who could not allow his sworn enemy to occupy a key position in the government. So Putin had to "exile" Sechin to the energy sector.

Medvedev and Sechin's mutual loathing was no secret. One day Sechin and his wife and friends gathered for a friendly dinner (the location was chosen by Sechin's wife, Marina). The others arrived earlier than Sechin, who was late. When he arrived, he angrily demanded that they go to a different restaurant: "You've picked a fine spot. Can't you see that's Medvedev over there in the corner?"

But publicly Sechin demonstrated absolute loyalty and even servility, not only to the former president but also to the new one. This was manifested in petty details. During long flights on foreign visits, officials usually dressed in more comfortable clothes, such as a track suit and slippers. So did Sechin, but never in the presence of the president. Accompanying Medvedev, he was always attired in a suit and tie.

Sechin's influence was not only due to his proximity to Putin. The latter had many dancing attendance on him, but it was Sechin who became the "spiritual leader" of the *siloviki*. After Sechin initiated the Yukos case and dispossessed Mikhail Khodorkovsky, he surrounded himself with an informal team of people from the security services, who considered it their duty to make the oligarchs share their ill-gotten gains, describing it as "velvet reprivatization."

"President Putin said that big business should be socially responsible to the state. So our colleagues from the FSB decided to set up an organization to bend the Khodorkovskys of this world into shape," explained Oleg Shvartsman, a businessman and an active participant in the scheme, in 2007 in an interview with *Kommersant*.[2] He said that Sechin managed to consolidate a vast number of active members and veterans of the security services and the Russian armed forces (around 600,000 people in total).

They were united less by the desire for profit than by common beliefs. The *siloviki* considered the "loans for shares" scheme to be a great evil, and the assets sold in the "wild 1990s," in their view, belonged to the state. Sechin and his associates never considered themselves to be raiders—they were saviors acting in the interests of the Motherland. The Yukos affair they had orchestrated was a desperate attempt to save Putin's regime from a US-led conspiracy: Khodorkovsky was financing the majority of parties in the Russian parliament and negotiating the sale of a significant stake in Yukos to ChevronTexaco or ExxonMobil. A company with a US majority shareholder could not be allowed to control the Duma.

However, Sechin's *siloviki* (the core of whom were from the FSB) were not the only secret superheroes of Putin's Russia. There existed a competing structure that set itself the same noble goals and was also guided by the ideals of serving the Motherland—although from the outside it looked like a racket. This was the Federal Drug Control Service (FDCS), headed by Viktor Cherkesov, a longtime friend and former deputy of Vladimir Putin, when the latter headed the FSB. Cherkesov's ally was the head of Putin's private security force, Viktor Zolotov, and both were at odds with the clan controlled by Igor Sechin and Nikolai Patrushev (Putin's successor as FSB head). It was Cherkesov and Zolotov who had managed, in 2006, to overthrow the prosecutor general, Vladimir Ustinov, by providing Putin with transcripts of his talks with Sechin, Luzhkov, and Fradkov. In 2007, at the height of "Operation Successor," the struggle between the security officers intensified.

In October 2007 Cherkesov went out on a limb. He published an op-ed in the liberal newspaper *Kommersant* (once owned by Berezovsky) entitled "Soldiers Must Not Be Profiteers." The most quoted passage is the one in which the author waxes philosophical about how the Russian security services single-handedly rescued the country from the brink in the late 1990s and early 2000s:

> Tumbling into the abyss, post-Soviet society grasped at the security services for support and clung to them for dear life. Some wanted society to fall and shatter into smithereens. But they were terribly disappointed. And they deeply resent the "Chekists" [security officers] for not letting society plummet to its death. . . .
>
> We saved the country from falling over the edge. This imparts meaning to the Putin era and historical merit to the Russian president. It imposes

> on our professional community an enormous responsibility that is wholly detached from conceited self-satisfaction.

The author goes on to say that there was a war inside the "Chekist corporation":

> For any corporation to be healthy, it must have standards. These standards should be all-encompassing. And they have to be proper standards. If they vanish and tyranny ensues, the corporation collapses. Experts and journalists are already talking about "warring factions" within the security services.

Viktor Cherkesov was in fact pointing the finger at Igor Sechin and the FSB heads, who had recently initiated criminal proceedings against Cherkesov's deputy:

> The current state of affairs within our "corporate" environment will determine the future. Infighting cannot be permitted. Standards cannot be arbitrary. Soldiers must not be profiteers. The "corporation" is dear to all who have dedicated their lives to it, myself included.[3]

The real reason for the article, as suggested by journalists, was the struggle between the FDCS and the FSB for control over the flow of smuggled goods from China. But perhaps both sides sincerely believed that they were simultaneously serving the Motherland.

The publication did not go unnoticed, but neither did it benefit Cherkesov. His aim was to get access to Putin, which was blocked by Sechin. But Putin decided that dirty laundry should not be washed in public. During the next reshuffle Cherkesov lost his post in the FDCS and was transferred to a less significant position at the Agency for Defense Contracts. Sechin's administrative clout only increased.

A REAL OILMAN

Prior to the Yukos affair Sechin had no experience of the energy sector. Only in July 2004 did he become chairman of the board of directors of Rosneft, so that come May 2008 he had less than four years' experience in the industry under his belt. However, the meticulous Sechin wasted no time. Whereas his rival Dmitry Medvedev, who headed the board of directors of Gazprom, had no interest in Russia's gas giant and effectively let Putin run it, Sechin delved into every detail of the management of Rosneft, Russia's oil giant.

In 2006 Sechin went further. At his request the investigative authorities began probing another major oil company, Russneft. Sechin's Rosneft wanted to buy the oilfields of this similarly named company, since it owned many promising greenfields. But the price could not be agreed, and Russneft owner Mikhail Gutseriev refused to sell. As a result, he was presented with a tax bill for 17 billion rubles and a criminal case. He eventually sold up (not to Rosneft, however, but to aluminum tycoon Oleg Deripaska) and left the country.

The story had an unexpected denouement. In 2010, when Medvedev was president, Gutseriev was pardoned. He returned to Russia and bought back his company. He had been helped by his friends German Gref, former economics minister and Sberbank head, and oligarch Vladimir Yevtushenkov.

Having found his feet as chairman of Rosneft, Sechin quarreled with the company's president, Sergei Bogdanchikov. In 2010 he replaced him with someone more amenable.

Sechin gradually became the most influential person in Russian industry and the Russian government, surpassing even Igor Shuvalov (although formally Shuvalov held a higher position as a *first* deputy prime minister, while Sechin was just a deputy prime minister).

Government colleagues said that Sechin had no economic theory, did not like private business, and believed that everything should belong to the state.

PUTIN'S RIGHT HAND

As deputy prime minister, Sechin began to pay more attention to Gazprom too. Since the New Year gas war with Ukraine in 2006, the company had been the Kremlin's main foreign policy tool. Putin essentially ran the company, and Sechin, as his trustee, was obliged to help him. Sechin complained bitterly about Gazprom CEO Alexei Miller. During visits abroad he would tell journalists that he had reached agreements galore, but nothing could be signed because Miller was asleep on the job.

Such criticism from Sechin probably would have toppled any other CEO, but Miller was also an old friend of Putin's. He too had worked in the St. Petersburg mayor's office in the 1990s. Moreover, he did not mind the fact that Putin made all Gazprom-related decisions. Putin viewed Gazprom not as a corporation but as a political tool and often did not care about the economic consequences of his actions.

Sechin, meanwhile, took his fight against the "wrong" oligarchs (those who had profited in the 1990s) to a new level. The year 2009 saw the worst industrial accident in post-Soviet Russia, at the Sayano-Shushenskaya hydropower plant. Seventy-five people died. Sechin arrived on the scene to find out what had happened and speak to relatives of the victims. There he uttered a memorable phrase. Pointing to a crowd of locals who had just buried their loved ones, Sechin said: "Give them everything." This meant that the owner of the plant had to bear full responsibility for the payment of compensation to the victims.

Later, Sechin headed the commission for the post-accident cleanup operation and reached the conclusion that the blame for everything lay with his longtime rival Anatoly Chubais, the architect of Yeltsin's privatization, which Sechin considered to have been unfair. It was Chubais who, at Putin's behest, had reformed the Russian power industry and eliminated the state-owned electric power monopoly RAO UES in 2008. Sechin decided to bring it back to life. He took charge of Inter RAO, the largest splinter of the former state-owned corporation, and began reassembling the pieces, undoing Chubais's liberal reforms.

The chairman of the board of directors of the disbanded RAO UES had been Alexander Voloshin, the former head of the presidential administration and the former boss and longtime enemy of Sechin. In 2003, during the Yukos affair, it was Sechin who had effectively brought about Voloshin's resignation. And after the 2008 crisis, the fortified Sechin declared war on the remnants of the Family and managed to get the better of Voloshin, Deripaska, Tanya and Valya, and even Medvedev.

Outwardly, it looked like a corporate conflict inside Norilsk Nickel, the largest steel company in the world. Until 2008 its major shareholders had been Vladimir Potanin, a former Russian deputy prime minister in the Yeltsin era and the architect of the loans-for-shares scheme, and his longtime partner Mikhail Prokhorov. On the eve of the crisis the partners decided to divorce—Prokhorov sold his stake to Oleg Deripaska, the aluminum king and son-in-law of Valya, who in turn was the son-in-law of Boris Yeltsin. The company's founder, Vladimir Potanin, lost control, and the new chairman of the board of directors was now Voloshin, who represented the interests of

Deripaska. It was then that Potanin turned to Sechin as the only force able to protect him from the resurgent Family.

And Sechin delivered. First, he helped the head of the Federal Tourism Agency, Vladimir Strzhalkovsky, become Norilsk Nickel's new CEO. It was a low-profile appointment, but Strzhalkovsky was another of Putin's St. Petersburg friends, something that no one else in the company, including Potanin, Deripaska, and Voloshin, could boast. Then in 2010, during the hot phase of the conflict, Sechin and Potanin connived to eject Voloshin from the board of directors. Voloshin had the support of President Medvedev, but that only postponed the inevitable.

At an extraordinary board meeting Voloshin was reinstated. But three months later he was gone again. Sechin had proved more durable. The combined force of Medvedev, Voloshin, Deripaska, and the Yumashevs, with their ties to the Family, could not beat him. The business community was disheartened, because these events clearly demonstrated that President Medvedev was not in control, and not even second in command. That position was occupied by Sechin.

THE BATTLE OF MOSCOW

In Medvedev's presence, Sechin always behaved impeccably, but he never missed an opportunity to humiliate Medvedev by proxy. The most scandalous public clash between Medvedev and Sechin took place in autumn 2010. On the surface, Sechin had nothing to do with it. The challenge to the president appeared to come from a third party—Yuri Luzhkov, the perennial mayor of Moscow and a veteran of Russian politics. However, the old dog Luzhkov never would have dared go against the president had he not been sure that he was immune from retribution. Sechin persuaded Luzhkov that his administrative clout outweighed Medvedev's. Plus, Putin would not let the president lay a finger on Luzhkov.

Mayor of Moscow since 1992, Luzhkov had supported Yeltsin during the constitutional crisis of 1993. In 1999 he had been sure that the presidency was his, but he had been undone by the Kremlin's black PR campaign.

Luzhkov himself recalls that conflict with Medvedev began in 2005, when the latter was the head of the presidential administration. He says that the trigger was the Kremlin's decision to raise wages for nurses across the country. On learning the news, Luzhkov immediately decided to raise the salaries of all Moscow health care workers—otherwise, he says, there would have been a serious imbalance. But Medvedev took offense. "What are you doing? You've reduced all the effects of our reforms to nothing," Medvedev allegedly shouted.

The next conflict Luzhkov recalls happened when Medvedev was already president. In November 2008 the mayor of Moscow gave an interview with TV host Vladimir Pozner in which he said that he believed that Moscow's mayor should be elected by popular vote, not appointed by the president (although he admits that after the Beslan tragedy in 2004 he supported Putin's decision to abolish gubernatorial elections).

The interview had some interesting moments. For instance, Luzhkov expressed support for Medvedev's (in reality Putin's) idea to lengthen the president's term. And he unexpectedly mentioned Crimea and Sevastopol: "Sevastopol has never belonged to Ukraine. . . . Crimea was given to Ukraine by the stroke of a pen . . . and it pains the heart of every Russian," lamented Luzhkov. Back then it was not a mainstream issue in Russian society and was raised only occasionally by Luzhkov, Sechin, and a few others. Therefore, no one paid attention, and people remembered only his critical comments about the lack of mayoral elections.

President Medvedev responded nervously to what he heard. Luzhkov irritated him, and he wanted to show who was in charge. "Anyone who disagrees can go," said Medvedev the following day. It was a clear sign that Luzhkov should put up or shut up.

Luzhkov remembers that he asked his family (his wife, Yelena Baturina, the richest woman in Russia, and their two daughters) for advice: "What shall I do? Just swallow it? Pretend nothing's happened?"

Having been persuaded not to bow to Medvedev, he wrote a mocking letter of resignation in which he accused Medvedev of returning to 1937 and the Stalinist repression of dissidents. Aware that dismissing Luzhkov for having called for democratic elections would be a mistake, Medvedev did not accept his resignation.

The next round came about, peculiarly enough, because of Stalin himself. In 2010 the Moscow authorities were preparing for the sixty-fifth anniversary of the Soviet victory in the Great Patriotic War. Luzhkov decided that Stalin's portrait should be on display.

"Stalin's role was great. He was one of the most powerful and decisive factors. It was Stalin who managed the country's resources and oversaw its strategy. The first period of the war was his fault, but the second was his triumph. He cannot be erased from history. Our soldiers went into battle under the banner 'For the Motherland! For Stalin!'" says Luzhkov. But the presidential administration was strongly opposed, and Medvedev banned the display of Stalin's image.

"It was insane," seethes Luzhkov to this day. "So I decided to create Stalin Alley on Poklonnaya Hill [in Moscow's Victory Park]."

Luzhkov claims that he is no Stalinist: "[Stalin] was responsible for 50 million deaths. The most hideous crime on his black conscience was the murder of 20 million kulaks—the country's strongest economic managers." Not for nothing does Luzhkov use the term "strong economic manager," since throughout his eighteen-year tenure as mayor of Moscow that was how the press described him. And he doesn't see any contradiction in his own words.

The denouement came in summer 2010. Central Russia suffered a drought, while forest and peat fires were raging around Moscow. In mid-August acrid smog enveloped the capital, causing panic. It was then that state news channels cited an anonymous source inside the presidential administration ("anonymous source" was a euphemism for Natalya Timakova), asking why the mayor was on vacation in the Austrian Alps while Muscovites were practically choking to death.

Luzhkov returned, offended and outraged. In an interview with the pro-Luzhkov Moscow TV station TVTs he said: "I got a kick in the teeth from the administration. 'He's back,' they're saying, 'but late.' Six days Comrade Mayor was on holiday." He responded to the "anonymous" source with an "anonymous" article in the newspaper *Moskovsky Komsomolets*. The text was credited to a certain Yuri Kovelitsyn, but everyone knew that the real author was Luzhkov. In it, he openly accused President Medvedev of an anti-Putin conspiracy:

> The Kremlin's persecution of the mayor of Moscow has gone far beyond the boundaries of political decency. . . . Replacing the head of Moscow, who is loyal to the prime minister and has worked with him to stabilize not only the capital, but Russia as a whole, would open the door to a "color revolution," whose deceptive euphoria could lead the Russian people astray.

> There are those in Russia who want to use their intellectual and financial capacity to exploit any cataclysm. They are courting Medvedev and inciting him against his own political mentor and pillars of support, one of which is the mayor of Moscow.

Medvedev was stunned by Luzhkov's arrogance. He knew that the mayor would not have behaved so provocatively had he not believed he had complete impunity—and such a feeling of impunity could only have been instilled by Sechin.

Technically speaking, Medvedev could have fired Luzhkov at any moment. No regional governor (which the mayor of Moscow officially was) had ever been dismissed by the president due to "loss of confidence," but the law did not prevent it. There was also the issue of explaining to Putin why the experienced and popular mayor had to be sacked. Putin did not like Luzhkov, but as president he had kept him on, since he believed that getting rid of Luzhkov would have provoked a backlash among Muscovites. The only way to convince Putin that Luzhkov had to go was to show that Moscow's love for the mayor was skin-deep.

Luzhkov now felt the full force of the propaganda power of NTV—the channel that ten years earlier had supported him and Yevgeny Primakov against the Family's very own Vladimir Putin. NTV broadcast two exposé documentaries: *Cap in Hand* (about Luzhkov himself, who always wore a cap) and *Dear Yelena* (about his wife).

Luzhkov was then summoned by the head of the presidential administration, Sergei Naryshkin, who suggested that he write a letter of resignation. Luzhkov promised to think about it and again went on vacation (again to the Austrian Alps) to celebrate his birthday. "It is clear that Yuri Mikhailovich [Luzhkov] is going through a difficult period in his life, and he needs time to think," an "anonymous source" in the Kremlin told news agencies.

On vacation Luzhkov wrote to Medvedev, accusing him and his administration of an "informational terror campaign" and (once more) of attempting to return to 1937 through the introduction of censorship. An example of such censorship, in Luzhkov's eyes, was the fact that the Kremlin had blocked a pro-Luzhkov documentary on TVTs (the fact that he had his own puppet TV channel seemed quite democratic to him).

In his letter Luzhkov referred to the "powerful protests" in support of him that would ensue. They turned out to be pie in the sky. Returning from vacation on September 27, Luzhkov told reporters that he had no plans to resign. Medvedev at the time was on a visit to China, but the next morning, September 28, a decree was published on Medvedev's official website announcing that Luzhkov had been "removed from office due to loss of trust." A couple of days later Putin weighed in, saying that Luzhkov should not have sought to undermine Medvedev. As a result, Medvedev was entitled to fire him.

Today Luzhkov says that the real cause of his dismissal was his unwillingness to back Medvedev for a second presidential term. He alleges that in February 2010 he was approached by a Medvedev emissary who asked the mayor if he would support Medvedev. Luzhkov said no.

He draws a parallel with another incident eleven years earlier. In February 1999 he was allegedly asked by Boris Berezovsky to become the Family's presidential candidate. Luzhkov says he refused because he wanted to undo the loans-for-shares scheme. However, according to the Family, Luzhkov thought that he was a shoo-in for the presidency and did not need the support of the weak Kremlin.

Medvedev's entourage denies ever asking for Luzhkov's support, since the mayor of Moscow was too closely linked to Medvedev's nemesis, Igor Sechin.

Luzhkov is absolutely right about one thing: in 2010 Medvedev did indeed begin to harbor ambitions for a second term as president. Sechin would have to nip them in the bud.

CHAPTER 12

IN WHICH RUSSIAN PRINCESS TATYANA YUMASHEVA COMES UP WITH A NEW DEMOCRATIC PARTY

No one has ever described Tatyana Borisovna Yumasheva as a princess, for she is nothing like a Disney heroine. In some ways Tanya does, however, resemble a British royal, such as Lady Di, Princess Anne, or even Camilla, Duchess of Cornwall: radiant smile, cold eyes, an overwhelming feeling of responsibility for one's family and reputation.

Yumasheva considers herself the keeper of her father's legacy. She fights to defend his name, his memory, his greatness. Any criticism of her father, Boris Yeltsin, she takes personally. She defends and greatly embellishes his view of what happened in the 1990s. Tanya (like her mother, Naina) says that Yeltsin did not drink alcohol. They remember him as a semi-mythical creature, a demigod, and believe all other versions to be nothing but lies and slander.

Yumasheva sees her father as a model of democracy and the 1990s a time of freedom. She believes herself to be a true democrat—she is her father's daughter, after all. For her, criticism of the 1990s tramples the sacred spirit of liberty and democracy. Her views and liberal values are so mixed up that for her Yeltsin is *democracy. For the sake of fairness, however, the entire Russian political elite was mixed up in the 1990s. In 1996, the year Yeltsin was reelected, Russian democrats mistook democracy for eternal rule by democrats.*

Yumasheva wanted to be a politician herself, and knows that she could have been. She has enough experience and charisma. But it was not to be. Instead she had to bear the burden of being the president's daughter. She sacrificed her own personal political ambitions for his and her family's sake. It was her choice—or at least she has convinced herself that it was.

THE FAMILY RETURNS

Boris Yeltsin, the first president of Russia, died in April 2007, before the end of Putin's second term and the start of "Operation Successor." It was then that the Family reentered big politics. Ever since Yeltsin's retirement the Family had kept out of the spotlight. The public had forgotten all about Tatyana Yumasheva and Valentin Yumashev.

After getting married in November 2001, Tanya and Valya disappeared for almost a decade. They did not give interviews or appear in the news. The journalists who had been on first-name terms with them were also gone. The anti-Yeltsin NTV was smashed in spring 2001, and its general director, Yevgeny Kiselyov, left for Ukraine.

Tatiana Yumasheva observed "Operation Successor" from the sidelines, but it was clear where her sympathies lay. The nerve center of Dmitry Medvedev's headquarters was Alexander Voloshin, a close friend and the last head of Yeltsin's administration, the man who had handed power to Putin in 2000. No one said it out loud, but many had the feeling that the Family was making a comeback. For a start, Medvedev lived at Yeltsin's former residence, in the neighborhood Gorki-9 (while Putin, as president, had chosen to live at Novo-Ogaryovo, the former residence of Gorbachev). That meant that the new president's neighbors were the Yumashevs, whose dacha in Gorki-10 was completed after Yeltsin's death.

On assuming office in 2000, Putin signed a decree entitled "Guarantees for Retired Presidents of the Russian Federation and Members of Their Family," permanently assigning the Gorki-9 residence to Yeltsin as one of the provisions. The decree did not mention any guarantees of immunity from prosecution. However, there was a tacit agreement that Yeltsin's family would refrain from political activity while Putin was president and that the Kremlin's new occupants would respect the Family's possessions. In the broader sense, the Family included not only Tanya and Valya but also Valya's son-in-law Oleg Deripaska, owner of the world's largest aluminum company,

RUSAL, and Roman Abramovich, not technically a member but nevertheless a close friend of the Family's.

When Medvedev became president, the Yeltsin family not only moved from Gorki-9 to Gorki-10 but also began to ruminate that perhaps some of the commitments of yesteryear no longer applied. On December 3, 2009, ten years after the first "Operation Successor," Yumasheva broke her silence, giving an interview to *Medved* magazine. She also started blogging, promising to write about weight loss and raising children. But within a week she was discussing politics.

On December 23 she wrote a detailed account of why her father had chosen Putin as his successor—because he was the best of a bad lot. The pro-democracy "liberals" (Chubais, Nemtsov, Chernomyrdin) had no chance of being elected, while Luzhkov and Primakov were dangerous, since they represented the previous generation of politicians who might restore the Soviet Union.

The next day Tanya went further, writing about the obligations that the Family and Putin had assumed during the transfer of power. "Did we stipulate living conditions? Staffing and economic policy? Were there agreements, written or unwritten? No. Apart from the phrase 'Take care of Russia,' Dad requested nothing from Vladimir Vladimirovich [Putin]. Nothing about family and relatives, or about policy, or about keeping on Dad's favorite members of staff. It's obvious to everyone that [Putin] had carte blanche when it came to staffing policy and future strategy. I believe it was right for the first president [Yeltsin] to step aside."

Although the blog was not critical of Putin, was it really about the Yeltsin-Putin succession? Or was Yumasheva in fact advising former president Vladimir Putin not to interfere in the new president's affairs?

Though she had chosen her words carefully, they were interpreted by many as a challenge to the ideology that the Putinist propaganda had crafted over the years. In 2007 state television often juxtaposed the new Russia with the "wild nineties" (NTV was now pro-Kremlin, but ironically still anti-Yeltsin). Putin had not only "lifted Russia from its knees" (i.e., restored its global prestige) but also ended the chaos and lawlessness that had prevailed under Yeltsin. That was the leitmotif of the 2007 parliamentary elections.

Yumasheva began to blog more frequently, the purpose seemingly being to rehabilitate her father's, her husband's, and her own good name and present an alternative version of the "wild nineties."

However, that was just at first glance. The end of the era of silence, even if it came via a modest blog, said only one thing: Yumasheva was reemerging as a public figure. She wanted to remind the public of her existence while repeatedly stressing that she had no intention of entering politics, thereby attracting politics to come to her. Her circle of friends talked only about Medvedev's chances of escaping Putin's custody and becoming a real president. Some said he had no chance, as the young president could not even appoint his own chief of staff and security heads. Putin, they said, would never allow his successor to take off the flotation device and start swimming for himself. Yumasheva herself held this view. She even placed a bet with friends (the stakes being a few crates of champagne) that Putin would return in four years. However, most in the Yumashevs' circle, including a few billionaires, believed that Medvedev was truly capable of something and would not give in so easily. Their argument was simple: no one in the history of Russia had ever given up power voluntarily, and Medvedev would not be the first.

The *siloviki* around Putin, of course, paid close attention to the reactivation of Tanya and Valya, supplying Putin, now prime minister, with regular reports on the Family's political ambitions and supposed machinations. Putin remained silent.

A NEW PARTY

A year before the 2011 parliamentary elections, Dmitry Medvedev came up with the idea to create his own party: a center-right platform to unite Russia's middle class and champion liberal reform. A previous entity with a similar agenda, the Union of Right Forces, had received 8.5 percent of the vote in the 1999 parliamentary election, but then in 2007 got less than 1 percent of the vote, failing to enter the Duma and ceasing to exist thereafter.

The idea of a new right-wing liberal party was gaining ground and frequently floated by Anatoly Chubais, the chief strategist of the Russian liberals and architect of the economic reforms of the 1990s, who under Putin had become head of the state energy company RAO UES, and Alexander Voloshin, former chief of staff of both Yeltsin and Putin, who had resigned in 2003 to chair the board of directors of that selfsame RAO UES.

By 2009 Chubais and Voloshin had completed their reform of the Russian energy sector, having transferred it into private hands and disbanded their own company. Both were seriously pondering a return to politics, albeit cautiously. In winter 2010 the media-shy Alexander Voloshin had become more public, opening an office in the former building of the Red October chocolate factory.

The location was symbolic—an island in the Moscow River directly opposite the Kremlin. It was here in the seventeenth century that one of Russian history's most infamous mutineers, Stepan Razin, was executed. At the beginning of the twentieth century, at the foot of Bolshoi Kamenny Bridge, a grand building was constructed on the waterfront for the elite of the new Bolshevik government. In the 1930s most of its tenants were purged—almost every night a police van came by to pick up one or more "enemies of the people." Fast-forward to the twenty-first century, when it was now the most fashionable area of the new Moscow. The red brick buildings of the former chocolate factory were inhabited by IT start-ups, restaurants, modern art galleries, and Russia's only independent TV channel, TV Rain, making it the capital's most freethinking quarter. Oddly enough, it was now the new part-time home of Alexander Voloshin. Sitting across the river from the Kremlin, he began scheduling appointments with popular bloggers, journalists, and writers to find out their views about the future of Russian politics, the prospects for a new liberal party, and who could and would join it.

Voloshin asked these questions so bluntly that his interlocutors got the feeling that it was not his own initiative, or even that of the notorious Family—new blogger Tanya and her husband, Valya. Voloshin never said so, but everyone got the impression that he had received a special assignment from President Medvedev.

A couple of months later the liberal Moscow crowd was buzzing. Almost all had had a meeting with Putin's former (and now Medvedev's secret) éminence grise. They spun yarns about how Tatyana Yumasheva had been spotted scribbling the new party's electoral list on a restaurant napkin. No one yet knew who the face of this new liberal party would be, since its creators were keeping their cards close to their chest. But everyone knew the cards were there.

The Yumashevs were indeed directly linked to the new project. Medvedev had summoned Valentin Yumashev to the Kremlin to ask him to help with recruitment policy. Yumashev liked the idea very much and proposed that the party should not have one specific leader, but rather a dozen people who would promote the party throughout the country. Medvedev disagreed. He thought it needed a figurehead.

SERFDOM

Thanks to President Medvedev, liberalism was suddenly in fashion. Tired of being Putin's faceless shadow, the new president was eager to make his mark as an enlightened figure. Having taken some tentative first steps, he believed that the time was ripe for an all-out PR campaign. So it was that in 2011 Medvedev organized a conference in St. Petersburg devoted to the 150th anniversary of the abolition of serfdom in Russia.

In the minds of Medvedev and his entourage, the conference and the president's speech were to be the starting point of his new political career.

"History has shown that Alexander II was right, not Nicholas I or Stalin," the president told the audience, adding that he considered himself the successor of the "tsar liberator"—Alexander II, who abolished serfdom in 1861. The audience gasped. Many understood "Nicholas I or Stalin" as code for Putin. Medvedev had always been careful not to publicly confront Putin, but now he was clearly heading that way.

There was less than a year to go before the next parliamentary election, and Medvedev's team was already targeting it. The campaign strategy was drawn up by none other than Vladislav Surkov, Putin's onetime political strategist.

Medvedev did not immediately trust Surkov, remembering that he had backed Sergei Ivanov to succeed Putin. For a long time Medvedev believed that Surkov was simply Putin's henchman. But Voloshin, who considered Surkov his disciple, persuaded the president otherwise, and in 2010 Medvedev assigned Surkov the task of coming up with a new party that could become a liberal counterweight to Surkov's other creation, United Russia.

Surkov believed he knew how Medvedev should act to secure a second term. To him, it was obvious there was no prior agreement between Putin and Medvedev dating back to 2007, when they had changed places. It had to be handled in such a way that Putin would not object to another Medvedev term. Medvedev had to demonstrate that he was a popular national leader and better adapted to the realities of the new world.

At that time Revolution 2.0 was in full swing. Oppositionists in the Arab world were overthrowing regimes, aided by Facebook and Twitter. To survive in the new environment, modern leaders had to know how to harness the power of social media for their own benefit. Medvedev, with his Moscow hipster image, fit the bill. He used Facebook, Twitter, and Instagram, posting pictures of his cat and demonstrating to Putin that he was an effective manager with his finger on the pulse of society and better placed than his predecessor to preempt a Twitter revolution in Russia.

Getting a million followers online was no problem for Medvedev. But creating a party required more tact. In order not to alarm United Russia and Putin's entourage, Medvedev explained to them that it was for their own good. But the real goal was to gently push them to the periphery.

Last but not least, to run for a second term Medvedev needed a strong group of followers, for electoral support and to provide graphic proof that he was in control.

COME SEPTEMBER

Surkov's plans ran into an unexpected obstacle: his client, Medvedev, was still bent on creating the image of a liberal, modern Western leader. Believing he was friends with the US president, Medvedev desperately wanted to be the Russian Obama—the epitome of the young, stylish leader.

In March 2011 Medvedev and Obama had to reach an agreement on what to do about Libya. The two leaders had similar feelings. Both deeply disliked the Libyan regime and found Muammar Gaddafi repulsive. Both had met the Libyan leader and concluded that he had lost touch with reality. Even his own son, Seif al-Islam, a secular young man who frequently haunted fashionable Moscow nightclubs in the company of Russian oligarchs and models, was ashamed of his father, who never parted company with his traditional Bedouin tent, even on trips abroad.

Medvedev and Obama were no less hostile to Nicolas Sarkozy, the main instigator of the anti-Libyan coalition. Everyone knew that the French president's election campaign had been partly funded by Gaddafi, yet that only spurred Sarkozy into showing the world that he was not in Tripoli's pocket, calling for the immediate bombing of Libya. Medvedev was loath to help Sarkozy, especially given the unpleasant memories of their joint settlement of the Georgian-Ossetian conflict in 2008. However, siding with Gaddafi would be even uglier. In the end, Obama and Medvedev agreed that they would not interfere with Sarkozy's efforts to oust the Libyan leader.

Libya's internal politics were of little interest to Medvedev. It was all about cultivating the right image inside Russia. His public speeches were meticulously prepared, and all mentions in the news and social media were counted and assessed. Who needed an old, senile Libyan dictator? Discussing the prospects of the Libyan operation, he glanced through the files on Russian-Libyan cooperation and concluded that Gaddafi never paid his debts and cadged new weapons on credit while giving nothing in return. The only major contract was with Russian Railways. Its head, Vladimir Yakunin, had always irritated Medvedev, so the president had no compunctions about sacrificing the deal. He cast aside Foreign Ministry pleas to veto the UN Security Council resolution for a no-fly zone over Libya. Russia abstained.

The next day Medvedev was surprised to see Putin on TV, speaking out on Libya. As prime minister, Putin rarely mentioned foreign policy. He ritually observed the constitutional norms, according to which foreign policy was the preserve of the head of state. But visiting a missile factory in Votkinsk in Central Russia, Putin described the UN resolution as "a medieval call for a crusade" and then delivered a thinly veiled reprimand to President Medvedev live on air: "What concerns me most is not the armed intervention itself—armed conflicts are nothing new and will likely continue for a long time, unfortunately. My main concern is the light-mindedness with which decisions to use force are taken in international affairs these days."

Medvedev was horrified. He really had blundered by not consulting Putin beforehand. But Putin's outspokenness was an unforgivable humiliation and demanded a response. The question was whether to do it privately or publicly. After reading online comments openly mocking him, Medvedev decided not to call Putin. Instead, having examined his schedule, Medvedev decided that his response would come that same day—during a visit to the OMON, Russia's special-purpose police unit. "It is entirely unacceptable to use expressions that effectively point the way to a clash of civilizations. The word 'crusade,' for instance. We must all remember that such language could make the situation even worse," he said didactically into the camera.

Russia's state news channels were aghast. What should they show? Could they possibly report that the "tandem" was split over Libya? TV bosses frantically rang the prime minister's and president's respective press secretaries. After a brief hesitation, Putin's office replied: "The head of state is responsible for foreign policy, so only his point of view should be reflected in state news broadcasts. Prime Minister Putin's statement should be forgotten."

But experienced players in Medvedev's camp knew that their man had made a huge mistake. Though Putin backed down, he did not forget.

The public squabble between the president and the prime minister was unprecedented. Relations between the Kremlin and the government had in fact been strained since 2008—the head of the presidential administration, Sergei Naryshkin, and the head of the government staff, Sergei Sobyanin, were not talking to each other—but Putin and Medvedev themselves never publicly demonstrated any hostility.

Whereas in the first years of Medvedev's presidency they found time to meet regularly and discuss all issues, their increasingly tight schedules and the silence between Naryshkin and Sobyanin meant that Russia's two leaders saw less and less of each other. As a result, by 2011 Putin and Medvedev met barely once a month. After the spat over Libya their advisers understood that the president and prime minister had to meet more often, otherwise things could end badly.

The tension was growing. Truce envoys from both camps tried to arrange more meetings to avoid misunderstandings and reckless action. Putin told them: "Don't worry, everything will be okay. Come September we'll do what we have to do, and everyone will breathe a sigh of relief." No one understood at the time what Putin meant by his reference to September.

A LIBERAL PARTY

By the end of March 2011 the minor blogging activity of Yeltsin's daughter had turned into a major historical project entitled "20 Years Ago." Every day Tatiana Yumasheva published her own reenactments of the collapse of the Soviet Union and its replacement by the new democratic Russia. The main point—that the end of authoritarianism had been a triumph of liberal ideas—penetrated every word. The symbol of democracy was, of course, her father, Boris Yeltsin. Clearly such a large-scale effort was not the work of one person. Tatyana Yumasheva had assembled a vast team of historians and journalists to contribute to her blog. Alongside that, she was laying the groundwork for a new liberal party and casting around for a leader.

Surkov decided to base the future party on Right Cause—a synthetic project built in 2008 on the debris of the former liberal party Union of Right Forces, which had dissolved in 2007 after failing to win any seats in the State Duma. However, the rump party could not be led by Medvedev himself, since it had little political weight. Therefore, a figure had to be found who would at once inspire confidence in the liberal electorate and prepare the ground for a second Medvedev term. The obvious candidates were past and present pro-democracy types in the government: finance minister Alexei Kudrin, first deputy prime minister Igor Shuvalov, and former economics minister and now Sberbank head German Gref.

Medvedev talked to each of them personally. The first was Gref, who refused. He was tired of the civil service after seven years as a minister and was happy with his newfound freedom at Sberbank. He was uninterested in oddball ventures.

Next up was Kudrin. The prospect of leading a new liberal party seemed enticing. However, he began to lay out his own terms and conditions. "It's all good and interesting," insiders paraphrase Kudrin's conversation with Medvedev, "but I don't want the party to be controlled by Surkov."

"You won't have time to change anything, I'm afraid," Medvedev allegedly replied.

"Well, so be it. I'm not going to lead a fake party," said Kudrin, according to his aides.

However, he did not deliver a final no until he had slept on it and, of course, consulted with Putin. The prime minister put an end to Kudrin's reflections: "We need to prepare for the elections. The government needs you. I personally ask that you stay on board. Your departure would weaken everyone," said Putin.

Kudrin had not expected such a gushing response and could not now defy the prime minister. So he rejected Medvedev's proposal. The president was deeply offended.

Medvedev's next candidate was Igor Shuvalov. He too failed to say yes (also on the advice of Putin). Medvedev was again offended—more than that, he was furious. It was becoming increasingly clear that none of the liberals in power dared to openly express support for him (although he himself had not yet risked declaring his ambitions) or to lead a new liberal party. With time running out before the parliamentary elections, the liberal idea looked doomed.

Meanwhile, Putin, who already had the backing of the conservative United Russia Party, suddenly got a taste for political engineering. His staff, headed by Vyacheslav Volodin, launched a party-building exercise of their own—and more successfully than Medvedev and Surkov at that. Ever since Surkov had aligned himself with Medvedev, Putin needed a "new Surkov," which he had found in Volodin.

Wanting to please his boss, Volodin came up with a new political project entitled People's Front. It was less a party than an alliance of different social organizations united around Putin. Rank-and-file members of United Russia were perplexed: why the need for a second structure duplicating the party? When they put this question to the long-standing head of the presidential administration, Surkov simply shrugged: the People's Front had nothing to do with him, and he resented the fact that Volodin had dared to trespass on his territory. Party building was his domain. But there was nothing he could do about it, since Volodin was acting on behalf of Prime Minister Putin. Surkov's only consolation was that the People's Front project was a crude and clumsy construction.

At first glance, the organization made no political sense other than to demonstrate to Medvedev that all efforts to create a new liberal party were futile. Society was well and truly on Putin's side, judging by news reports, which had begun to resemble Soviet newsreel footage of rooms full of workers and rural laborers giving the leader a standing ovation (even though it looked artificial and phony, like clunky propaganda). Trade unions across the country scrambled to join Putin's People's Front (though not without the odd scandal along the way), while the president's team could not even muster a handful of intellectuals able and willing to lead a Medvedev-affiliated party.

A NEW FACE

Luck finally smiled on Surkov. Instead of looking for a politician, he turned his gaze on big business. His eye was caught by Mikhail Prokhorov, once Russia's richest man and former co-owner of Norilsk Nickel, who had successfully sold his stake on the eve of the 2008 crisis, earning a reputation for having the best business acumen in Russia.

Rich and somewhat arrogant, this unmarried tycoon led a wanton existence. In 2009 he bought the New Jersey Nets basketball team and moved them to Brooklyn, where he was a key investor in the arena built for them there (Barclays Center) and became something of a celebrity in the sports world. But he hasn't always been that lucky. In January 2007 he had been arrested by French police at the Courchevel ski resort on suspicion of pimping, since he had brought with him too many models. It was hard to think of a less electable person. But Surkov discovered that Prokhorov had a great enthusiasm for the project. Bored with business, the oligarch plunged headfirst into the new venture and began spending money on the party-building enterprise.

Later, Prokhorov said that Surkov and Medvedev had tried to use him to create a powerful party, while planning all along to ditch him at the last minute to enable Medvedev to turn the party into a platform from which to run for a second term. They calculated that Prokhorov would invest money and then, when the time came, dutifully step aside.

In the first two months Prokhorov did indeed invest around $20 million in Right Cause and brought in a few celebrities, including Alla Pugacheva, Russia's best-known singer since the days of Leonid Brezhnev. Never previously a member of any party, she was now suddenly supporting Prokhorov. It was rumored that the aging star agreed to a generous salary ($20,000 per month) for the occasional appearance at party congresses to sing the party anthem.

But the independent-minded Prokhorov soon ran into problems with Surkov. The former CEO of Norilsk Nickel was loath to coordinate every step with the presidential administration. The feeling was mutual. Prokhorov's management style irritated Surkov. The latter was used to total control and a hands-on approach to party building. He was hurt that his protégé Vyacheslav Volodin had flown the nest without looking back, and he would not allow his new offspring, Mikhail Prokhorov, to do the same.

In early September Surkov put forward a number of conditions, one of which was that Prokhorov had to remove Yevgeny Roizman, a popular antidrug campaigner in the Urals, from the party list. The demand was excessive, since Prokhorov had repeatedly stated publicly that Roizman would be listed. To bow to the Kremlin meant to go back on his word.

It was then that Surkov tried to persuade Medvedev that Prokhorov was uncontrollable and, hence, unsuitable. The president did not demur, whereupon Surkov's spin-doctoring weapons, which had been helping Prokhorov to build the new party, were now turned against the oligarch.

The operation to seize control of the party had already been worked out in detail by Surkov and practiced on smaller parties. On the eve of Right Cause's next congress, opponents of Prokhorov persuaded the party committee to raise the issue of the oligarch's resignation. A significant number of heads of the party's regional branches had been recruited in advance and were ready to carry out any instruction from the presidential administration. On the second day the party split in two. Prokhorov's opponents met in Moscow's World Trade Center on Krasnaya Presnya (hastily rented by the presidential administration), where they formally deposed the billionaire leader.

Meanwhile, Prokhorov's supporters, including Alla Pugacheva, gathered in the building of the Academy of Sciences (which had been rented by the oligarch). Prokhorov went onstage and told his audience and the cameras that he would fight. He accused Surkov personally of raiding the party and said that he would not tolerate any more Byzantine politics. However, instead of fighting, the very next day he went on vacation to Turkey and was not seen for a month.

Surkov was adamant that it was not the end of the liberal project—he had simply gotten rid of an unyielding leader who now needed replacing. But he had miscalculated. The fallout was so toxic that Medvedev, Voloshin, and the Yumashevs' year-old liberal project was no more. Right Cause effectively ceased to exist. Prokhorov's replacements were cartoon figures hired by Surkov to create the appearance of political activity. In the end, the party that was supposed to unite all of Russia's liberals came in last in the 2011 parliamentary elections.

The collapse of this powerful right-wing pro-democracy party was observed by one man in particular. Prime Minister Putin, sitting in his residence, watched Prokhorov's speech at the Academy of Sciences and chortled. "Serves you right!" he said, mentally addressing Surkov. "Prefer dealing with weaklings? Can't handle a real fight?" The fact that the president's team, even with all the vast resources available to it, could not create a party to support him was proof that Medvedev was not ready for the greater challenge ahead.

WAR BREAKS OUT

Medvedev had no bitter feelings about Libya, but Putin was still seething. For him, it was war. He had been personally acquainted with Gaddafi, who had visited Moscow, pitched his Bedouin tent right inside the Kremlin, and accompanied Putin to a concert by French singer Mireille Mathieu. Gaddafi's talks with Putin had been solely about the Americans, whose true goal, Gaddafi said, was to kill the Libyan leader and establish world domination. He praised Putin's resistance to Washington.

For Putin, Medvedev's decision not to veto the UN's anti-Libyan resolution was an unforgivable act of weakness. In the aftermath Putin received a string of reports from the Foreign Ministry and the SVR (the Foreign Intelligence Service) about what Russia stood to lose from betraying Gaddafi. Until then, no one in Putin's entourage had dared to make any accusations against Medvedev, but now the taboo was lifted. "Medvedev betrayed Libya. He'll betray you as well," they whispered in the prime minister's ear.

Putin became increasingly irate. On the issue of Libya, he began to forget that foreign policy was the prerogative of the president: "They [NATO] talked about a no-fly zone, so why are Gaddafi's palaces being bombed every night? They say they don't want to kill him, so why are they bombing him? What are they trying to do? Scare the mice?" he said on television.[1]

When Gaddafi was finally killed, Putin was apoplectic. Above all, he resented the perfidy of the West. As an anti-Western pariah, the Libyan leader had headed a strong regime. The problems began only when he made concessions, confessed his sins, and paid compensation to the relatives of the victims of the Lockerbie bombing. Sanctions were lifted and he even attended the G8 summit in 2009 at L'Aquila in Italy (as chairman of the African Union), where he shook hands with Barack Obama. However, his obedience and tractability were soon to be punished. At the very moment when Gaddafi came in from the cold and put his trust in the West, he was stabbed in the back. When he was a pariah, no one had touched him. But as soon as he opened up, he was not only overthrown but killed in the street like a mangy old cur.

Putin laid part of the blame for Gaddafi's murder on Medvedev, since Medvedev had been promised by his Western partners that they would simply establish a no-fly zone over Libya to prevent the dictator from bombing rebel positions. And he had gullibly believed them.

Observing Medvedev and Surkov's fascination with the US-controlled Twitter and Facebook, the *siloviki* around Putin suddenly had a discomfiting thought: What if all this social media hippie nonsense was not to *prevent* a "color revolution" but to *prepare* for one? Could it be the start of an American plan to do to Russia's political elite what had been done to Libya's?

In late summer Putin invited Medvedev on a fishing trip. They went to the Zhitnoe resort near Astrakhan, which had originally been built for the Russian defense minister. They fished for three days and showed their catch to reporters. Both looked content. The president believed that the prime minister no longer harbored a grudge. The "tandem" was strong.

But it was during that fishing trip that Putin suggested to Medvedev that it would be better if he relinquished the presidency. "The global situation is complex, Dima. You could end up losing Russia," is how the fateful conversation went, according to accounts.

"But why?" asked Medvedev, confused. "Why will I lose Russia?"

"Because the world is mixed up, Dima. Gaddafi thought he would never lose Libya, but the Americans tricked him," Putin reportedly explained. "In 2008 I was Russia's number one politician. I could have gotten reelected, but the constitution didn't allow it. I played by the rules and handed power to you. But we agreed that when the day came, we'd sit down and decide what to do next. And now the day has come. I'm still the number one politician, you're in second place. The law allows both of us to run for the presidency. You're younger, that's a plus. I'm more experienced, that's a plus for me. There's one key difference—my poll numbers are higher. I have the People's Front behind me. The ruling party in any country always nominates the more popular candidate. We'll be stronger if we go to the polls as one team. You'll be prime minister like I am now. And then you'll have another chance to return to the Kremlin."

Medvedev had no reply.

The denouement came quickly. In the run-up to United Russia's next congress, everyone was expecting an earth-shattering statement. But no one knew exactly what it would be, not even Medvedev's aides. On September 24 the congress met at Luzhniki Stadium in the early morning, a few hours before the day's events were due to start. Warm-up guys traversed the arena, getting everyone to practice chanting "Pu-tin! Pu-tin!" and (just in case) "Med-ve-dev! Med-ve-dev!"

Putin spoke first. He said enigmatically that "Dmitry Anatolievich [Medvedev] has some suggestions for the future configuration of power" and then gave the floor to the president. Medvedev gave a long speech, summing up his presidency, and then proposed Putin as the next head of state. The audience erupted in applause and well-rehearsed chants.

Next Medvedev said, "This applause gives me the right to refrain from further elaborating on Vladimir Putin's experience and authority. A few more words on this subject. I was always asked when we would decide, when we would tell people, and sometimes Vladimir Putin and I were asked: 'Have you two fought?' I want to fully confirm what I just said. What we are proposing to the congress is a deeply thought-through decision. And even more, we already discussed this scenario back when we first formed a friendly alliance."[2]

Medvedev's team was inconsolable. "No reason to rejoice," tweeted Medvedev's closest aide, Arkady Dvorkovich.

CHAPTER 13

IN WHICH OPPOSITION LEADER ALEXEI NAVALNY THINKS HE CAN LEAD THE PEOPLE TO THE KREMLIN

Alexei Navalny is an alien. At first glance he looks like an ordinary person, and watching him walk the streets or ride public transport, you might think he is an ordinary man. In short, he does everything that ordinary people do and which top government officials and superstars do not. But appearances are deceptive. Navalny wears a human mask for the same reason an extraterrestrial in a sci-fi film does, to hide his real identity—that of a politician.

Navalny's life is hard. The state machine is out to get him, and he has to deal with that somehow. For instance, he does not drive, for fear that a "provocateur" might jump in front of his car and be hurt or killed, whereupon he could be prosecuted.

Navalny is certainly aware that he is a superstar. Jail is perhaps the last place Putin wants him to be, since that would make him a martyr and increase his popularity. Navalny understands his exclusivity. He is probably the only real politician out of Russia's 143 million inhabitants.

The likes of Putin, Sechin, Kudrin, and Chechen leader Ramzan Kadyrov are politicians of a different sort. They never aspired to government or dreamed of a political career. They never intended to sacrifice everything for the sake of power. It simply fell into their hands. Some (though not Kadyrov) perhaps even regret that they were forced to swap a normal life for the trappings of high office.

Navalny, though, is unique: he made a conscious choice. As yet he has no power, and may never have. But he has certainly sacrificed the chance to lead a normal life, although he describes it as an opportunity to change Russia for the better.

If Russia had an open political system, Navalny would probably not be alone. But because it does not, there seems to be no one else crazy enough to trade real life for politics. Why does Navalny continue to believe that his time will come and that one day he could succeed Putin as president? There's only one rational explanation—he's an alien.

CROOKS AND THIEVES

In February 2011 the popular young opposition leader Alexei Navalny held radio debates with an unknown MP from United Russia called Yevgeny Fyodorov, whose only distinguishing feature was his readiness to represent the ruling party in a debate with Navalny. By that time Navalny had become an online hero, the country's most popular whistle-blower calling out corruption, and the only major new face of the opposition. The authorities tried hard to ignore him, so as not to increase his popularity. But his scathing blog, in which he published the results of anti-corruption investigations, made that impossible.

The debate between Navalny and Fyodorov is memorable for one thing in particular. It was during this head-to-head that Navalny first mentioned the phrase "United Russia is the party of crooks and thieves." This slogan was to form the backdrop of the entire election campaign for the State Duma in 2011. The powerful state propaganda machine behind the "party of power" (the official slogan) made every effort to quash this Internet meme but failed.

Yevgeny Fyodorov would also become an online star. Four years after the annexation of Crimea he set up the National Liberation Movement, an organization of conspiracy theorists convinced that Russia was controlled externally by the United States, and called for a referendum to amend the Russian constitution to reintroduce state ideology. But back in 2011 he was a little-known MP who for some reason agreed to hold a debate with Navalny and inadvertently helped him.

Navalny recalls that his first fight was with fellow members of the opposition. In autumn 2011 Moscow hosted an event entitled "Last Autumn." At the top of the bill was a debate between Russia's three main opposition leaders:

former Yeltsinite and deputy prime minister Boris Nemtsov, former world chess champion Garry Kasparov, and Alexei Navalny. Nemtsov presented a mock project with the name Nah-Nah (in Russian that sounds like a name of one of the Three Little Pigs, but it also resembles a very rude variation of the phrase "go to hell"), suggesting that people should write in these words to spoil their ballots in the upcoming elections. Kasparov urged that the elections should just be boycotted. Navalny, meanwhile, insisted that both proposals would only increase the number of parliamentary seats for United Russia's "crooks and thieves," so the best option, in his view, was to vote for any party that could feasibly enter the Duma except United Russia.

Navalny won hands down. It was not surprising, since none of the other opposition leaders, including even the most well-known, such as Nemtsov and Kasparov, were popular. All opinion polls showed that the public had no empathy for real opponents of the government—voters were still attracted by officials in power. The example of Yuri Luzhkov demonstrated that no office meant no support. But Navalny's position was fundamentally different. All of a sudden he was Russia's most popular politician since Boris Yeltsin and his tussle with the Communists in the early 1990s—more precisely, the most popular *opposition* politician since Yeltsin.

Navalny's popularity was, of course, confined to his audience—young forward-thinkers who used the Internet and read his blog. Among this stratum his influence was undeniable and absolute—no one else could boast such a core group of supporters. And it was Navalny's campaign against the "crooks and thieves" that dominated the political scene in autumn 2011.

Up to this point the political initiative had always belonged to the Kremlin. It (represented by Vladislav Surkov) had kept abreast of society and even tried to shift the public mood and distract their attention through the creation of synthetic parties. Autumn 2011, however, took the ruling class by surprise. Medvedev's camp was demoralized and its hopes were fading. The "Medvedites" were still reeling from the United Russia congress and Medvedev's capitulation. They had been expecting at least some form of resistance, not abject submission.

Vladislav Surkov still held the post of deputy head of the presidential administration and had to manage the Kremlin's election campaign. He too was dismayed by Medvedev's "betrayal" and had lost much of his appetite for political activity. Moreover, the election campaign had already begun without him. Leading the charge was People's Front, whose "supervisor" was

Surkov's former pupil Vyacheslav Volodin. Putin's election campaign had in fact started in the summer, and Surkov knew that he had too much ground to cover.

As a result, United Russia had to do very little. Party functionaries simply squabbled among themselves for the top places in the party list, which would guarantee a seat in the new Duma.

But Navalny's campaign was exploited by A Just Russia (AJR), a puppet party that had been created by Surkov as part of his "two legs" concept—a kind of center-left, social democratic counterweight to the center-right United Russia. In the run-up to the campaign almost all the party's sponsors and stars had fled to the "party of power," so its spin doctors co-opted Navalny's line and began to urge its online audience that the only way to reduce the number of "crooks and thieves" in parliament was to vote for AJR.

The party, which had never been considered part of the real opposition, took another bold step in an effort to increase its support: it began to offer all and sundry the chance to represent the party in precinct election commissions as observers or even as members with decisive voting rights. The 2011 parliamentary election, which till then had been devoid of all opposition, suddenly became interesting. Out of curiosity, intelligent but hitherto apolitical young people began registering as observers to see how the electoral process worked or, more precisely, to see how the authorities would falsify the elections, since everyone believed that was what would happen. The thousands of newly signed-up observers saw it as a kind of combination of interactive theater and intellectual exercise. The experiment exceeded expectations to such an extent that it changed the course of Russian politics.

THE "DIRTY BOOTS" REBELLION

As voting ended in Moscow on December 4, the day of the parliamentary election, unofficial reports began appearing about the results in Russia's Far East and Siberia, which were several time zones ahead. Navalny remembers that there was a feeling that United Russia was in trouble. Preliminary figures indicated that the party was hovering around 35 percent of the vote—a long way off from even a simple majority. Back in Moscow, order had to be restored. So toward evening, independent observers in the capital were asked or forced to leave polling stations under a variety of pretexts. The Internet was flooded with videos captured on mobile phones, showing observers being expelled or ballot papers manipulated.

The next morning the head of the Central Election Committee, Vladimir Churov, announced nationwide that United Russia had received 49 percent. Later, thanking Churov for a good job, President Medvedev said, "You're a magician."

On Monday evening, the day after the election, a previously planned rally by the Solidarity opposition movement took place at Chistye Prudy in central Moscow. Navalny says that he was not initially planning to go, since it was likely to be yet another drab, sparsely attended anti-Putin event. But, invigorated by the results of the election, he decided to go—and called upon his blog followers to do likewise.

The gathering went down in history as the "rally of the dirty boots." Moscow's streets were covered with slush and everyone was standing in puddles. The darkness made it hard to assess exactly how many people were there, but the feeling was that the turnout was very large indeed.

"Back then it was the biggest rally I'd ever seen. After what followed it might not seem much, but at the time it was awesome. The mood was zany," says Navalny. He considers it the most important rally the opposition ever held, and there were a few more to come.

In a buoyant mood, Navalny delivered a blistering speech (which critics at the time described as "Fuhrer-esque"): "They call us 'Internet hamsters.' Yes, that's right. I'm an Internet hamster and I'm going to gnaw the throat of every one of those beasts!"[1] Navalny's trademark was to strike up Q&A-style chants: "Did you vote for United Russia?" he asked. "No!" shouted the crowd. "What's the party called?" was the next question. "The party of crooks and thieves!" responded the crowd. At the end of the speech, with no cue from Navalny, everyone began chanting "Putin is a thief!"

"I thought it would be a shame if that was that. So I suggested to [fellow opposition figure Ilya] Yashin that we should announce a march right away," says Navalny. Yashin did not want to ("I have an important meeting tonight, and anyway we'll get arrested"), but nevertheless from the stage he urged the crowd to march on the Central Election Commission.

The march was short-lived. The police managed to split the crowd, separating the vanguard from the majority of the protesters. Most of the people remained on Turgenev Square at Chistye Prudy, while those who did go were easy pickings for the police. About 100 people were arrested in total, including Navalny and Yashin. The majority of them were electoral observers: "Of the twenty people with me in the detention cell, eighteen were observers who'd come to the polling stations and been dragged away," says Navalny. "Those first arrests were the trigger. No one had been arrested before that."

The following week was spent preparing for the next rally. The Kremlin was at a loss to understand what was happening. Had the "color revolutionaries" invaded after all, despite Surkov's efforts? Or was it a homegrown conspiracy? Some viewed the situation with interest, some with schadenfreude, most with bemusement.

Only on the second day, December 6, did Surkov's youth organization, Nashi, try to break up the protests. The demonstrators made their way to Triumphal Square in central Moscow and came face-to-face with regional divisions of Nashi brought in specially—they were beating drums and chanting "Russia!" and "Putin!" Their opponents shouted back: "Russia without Putin!" and "Shame on the Nashists!" That evening about 200 protesters were detained. The next day Vladislav Surkov's Nashists disappeared from the streets.

The only official entrusted with somehow regulating the situation was the deputy mayor of Moscow, Alexander Gorbenko. He was the most senior figure to take part in the negotiations about where the rallies would be held. Gorbenko tried to reason with the protestors, explaining that the Americans were weaving a conspiracy against Russia and paying electoral observers to cast doubt on the results. It was all a calculated plot, he said. Back then the "US conspiracy" theory was popular among officials of all stripes. Rumors circulated among them that US surgeons had deliberately botched Botox injections in Vladimir Putin's face in order to undermine his authority.

Gorbenko's talks with the opposition ultimately bore fruit. The Moscow authorities allowed a rally to be held on Bolotnaya Square, across the river from the Kremlin, a symbolic place where historically riots had broken out and rebels had been executed.

It should be noted that not all the stories of US machinations were pure fiction. In 2011 the US Agency for International Development did indeed channel all funds intended for pro-democracy programs in Russia to the nongovernmental organization Golos, which oversaw the elections and carried out an independent vote count. That said, Golos observers numbered fewer than 3,000—less than 10 percent of the number of volunteers who registered with the official election committees.

MEDVEDEV'S RENAISSANCE

The rally scheduled for December 10, 2011, in Bolotnaya Square did in fact take place. According to independent estimates, 50,000 people attended, including not only the regular opposition but former observers, young "Internet hamsters," and pretty much half the presidential administration, including, for instance, Mikhail Abyzov, a billionaire associate of Medvedev's, who would become a minister in the latter's government just a few months later. Almost everyone present felt a strange sense of euphoria.

Medvedev's camp experienced a kind of renaissance. "If we'd known that so many people would come out in support of us, we'd have acted differently in September," Natalya Timakova, Medvedev's press attaché, is supposed to have said. Whether or not she said it, the Medvedites certainly felt at one with the protesters in Bolotnaya Square. Moreover, they believed, not without reason, that the protests were the consequence of Putin's return, announced on September 24. The progressive intellectuals wanted to see the back of him.

Navalny relates that in actual fact most of the protesters hated Medvedev and Surkov no less than they did Putin. "We don't want our president to be pathetic or puffed up," shouted Navalny from the stage at Chistye Prudy to the approving roar of the crowd. Whereas "puffed up" was Navalny's own description of Putin, the word "pathetic" was already Medvedev's established epithet and was hashtagged in many tweets about him.

Today Navalny believes that the protest was a little unfair to Medvedev. "Medvedev believed he was doing the right thing. He would have continued to be a better president [than Putin]. He was weak, cowardly, and comical, but all that he did was a step in the right direction. His reforms of the judiciary, for instance. They were halfhearted, perhaps 10 percent of what was needed, but all the same," reflects Navalny. Humiliated by having to switch places with Putin, Medvedev and his team were initially delighted by the protests, says Navalny. They wanted modernization and believed they would have coped better with the protests, according to Navalny.

A second, larger rally was planned for Saturday, December 24, two days after Dmitry Medvedev was due to deliver his final address to the

Federal Assembly. Having reported on his main achievements (judicial reform, accession to the World Trade Organization, mandatory declaration of officials' income, the creation of the Skolkovo Innovation Center), the president commented on the incipient protests, saying that public opinion should be heeded and the electoral law amended accordingly. Medvedev proposed reintroducing elections for governors (abolished by Putin in 2004) and the mixed electoral system for the Duma (abolished by Surkov in 2005 to avert a "color revolution"), as well as simplifying the procedure for registering parties.

Interestingly, the Kremlin did not implement any of the actions specifically demanded by the protesters. The head of the Central Election Commission, Vladimir Churov, was not dismissed, and there was no rerun of the recently held parliamentary elections. But having announced new political reforms, the authorities (or at least Medvedev) could not completely ignore society. "We knew they were trying to fob us off. But it didn't really matter at the time, because they were clearly on the way down, while we were in the ascendant. They were falling apart. I gave the system another eighteen months in power, no more," remembers Navalny.

Medvedev's political reforms coincided with an act of penance from Surkov. The same day as Medvedev's speech, December 22, the newspaper *Izvestia* published a major interview with the Kremlin strategist and "color revolution" slayer in which he praised the Bolotnaya movement, albeit in his customary dialectical style.

He asserted that the protests were not actually protests ("The tectonic structures of society have begun to shift. The social fabric has acquired a new quality. The future is already here, and it looks troubled. But do not be afraid. Turbulence, even if very strong, does not mean disaster or instability"). Surkov described the protesters as "the most productive part of our society," adding, "We cannot arrogantly dismiss their opinions. Of course, one could argue that they are a minority. But what a minority!"

FOR YOUR EARS ONLY

The unexpected protest made an impression not only on Kremlin liberals. Suddenly everything came to life. The "sleeper cells" of Russian political life, those people who only meditated upon politics in the privacy of their own thoughts, sensed that their time had come.

Mikhail Prokhorov's interest in politics was suddenly revived. Having said goodbye to Right Cause and skipped the Duma elections, the day after the Bolotnaya Square rally he rematerialized after a six-month absence and announced his intention to run for president. In his new campaign blog, set up on December 14, he wrote: "No doubt the Kremlin will try to use me in the elections. Of course, they'll try to exploit Bolotnaya. They want to play at democracy and show that the people have a choice. It's clear that Peskov [Putin's press secretary], the Kremlin spin doctors, and the state TV channels will all try to exploit us."[2]

By December another unexpected figure had joined the protest—Alexei Kudrin. Russia's finance minister and Vladimir Putin's closest aide was the first victim of the shift announced on September 24.

On the day of the United Russia congress at which Medvedev and Putin had announced their role reversal, Alexei Kudrin was in Washington, at a meeting of the IMF board of governors. The news came as a surprise, as it did for many members of Putin's inner circle. For Kudrin, it was an unpleasant one, especially the revelation that in May the new government would be headed by Medvedev, with whom Kudrin had a long-standing conflict.

Kudrin had long eyed with envy his comrade German Gref, who had been able to leave his position as minister of economic development and become the head of Sberbank. Kudrin was tired of the government and the Ministry of Finance. The reforms had stopped. He was powerless to change anything and had to waste his energies on resolving internal departmental strife. Having watched the congress in his hotel room in Washington, he delivered an unusual impromptu press conference in the lobby of the hotel. "I do not see myself in a new government. It is not just that no one has offered me a job. I feel that the disagreements I have will not allow me to join any future government," he said.[3]

For Medvedev it was a slap in the face. Kudrin's statement that he would not work with Medvedev when he became prime minister was suddenly headline news. Medvedev, still president, decided to hold an unscheduled meeting on economic issues, not in Moscow but in the Ulyanovsk region, which he was due to visit that day.

On the eve of the meeting Kudrin received a phone call from Surkov, who wanted to make sure that Kudrin would be there, offering him a seat on the presidential plane. The next call was from Putin: "I saw your speech. You shouldn't have said that."

The meeting turned into a public showdown between Medvedev and Kudrin.

"Alexei Leonidovich [Kudrin], who is present here today, recently gave us the glad tidings that he has no plans to work in the future government. And that he has some major disagreements with the president. You have only one option. And you know what it is. Are you going to write a resignation statement?" said Medvedev.

"Dmitry Anatolievich [Medvedev], I do indeed have disagreements with you, but I will only make a decision regarding your proposal after consulting with the prime minister," replied Kudrin.

"You can consult with whoever you like. But as long as I'm president, I will continue to make the decisions," retorted Medvedev.[4]

The skirmish happened in front of the television cameras. Having been humbled by Putin at the United Russia congress, Medvedev took his vengeance on Putin's old friend. The meeting ended with Medvedev ordering Kudrin to phone Putin to get his "consultation" over and done with. Kudrin packed up and left, but he did not make a phone call—there was no secure line available, and Putin never talks if his conversations can be eavesdropped upon. But Medvedev was persistent. Later, having found a secure channel, he contacted Putin himself. That evening the finance minister's resignation was announced. Still, despite having been dismissed live on air, Kudrin retained all his former influence. He was Putin's closest adviser, after all. He didn't even vacate his office at the Ministry of Finance.

Ever since the start of the December rallies, Kudrin had begun to show great interest in them. On the eve of the first rally at Bolotnaya Square, several members of the organizing committee met with him at a restaurant not far from the Ministry of Finance. The protest leaders wanted to know if they would be allowed to stage the rally without any provocations from the authorities. The officially unemployed Kudrin offered to help. Having listened to their questions over dinner, Kudrin said: "I just need to make a secure phone call." And he headed off in the direction of the Ministry of Finance to give Putin a ring.

Despite continuing to communicate regularly with Putin, Kudrin managed to win the trust of the opposition. Although the prime minister was using Kudrin to study the opposition, the opposition likewise was using him to find out what was going on in Putin's mind. One day he met with Alexei Navalny himself, who questioned him about what Putin really wanted. Was it true that he was worn out by everything? Was it true that he had long wanted to pack up and leave for somewhere quiet in the south, where he could live the life of an oligarch, with a yacht, a villa by the sea, and beautiful women? But Kudrin, according to Navalny, assured him that it was not so: Putin believed that Russia would fall apart without him. His mission was to save Russia, and "you oppositionists" are getting in the way—that was how the former finance minister summed up Putin's thoughts.

PEAK OF POLITICS

December 24, 2011, saw the biggest rally yet. More than 100,000 people congregated on Sakharov Avenue in Moscow. "That was when politics peaked," says Navalny. Before the rally there had been arguments about who should be allowed to attend, and whether or not nationalists and leftists should be invited. Some were deeply hostile to the nationalists, while others were more opposed to Ksenia Sobchak, the rich socialite daughter of Anatoly Sobchak, Putin's former boss in St. Petersburg. In the end it was a free-for-all. The rally was even attended by Mikhail Prokhorov, who had avoided the Bolotnaya Square protests. He did not get up onstage, but remained in the crowd. Still, the most unexpected participant in the rally was not Prokhorov or Ksenia Sobchak but Alexei Kudrin, Putin's closest ally and economic adviser. Moreover, Sakharov Avenue gathered together not only those with newly awakened political ambitions but also the most circumspect people in Russia—bankers and representatives of big business.

Putin's entourage began to view the Bolotnaya Square protests in a different light. The prime minister was supplied with regular transcripts of conversations between members of Medvedev's team, which showed that many inside the presidential administration actually welcomed the demonstrations. Moreover, evidence emerged that those in receipt of public funding through connections with Surkov were actively engaged in the protest movement. An example was the state-run news agency RIA Novosti, which provided live coverage of all the protest rallies; two years later it would be effectively shut down, then rebranded and placed under new management.

Vyacheslav Volodin, Surkov's former protégé and now direct competitor, kept the prime minister up to speed. It seemed that, having lost out to Putin in the struggle for the next presidential term, Medvedev had elected not to go quietly but to use Surkov to shake things up and perhaps even disrupt the presidential election scheduled for 2012. Surkov, who had done everything to suppress a "color revolution" in Russia, was now seemingly orchestrating one in the interests of his new patron, Dmitry Medvedev.

Putin found it all perfectly plausible. With one foot already back in the Kremlin, on December 27 Putin moved Surkov from the presidential administration to a post in the government in charge of innovation and new technology, where he would be easier to monitor. Medvedev did not demur. Surkov's place as deputy head of the presidential administration was taken by the country's new chief political strategist, the selfsame Vyacheslav Volodin. However, members of Surkov's circle say that he did not see it as a punishment. He was apparently tired of being the Kremlin's top villain and wanted to focus on something more positive. Now he had a chance to go down in history as an innovator.

The end of the Medvedev era was symbolized by the return of his once-vanquished opponent Sergei Ivanov, who became the new head of the presidential administration. His candidacy was reportedly proposed by Medvedev himself, since he was at least on speaking terms with Ivanov. The other options, Sechin or Volodin, would have been far worse.

The next opposition rally, on February 4, 2012, was again held at Bolotnaya Square. Volodin was ready. He staged an "anti-protest" on Poklonnaya Hill with about 100,000 participants, mainly state employees, who held up placards with the slogans "No to the Orange Revolution," "Everything's at Stake," and "Who if Not Putin?" Putin approved.

Another symbol of Volodin's struggle against the liberal protests was Igor Kholmanskikh, foreman of the Uralvagonzavod railroad cars plant. On December 15, shortly after the first rally on Bolotnaya Square, Putin held his annual live phone-in, during which he answered questions from members of the public for four hours. The questions were, as always, prepared in advance and rehearsed. Volodin's masterstroke was a question from a "laborer" from Nizhny Tagil in the Ural region—that is, Kholmanskikh. Standing among his team of blue-collar workers, Kholmanskikh told Putin said that they cherished the stability he had brought and did not want to return to the bad old days. He did not actually ask a question, but simply stated: "If the police can't cope with the demonstrations, my lads are ready to come and lend a hand," adding that they would, of course, act "within the law."

Putin expressed his gratitude, and just a few months later appointed Kholmanskikh as the presidential envoy to the Urals Federal District, despite his lack of political experience. The appointment was extremely symbolic. It marked the end of Putin's flirtation with the liberal intellectuals. The "creative class" (in the words of Vladislav Surkov), which made up most of the protest movement, could go to hell. They had betrayed Putin. Moreover, they were Medvedev's people, not his. Henceforth, Putin stopped trying to find common ground with the intellectuals. He decided that the middle classes, whom he had given stability and prosperity, were backstabbers. They did not appreciate what he had done for them and were not satisfied that they had just enjoyed the most prosperous decade in the entire history of Russia. The middle classes, the supposed bedrock of Putin's support as conceived by Surkov, had not kept their side of the bargain. They and Surkov would pay for their disloyalty.

RUSSIA'S MAIDAN

The presidential elections were remarkably calm. Thousands of the Bolotnaya and Sakharov protesters again registered as observers, but no large-scale fraud was uncovered. Vladimir Putin received 64 percent of the vote.

On the evening of election day a crowd assembled near the Kremlin on Moscow's Manezh Square. The jubilant pro-Putin onlookers were presented, as they had been four years previously, with the incoming and outgoing presidents. The first thing that caught the eye was that Putin was in tears. His spokesman Dmitry Peskov later explained that there had been a very strong wind. However, this force of nature curiously had no effect on Medvedev, who was standing alongside him.

"This was about more than simply electing the next president of Russia. It was a vital test for all of us, for all our people. It was a test of our political maturity and sovereignty," said the tearful Putin. "We have shown that no one can impose anything upon us—absolutely no one! We have shown that the Russian people understand that these political provocations have only one goal—to destroy the Russian state and usurp power. Today the Russian people have decisively rejected any notion of that."

It seems that Putin really believed that he had miraculously rescued Russia from the "usurpers." Whom exactly did he have in mind? The United States? Medvedev? Navalny?

Nevertheless, Putin's touching speech left the protesters unmoved. All was not lost, they thought. "We knew that they were still in power, that Churov [head of the Central Election Commission] would not be fired, that our demands would not be met, and that they would try to defuse the situation with token reforms. But we also knew that we would overcome them, because of the force behind us," says Navalny.

The opposition's next move was scheduled for May 6—the day before Putin's inauguration.

"Before every rally, this one included, I restated our core strategy—escalation," recalls Navalny. "People were saying they were fed up with peaceful rallies and wanted something more hard-core. They were up for a fight with the cops."

It was certainly clear that the rally on May 6 would be no sing-along. Ksenia Sobchak, who had attended all the previous rallies, did not come to this one for fear of the backlash from the authorities. Navalny says that he knew in advance that 600 people were planning to descend from the regions and set up camp in Bolotnaya Square.

It is obvious in retrospect that there was a traitor on the opposition's organizing committee. Konstantin Lebedev, an assistant of left-wing activist Sergei Udaltsov, was an agent of the security services. Navalny believes that Lebedev found out about the opposition's plans and informed the FSB, embellishing them in his telling. The authorities arrived at Bolotnaya Square expecting trouble.

The protesters were caught in a trap. The police closed off a bridge, cutting the rally in two. Scuffles broke out. It was the first major clash between the protestors and the law. The next morning, however, the opposition was still in high spirits. "Everyone thought, 'Good job, we rattled them,'" says Navalny.

The next day also happened to be Putin's inauguration. Moscow's entire center was blocked off all the way from the government building, where Putin had been prime minister, to the Kremlin, Putin's new (and old) workplace. The police took no chances. There was not a soul to be seen anywhere. No passers-by, no random onlookers. The center of Moscow was eerily deserted, as if after a nuclear explosion.

The opposition got as close as they could. A symbolic rally was held on Nikitsky Boulevard beyond the cordon. Although the demonstrators posed no threat of disrupting the ceremony or being shown on state television, riot police in any case broke up the rally and arrested the participants. They also raided the nearby Café Jean-Jacques, where many sympathizers of the protesters were enjoying a cup of coffee. All TV stations broadcast rosy footage of Putin's motorcade moving through the empty streets. The only exception was TV Rain, which split the screen in two—one half showing the inauguration, the other the assault on the café. This image would become the symbol of Putin's new term, although no one realized it at the time.

THE FORCE AWAKENS

"None of us expected Putin to go so far. No one expected him to sacrifice all he'd done before simply for the sake of holding on to power," says Navalny about the events of 2012. "We all thought his sense of historical mission was the most important thing for him—his desire to go down in history as the new Peter the Great. No one expected that he'd pick a fight with the cream of society and appeal to grassroots fundamentalism to get back into the Kremlin."

It was a quite a while before it finally dawned on Navalny and the protesters that the fight was in fact lost. Summer 2012 had been marked by romantic rebelliousness. There had been a festive mood on the streets of central Moscow, including Occupy Abai (part of the global Occupy movement), which had set up camp for several days by the statue of Kazakh poet Abai Qunanbaiuli at Chistye Prudy. It was a carnival atmosphere. Even in late May, when the arrests began, there was still a sense of giddiness in the air.

The Investigative Committee launched what became known as the "Bolotnaya case," followed by the arrest of a cross-section of those involved in the May 6 protests for allegedly fighting with the police.

The opposition, meanwhile, in the words of Navalny, was struggling with a "leadership crisis." In autumn the most prominent activists and show business stars supportive of the protests had been elected to the Opposition Coordination Council (OCC). First place in the elections had gone to Navalny, followed by poet Dmitry Bykov, former chess world champion Garry Kasparov, and Ksenia Sobchak. But the OCC soon became mired in internal squabbling. "It was outdated as soon as it was elected. The times and regime had changed," says Navalny. About six months later the OCC was dissolved.

In October NTV showed a documentary film entitled *Anatomy of Protest 2* (the first part had been aired in March), which claimed that the protests in Moscow had been organized with a helping hand from abroad. The film showed a clandestine recording of a meeting between OCC member Sergei Udaltsov and Georgian politician Givi Targamadze where they allegedly discussed ways to finance the Moscow protests. The meeting was organized by Konstantin Lebedev, the aforementioned mole.

Udaltsov was subsequently charged with inciting mass disorder and sentenced to four and a half years in prison. The other members of the OCC distanced themselves from him, and there was no large-scale rally in his defense.

"Today people say the protests achieved nothing," reflects Navalny. "But they toppled the Putin-Medvedev Russia—like the 1905 revolution provoked a reaction that swept away tsarist Russia. Alas, the protests also led to the war in Ukraine."

The methods applied to the opposition became increasingly authoritarian. As of autumn 2012, arrests, court proceedings, and prison sentences became commonplace. In 2012 three criminal cases were opened against Navalny himself, one in May and two in December.

Navalny says: "Putin had no other option. He knew that if he didn't return to the Kremlin, Navalny would not be the one to go after him. He would be hounded by members of his own team—Ivanov, Kudrin, Medvedev, or Surkov. Those he worked with would be the first to turn on him. If he weakened, they would arrest him. He understood the system that he himself had built—it would have devoured him. Putin's aim was not to scare the opposition. He needed to strike a blow to those around him."

DE-MEDVEDIZATION

After his inauguration Putin kept the promise he had made six months earlier and duly appointed Dmitry Medvedev as prime minister. Despite all Putin's suspicions about Medvedev's role in the Bolotnaya protests, the latter had at least kept his word and returned the keys to the Kremlin.

However, the "tandem," which had been trumpeted by state propaganda for the past four years, was no more. Gleb Pavlovsky, Surkov's former right-hand man, who had been dismissed in 2011 and stripped of his Kremlin pass for showing too much allegiance to Medvedev, coined the term "de-Medvedization."

To begin with, the Duma set about methodically abolishing all laws passed under Medvedev. The next and most humiliating part came when Medvedev's initiatives were scrapped by the very government that Medvedev himself now headed. In summer 2012 the parliament was hyperactive, passing a clutch of repressive laws that tightened the procedures for holding rallies and reintroduced prison sentences for those found guilty of libel (which Medvedev had decriminalized several years before). Vyacheslav Volodin, Putin's new political strategist, is said to have penned the laws, which were readily rubber-stamped by the Duma. Journalists nicknamed the new convocation of the Duma the "crazy printer" for the sheer volume of paper it churned out.

The climax of the Duma's belittling of Medvedev occurred during his annual report to parliament in April 2013. MPs, even members of the Medvedev-led United Russia, described the government as ineffective. The Kremlin-loyal (i.e., fake) opposition figure Vladimir Zhirinovsky accused Prime Minister Medvedev of having had a hand in the Bolotnaya protests: "How come they were so well organized? They must have had outside help. Not only from the West, but from inside the government!"

Medvedev was publicly discredited too. In August 2012, on the anniversary of the war in Georgia, there appeared an online documentary entitled *The Lost Day* (with the tag line "How Medvedev's cowardice killed a thousand people"). The film was well made, obviously the work of a national TV station. The film's protagonists were retired generals, one of whom was the former head of the General Staff, Yuri Baluyevsky, who accused Medvedev of cowardice, indecision, and failing to respond to Saakashvili's provocations in South Ossetia "until he got a kick up the rear from Putin." A few months later a second film appeared in which Medvedev was accused of surrendering Libya to the Americans. One of the interviewees was the wizened former prime minister Yevgeny Primakov. It was open season.

The old guard's attack on Medvedev was in fact a prelude to the next step: the toppling of defense minister Anatoly Serdyukov. Initially Serdyukov had been Sechin's man. Back in 2004, in the midst of the Yukos affair, Sechin had pushed Serdyukov's candidacy for the post of head of the tax service. Since Mikhail Khodorkovsky stood accused of tax evasion, the role of top taxman was significant. Serdyukov coped with the task, which later earned him a promotion. In 2007, on the eve of "Operation Successor," Serdyukov took charge of the Russian Ministry of Defense.

Following the case of Private Sychev and the demands to "amputate Sergei Ivanov's legs," the role of defense minister was considered a political graveyard. Serdyukov had to take the flak for past mistakes, focus the public's attention elsewhere, and carry out unpopular military reforms, all at the same time. He set about his duties with gusto and immediately alienated the old generals, whom he did not like anyway, deriding them as "little green men."

Serdyukov's army reforms were quite radical and hence internally unpopular. Even the fact that the new minister secured a huge budget for rearmament did not cause the generals to warm to him. They despised him and his entourage—mostly smart young women, who took over the Ministry of Defense and ran it like an accounting firm.

In 2008 Serdyukov locked horns with then finance minister Alexei Kudrin. They had had an uneasy relationship ever since Serdyukov's days as Russia's tax chief, when he was essentially the treasury's main source of income. Having analyzed the Five-Day War with Georgia, the new defense minister demanded the allocation of 28 trillion rubles (about $1.12 trillion) over the next decade for rearmament. The Ministry of Finance offered 9 trillion rubles, whereupon the Ministry of Economic Development came up with a compromise figure of 13 trillion. In 2010 Prime Minister Putin seemingly approved the compromise. But just when everything looked settled, Serdyukov went to President Medvedev in person and convinced him that 13 trillion rubles would not go far. In late 2010 Medvedev convened a meeting on defense spending and in front of the cameras announced that the government was ready to allocate 20 trillion rubles.

"We'd already agreed on a figure," said Putin with barely concealed irritation.

Military spending was Kudrin's main gripe about Medvedev. It was the announcement about defense spending, he says, that prompted him to say he would not serve in a future Medvedev government.

Not only Kudrin but the entire state apparatus was at a loss. With a budget of 20 trillion rubles, Defense Minister Serdyukov was now the most powerful *silovik* at the core of the new power structure. Kremlin and government insiders began to whisper that Medvedev's generosity was a "loyalty fee" to keep Serdyukov on his side. Putin was later supplied with a transcript of a conversation that allegedly took place between President Medvedev and Defense Minister Serdyukov. "We'll be your power base," Serdyukov supposedly said, clearly referring to a possible confrontation between Putin and Medvedev. However, since no such confrontation ever ensued and Medvedev did not seek one, the conversation is most likely a myth cooked up to discredit Serdyukov.

Another of Serdyukov's ill-wishers was Sergei Ivanov, his predecessor as defense minister and now the head of the presidential administration. Serdyukov did not mince words when speaking of Ivanov, blaming him for failing to carry out the necessary reforms and describing him (when feeling polite) as an "ineffective minister." Serdyukov did not expect Ivanov to make a comeback after losing out to Medvedev and clearly overestimated his own influence.

In autumn 2012 the Investigative Committee opened a criminal investigation into embezzlement at the Ministry of Defense. There were several women involved in the case, including Yevgenia Vasilyeva, Serdyukov's alleged mistress and the former head of the Department of Property Relations under the Defense Ministry. The story unfolded like a medieval tale of dastardly intrigue.

On the morning of October 25 in the most expensive area of Moscow, the so-called Golden Mile, members of the Investigative Committee and a team of Russian *spetsnaz* (special forces) almost came into collision. The former had come to search the apartment of Yevgenia Vasilyeva on Molochny Lane, only to find that the entrance to the building had been blocked off by commandos. The investigators were preparing for a tactical retreat when the chief of staff, Sergei Ivanov, intervened. He insisted that the commandos let the investigators through. They entered Vasilyeva's apartment and found the minister of defense there. This juicy tidbit was immediately leaked to the tabloids, which was remarkable. Russian media never write about the private lives of members of the government, yet suddenly newspapers and websites were having a field day with the defense minister. The situation was compounded by the fact that Serdyukov was married to the daughter of former prime minister Viktor Zubkov.

After the scandalous raid, Putin summoned Serdyukov and warned him not to interfere in the investigation. Putin had already decided that the minister had to go, but his style is to avoid knee-jerk decisions, preferring to wait awhile in order to weaken the link between cause and effect.

When the time was right, Serdyukov was duly dismissed. No one tried to protect him. His former patron Medvedev was helpless to intervene, while all other influential figures were baying for Serdyukov's blood. On November 6 Putin announced that Sergei Shoigu would be Russia's new defense minister. A former head of the Ministry of Emergency Situations, in 1999 Shoigu had helped Putin become president by agreeing to lead the pro-Kremlin party Unity.

The rout of Medvedev's clan was wrapped up in April. In spring 2013 the Investigative Committee began to look into the activities of Medvedev's brainchild, the Skolkovo Innovation Fund, which was overseen personally by

Vladislav Surkov, now deputy prime minister. The former Kremlin strategist refuted the charges against his Skolkovo subordinates. "The zeal with which the Investigative Committee published its hypotheses created the impression that a crime had been committed. But it's just hyperactivity on the part of the investigators. If someone's guilty, let's see the evidence," Surkov lashed out during a talk at the London School of Economics.[5] But the Investigative Committee no longer considered the once all-powerful Surkov someone to worry about. A day later Investigative Committee press secretary Vladimir Markin wrote an article for the newspaper *Izvestia* entitled "The View from London: Don't Blame the Mirror if Your Face Is Ugly," in which he slammed the deputy prime minister:

> Officials and "effective managers" have a new fad. As soon as their multistory mansions are searched, they immediately scream about orders from the higher-ups. It's highly fashionable these days to be a political prisoner. You immediately attract the attention of the BBC and the support of Amnesty International. Perhaps that's why these effective managers' supervisors prefer to speak out in London in front of their target audience. Their plaintive cries are music to liberal ears: "The Investigative Committee is too hasty in its accusations against Skolkovo," they say. A rhetorical question arises: how long would a British cabinet minister survive if during a private visit to Moscow he publicly condemned Scotland Yard for performing its duties? Moscow, it seems, is too lenient.[6]

The press secretary's tone was so unbridled that it was clear that the article was not his. That meant that Surkov's days in the government were numbered. The next day President Putin signed a decree relieving Surkov of his position.

The cleansing of the Kremlin and the government of disloyalists, or anyone casually suspected of disloyalty, was complete. Dmitry Medvedev, who still considered himself the leader of the top-placed liberals, looked on in silence. Perhaps he saw it as a test of his own character. He did not, however, venture to intercede on behalf of any of his former allies.

PART FOUR

PUTIN THE TERRIBLE

CHAPTER 14

IN WHICH PATRIARCH KIRILL GIVES FATHERLY ADVICE TO RUSSIA'S CABINET OF MINISTERS

His Holiness Patriarch Kirill of Moscow and All Russia, the head of the Russian Orthodox Church, was long considered to be just about the most educated person in Russia. In the "wild nineties" he hosted a talk show on Channel One entitled The Pastor's Word, *which displayed his eloquent command of the Russian language. His programs were at once lucid, philosophical, profound, and modern. Indeed, he seemed such a modernist and reformist that the conservative church hierarchy began to accuse him of heresy, sympathy for Catholicism, and excessive Westernism and liberalism. The incriminations intensified when liberalism went out of fashion.*

For the Russian Orthodox Church, "sympathy for Catholicism" was tantamount to treason. After becoming patriarch, the head of the Church, Kirill assembled a team of top theologians and intellectuals. But no reformation followed. The Kremlin demanded that the church be the guardian of moral principles and traditions—and the patriarch's rhetoric changed accordingly.

I first glimpsed the future patriarch in 2008 in Kiev during the sumptuous celebrations marking the 1,020th anniversary of the Baptism of Rus. At the time Ukraine was led by the pro-Western Viktor Yushchenko, who invited the Archbishop of Constantinople and Ecumenical Patriarch Bartholomew to the feast. The Moscow patriarchate sensed danger. They feared the Ukrainian authorities wanted to encroach on the canonical territory of the Church and lead the

Ukrainian flock away from Russia. So Russia sent a huge delegation to Kiev, headed by the already infirm Patriarch Alexis II.

On the main day of the celebrations Kiev's two central squares, as often happens in Ukraine, hosted two competing events. President Yushchenko and Patriarch Bartholomew went to Sofia Square, where the city's main cathedral is situated, but down the road on Independence Square was a rock concert organized by the Church. Musicians and members of the church hierarchy alternated onstage. The headliners were Russian rock band DDT, who made no effort to hide their opposition sentiment. During a break between songs, the announcer loudly declared: "And now, please welcome Metropolitan of Kaliningrad and Smolensk, Kirill!" Metropolitan Kirill literally ran onstage, looked out over the perhaps 100,000-strong crowd, raised his arms, and shouted rocker-style into the microphone: "Hey, Maidan!" The crowd shouted in reply, "Hey, Metropolitan!" Kirill delivered a short but inspired speech, after which the chant "Metropolitan! Metropolitan!" rang out for several minutes.

The Moscow patriarchate understood that its influence on Ukraine had not waned, largely thanks to the energy of Kirill. But on becoming patriarch, he adopted a very different tone. Church leaders began to champion morality and ethics. During one incident in 2015, for instance, a priest led his congregation from the church to disrupt a concert that was taking place in the street, since the music was interfering with their prayers.

"THE PATRIARCH BELIEVES IN PUTIN"

On February 21, 2012, two weeks before the presidential election, a group of women in multicolored balaclavas entered the Cathedral of Christ the Savior in central Moscow, the country's principal cathedral, to film a video for their new song, "Mother of God, Get Rid of Putin." Two days previously they had tried to do likewise at Yelokhovo Cathedral, the second most important place of worship in the Russian capital, but had been ejected by security. Their second attempt was only marginally more successfully—they managed to jump on the soleas in front of the iconostasis and dance for a few seconds before being removed.

The "punk prayer" (as they called it), performed by members of the group Pussy Riot, brought them fame. Suddenly the Russian media was awash with stories about them. Their previous stunts had not provoked any such reaction. The previous month, for instance, they had gone to Red Square to record a video for another track, "Rebellion in Russia—Putin's Wetting Himself." That time they got off with a fine and a few online mentions.

To call Pussy Riot a musical group would be a stretch. Their main preoccupation has always been political performance art.

For ten days after the punk prayer, nothing happened. But on March 3 the police woke up. On the eve of the presidential election, two members of the group, Nadezhda Tolokonnikova and Maria Alekhina, were arrested. The next day, the day of the election itself, a third participant, Ekaterina Samutsevich, was detained. The remaining two members were overlooked.

According to rumor (which the Church denies), the arrests were made after the intervention of Patriarch Kirill. He allegedly telephoned Vladimir Putin and asked him to punish the "wenches" for profaning a holy temple. According to members of the patriarch's entourage, he was utterly dumbstruck by the stunt—no one had ever seen him in such a state.

Patriarch Kirill, whose secular name is Vladimir Gundyaev, was perhaps personally offended by the lyrics sung in the clip. In it, for example, there is the line: "Patriarch Gundy believes in Putin. Would be better to believe in God, you bitch."

Thus began the lengthy trial of Pussy Riot, which made them world famous. No one at that time could have imagined such a reaction. During this time they became global pop-art icons. The senior church hierarchy, including the father superior of Sretensky Monastery, Archimandrite Tikhon Shevkunov, who is often described as Putin's confessor, began murmuring that the members of Pussy Riot were clearly puppets in a plot against the Russian authorities. "I am not fond of conspiracy theories, as they say. But I think we will soon discover how much cynical and frightful preparation went into this act," said Father Tikhon.[1]

The Pussy Riot affair was the most sensational, but it was not the only scandal that the Church and Patriarch Kirill were involved in at the time.

Ironically, just when the rallies on Bolotnaya Square were taking place, in autumn 2011, a Moscow court examined a case concerning a five-room apartment owned by the patriarch in the renowned House on the Embankment, which overlooks Bolotnaya Square and the Kremlin. In this apartment (which the Moscow mayor's office gave to the future patriarch in the 1990s) there lived a woman named Lydia Leonova, who the patriarch said was his second cousin. Their neighbor was Yuri Shevchenko, a former health minister and the former private doctor of Lyudmila Putin. During repair work to Shevchenko's apartment, the ventilation system was damaged, causing a thick layer of dust to gather inside the patriarch's apartment. The patriarch's relative sued the former minister for 20 million rubles ($575,000) to cleanse the patriarch's unique library of the "nano-dust."

To wash his hands of sin, the patriarch met the toadying TV and radio host Vladimir Solovyov in private and instructed him to tell Kirill's version of events during one of his radio monologues. However, Solovyov's intercession only made matters worse. He reminded his audience of another forgotten scandal, when the patriarch was photographed apparently wearing a Breguet watch. In conversation with Solovyov, Kirill had asserted that the photograph was a fake, although he did admit to owning a Breguet—it was a gift and still lay inside its unopened box.

A week later the scandal went into overdrive. Bloggers discovered photographs on the patriarch's official website of a meeting between him and the justice minister. In the photos the patriarch's watchless wrist was at odds with the reflection of an expensive Breguet in the polished surface of the table in front of him—a badly botched Photoshop job. The Church was forced to apologize, restore the original image, and then dismiss the incompetent press office employee who was responsible for the manipulation of the photograph.

The scandals were piling up and being distributed through social media. So the Church went on the counterattack. The Church hierarchy, including the patriarch himself, claimed to be the victims of a planned campaign. "We were warned that we would be attacked," said the Church's official spokesperson, arguing that the campaign against the patriarch was being waged by various past and present members of the ruling elite.

It did indeed feel like a coordinated action. And it is curious that the incidents were reported not only by the liberal media but by state-funded sources too. As the protests gathered pace and the Pussy Riot affair evolved, ever more photo collages of the patriarch wearing a watch appeared online. It seemed as if the focus of public outrage had shifted from Putin to the patriarch. That led to a split in the protest movement.

Before the scandal Kirill had practically given his blessing to the protesters. "If the authorities remain insensitive to the protests, it is a very bad sign, a sign of their inability to self-adjust," he said in his Christmas message. "The authorities must pick up the signals from outside . . . and alter their course." But a couple of months later his rhetoric changed.

As a result, the protesters divided into two camps. Nearly all agreed with the slogan "For fair elections"; the slogan "Putin is a thief" was more controversial, while the anti-Church rhetoric was too much for some. It was one thing to oppose the Kremlin, on which point the movement was unanimous. But it was another thing entirely to attack the Church. Some protesters were alienated.

The anti-Church campaign, which came to an end in autumn 2011, did not weaken the position of Patriarch Kirill and the clerical establishment. On the contrary, it strengthened it. The church in fact helped Putin consolidate society and defeat the Bolotnaya protests.

After a long trial, the three members of Pussy Riot who had been arrested were sentenced to two years in prison. "Just two years of porridge," Vladimir Putin jokingly commented on the harsh sentence. They served eighteen months before being amnestied in December 2013 in honor of the twentieth anniversary of the Russian constitution.

WORD AND DEED

The close relationship between the Church and the state began in the late Soviet period. In the early 1990s, when the wraps came off the KGB archives, a special commission published extracts from internal documents, according to which almost all the higher echelons of the Church seemed to have collaborated with the KGB. Potential KGB agents included Patriarch Alexis II (code name "Drozdov") and his successor, Patriarch Kirill (code name "Mikhailov"). Neither the patriarch nor any Church representative has ever commented on this information. President Boris Yeltsin was not a deeply religious man, yet he felt obliged to attend church at Easter and Christmas, which became a tradition for Russia's post-Soviet leaders. Someone far closer to the Church was banker Sergei Pugachev, who had Family connections. Pugachev still has a letter from the patriarch to President Yeltsin in which the head of the Church proposes that the banker be an intermediary in relations between the Church and the state.

It was Pugachev who introduced the Church hierarchy to Vladimir Putin when the latter moved to Moscow in 1996. Pugachev took him to Sretensky Monastery, located near the FSB building at Lubyanka Square. In 1998 Putin became head of the FSB, and his visits to the monastery became more frequent.

Sretensky Monastery became a focal point for officialdom, particularly the heads of the security services. Back in the 1990s it had been a rendezvous point for the *siloviki*, while in the 2000s it became the favorite haunt of just about all the country's top officials. Members of Putin's entourage were often found there. That was when Father Tikhon Shevkunov became known as "Putin's confessor." He turned into one of the most influential members of the Church hierarchy, maintaining close contact with the heads of the security services, above all FSB director Nikolai Patrushev. Even more influential was Metropolitan Kirill, the head of external Church relations—the Church's "foreign minister."*

Patriarch Alexis himself did not seek close ties with Putin, says Pugachev. The patriarch did not like the "KGB-ists" and wanted nothing to do with them. However, other Church leaders actively embraced relations with the state.

Pugachev says that Putin's fascination with the Church was quite rational. The president saw Orthodoxy as the pure embodiment of the national idea, with a greater capacity to unify the people than any political party. According to surveys, 80 percent of Russian people do not understand anything about Orthodoxy and do not read the Bible or other religious texts, yet consider themselves Orthodox Christians.

In his first term as president Vladimir Putin became very involved in Church politics. In 2003, on a visit to New York, he initiated talks between the Church and the so-called Russian Orthodox Church Outside Russia, which had broken away in 1917. One of the guiding hands behind the negotiations was Father Tikhon Shevkunov, who accompanied the president. In 2007, a year before the end of Putin's second presidential term, the talks ended with the unification of the two churches, restoring the canonical link between them. In a bid to make history, Putin and his administration oversaw the entire process.

A few months before the end of Putin's second presidential term, state television (today's Rossiya One) aired a documentary film entitled *The Fall of an Empire: The Lesson of Byzantium*, by none other than Tikhon Shevkunov. The film was nothing short of an anti-Western manifesto. The spiritual father

*Patriarch Kirill is a passionate skier and often joined the president (be it Medvedev or Putin) at the presidential resort Lunnaya Polyana near Sochi. However, he generally preferred Switzerland.

of FSB director Nikolai Patrushev (and possibly President Putin) cautioned viewers and the state against headstrong reforms and rapprochement with the West. The narrative of Father Tikhon's heavily distorted history of the Byzantine Empire ran thus: a great and wealthy empire had been brought down by the intrigues and machinations of the West; Byzantine oligarchs had plundered the national wealth and taken it to Western Europe; military reforms had weakened the army; and Byzantium itself had been undermined by Western sympathizers lured by vice, consumerism, and individualism. It was, in short, a thinly disguised reference to Russia and echoed the conspiratorial tone so beloved of the *siloviki*, including Patrushev.

Things began to change in 2008, after the death of Patriarch Alexis II. His successor, Metropolitan Kirill, was chosen in what was possibly the most democratic election ever held in Russia.

Although Metropolitan Kirill was considered the favorite and was in fact the rightful heir to Patriarch Alexis II, the campaign proved extremely controversial. Opponents of Kirill dug up dirt on him, raking up stories from the 1990s about his alleged misuse of church tax exemptions and involvement in tobacco and alcohol smuggling. Meanwhile, the presidential administration (which still danced to the tune of Vladislav Surkov) actively supported Metropolitan Kirill and sought to discredit his rivals.

Even before his elevation to the patriarchy, Kirill was considered a liberal Westerner and a highly educated, progressive thinker. However, his election coincided with a rise in homegrown Orthodox fundamentalism. The phrase "spiritual brace" (used to describe the unifying effect of the church on the Russian people) may have been thought up by the presidential administration, but the Church eagerly adopted it.

Kirill was a long-standing member of the bureaucratic elite. Moreover, in the words of the presidential administration, he "displayed unprecedented activity," that is, he was ready to assist the Kremlin in achieving its political objectives. Orthodoxy was well on its way to becoming the official state ideology and a means to cement Putin's electorate.

During Putin's third term Patriarch Kirill acquired unprecedented political influence. He had access to Putin at the drop of a hat and could appoint his own people to high positions. In 2015, for example, at his request the Russian culture minister dismissed the director of the Novosibirsk Opera and Ballet Theater for staging a blasphemous version of Wagner's *Tannhäuser*. The patriarch's favored nominee was duly appointed in his place.

A CHANGE OF FLOCK

In January 2012, shortly before the scandals erupted around the patriarch, the head of the Russian Orthodox Church received a letter from Boris Berezovsky, who had long been living in London. They were not intimately familiar, having met only briefly in the 1990s. Although of Jewish descent, Berezovsky was a baptized member of the Russian Orthodox Church, which is why he appealed to the patriarch. The rambling letter made little sense. "Help Putin to recover his wits," Berezovsky wrote. "Convey to him the will of the people. And when Putin hears you, take the reins of power from his hands and give them to the people in a wise, peaceful, Christian manner." It was a strange missive, and the press service of the Church announced that the patriarch did not intend to respond.

By that time the former oligarch had become almost completely severed from Russian political reality. In 2010 he attended a rally in London holding a banner that said "I created you and I will stop you" (referring to Putin). Along with his sense of reality, Berezovsky had also lost much of his fortune. After the death in 2008 of his business partner Badri Patarkatsishvili, it turned out that all their joint assets were registered to the deceased and duly went to the latter's family. Berezovsky tried to recover half of Patarkatsishvili's $11 billion estate, but to no avail.

Late 2011 saw the start of a momentous court case for Berezovsky. Back in 2007 he had filed a suit with a London court against his former partner Roman Abramovich, but only in 2011 did the case finally come to trial. Having arranged the privatization of Sibneft as part of the loans-for-shares scheme in the mid-1990s, as well as the purchase of various metallurgical assets later taken over by RUSAL, Berezovsky claimed that he was the co-owner of these assets. Abramovich, said Berezovsky, had even paid him dividends up until Berezovsky's forced emigration to London in 2000. Abramovich had later paid him $1.3 billion for 43 percent of Sibneft, which, Berezovsky opined, was a serious undervaluation. He demanded $5.5 billion in compensation. Abramovich asserted that Berezovsky had never been a co-owner of the companies and had received the money in exchange for "political protection." Testimony was also given by Alexander Voloshin and Oleg Deripaska. During the proceedings Berezovsky was nervous and confused, while Abramovich was calm and meticulous.

In summer 2012 Judge Elizabeth Gloster ruled as follows:

> On my analysis of the entirety of the evidence, I found Mr. Berezovsky an unimpressive, and inherently unreliable, witness, who regarded truth as a transitory, flexible concept, which could be moulded to suit his current purposes. At times the evidence which he gave was deliberately dishonest; sometimes he was clearly making his evidence up as he went along in response to the perceived difficulty in answering the questions in a manner consistent with his case. At other times, I gained the impression that he was not necessarily being deliberately dishonest, but had deluded himself into believing his own version of events.[2]

Mikhail Khodorkovsky says that he has no doubt that Berezovsky was indeed Abramovich's partner: "I could have testified at any moment that they were partners in the late 1990s. Moreover, it was Boris who invited Roman to join him. When the merger of Yukos and Sibneft was first mooted, they talked to me as partners. There was no talk of 'political protection.' They were 50-50 partners." Khodorkovsky was unable to testify, of course, because at that time he was in prison.

Berezovsky lost the case and was ordered to pay £100 million in legal costs. According to friends, he became depressed and longed only to return to Russia. He even wrote two letters to Putin in which he asked to be pardoned, one of which was personally delivered by none other than Abramovich (Putin publicly admitted that Abramovich had given him the letter in February 2013), the other through German businessman Klaus Mangold. In March 2013 Berezovsky was found hanged in the bathroom of a house owned by his ex-wife. Many of his friends believe it was suicide.

In the final months of his life Berezovsky came into contact with another political refugee from Russia, who also considered himself to be Putin's "creator." Sergei Pugachev, a former Kremlin insider who in the 2000s was known as the "Orthodox banker" for his contributions to the Russian church, moved to London in 2012. A year later criminal charges were brought against him in Russia and he was put on the country's international wanted list.

According to Pugachev, all his Russian assets—worth approximately $30 billion, including shipyards, a coal deposit in Tuva, and a development project on Red Square—were expropriated by the state. The Russian authorities asserted that Pugachev's bank siphoned 68.5 billion rubles (about $2.75 billion) abroad through loans to dummy organizations. Pugachev was initially planning to fight Moscow in a British court, but he lost a lawsuit against the

Russian Deposit Insurance Agency. After complaining to Scotland Yard that the Kremlin was preparing a KGB-style hit, he moved to France, where he is now a citizen; any further question of who robbed whom is likely to be for a French court to decide.

Pugachev's fall from grace was a sign of the times. Unlike Berezovsky, Gusinsky, and Khodorkovsky, he had never displayed political ambitions and had never openly opposed the Kremlin—at least not until criminal charges were brought against him. On the contrary, he had been a member of Putin's inner circle.

But by the late 2000s the inner circle had been updated. Putin distanced himself from acquaintances made before and during his first presidential term and surrounded himself instead with friends from earlier days, such as Arkady Rotenberg, his former judo partner. In the 1990s Rotenberg had worked as a judo instructor before blitzing his way into business in the 2000s, becoming known as the "king of state procurements" and one of the most influential businessmen in Russia. Other such people include Vladimir Yakunin and Yuri Kovalchuk, Putin's friends from the mid-1990s, who together set up the Ozero dacha cooperative. In the first decade of the 2000s Kovalchuk became Russia's number one media mogul: the largest private TV channels (Channel One, NTV, Ren-TV, Channel Five, and TNT) and the newspaper *Izvestia* all came under his control. Yakunin, meanwhile, took charge of Russian Railways, the state rail monopoly.

Incidentally, Yakunin was even more Orthodox than Pugachev. He too became friends with Father Tikhon Shevkunov and brought numerous holy relics to Russia for display at the Cathedral of Christ the Savior in Moscow, most noticeably the Cincture of the Theotokos, which brought so many visitors that lines stretched for several miles. Together with the new governor of St. Petersburg, Georgy Poltavchenko (also a former KGB-ist), Yakunin established the tradition of making regular pilgrimages to Mount Athos in Greece and Valaam Monastery, located on the largest island in Lake Ladoga, in northern Russia.

CHAPTER 15

IN WHICH KREMLIN STRATEGIST VYACHESLAV VOLODIN INVENTS A NEW NATIONAL IDEA

"Don't impose your agenda on me," says Vyacheslav Volodin when asked a question he does not like. As for Volodin's own agenda, it is based almost entirely on the man in the street. He is very fond of opinion polls, which he looks into like a crystal ball.

Volodin is well versed in US politics and can turn any conversation into a discussion of America's problems. Things aren't too bad in Russia, he suggests; over in the United States everything's much worse.

He is said to be single-minded and very careful never to do anything that could hurt his political career. In recent years, for example, he has practically stopped talking to the press—and if he does grant an interview, he will ask you not to impose your agenda.

He is also said to be very unforgiving. It's as if Volodin keeps a to-do list that includes settling old scores.

He considers himself a man of action and sincerely believes that he alone knows what people want and that only he is capable of listening to them. He probably believes himself to be a real democrat, aided as he is by private opinion polls that allow to him divine the true will of the people.

Moreover, he sometimes openly doubts himself: What if my domestic policy is wrong? What if I'm doing more harm than good? *But he does not develop these thoughts. That's not his agenda.*

ASYMMETRIC RESPONSE

In December 2012 Vyacheslav Volodin, then deputy chief of staff of the presidential administration, gathered together all the leaders of the State Duma in his office, including Duma Speaker Sergei Naryshkin (until recently head of the presidential administration) and the leaders of all four party factions. The purpose of the meeting was to discuss how to respond to the Magnitsky Act, a law recently passed by the US Congress to impose targeted sanctions on various Russian government officials who, according to the US State Department, were guilty of human rights violations. Volodin started by delivering an impassioned diatribe about the duplicity of the United States and how it tramples on human rights around the world and therefore has no moral right to reproach others. Volodin's audience themselves often spouted anti-US rhetoric, and so they wondered why he was preaching to the converted.

The law could have buried Russian-US relations. To avoid such an outcome, the Obama administration watered it down somewhat, thinking that the Kremlin would appreciate Obama's leniency. But the new gray cardinal of the Kremlin, Vyacheslav Volodin, was livid. His current dogma stipulated no concessions whatsoever to the West, and he had been urging Putin to be strong and popular without flirting with the intelligentsia. This meant that the Russian parliament had to come up with a clear response to the Magnitsky Act.

However, the situation was complicated by one detail: Volodin could not get instructions from Putin. The latter had not been seen at the Kremlin for more than a month. The president, without whose opinion nothing could be decided, was ill, and no one dared to disturb him.

That is why Volodin, having drafted a response to the Magnitsky Act, decided in any case to shift responsibility by making it collective. It was like the crime scene in Agatha Christie's *Murder on the Orient Express*, when each of the twelve associates stabs the victim to assuage individual culpability. The leaders of the Duma factions agreed that Russia's response to the Magnitsky Act should be a consolidated gesture. They would be named as coauthors, whereupon rank and file members would add their signatures. No law in the history of Russia had ever enjoyed such parliamentary solidarity.

The first draft of the response was fairly standard, stipulating visa bans and the expulsion of US employees from Russian NGOs. But ahead of the second reading Volodin added an amendment: henceforth US citizens would not be allowed to adopt Russian children. He cited Putin's frequent off-the-record comments about Russia's deplorable practice of "selling children."

WHO'S IN CHARGE OF RUSSIA?

Volodin was not the only one discomfited by the Putin blackout. The Russian leader had not been seen by ministers, business leaders, or even old friends. A German businessman named Matthias Warnig, Putin's closest foreign acquaintance, tried several times to fly home to Germany for Christmas after failing to meet with Putin. Each time he set off for the airport his mobile phone rang and he was politely requested not to leave and to come immediately to the Kremlin. Each time Warnig turned his car around and waited for hours in the Kremlin reception area. But Putin never appeared.

In terms of business and political influence, Warnig was probably more powerful than the Russian prime minister. Warnig held directorships in practically every large Russian company, both private and public. He sat on the board of RUSAL, the largest metals company in the world. He headed the board of Transneft, Russia's state-owned pipeline monopoly. He was a member of the supervisory boards of two major Russian banks—the state-owned VTB and the private Rossiya. He also sat on the board of Rosneft, Russia's largest state-owned oil company. Lastly, he was an important top manager at Gazprom, responsible for operations in Europe as head of the company's European subsidiary.

Yet despite his reach, Warnig had no choice but to sit in a leather chair for hours on end in the Kremlin reception area, staring at the parquet floor, the walls, and the faces of the Federal Security Guard members on duty. He realized that no one knew where Putin was or why the president was unable to see even his closest companions. But since all his power and all his appointments to the boards of Russia's top companies derived solely from Putin, Warnig had to sit patiently just in case his boss showed up.

All visitors to the Kremlin at that strange time asked the same question: *Who's in charge of Russia?* In the space of twelve years Putin had built a system in which his word was law. How could matters be resolved when there was no command from Putin? Subordinates, of course, learn how to guess the thoughts of their superiors, how to conjecture and extrapolate. But Putin had been absent for a long time. Who was sitting in for him? *Was* anyone sitting in? Or was everyone twiddling their thumbs waiting for him to reappear?

Was Putin's spokesman, Dmitry Peskov, who continued to deliver comments and statements on Putin's behalf, in charge? Probably not, because Peskov was clearly worried. In particular, he was concerned about how—or even whether—he could arrange the traditional annual phone-in with the Russian public held every autumn or early winter, during which the president took questions from a live audience for several hours. In October 2012 Peskov told reporters that it would not take place, so as not to "freeze" whole villages of people who usually turned out in the harsh Russian winter to ask the president a question. Instead, it would be held at a more clement time of year. But one thing that Peskov could not scrap was the president's New Year address. And the New Year was fast approaching.

Could Russia's secret ruler be chief of staff Sergey Ivanov? But everyone inside the presidential administration knew that Ivanov was making every effort not to rule anything. They remembered how he had been burned in 2007 during "Operation Successor," when he had lost out because he was too sure of himself. Four years later Ivanov unexpectedly found himself once again at the top of the state pyramid. After Putin, he was de facto the most powerful person in Russia. But he could not bring himself to act for fear that it was a test. The thought plagued him that Putin might be waiting in the wings, ready to reappear at any moment. Therefore, it was better to wait and avoid making any rash decisions.

Then there was Vyacheslav Volodin himself. He had replaced Vladislav Surkov as the Kremlin's gray cardinal just one year earlier. Volodin was not an old acquaintance of Putin's. He was only a hired hand who had been offered the chance to shape the Kremlin's new strategy.

Lastly, of course, there was prime minister Dmitry Medvedev, who was de jure, if not de facto, second in command. But officials did not go to him on pressing matters. After he resigned as president, his reputation was so dented that he had ceased to be a real center of power.

As a result, for around two months no one was in charge of Russia. The public did not even know about it, since it was not mentioned by the national media. Even foreign leaders did not suspect the full extent of the situation, noting only that the Russian president was unwell; they were not aware of the extent to which the entire Russian political elite was disoriented by Putin's lack of visibility. "I have had to postpone my visit to the Russian Federation because President Vladimir Putin is not feeling too good," Japanese prime minister Yoshihiko Noda told reporters. "He injured his back during judo training," said Belarusian president Alexander Lukashenko. And in August Putin, an animal lover and fan of extreme sport, had flown in a motorized hang glider with white cranes that had been raised in a nursery, leading the flock as they learned how to fly; soon afterward, at the APEC summit in Vladivostok, Putin was visibly limping. However, members of Putin's inner circle said off the record that the president had been injured before, not during, the flight—on the judo mat, as Lukashenko had said. At any rate, it was after the summit that he went missing, and all of his foreign visits that autumn were canceled.

THE RISE OF THE CHILDREN

Putin's absence, oddly enough, did not cause much reaction in Russian society. The Kremlin did not comment on the canceled visits, and foreign leaders' comments about the president's ill health did not particularly bother anyone.

But there was an incredible uproar when Volodin submitted the proposed ban on foreign adoptions to the Duma. The government unexpectedly opposed the law. Such open and pointless confrontation with the United States would be damaging, many MPs thought, especially since the US State Department had not yet published the names of the Russians on its sanctions list and planned to do so no earlier than February. Assuming that the absent Putin would not be in favor of the bill, ministers began to publicly criticize it. The bill was unofficially called the "Dima Yakovlev law," in honor of a Russian boy who had died in the United States through the negligence of his American adoptive parents.

Among the critics were deputy prime minister Olga Golodets, education minister Dmitry Livanov, finance minister Anton Siluanov, and minister without portfolio Mikhail Abyzov. Even foreign minister Sergei Lavrov, who never in his career had expressed a personal opinion, spoke out against the law, saying that he pitied his Foreign Ministry colleagues who had only just agreed on a bilateral agreement with the United States on adoption, as the new law threatened to undo all their efforts. Such mass ministerial revolt was unprecedented in the history of Putin's Russia. On one hand, the ministers disagreed with Volodin and did not want to become victims of possible US sanctions as a result. On the other, they were confident that Volodin's amateurish bill would be slapped down by Putin, as often happened whenever an oddball idea met with resistance inside the elite.

The elite had never before been so outspoken. But in Putin's absence that was the only way to contact the president. Only one key liberal member of the government kept quiet: prime minister Dmitry Medvedev.

In the end, Putin's annual press conference was scheduled for December 20. Everyone froze. There was still no word from Putin himself, and it was not clear which side of the adoption argument he would take. The liberals were convinced that the president was deliberately biding his time so as to take all the credit for saving the children. He would scrap the law, thereby demonstrating to the world community as well as to the liberal elite that he was merciful (as well as to remind everyone that he alone was Russia's supreme arbiter).

But things turned out differently. When Putin appeared at the press conference, half the journalists assembled there asked him about the anti-adoption law. Clearly irritated, despite knowing about the question in advance, Putin delivered an anti-US lecture: "When our representatives try to fulfil their obligations under the agreement, they say, 'This is not a federal case, it's a state case, and you do not have any agreements with the individual states. Go to the State Department and sort it out with them because you signed an agreement with them.' But the federal government refers them to the states. So what is the point of this agreement?"

Then he gave vent to his pent-up enmity:

> What concerns do our partners in the United States and their lawmakers voice? They talk about human rights in Russian prisons and places of detention. That is all well and good, but they also have plenty of problems in that area.
>
> I have already talked about this: Abu Ghraib, Guantanamo, where people are kept jailed for years without being charged. It is incomprehensible. Not only are those prisoners detained without charge, they walk around shackled, like in the Middle Ages. They legalised torture in their own country.
>
> Can you imagine if we had anything like this here? They would have eaten us alive a long time ago. It would have been a worldwide scandal. But in their country everything is quiet. They have promised many times that they would close down Guantanamo, but it's still there. The prison is open to this day. We don't know, maybe they are still using torture there. These so-called secret CIA prisons. Who has been punished for that? And they

> still point out our problems. Well, thank you, we are aware of them. But it is outrageous to use this as a pretext to adopt anti-Russian laws, when our side has done nothing to warrant such a response.[1]

Putin signed the Dima Yakovlev law on December 28, 2012. Ironically, that date in the Christian calendar is Holy Innocents Day, in memory of the killing of newborn babies by King Herod. Russian Internet users immediately called the new legislation "Herod's law." And the hashtag "#putineatschildren" started trending in the Russian-language Twittersphere.

Afterward Putin did not receive any of his long-suffering government officials. He did not offer an explanation to the members of the Russian cabinet as to why he had supported the illogical bill and approved the anti-Western path proposed by Volodin.

Government members were in shock. For them, the Dima Yakovlev law was a lesson about the futility of trying to second-guess the president, let alone influence him. For Volodin, the law was a major victory. He had cottoned on to Putin's irritation and found a means to express it—henceforth, foreigners would not be allowed to adopt Russian children.

It was another couple of months before Putin became fully reimmersed in politics and government. Over these two months any criticism, counterarguments, or protests, including the winter rallies in Moscow against the Dima Yakovlev law, provoked only irritation.

HOME SWEET HOME

"In February 2013 it became clear that open politics was over," said a businessman close to Putin. The president had recovered both his strength and his suspicions.

The news from abroad intensified his paranoia. In Venezuela, President Hugo Chávez had died of cancer. Although the two presidents were never close friends, there were parallels between them: they had become president at roughly the same time, both had struggled with oligarchs and subjugated the media and the oil industry, both had set up youth organizations and opposed the United States, and both had fought against the "fifth column," although the demagogue Chávez had started his campaign a few years before Putin. Moreover, Venezuela was the only country (with the exception of Nicaragua and Nauru) to recognize the independence of Abkhazia and South

Ossetia. Chávez had become friends with Igor Sechin after the latter became the unofficial head of the Russian oil industry.

The Kremlin discussed not only Chávez but also the "cancer epidemic" that was the scourge of Latin American presidents. Two Brazilian presidents (Lula da Silva and Dilma Rousseff), Argentine president Cristina Kirchner (later given the all-clear), Paraguayan president Fernando Lugo, Colombian president Juan Manuel Santos, and Bolivian president Evo Morales had all been diagnosed with the illness. Privately Chávez asserted that the Americans had irradiated him during a visit to the UN General Assembly in New York. There had been cases of cancer among top Russian government officials as well. Almost everyone believed Chávez's conspiracy theory.

Chávez's funeral was attended by an impressive delegation, including Federation Council Speaker Valentina Matviyenko, foreign minister Sergei Lavrov, Chávez's friend Igor Sechin, and Sergei Chemezov, the head of Rostec (Russia's monopolist arms manufacturer).

After Chávez's death, Putin's advisers from the security services recommended that the president pay attention to the "fifth column," in particular the many Russian senior government officials who had property and bank accounts abroad; quite a number of their children studied overseas, and some even had residence permits for other countries. If the situation worsened, such officials could be exploited by Western intelligence agencies for blackmail purposes. Putin unexpectedly heeded the warning and gave the go-ahead for Volodin to draft a bill banning high-ranking officials and Duma MPs from owning accounts and financial assets abroad.

Putin signed the new law in May 2013. It took everyone by surprise. No government ministers wanted to part with their numerous properties. Many made no secret of such possessions. First deputy prime minister Igor Shuvalov, for instance, listed homes in the United Arab Emirates, Austria, and Britain, and other members of the government declared apartments and houses in Spain, Italy, Bulgaria, and Switzerland. Nor was it possible to own real estate abroad without opening a foreign bank account. Nevertheless, government officials were confident that the new law would not apply to them. Many joked that they would prefer to resign than to close their accounts and sell their property.

Some did just that. One of them was billionaire Roman Abramovich, who used the law as an excuse. From 2000 to 2008 Abramovich was the governor of Chukotka, in the far northeast of Russia, the most distant region from Moscow. In 2008 he asked for permission to go live permanently in London. Putin initially said yes, but then decided that Abramovich had not spent enough of his fortune in Russia and demanded that he retain the nominal position of speaker of the Chukotka parliament. The new law of 2013 helped Abramovich escape the dangerous and uninviting world of Russian politics—and Russia itself.

SNOWDEN VERSUS OBAMA

Most officials rejected the notion that the ban on accounts and assets abroad had been introduced in advance of a major confrontation with the West. To prove their point, they highlighted the fact that Barack Obama was preparing to pay a visit to Russia in September, which was due to include the G20 summit in St. Petersburg.

And not just a visit, but a state visit. Everything was planned in meticulous detail. Obama and Putin would start by holding talks in Moscow and then fly to St. Petersburg together to meet with business leaders. Russian liberals in the government pinned great expectations on the face-to-face meeting and persuaded Putin that even if a political partnership was unattainable, an economic alliance was possible.

The visit went ahead, but not as planned. In June a contractor for the US National Security Agency by the name of Edward Snowden boarded a flight in Hong Kong bound for Moscow. Washington demanded his arrest at Moscow's Sheremetyevo Airport and immediate extradition. Moscow refused. A major row broke out, during which Snowden took refuge in a hotel at the airport.

A telephone showdown took place between Putin and Obama. The US president said that Moscow underestimated the threat posed by Snowden and that Russia's noncompliance would jeopardize the state visit. Putin replied that the Americans had only themselves to blame. Why had they kicked up such a fuss when he landed in Moscow? After all, he had been planning to fly on to Cuba, where the US authorities could have picked him up easily. Obama pleaded, saying that the US public and political establishment would be outraged if the fugitive Snowden was not extradited. Putin replied that the Russian public would be outraged if he *was* extradited. There the conversation ended.

"If he wants to stay here, there's one condition: he must stop all activity intended to inflict harm on our American partners—strange as that may sound coming from me," said Putin a short while later, trying to alleviate US suspicions that Snowden was a Russian agent.

The government team preparing for Obama's visit was horrified. Caught up in the conspiratorial atmosphere, the liberal section of the Kremlin and the government explained to Putin that it was all a Chinese plot. The Chinese, they said, had dispatched Snowden from Hong Kong to the Russian capital with the specific aim of embroiling Moscow and Washington. But it was too late.

The Obama administration decided to cancel the full state visit, limiting the president's time in Russia to the G20 summit in St. Petersburg. Instead of Moscow, he stopped over in Sweden for two days.

Whether or not the failed visit would have rescued Obama and Putin's relationship and US-Russian relations remains unclear. In any case, all negotiations thereafter between the two countries turned into a public swearing contest. On the eve of the G20 summit Putin described US allegations that the Syrian government had used chemical weapons against rebel fighters as "complete claptrap" before accusing US secretary of state John Kerry of "lying" about there being no al-Qaeda militants in Syria.

If this rhetoric was intended to persuade Obama not to visit Russia at all and to skip the summit in St. Petersburg, it did not work. A meeting between the two leaders was duly arranged, during which Obama kept his cool in the face of Putin's coarseness. On the sidelines of the summit the Americans made it clear to the other participants that Putin was not a team player. He was so unconstructive that Washington had given up on him. The United States would wash its hands of Putin, they said.

DIFFERENT VALUES

Volodin's domestic PR was quite successful. The Kremlin's new policy architect was the opposite of Surkov. He did not try to build complex structures, preach new values, or invent new systems. He believed that people should be given what they wanted. Volodin pored lovingly over polling data and surveys. They confirmed that the government was doing everything right and that Putin was popular and his actions had public backing. What's more, Volodin loved to be guided by public preferences and pursued policies that were sure to be popular. This new populism meant a return to traditional conservative values.

"It hurts me now to talk about it, but say it I must. Russian society today lacks a 'spiritual brace,'" said Putin in his annual speech to the Federal Assembly in December 2012. This rather archaic phrase became the key concept for his third term as president.

During his first term Putin had been fond of expounding his worldview to Western leaders—everything from the situation in the Caucasus to why Russia should not be criticized for human rights abuses but treated as an equal and strategic partner. On failing to convince his counterparts, he changed his agenda. In his second term he went on the offensive, accusing Western leaders of insincerity and breaking their own promises.

By the time of his third term the world-weary Putin had transmuted into a Slavophile philosopher. "Do not harbor any illusions," he once told US vice president Joe Biden, according to a civil servant who was a part of the negotiations. "We are not like you. We only look like you. But we're very different. Russians and Americans resemble each other only physically. But inside we have very different values." It was in fact the complete opposite of what Putin had said a decade previously.

"Imagine you are sitting here in the Kremlin," he told Angela Merkel. "And you have voters who live in Kaliningrad and others who live in Petropavlovsk-Kamchatsky [in the Russian Far East]. And all these lands, languages, and lifestyles have to be united. People need something to unite around. One of your compatriots was our great empress Catherine II. She initially wanted to abolish serfdom, but then studied the foundations of Russia in more detail. And do you know what she did? She strengthened the rights of the nobility and destroyed the rights of the peasantry. Nothing has changed [in Russia]: one step to the right or to the left and you lose power."

According to one of his closest aides, Putin thought long and hard about traditional Russian values. "Putin was more concerned about values than about Russia's unique path," says the aide. "He believed that building capitalism was every country's destiny." The main source of Putin's contemplations was the philosopher Ivan Ilyin. Based on Ilyin's works, Putin placed the basic values of Russian society in this order: God, family, property.

"In the face of external fluctuations," says one of his advisers, paraphrasing Putin, "Russians must defend their conservative agenda to protect other nations and peoples, too. We are Orthodox Christians for a reason. Our identity has been shaped by Orthodoxy. By adopting Orthodoxy, we are to some extent in opposition to the Western world."

Another aide says that at some point Putin realized that the most important "brace" with which to bind the Russian people from Kaliningrad to Kamchatka was his own good self. Putin believed that everything would fall apart without him.

Since the defense of "traditional values" was popular with the people, Volodin eagerly embraced it. As an extra fillip, the consolidation of a patriarchal society helped combat the liberal opposition. A useful target was homosexuality, which in 2013 suddenly became an important domestic political issue. It chimed with the idea of the Church's role as a "spiritual brace." Back in the mid-2000s various Russian regions had started to adopt laws banning "gay propaganda." In 2012 it was the turn of St. Petersburg. Russia's capital of culture under governor Georgy Poltavchenko became the capital of Orthodox Russia by adopting its own "anti-gay law," which caused quite a stir in the press.

In December 2012 Prime Minister Medvedev, in response to a direct question about whether such a law would be passed at the federal level, said, "You simply cannot regulate all of people's moral behaviour and neither can you regulate all the interaction between people through legislation. This is my position and this is the United Russia position."[2]

However, a month later such a law was indeed submitted to the Duma and adopted in the first reading almost unanimously (with just one nay and one abstention). A wave of protest swept across the globe, which was actively covered by Russian state media, whose interpretation of events was unambiguous: the Western gay lobby could not stomach Putin's defense of traditional values. Russia's state-owned Channel One even coined the term "Gayropa" ("gay" + "Europe") to characterize Putin's opponents in the West (and inside Russia), who were all viewed as "representatives of sexual minorities" themselves.

BACK TO POLITICS

The protests of 2011 had rattled the Kremlin, but by 2013 Volodin was fully confident that the leaders of the Bolotnaya movement had been discredited and defeated. Criminal charges had been brought against most of the leaders, which effectively negated their political activity.

The strangest was the criminal case against Alexei Navalny. Back in 2011 the Investigative Committee had accused him of fraud in connection with the timber company Kirovles, but in April 2012 the case was closed for lack of evidence. But then in June the head of the Investigative Committee, Alexander Bastrykin, publicly chastised the investigator in charge for having closed the case, and demanded that it be reopened.

Navalny responded with his own investigation of Bastrykin. He published information that Bastrykin owned a law firm in the Czech Republic, plus had a Czech residence permit and an apartment in Prague—all of which were illegal for a member of the security services. None of this had ever been mentioned by the head of the Investigative Committee himself. Navalny wrote a complaint to both the Investigative Committee and the presidential administration asking for an investigation into Bastrykin's activities. But Bastrykin was safe. He had known Putin since university. Moreover, Bastrykin had been the student monitor of Putin's cohort at university, for which in Kremlin circles he was known as the "elder." The powerful "elder" had almost daily access to Putin, and no one doubted that the order to resume the investigation of Navalny had the backing of the president.

The trial came to a close on July 18, 2013. Its end coincided with the beginning of the campaign for Moscow's upcoming mayoral elections, and Navalny announced his intention to run. However, he had no chance of registering his candidacy, since he had just been sentenced to five years in prison. In the evening on the day of the verdict, a huge unauthorized rally gathered in the center of Moscow on Manezh Square in support of Navalny. The protesters blocked the traffic on Tverskaya Street and climbed onto the windowsills of the Duma building, plastering it with pro-Navalny leaflets.

The Navalny verdict, handed down by a court in Kirov, had undoubtedly come from Moscow. But even Moscow officialdom was shocked by the severity. Volodin, for instance, was sure that he had received Putin's personal approval for Navalny to run as mayor in order to undermine the popularity of the incumbent, Sergei Sobyanin, and to add an element of competition, if only for show. The verdict puzzled Volodin, and he went to Putin to figure out what to do with Navalny. Putin, in his usual manner, did not give a straight answer. Even when dealing with his closest aides, he always eschews direct language in favor of winks and nods. "Shall we do as agreed?" asked Volodin, trying to elicit an answer.

"Do as you think is best," answered Putin vaguely.

On that same day the general prosecutor contacted Navalny's lawyers and advised them to appeal both the verdict and their client's detention pending appeal. The lawyers could not believe their ears, as it was unprecedented in Russian court practice for a sentenced person to be released pending an appeal, and they considered such an effort pointless. So the Prosecutor's Office appealed the court's decision itself. The next day Navalny was released.

When the following morning Volodin reported to Putin that his instructions had been followed and Navalny had been released, Putin unexpectedly retorted with a sardonic grin: "What a bunch of ass-lickers."

Then began an exotic experiment: the first completely fair and competitive elections in the history of Putin's Russia. Moreover, the presidential administration demonstrably helped Navalny get registered in time. The signatures of municipal MPs required for registration were supplied by members of United Russia.

Volodin wanted to prove that Navalny's popularity was solely the result of his online activity and that he would flop in a real election. On the eve of the election he reported to Putin that Navalny would get no more than 10–15 percent of the vote. But the pollsters were wide of the mark. Navalny received 27 percent, while the incumbent, Sobyanin, secured 51 percent, enough to claim a first-round victory.

But Volodin was still satisfied. He had proven to Putin that everything was under control. It was simply a matter of time before the protest movement petered out of its own accord. In any event, the Kremlin's media machine would soon destroy Navalny's popularity, he was sure.

CHAPTER 16

IN WHICH PUTIN'S PRESS SECRETARY DMITRY PESKOV REALIZES THE FUTILITY OF TRYING TO PLEASE THE WEST

Hanging in Dmitry Peskov's office on Staraya Square is an amusing photograph of the aged Leonid Brezhnev sitting under a parasol, reading the newspaper Pravda. *It would have provided a good backdrop to an interview given by Peskov in 2012. Speaking to TV Rain, he said that Brezhnev was underestimated as a political leader, that the Brezhnev era had been the golden age of the Soviet Union, and that much good had in fact come from the period of "stagnation." Perhaps Peskov had something else in mind when he put up the picture. Maybe it wasn't he who put it up. Maybe he's never even noticed it.*

Dmitry Peskov is bored. He is a very bright and energetic man who seems to have nothing to do. Vladimir Putin does not need a bright and energetic PR guy. His popularity at home is off the charts, while his image abroad . . . well, the less said about that the better. The days when Peskov hired the PR agency Ketchum to promote Russia's international image are long gone. He is under no illusions: Russia's image abroad is shattered, and it is probably not worth trying to piece it back together.

Peskov is always on the move, both literally and verbally. Once a day via the messaging service Telegram he holds a Q&A session with reporters from the Kremlin pool. He's very open with the press, and tries to be honest and straightforward.

Peskov leads an active social life and enjoys it. In August 2015 he married Olympic figure-skating champion Tatyana Navka. The wedding took place in Sochi—maybe the very same place where forty years previously Brezhnev was snapped with Pravda *and parasol.*

"THE GAMES WE DESERVE"

The saga of the Winter Olympics in a subtropical region began in 2005, when Russia was not just rich but super-rich. A time when money grew on trees. And it began without Putin's involvement.

Russia already had the experience of bidding for major sporting events, including the 2008 European Football Championship and the 2012 Summer Olympics. But little money was allocated to the bidding process, and in any event the cash usually disappeared without a trace. The idea of holding the Olympics in Sochi belonged to the most enthusiastic skier among Russia's oligarchs, Norilsk Nickel owner Vladimir Potanin. It was the second scheme (after the loans-for-shares deal) that changed the course of Russian history.

Potanin loved to ski at Krasnaya Polyana, where he had a house, and he set about developing the Rosa Khutor resort nearby. The idea greatly appealed to the head of Rossport, Russia's government sporting body, the legendary Soviet ice hockey player Vyacheslav Fetisov. Together they set up a bid committee.

Both realized that the idea might also appeal to Putin, who spent much time in Sochi and also skied at Krasnaya Polyana. Potanin discussed it with him, but the president's initial reaction was lukewarm. So the bid committee turned to Dmitry Peskov, who was then the deputy of presidential press secretary Alexei Gromov.

It is said that Peskov proposed a low-cost advertising campaign focused on one man: Vladimir Putin. The bid committee produced billboards and radio spots advertising the Sochi bid. Peskov gave clues as to the route that the president's motorcade took to the Kremlin, as well as what radio stations he listened to while on the move and at what times, and the media buys were targeted accordingly. The slogan for the public (i.e., for Putin) was "The Games We Deserve."

A stooge caller was hired to call in during the president's annual live Q&A session with the public and ask about when Russia would finally host the

Olympics. It made Putin think that the people really wanted the Olympics and that, moreover, they wanted them in Sochi, so he gave the go-ahead. All the state TV channels immediately climbed on board, and the bid committee's money trough became bottomless.

"Putin saw it as an opportunity," says Peskov. "He had the idea that Russia's innate slowness and inflexibility meant that the state couldn't handle such projects. We hadn't built a new city for ages. To get everything done on schedule, Russia needed to be set an international deadline."

Peskov explains why no one objected to hosting the Winter Olympics in the subtropical city of Sochi: "It was Soviet Russia's number one health resort. But there was no sewage system and no airport. How else would we have found a way to rebuild the country's main resort?"

No efforts were spared to impress the International Olympic Committee (IOC) inspectors. Even the unfinished Sochi Airport was made to look fully operational. It would perhaps have been better to openly admit that the airport was not yet running, since the lead time to the Games was seven years. But economics minister German Gref decided to create a Potemkin village. Students were brought in to simulate passengers, kiosks and restaurants were temporarily opened, and the arrival and departure boards displayed nonexistent flights. Fortunately for Russia, the sham was exposed only after the IOC vote.

The competition (South Korea's Pyongchang and Austria's Salzburg) was not difficult to defeat with an unlimited budget. The secret was simple, says a member of the bid committee: just make the best of everything and spend the money well. The same consultants who had produced the London and Paris bids for the 2012 Summer Games were hired, plus an individual approach was devised for each IOC member.

"It's much more complicated than bribing, say, members of the FIFA executive committee. Those are faceless bureaucrats, but the IOC contains celebrities and royalty," says a member of Russia's bid team. How, for example, was it possible to entice Prince Albert II of Monaco? He already had everything. But the ad hoc working group discovered that he was fond of nightlife. So it was that the prince became a regular at Diaghilev, the most expensive club in Moscow, to which he was chauffeured for all the best parties. The other members were more of a challenge: "We'd hear, for example, that someone had a relative who sold stoves and was looking to expand into Russia. We said we'd help, of course."

On the eve of the vote, which was held in Guatemala, the largest Russian companies were "encouraged" to chip in a few million dollars each. Where the money went is unknown.

The climax was the presentation of the Russian bid. The Ministry of Emergency Situations chartered a private plane to fly an artificial ice rink to the hot Latin American country. Locals and even IOC members were stunned. Next came Vladimir Putin. His demeanor was a carbon copy of Tony Blair's before the 2012 Olympic vote, when London was selected. Putin held individual meetings with each member of the IOC. The conversations were quite intimate. "How are your three children?" he asked one, glancing at the dossier in front of him. "Bring them to Moscow as our guests." The IOC members were delighted by such attentiveness.

Without waiting for the results of the vote, Putin departed from Guatemala immediately after his speech. Victory was certain. However, just as a precaution, Peskov warned the press that if Sochi lost the bid, only he would be available for comment. In case of victory, everyone would be on the record.

Whereas the maneuvers surrounding the bid were costly but effective, the construction work was hypercostly and ineffective. "Sure, it was expensive, but that's Russia," says Peskov.

Putin admitted that 214 billion rubles (about $7.2 billion) was spent directly on Olympic facilities, of which 100 billion came from the state treasury and the rest from private investors. However, according to figures from Olympstroy, the state corporation in charge of the Olympic project, the total cost of the Games (including railways, roads, power plants, and other infrastructure) amounted to 1.524 trillion rubles, or $36 billion. According to independent estimates, the cost set an Olympic record, in not only absolute but also relative terms. On average, the total cost for Olympic hosts comes to around 180 percent of the initial estimate, but for the Sochi Games the figure was 300 percent.

But for Peskov such criticism seems like nitpicking. "The road from Sochi to Krasnaya Polyana was also part of the Olympic project, I guess. The Olympics provided an opportunity to develop the region. So we combined the costs. The naysayers didn't like it," says Peskov.

Peskov cites examples of how money was overspent not by malice but by mistake. For example, Fisht Stadium, which was due to host the opening and closing ceremonies, was designed as an open stadium, because it was also intended as a venue for the 2018 FIFA World Cup and grass does not grow very well inside closed arenas. But the architects quite literally failed to see which way the wind was blowing. When construction was in full swing, they realized that the flow of air from the sea to the land was so strong that people holding flags would be blown away. So a roof was added at enormous cost.

"OR ELSE WE'LL LOSE IT"

While Russia was preparing for the Olympics, Ukraine was getting ready to sign an association agreement with the European Union. This less significant event subsequently cost Russia far more than the Olympics did. The signing was initiated by Ukrainian president Victor Yanukovych, whom Putin considered to be under the Kremlin's thumb.

Viktor Yanukovych and Vladimir Putin had a long history. In 2004 Putin was convinced that Yanukovych would be the next president of Ukraine. Yanukovych was less sure. An official close to him says that Yanukovych asked Putin for a Russian passport in case he was suddenly forced to flee the country. What Putin replied is unknown.

The Orange Revolution was a disaster for Yanukovych. He himself said so. It is also alleged that on January 19, 2005 (the Feast of the Epiphany for Russian and Ukrainian Orthodox Christians), he decided to kill himself. At that time he was living in the Mezhyhirya residence near Kiev. That night he took a rifle and went to the nearby lake. Standing there on the shore, gun in hand, he suddenly noticed the moonlight falling on the frozen surface of the water in the shape of a cross. He took it as a sign. He got some locals to make a cross-shaped hole in the ice, then he stripped and plunged in. Back at the house there was no one except his two sisters, a cook, and a waitress (everyone else had long gone). Yanukovych ordered dinner. The waitress later became his common-law wife. It's hard to say how true this story is, since we only have Yanukovych's word for it via those close to him.*

In the end Yanukovych not only survived the first Maidan uprising but managed in the aftermath to consolidate all the discontented. Eighteen months after the Orange Revolution, he won the parliamentary elections and became prime minister. Three and a half years later, in 2009, he finally became president.

---

*Incidentally, he is known to be fond of telling shocking stories, even to people who aren't so close.

Vladimir Putin had never been a friend of Yanukovych's. He did not entirely trust him, but he gave Yanukovych his support. Throughout 2013 President Yanukovych spoke about Ukraine's intention to move closer to Europe by signing an association agreement with the EU. It was a pragmatic aim, since it had the support of all Ukrainian politicians—bar one. That was Viktor Medvedchuk, Putin's closest friend and the mouthpiece for the Russian president inside Ukraine. Everyone said that Ukraine was a European country, while only Medvedchuk insisted that Ukraine's future was with Russia. He created the pro-Russian movement Ukrainian Choice and plastered posters about it all over bus stops across the country. But Putin's hopes that the movement would acquire grassroots support were premature. The former head of the Kuchma administration had negative popularity ratings.

On July 27, 2013, Putin arrived in Kiev to celebrate the 1,025th anniversary of the Baptism of Rus. Visiting a prayer service at St. Volodymyr Hill, in the center of the city, he met with Yanukovych. The meeting lasted fifteen minutes and was covered by all the Ukrainian media. Next he went to a roundtable discussion organized by Medvedchuk, entitled "Orthodox Slavic Values: The Basis of Civilized Choice in Ukraine." The discourse revolved around what was best for Ukrainian society: European values imposed by Eurocrats, or Orthodox Slavic spiritual principles and traditions.

"We, Russia and Ukraine, have always been united and our future lies in this unity," Putin said in his address. "The Baptism of Rus was a great event that defined Russia's and Ukraine's spiritual and cultural development for the centuries to come. We must remember this brotherhood and preserve our ancestors' traditions. We will respect whatever choice our Ukrainian partners, friends and brothers make. The question is only one of how we go about agreeing on working together under absolutely equal, transparent and clear conditions."[1] Unlike 2004, when Putin was popular in Ukraine and his words were heeded, this time his speech made no impression whatsoever on the Ukrainian public.

In the run-up to the autumn summit in Vilnius, where Yanukovych was due to sign an association agreement with the EU, Putin made it increasingly clear to the Ukrainian president which choice was the "right" one. For Putin, it was a matter of principle that Ukraine should not sign an agreement. Since the beginning of his first term back in the early 2000s, he had often said at meetings, "We need to deal with Ukraine or we'll lose it." Inside the Kremlin he was in charge of the "Ukrainian vector," since no one else could be trusted with such an important project. In autumn 2013 he began to put pressure on Yanukovych to abandon the EU plan. Three times in late October and early November Yanukovych flew to Russia for talks.

One of Moscow's levers was money: Russia promised Ukraine a loan of $15 billion. Another one was Yulia Tymoshenko. Having vanquished his sworn enemy in the 2010 presidential election, Viktor Yanukovych immediately initiated criminal proceedings against her. Among the charges were the gas agreements of 2009 she made with Putin, and in autumn 2011 she was imprisoned. Yanukovych was clearly afraid of Tymoshenko, which was why he had declined to join her in a "grand coalition" in 2009—he feared that she would bend him to her will. Even Yanukovych's inner circle was against Tymoshenko's prison sentence, but he was convinced that it was the only way to prevent another Maidan uprising and a new revolution. If Tymoshenko remained at liberty and able to negotiate with Putin, sooner or later she would overthrow him, thought Yanukovych.

Tymoshenko's jail term deeply troubled the West, in particular Angela Merkel. Every meeting she held with Yanukovych began and ended with a discussion of Tymoshenko and a request that she be moved to Germany for treatment of her back injury. Eventually German doctors were allowed to examine Tymoshenko in the hospital wing of the Kharkiv prison. The medical examination revealed no serious illnesses, which somewhat surprised Merkel. However, Tymoshenko was afraid for her life, especially poisoning (a common phobia among Ukrainian politicians after the Viktor Yushchenko affair). In the prison hospital Tymoshenko ate and drank only what her daughter brought her. The authorities complicated things by delaying the food packages, so Tymoshenko was forced to stage several involuntary "hunger strikes."

All this shocked Chancellor Merkel, and she insisted that Tymoshenko's release must be a precondition for any EU-Ukraine association agreement. This principled stand was exploited by Putin. He told Yanukovych that the Europeans wanted to overthrow him and would not accept him into their club even if he did sign an agreement. Instead they would secure Tymoshenko's release and install her as Ukraine's next president. Yanukovych was in a quandary. On one hand, he understood that signing an agreement with the EU would guarantee him reelection in 2015; on the other, he was terrified of Tymoshenko.

Most likely the Kremlin had other levers of influence on Yanukovych. In any case, at the last moment he pulled a U-turn. On November 21, 2013, a week before the summit in Vilnius, Ukrainian prime minister Mykola Azarov announced that the signing of the agreement would be delayed. Protesters immediately began to gather on Independence Square, mainly students demanding European integration for Ukraine.

On November 27, writes Ukrainian journalist Sonia Koshkina, Yanukovych attended the birthday party of Ukrainian oligarch Igor Surkis, the owner of the soccer club Dynamo Kiev and a business partner and friend of Medvedchuk's. Seated at the table were Ukraine's top businessmen (members of the "Ukraine management committee" set up after the Orange Revolution, including Dmitry Firtash and Igor Kolomoisky). Instead of birthday greetings, Yanukovych started the evening with an announcement that the European integration project had been canceled. He spent the rest of the evening explaining his decision purely in terms of economics.[2]

All Yanukovych's supporters were shocked. The decision was unexpected, since up until that moment members of the ruling party who had publicly questioned the idea of European integration and opposed the EU agreement had been excluded from the party and expelled from parliament. Some were even prosecuted.

At the summit in Vilnius on November 28 Yanukovych refused to sign the EU agreement and proposed that Russia join the talks (EU leaders rejected the proposal). An online video later showed a "private" conversation among Yanukovych, Merkel, and Lithuanian president Dalia Grybauskaite in which Yanukovych can be heard saying: "I'd like you to listen to me. For three and a half years I've been alone. I've been face-to-face with a very strong Russia on a very unlevel playing field."[3]

On the night of November 29–30 a unit of Ukraine's Berkut special police force tried to clear the protest camp from Kiev's main square. The demonstrators braved beatings from the police before fleeing and taking refuge in St. Michael's Monastery, where the monks gave them shelter. That marked the start of the second Ukrainian revolution.

LET THE GAMES BEGIN

The Olympic Games in Sochi were a trying experience. Relations with the international press were critical. Putin and his entourage were particularly worried that an accident might happen. "There were fears that the hastily constructed buildings would be of poor quality and collapse," says a senior official inside the presidential administration. There were also fears that there would be power outages and blackouts. Something was bound to go wrong, thought the Kremlin.

But in the end everything went off almost without a hitch. Perhaps the only oddity was the strange design of the toilets in the luxury hotel complex built by Gazprom. Instead of one toilet and one bidet, for some reason each booth contained two toilets. They were the main online meme during the first days of the Olympics. The organizers' more serious concerns were unfounded.

Two of the torchbearers on the Olympic flame's last leg into Sochi were defense minister Sergey Shoigu and foreign minister Sergey Lavrov. The opening ceremony of the Olympic Games was very impressive, but one key scene planned by the organizers was canceled at the insistence of the IOC. A package with photographs of someone who had perished during the Great Patriotic War was to be placed on every seat in the venue, including the person's name, date of birth, and date of death. A minute's silence was to be announced, whereupon all the spectators would hold up the photos. The master of ceremonies, Channel One head Konstantin Ernst, was very keen for it to happen. But the IOC decided that such political action would set an undesirable precedent. If Sochi were allowed to do it, then all subsequent Olympics organizers would arrange their own minutes of silence.

The opening ceremony was attended by around forty foreign leaders (including those of Italy, Japan, Turkey, and China), which Russian state media portrayed as a sign of broad international recognition. One of the guests was Ukrainian president Viktor Yanukovych. His visit to Sochi was a rather risky move, since the standoff between the opposition and the security forces in central Kiev had already claimed its first victims—in late January some Maidan activists had been shot dead by unidentified snipers. But Yanukovych's main objective was to secure the second tranche of a $15 billion loan promised in December. Putin was in no hurry to allocate the money, however.

Dmitry Peskov says that even when Yanukovych returned to Kiev he remained in constant contact with Putin. They called each other several times a day. The events in Kiev had spoiled Putin's festive mood. He kept trying to give advice to Yanukovych and offered him help, but the latter replied: "Don't worry, Vladimir Vladimirovich, everything's under control." Putin did not believe him, and so withheld the cash.

At that moment, the start of the Olympic Games, nothing was under control. Back on January 16 the Verkhovna Rada, Ukraine's parliament, had hastily adopted several laws intended to prevent unrest. The opposition called them "dictatorial." In fact, they were carbon copies of the Russian laws passed in the wake of the Bolotnaya rallies, including criminal liability for libel, tougher penalties for extremism (calls for the overthrow of the government were classified as such), the designation of NGOs as "foreign agents," and a ban on Internet media operating without state registration.

In Russia the laws had been phased in gradually and did not provoke any protests, only a slight murmur in the liberal media. In the febrile atmosphere of Kiev, however, they caused an earthquake. Yanukovych was caught unawares. Grushevskogo Street, which leads to the Verkhovna Rada and government buildings, saw the first bloodshed: Berkut units and Maidan activists, including a military wing known as Right Sector, started shooting at each other.

A week later Yanukovych proposed that opposition leader Arseniy Yatsenyuk become prime minister and form a government of "national trust." But that only made matters worse. Yatsenyuk refused, and Yanukovych had not bothered to warn his own party, including MPs and the current prime minister, Mykola Azarov, of his idea. They learned about the proposal from news reports. It was then that the president's supporters began to desert him, and the pro-Yanukovych Party of Regions also became estranged.

On January 28, 2014, Prime Minister Azarov resigned. That same day the parliament abolished the "dictatorial" laws, and Yanukovych appointed Sergei Arbuzov, a friend of his son Alexander's, as acting prime minister. This caused even greater irritation throughout the entire Ukrainian elite, including the Party of Regions.

The Kremlin was not really up to speed on what had been going on during the years of Yanukovych's presidency. Having come to power with the support of the Ukrainian oligarchs, Yanukovych had decided to end his dependence on them. The only way to secure full independence from the grandees of Ukrainian business was to become one of them—and the biggest at that. This task was entrusted to his son Alexander, a doctor by training who was nicknamed "Sasha the stomatologist." His behavior was so rude and aggressive that it shocked even hard-boiled business sharks. He seized not just businesses that were small or unfriendly but also the businesses of friends and sponsors of his father. One of Alexander Yanukovych's victims was Vladimir

Yevtushenkov, a major Russian business figure, who considered himself a friend of the Ukrainian president's.

According to hearsay, after his inauguration in 2010 Viktor Yanukovych, in the company of friends, gave the following toast: "No eating for two years! Everyone must work for the good of the country!" Ironically, Yanukovych spent those two years enriching himself. The symbol of his personal wealth was Mezhyhirya, his personal residence, which was rumored by the liberal press to be opulent to the extreme. "You like your dacha more than your country," Donetsk oligarch Rinat Akhmetov, the main sponsor of all Yanukovych's preelection campaigns, once chided him.

The president was very attached to his infamous dacha. Since 1935 Mezhyhirya had been a government residence, where the leaders of the Soviet Ukraine (including Nikita Khrushchev) had lived. Yanukovych himself had lived there since 2002, and in 2007 he was able to privatize the estate. At that time Viktor Yushchenko was president and Yanukovych prime minister. Yushchenko wanted to dissolve parliament and hold early elections. In order to buy Yanukovych's compliance and as compensation for the fact that he might lose power, Yushchenko gave him the grand residence.

The 140-hectare complex was surrounded by a 5-meter-high perimeter fence. The property contained a marina, a zoo, an equestrian club, an archery range, tennis courts, and hunting grounds. In February, after the overthrow of Yanukovych, the opposition rebels found on the grounds of the complex a collection of retro cars and a gold paperweight in the form of a baguette, among other things.

APOGEE

Vladimir Putin spent only the first weekend of the Games in Sochi before returning to Moscow on February 11, 2014. There he appointed a new commissioner for human rights and met with Egyptian defense minister Abdel Fattah el-Sisi, who six months earlier had defeated the "Egyptian spring" by overthrowing President Mohamed Morsi and staging a military coup. It was in fact at the Kremlin that el-Sisi officially announced his intention to run for president for the first time. Putin openly endorsed his nomination.

Still in constant communication with Yanukovych, Putin was convinced that what was happening in Kiev was the result of a US-led operation. Back in December US assistant secretary of state Victoria Nuland and Senator John

McCain had visited Ukraine. Nuland handed out biscuits and sandwiches on Independence Square to both the protesters and the police, while McCain spoke from a makeshift stage.

Peskov says that there was compelling evidence of US intervention. "It was an uncontrollable descent. Yanukovych's mistakes were compounded by Washington's provocations. People flew in with money, while day and night there were lights in all the windows. Everything played out according to plan. It was a direct challenge to Russia's security."

On February 14 Putin held a Security Council meeting at his Novo-Ogaryovo residence outside Moscow, and the next day returned to Sochi. There, the confrontation with the United States was also simmering. On February 15 the two countries faced each other in an ice hockey match. President Putin, Prime Minister Medvedev, and chief of staff Sergey Ivanov were in the stands. The match ended in scandal: with the score tied at 2–2 in overtime, Russian forward Fyodor Tyutin scored a third goal, but the referee Bradley Mayer (who was American) disallowed it because the net had been dislodged. Russia lost the penalty shootout.

Putin and the Russian fans were furious. Why was a match against the United States being refereed by an American? They were indignant. It was another anti-Russian conspiracy. They were equally outraged by the congratulations tweeted by the White House: "Congrats to T.J. Oshie and the U.S. men's hockey team on a huge win! Never stop believing in miracles. #GoTeamUSA—bo." The initials "bo" appended at the end meant that President Obama had written the tweet himself, not his press service.

"It's a pity that the referee didn't notice the dislodged net earlier, because it always helps the defending team if the ref can't see it," jibed Putin, commenting on the match. "Because if they concede a goal they can always dispute it, and if they don't they can launch a counterattack. But referees makes mistakes, so I'm not going to pin the blame, but simply say that we were the better side."[4]

After the game Putin went to a meeting with veterans to mark the twenty-fifth anniversary of the withdrawal of Soviet troops from Afghanistan, the war that effectively killed the Soviet Union. Immediately afterward Putin met with athletes and coaches from the Ukrainian national team. During the meeting one of the coaches told Putin on camera that he supported the Russian ice hockey team and had been gutted by the goal disallowed by the US referee. "It's very nice to hear that from you," replied Putin.

THE NEW AFGHANISTAN

Because of the Olympics, the twenty-fifth anniversary of the Soviet withdrawal from Afghanistan went almost unnoticed. That fateful war had begun in 1979, the invasion triggered by prime minister Hafizullah Amin's coup in Kabul, as a result of which the Afghan president, Nur Muhammed Taraki, was overthrown and murdered.

Brezhnev reacted badly to the death of Taraki, who had only recently visited Moscow. He called Amin a "dishonest person." What's more, following the assassination of Taraki, the KGB began to report that Amin was allegedly planning to switch allegiance to the United States, secretly meeting with US diplomats and intelligence services and giving instructions to conduct surveillance of Soviet citizens working in Afghanistan. For the most part, these were only rumors emanating from Amin's opponents. But they were enough to make the Politburo ponder the threat. KGB head Yuri Andropov and defense minister Dmitry Ustinov claimed that Afghanistan risked becoming hostile to the Soviet regime. The only possible course of action was to send in the troops.

Chief of the General Staff Nikolai Ogarkov was strongly opposed, but Andropov silenced him by saying, "You were invited not to give your opinions, but to note down and implement the Politburo's instructions." Another opponent of the invasion was the chairman of the Council of Ministers, Alexei Kosygin. But at the historic meeting of the Politburo on December 12, 1979, he was absent, and the decision to invade was made unanimously.

The war lasted ten years. It became known as the "Soviet Vietnam" and was in fact the prelude to the disintegration of the Soviet Union. The Americans, of course, played a huge role. They actively supported the mujahedeen against the Soviet army. To distribute funds and enlist regional volunteers they recruited a certain Saudi by the name of Osama bin Laden.

In 1989 Mikhail Gorbachev decided to withdraw the troops. Three years later the pro-Soviet Afghan leader Mohammed Najibullah was overthrown. For the next four years he lived inside the building of the UN mission in Kabul. In 1996, when the Taliban took the Afghan capital, they broke into the UN office and captured and killed Najibullah. The Taliban government was never recognized by the international community, but over the subsequent five years it established de facto rule over the country. Only in 2001 was it overthrown—this time by a US-led international coalition with the support of Russia. That, however, was not the end of the war in Afghanistan.

One year after the Sochi Olympics in February 2015, the twenty-sixth anniversary of the withdrawal of Soviet troops from Afghanistan, Putin acknowledged that he now understood Brezhnev's frame of mind: "As the years go by and more and more facts become known, our understanding of the reasons and motives for the Soviet invasion of Afghanistan increases. Many mistakes were made, of course, but there were genuine threats that the Soviet leadership tried to head off by invading Afghanistan."

It is symbolic that Afghan war veterans would play a crucial role in the subsequent events in Crimea.

DENOUEMENT

For Russia, the most important part of any Olympics is not individual victories but the team results—the country with the most gold medals is the winner. For much of the Games, however, the Russian team was not sitting pretty. Five days before the end of the Olympics, the host country was in fifth place, behind Germany, Norway, the Netherlands, and the United States. Putin again left Sochi—for reasons more important than the Olympic medal standings. On February 18 the hostilities in Kiev had resumed. The Maidan activists had launched a daylight attack on the government quarter, and at night the security forces had tried to clear the central square, during which action twenty-five people had been killed. Every day Putin phoned Victor Yanukovych (who still maintained that everything was under control) and Angela Merkel, telling her that the radical opposition was to blame for the tragic violence, not the Ukrainian president.

Meanwhile, as the Games drew to a close the Russian national team was edging up in the medal count. On February 19 the Russians won gold in men's snowboarding; the day after, they picked up another gold medal in women's figure skating.

But in Kiev the news was less sanguine. On February 20 clashes in the center of the city killed more than ninety people. Several Ukrainian athletes left Sochi in protest at the bloodshed in their homeland.

It was on that day in Kiev that negotiations began with the participation of the foreign ministers of Germany, France, and Poland—Frank-Walter

Steinmeier, Laurent Fabius, and Radoslaw Sikorski—as well as the recently retired Russian ombudsman for human rights, Vladimir Lukin.

Putin aide Vladislav Surkov also arrived in Kiev. His mission was different from Lukin's. Whereas Lukin had to work with foreign diplomats, Surkov had to deal with Yanukovych and his entourage and ensure that the Ukrainian authorities were coping. After two months of hearing "everything is under control" from Yanukovych, Putin had serious doubts.

European ministers made it clear to Yanukovych that as a result of the bloodshed he was effectively a pariah; therefore it was in his interests to make as many concessions as possible. The United States imposed individual sanctions on Yanukovych and his security forces responsible for the Maidan massacre, followed thereafter by EU sanctions. French foreign minister Laurent Fabius promised to "hit the wallet of those responsible for the violence."

While European ministers, Ukrainian opposition leaders, and Yanukovych were negotiating, February 20 was a very busy day for Kiev's airports. Private jets were lining up on the runways with government officials and their families, cash and valuables on board. Kiev International Airport alone saw the departure of sixty-four VIP flights that day.

During the talks Yanukovych agreed to everything, promising constitutional reforms and early presidential elections in December 2014. At the crucial moment he again telephoned Putin, who insisted that Yanukovych sign an agreement with the opposition. Putin then called Angela Merkel, Barack Obama, French president François Hollande, and British prime minister David Cameron.

However, the Maidan activists did not want to sign an agreement. When the leaders of the Ukrainian opposition went to Kiev's main square to inform the crowd of the agreement with Yanukovych, they were met with boos. During a speech by champion boxer Vitaly Klitschko, who considered himself the sole leader of the opposition, the activist Volodymyr Parasyuk forced his way onto the stage and shouted: "Our leaders shake hands with murderers! Shame on you! No more Yanukovych. He must be gone by 10:00 a.m. tomorrow!"

The Maidan crowd began chanting, "Criminals out!"

Parasyuk continued: "If by 10:00 a.m. tomorrow our politicians do not call for Yanukovych's immediate resignation, I swear we will storm the government!" At that moment coffins containing the bodies of the deceased protesters were brought out onto the square, and all the opposition leaders, including Klitschko, knelt down.

The most unexpected event of February 21 was not the eventual signing of an agreement but the sudden withdrawal of the security forces. The internal troops guarding government buildings and the Verkhovna Rada and the Berkut special police units surrounding the building of the presidential administration also departed. The order to leave was given by interior minister Vitaly Zakharchenko. It was a blow to Yanukovych and his administration. They suddenly found themselves without protection, one-on-one with the rebels.

Yanukovych called Putin to tell him that he had signed an agreement and intended to move to Kharkiv. "You're going where?" Putin shouted at him. "Sit still! Your country is out of control. Kiev is at the mercy of gangs and looters. Are you insane?"

"Everything is under control," replied Yanukovych.

"I never imagined that he was such a cowardly piece of shit," Putin is alleged to have said of his former colleague.

Surkov had effectively failed in his mission to prevent Yanukovych's flight from Kiev and the collapse of his regime. That made his resignation a foregone conclusion. Only Putin's dislike for knee-jerk decisions delayed it slightly. In March Surkov went abroad on vacation, and his wife began to post Instagram photos of their trip. Expecting to be fired, Surkov thought he could now live the life of an ordinary individual. But he was inadvertently rescued by the West when he was included on the EU sanctions list, issued on March 21. Putin could not punish someone who had been punished by his enemies. So Surkov was retained as a presidential aide for Ukraine, and a short while later was sent back to that country, this time with the task of sorting out the situation in the Donbass region.

THE PLASTIC WRAP COMES OFF

On the evening of February 21, 2014, Yanukovych went to his Mezhyhirya residence, which he did indeed value more than his country, it seems. His aides had been emptying out the residence since February 19, shipping out valuables, cash, and gold bars by the bucketload.

Yanukovych summoned the head of his administration and the Speaker of the Verkhovna Rada for a farewell dinner. Seemingly loyal, they had not yet resigned and fled the country. However, the Speaker, Volodymyr Rybak, arrived at Mezhyhirya simply to tender his resignation. He knew that he was on the way out, as did most MPs from the Party of Regions, who followed suit the following morning. After that "last supper" everyone climbed inside their jeeps and headed for Kharkiv in eastern Ukraine, where a separatist congress was due to be held. This "congress of deputies of all levels" was intended to challenge the Maidan rebellion, demand federalization, and even bring about the secession of the eastern provinces. Yanukovych had already tried something similar back in 2004 in the midst of the Orange Revolution, but his attempts had failed.

This time the attempt failed once again. As described by Sonia Koshkina, Yanukovych was still behaving as if nothing had happened. He still thought of himself as president and all others as subordinates. The governor of Kharkiv, Mikhail Dobkin, took offense and urged Yanukovych not to appear at the congress. Moreover, he said, he could not guarantee Yanukovych's personal safety.[5]

However, Yanukovych was seriously considering the idea of breaking up Ukraine. In the evening he gathered his old associates and posed them a question: "What could be the name of this new country?"

"China," joked one of them.

"There already is a China," said another without irony.

"Are you all making fun of me?" fumed Yanukovych.

On the morning of February 22 Yanukovych learned that his beloved Mezhyhirya had been seized by a crowd during the night. He then recorded a televised address in which he described the goings-on in the country as "gangsterism, vandalism, and a coup d'état."

Then came perhaps the final turning point. The fleeing president arrived at the Kharkiv Palace of Sport for the planned congress. He got out of his jeep and headed to the door. At that moment his phone rang. After a short conversation Yanukovych turned around, went back to his car, and drove away. Someone had tipped him off that pro-Maidan soccer fans had broken through the cordon around the building. The Kharkiv elite inside fled immediately, and the congress did not take place.

Yanukovych went to Donetsk Airport, but local border guards refused to let his Falcon jet fly to Russia. That was a shock for him. So he went by car to Crimea. There on the coast he was picked up by a Russian helicopter.

Yanukovych's next public appearance came a week later, on February 28. During a press conference in Rostov-on-Don in southern Russia he seemed unhinged, still claiming that he was the only legitimate president of Ukraine. He blamed the radical opposition and "fascist thugs" for what had happened, as well as the "international mediators" who had betrayed him.

Despite its despair over Yanukovych, the Kremlin shared his opinion of Western mediators. "He signed an agreement, ordered the withdrawal of the police, and remained in the country. The European mediators promised to guarantee the implementation of the agreement. What happened was simply appalling and absolutely unprecedented. It was a direct threat to Russia," concludes Dmitry Peskov.

On February 23 the Sochi Olympics came to a close. Over the last three days of competition the Russians won two golds per day and wound up leading the team gold medal count. It was a national triumph.

However, the Kremlin's mind was elsewhere. Putin was already plotting an operation in Crimea.

"The paradox of Sochi is that they were one of the best Games in history. But they lived in the global consciousness for just a few days. The fat imprint of Ukraine smothered everything," sighs Peskov.

Putin himself, summing up the Olympics, said that he had no doubts about the ingrained bias of the West: "There is a cohort of critics far removed from sport whose battleground is international politics. They used the Olympic project for their own anti-Russian propaganda purposes. Whatever we say, we cannot convince anyone because they have their own agenda."[6]

"Their goal was to get rid of Putin," Peskov says, sounding sure. "They [the West] do not like him. Russia is too obstinate under Putin and unwilling to make concessions. They are ready to do anything to get rid of him. We sensed this even before Ukraine, but afterward it was a different matter. After Ukraine the diplomatic masks came off. Before that, the confrontation was wrapped up in diplomatic plastic wrap, but now the plastic wrap was removed."

In 1980 the outbreak of war in Afghanistan spoiled the Soviet Union's Moscow Olympics. Sixty-five countries, including the United States, Britain, Canada, Germany, Turkey, Japan, and even China, boycotted them. There was no boycott of the 2014 Sochi Games, since the events in Crimea began immediately afterward. However, the Kremlin's feast of sport had been ruined once again.

CHAPTER 17

IN WHICH DEFENSE MINISTER SERGEY SHOIGU TAKES REVENGE FOR AFGHANISTAN AND NICHOLAS I

Sergey Shoigu likes to tell how his childhood dream was to be a truck driver: someone completely free and dependent only on himself. The current defense minister holds the record for staying in power in modern Russia—he lost his freedom and independence back in 1991.

Even before being appointed defense minister, Shoigu always behaved like a military man. He was fond of army jokes, discipline, tough talk, and rigor. He even manages to look more brutal than the other siloviki*—he is not a philologist by training, like Sechin or Ivanov, but a builder.*

Shoigu's reputation as a politician is unblemished, but he never exploits that fact. He is more soldier than politician. As a military man, his task is to execute orders.

In 2006 during a TV broadcast, a teenager asked Shoigu, then head of the Ministry of Emergency Situations, the following question: "What would you do if you were on a plane that was falling from the sky?"

Shoigu answered without hesitation: "Nothing. It would keep falling regardless."

THE BOSS

To better understand potential opponents, Vladimir Putin advised Shoigu to watch two American TV series: *Boss* and *House of Cards*. "You'll find them useful," the president recommended. It is clear why Putin liked them: they affirmed his belief that Western politicians are all cynical scoundrels whose words about values and human rights are pure hot air and simply a tool to attack enemies. Shoigu agreed with that assessment.

The new defense minister has always been Putin's most loyal ally, even though his career began long before Putin moved to Moscow. Shoigu's longevity inside Putin's inner circle is unmatched. He became a federal minister back in 1991, when Putin was working as an aide to the mayor of St. Petersburg, Anatoly Sobchak. To begin with, Shoigu created a "rescue corps" that later morphed into the splendidly named Ministry of Disasters (which was in fact a powerful security service). In 1992 Shoigu was a mediator in the settlement of the Georgian-Ossetian conflict, and he assisted in the evacuation of Russian refugees from Tajikistan.

Shoigu has never tried to stand out from the crowd—all the more remarkable given that Putin partly owes his presidency to him. In 1999 the popular head of the Ministry of Emergency Situations headed the electoral list of the pro-Putin party Unity, the brainchild of Boris Berezovsky and Alexander Voloshin. The success of Unity (which took second place in the 1999 Duma elections, behind the Communists) effectively guaranteed Putin's subsequent victory in the 2000 presidential election, since his main rival, the Primakov-Luzhkov team, had been destroyed. However, the creators of the party reaped neither dividends nor Putin's gratitude. A year later Berezovsky went into self-imposed exile in London, and almost all the governors who had backed Unity lost their jobs. In the early years of Putin's presidency Shoigu too was out of sorts.

The leader of Unity opposed Vladislav Surkov's idea of merging his "offspring" with the Fatherland–All Russia party. The Kremlin ignored his objection, but to sweeten the pill Shoigu was given the symbolic post of co-chairman of United Russia (along with defeated Moscow mayor Yuri Luzhkov and the governor of Tatarstan, Mintimer Shaimiev).

Even more complex were Shoigu's relations with the new elite, most of whom were Putin's former colleagues from the FSB, who now controlled the presidential administration. As a Yeltsin-era *silovik*, Shoigu was a natural enemy. Therefore, Shoigu was not chosen to lead United Russia in the 2003 Duma elections, ceding the position to the uncharismatic but servile interior minister, Boris Gryzlov, a former classmate of FSB director Nikolai Patrushev. Six months before the election, in June 2003, Gryzlov launched a powerful PR campaign against corruption inside his own department. The image of a strict but fair policeman was intended to please voters. He discovered a gang of "werewolves in epaulets" inside the Interior Ministry. However, it turned out that the head of this alleged criminal group inside the department was not a police official but a general from the Ministry of Emergency Situations with close links to Sergey Shoigu. Earning brownie points ahead of the election, Gryzlov simultaneously managed to bury his fellow party member.

The party was shaken to the core. It was rumored that Shoigu's subordinate testified against his boss and even admitted during his interrogation that aircraft belonging to the ministry had been used to import drugs to Russia from Tajikistan. The rumors remained just that, but for a moment Shoigu looked vulnerable.

Shoigu's loyalty and patience helped him through. He knew that the key to survival was to retain access to Putin. For that, Shoigu was able to exploit the president's love of hunting and extreme sport, as well as the unique resources of the Ministry of Emergency Situations. Shoigu effectively became Putin's one-man tour operator, arranging trips for the president across the length and breadth of Russia, including, for instance, Shoigu's homeland, Tuva—a small, picturesque republic on the border of Mongolia. Shoigu became Putin's permanent hunting and fishing companion. It was he who organized a fishing expedition to Tuva for Putin and Prince Albert II of Monaco back in 2007, when the president first posed for photographers with a naked torso. And the even more famous August 2009 photo of a bare-chested Putin wearing a cowboy hat and riding a horse was also the product of a Shoigu-inspired trip.

Shoigu even "directed" the photo shoot. It was he who selected Putin's cowboy hat from the wardrobe of the Ministry of Emergency Situations and chose the tree that Putin climbed up that day. Eyewitnesses say Putin tried very hard. Three times he swam across the cold, narrow Khemchik River to make sure his butterfly stroke was properly captured on film.

Six months later tragedy struck: a fire at a nightclub in Perm in central Russia killed 156 people. It immediately became clear that the fire safety service was to blame. It had repeatedly inspected the club and on each occasion had given the all-clear in exchange for a bribe. The media wrote that it was typical of Shoigu's Ministry of Emergency Situations, which was responsible for fire safety. But the tragedy had no effect on Shoigu personally.

In 2009 Shoigu and Putin's joint recreation reached a new level when Shoigu was named the president of the Russian Geographical Society, which had existed since the mid-nineteenth century, and Putin became the chairman of the board of trustees (his predecessors in the role were emperors Nicholas I, Alexander II, Alexander III, and Nicholas II).

Shoigu's aides maintain that he does indeed enjoy extreme sports and goes on annual expeditions to the forest, every one of which is a huge headache for his bodyguards, who must not lose sight of their charge. The minister is also pursued through the Tuvan taiga by Defense Ministry officials with a special communications link and a nuclear suitcase.

The acid test for Sergei Shoigu came in 2012 on Putin's return to the Kremlin. The irreplaceable head of the Ministry of Emergency Situations was appointed governor of the Moscow region. It was an obvious demotion, but Shoigu took the blow stoically and carried out Putin's instructions. The president noted Shoigu's uncomplaining attitude, and so his Moscow exile lasted only six months. When Anatoly Serdyukov was fired from his post as defense minister, Putin replaced him with Shoigu, who was neutral and had no connection to the attack on Serdyukov for alleged corruption. It was Putin's traditional system of checks and balances. Though he can be swayed in part by his entourage, he only ever half follows through on the advice given. If someone actively lobbies for another's resignation, Putin never appoints the lobbyist's preferred choice. Serdyukov's ousting was orchestrated by chief of staff Sergey Ivanov and the "weapons king," Rostec CEO Sergey Chemezov, which meant that the new minister had to be someone with no connection to them.

An important mission for Shoigu in his new role was to establish relations with the generals. They had despised Serdyukov for ignoring their opinion and viewing them as an obstacle to army reform. Shoigu disbanded Serdyukov's entire team of female bean counters.

EVERYTHING'S SHIPSHAPE

In the propaganda film *Crimea: The Way Home*, made by Russian state television, Putin relates that he spent the night of February 22–23 directing the operation to save the life of Viktor Yanukovych. He phoned the fleeing president several times, kept in touch with his bodyguards, and instructed Russian *spetsnaz* special forces to locate Yanukovych's motorcade. Putin said that he had information that the new Ukrainian authorities intended to kill the deposed president. The source of this information was most likely Yanukovych himself, who in his last televised address to the Ukrainian people claimed that his vehicle and that of Verkhovna Rada speaker Volodymyr Rybak had been fired upon (which Rybak denied).

Putin spent that sleepless night at his Novo-Ogaryovo residence in the company of his closest advisers: defense minister Sergey Shoigu, Security Council secretary Nikolai Patrushev, FSB head Alexander Bortnikov, and chief of staff Sergey Ivanov.

"I told my four colleagues that the events in Ukraine had unfolded in such a manner that we had to start planning how to return Crimea to Russia. We could not leave the region and its people to the whim of fate and the nationalist steamroller," Putin said, summing up the events of that night.[1]

The idea was not unanimously welcomed. Patrushev was passionately in favor and urged Putin to act without delay. Shoigu, however, reacted with extreme caution. He would be responsible for carrying out the planned operation, so he listed numerous arguments against. But Putin did not listen.

One of the planners of the operation in Crimea says that Putin mixed up his dates. The Russian special forces boarded ships at Novorossiisk and were sent to Sevastopol a little earlier, on February 20—that is, *before* the overthrow of Yanukovych. However, at that moment his fate seemed a foregone conclusion to the Kremlin, since the Ukrainian president had begun talks with European ministers and was ready to accept their terms and conditions. This explains why Putin instructed his representative, Vladimir Lukin, not to sign an agreement.

The Kremlin says that a specific plan of action in respect to Crimea was first discussed in December 2013, when the head of the Supreme Council of Crimea, Vladimir Konstantinov, paid a visit to Moscow. He told Security Council secretary Nikolai Patrushev that in the event of Yanukovych's overthrow the autonomous republic of Crimea would be ready "to join Russia." Patrushev was pleasantly surprised by such resoluteness, says an eyewitness.

The idea to return Crimea to Russia's fold was not spontaneous. Back in 2008, at the NATO summit in Bucharest, Putin had said that if Ukraine joined NATO it would risk losing Crimea and the East. As time passed, the idea of annexing Crimea took shape. Putin's age-old mantra of "we have to deal with Ukraine or we'll lose it" turned into "if Ukraine joins NATO, we'll take Crimea." After all, Russia's Black Sea Fleet was stationed in Crimea at Sevastopol, the "city of Russian glory." The base had been on lease from Ukraine since 1991.

In 2010 Dmitry Medvedev and Viktor Yanukovych signed the so-called Kharkiv agreements: Russia cut the high price of gas for Ukraine (for which Yulia Tymoshenko had been prosecuted) in return for an extension of the twenty-five-year lease of the base at Sevastopol for the Black Sea Fleet and an increase in the number of Russian troops stationed there.

By the fall of 2013, when the Maidan protests began in Kiev, the daily talk inside the Kremlin and among the *siloviki* and patriotic businessmen was all about Crimea. The phrase "*Krim nash*" (Crimea is ours) was on their lips. Particular fans of the slogan were Rosneft head Igor Sechin and Russian Railways head Vladimir Yakunin.

The decision to return Crimea to Russia (which, according to Putin, was made at 7:00 a.m. on February 23, 2014) was very risky. Yet Nikolai Patrushev and Sergey Ivanov, backed by FSB head Alexander Bortnikov, told Putin that private polls conducted by the Federal Protective Service showed that the Crimean population was overwhelmingly in favor of joining Russia. What's more, there would be no resistance: the Ukrainian government was in disarray, and there was no one to give any orders to the military to defend the peninsula. As a result, it was decided that the operation to "return" Crimea should go ahead, but with great care. The task was entrusted to Sergey Shoigu. All understood its enormous size. The fear of failure was real, because despite the years of talk about the need to retake Crimea, there was in fact no concrete plan. It had to be played by ear.

The political part of the Crimean operation was directed by the almost completely unknown Oleg Belaventsev, Shoigu's former assistant, who for many years had been in charge of top-secret assignments. Inside the Ministry of Emergency Situations he led the Emercom agency, which carried out the Ministry's overseas operations. When Shoigu was appointed governor of the Moscow region, Belaventsev became his executive secretary. And when Shoigu moved to the Defense Ministry, he appointed Belaventsev as the new head of the subcontractor company that had been suspected of corruption in the Oboronservis case, which led to Serdykov's dismissal.

On February 23 Belaventsev went to Crimea to get a grasp of the situation for himself. The plan to seize Crimea initially involved the help of the prime minister of the republic, Anatoly Mogilev, who was a protégé of Viktor

Yanukovych. He agreed not to get in the way of Moscow's operation, but then got cold feet and fled to Donetsk.

Belaventsev's next move was to approach the leader of the Crimean Communists, the sixty-six-year-old former head of the Supreme Council of Crimea, Leonid Grach. In Moscow he was the most recognizable of Crimea's pro-Russian politicians, while at home he had something of a reputation as a nut job. A few days after speaking to him, Belaventsev proposed that he become the new prime minister. Grach even spoke over the phone with Shoigu, who told him that Russia was about to assert control over Crimea and asked him to take responsibility. Grach readily agreed. But Shoigu soon realized that Grach had no influence in Crimea whatsoever and was unreliable. So the old Communist was forgotten.

On February 26 unrest broke out in Simferopol. Two opposing rallies took place outside the building of the Supreme Council—one Crimean Tatar, the other Russian. Word had got round that the Supreme Council was going to ask Putin to accept Crimea into the Russian Federation. The Russians came out in support, the Tatars in protest. A fight ensued in which two people were killed (one was crushed, the other died of a heart attack). But the leaders of the Russian and Tatar rallies managed to disperse the crowd. The Russian leader was forty-one-year-old local MP Sergey Aksyonov.

That same night Shoigu ordered the deployment of Russian paratroopers from the Pskov 76th Guards Division to Crimea. Ten aircraft landed in Sevastopol, whereupon the troops carried out a nighttime operation to seize the Supreme Council, the government of Crimea, and close the peninsula's airspace. The Russian flag was raised over the building of the Supreme Council. The troops were in unmarked uniforms, thus earning them the nickname "little green men." The Russian authorities did not acknowledge them as their own, and the Russian military officially denied any involvement. The troops who took control of the Supreme Council in Simferopol were operating blindly—they were not told in advance where or why they were being dispatched. Their task was to establish control over the building, and some did not know which city or country they were in. The new lord of the manor—that is, of the Supreme Council building—was now Belaventsev.

In *Crimea: The Way Home* Putin says that he did not need permission from the Federal Council (the upper chamber of the Russian parliament) to deploy troops to Ukraine: "According to the relevant international agreement, we had the right to station 20,000 troops at our military base in Crimea, even slightly more. Even with the extra forces we sent, that figure was not reached. Strictly speaking, we did not violate anything." However, the acting president of Ukraine at the time, Aleksander Turchynov, stated that there were 46,000 Russian troops in Crimea. Putin requested permission from the Federation Council to deploy troops much later, on March 1, when the Crimean operation was already finished.

Before the clash outside the building of the Crimean Supreme Council on February 26, advisers from the FSB and the GRU (the Russian military intelligence service) arrived in Crimea, including Igor Girkin, who would later become known as Igor Strelkov, the leader of the Donetsk People's Republic independence movement. Their goal was to organize an emergency session of parliament and elect a new prime minister. Crimea's parliamentarians refused to attend, so plainclothes officers took them to the building by force.

The head of the Crimean Supreme Council nominated the aforementioned Sergey Aksyonov as the new prime minister. This little-known MP was the leader of the Russian Unity party in Crimea and was reputed to have criminal connections. He had instigated the brawl outside the Supreme Council building, after which the Russian troops landed at Sevastopol. "The speaker of the Crimean parliament told me he's our Che Guevara—just what we needed," Putin says in *Crimea: The Way Home*, describing his first encounter with Aksyonov.

"The parliament was the absolutely legitimate representative body of the Crimean authorities," Putin said in a TV interview. "People voted and elected Sergey Valerevich Aksyonov as the new prime minister of Crimea. The legally incumbent Ukrainian president Yanukovych approved it. From the point of view of Ukrainian law, it was all satisfactory. Whatever might be said or construed, everything's shipshape."

After being delivered by helicopter from Crimea onto a Russian warship on February 23, Yanukovych was now ensconced at the Barvikha resort outside Moscow. However, according to Putin, he returned once more to Crimea at the end of February before finally realizing that there was "no one to negotiate with."

On the afternoon of February 27 the speaker of the Crimean parliament put the resignation of Prime Minister Mogilev and the election of Sergey Aksyonov as the new prime minister to a vote. According to official data, sixty-one out of sixty-four MPs voted in favor. However, according to the

MPs themselves, the real figure was forty-two out of fifty-three, which was not enough for a quorum.

On February 28 an Il-76 military transport aircraft brought 170 veterans of Afghanistan and Chechnya to Crimea, as well as athletes, members of motorcycle clubs, and members of "patriotic clubs." They were put up at a resort in Crimea that was the property of the Ministry of Defense at the behest of Duma MP and leader of the Veterans of Afghanistan Union Franz Klintsevich, a longtime friend of Shoigu. In 1999, at Shoigu's request, he and his "Afghans" had joined the pro-Putin Unity party. After Shoigu's appointment as defense minister Klintsevich said, "Shoigu and victory go hand in hand."

The "tourists," who received their instructions from Klintsevich, were all eager for Crimea to return to Russia and had a strong nostalgia for the Soviet imperial past. They were willing to fight, but their role was simply to play the part of ordinary Crimeans, protesting and demanding that Russia retake control of the peninsula. It was an improvised Maidan, just as heartfelt as the one in Kiev, but with the crucial difference that most of the activists were Russian—that is, foreign nationals (at the time)—even though physically and linguistically they were no different from the locals.

Within days the Russian troops, with the support of local militias, took control of all the Ukrainian military bases in Crimea. There was no resistance, since almost all the bases were manned by contract service personnel from the local community. And almost all of them were pro-Russian.

THE GHOST OF NICHOLAS I

Crimea has a long and complicated history. It became part of the Russian Empire under Catherine the Great in 1783. But the most dramatic events on the peninsula occurred seventy years later, during the reign of Tsar Nicholas I.

Nicholas I should have been the greatest Russian emperor of the nineteenth century. His elder brother, Alexander I, had defeated Napoleon, but he remained "a weak and wicked ruler" in the memory of future generations. Nicholas I was not like that. In 1825 he suppressed the revolt of the Decembrists, and his court ideologue, education minister Count Sergey Uvarov, formulated the Russian national idea: "Orthodoxy, autocracy, nationality." The emperor suppressed separatism in Poland with an iron fist. Poland for him was like Chechnya for Putin. Nicholas helped Austria crush the revolution in Hungary—which earned him the nickname "Gendarme of

Europe." Lastly, Nicholas, who considered himself a great Orthodox monarch, believed it his mission to liberate the Slavic peoples under Ottoman rule. Moreover, he wanted to take Constantinople, though he understood the perils of doing so.

Putin has often been compared to Nicholas I, not least by former Czech foreign minister Karel Schwarzenberg: "It was under Nicholas I that the great part of Central Asia was conquered by the Russians. Putin is quite successfully getting them under the control of Russia again, and the West is losing," he opined.[2]

The downfall of Nicholas I was the Crimean War—the first and only time in history Russia found itself alone against the rest of the world. In the period 1853–1856 Russia faced an alliance consisting of Britain, France, Turkey, and even Sardinia. In the post-Soviet years anti-Western Russian journalists would resurrect the stereotype according to which the whole of Russian history is one long confrontation with the West. In fact, there was only one such confrontation with the West: the Crimean War.

The war was provoked by Russia's rising ambitions and Britain and France's decision to save Turkey from the Russian onslaught. The pretext for the Crimean War was a diplomatic conflict over the Church of the Nativity in Bethlehem, then under Ottoman rule. To put pressure on Turkey, Russia sent troops into Moldavia and Wallachia (also under the control of the Ottoman Empire). In response, France and Britain sent their fleets to the Sea of Marmara. When Russia's troops crossed the Danube, the British and French declared war on Russia.

The European press was brimming with anti-Russian propaganda. Nicholas I was called the "Dictator of the North," and British newspapers claimed that Christians in the Ottoman Empire enjoyed greater religious freedoms than Catholics and Protestants in Orthodox Russia (despite the fact that in 1844 Nicholas had visited London as the personal guest of Queen Victoria). At the same time, Russia unrolled its first-ever large-scale anti-Western propaganda campaign.

During the Crimean War the technological gap between Russia on one side and Britain and France on the other became apparent. The war ended in humiliating defeat and the death of Nicholas I. According to one version, the tsar committed suicide after a failed attack on the Crimean city of Yevpatoria and the doomed defense of Sevastopol.

The defense of Sevastopol was glorified thanks largely to the memoirs of someone who took part in it—Leo Tolstoy. Sevastopol was later sanctified as the "city of Russian glory" on the hundredth anniversary of its defense.

It was during the centenary event that the Soviet leadership decided to transfer Crimea from Russia to Ukraine. In 2014, after the operation to retake Crimea, Putin said that the original decision had been made personally by Nikita Khrushchev. But in 1954, when the deed was done, Khrushchev did not have enough power to made such decisions alone. A year after Stalin's death the country was ruled by a team of the dictator's heirs. Khrushchev, who was first secretary of the Central Committee of the Communist Party, had to deal with each of them, in particular the prime minister, Georgy Malenkov, who was first among equals. Khrushchev managed to become supreme leader only in 1957. To this day there is still no entirely plausible explanation as to why Crimea was handed over to the Ukrainian SSR. The most convincing theory seems to be agricultural: Khrushchev wanted to irrigate the Crimean steppe with water from the Dnieper, which flows through Ukraine, and planned to make the Ukrainian leadership responsible for farming the peninsula.

"CRIMEA IS OURS"

Having elected Aksyonov as the new prime minister in late February 2014, the Crimean parliament decided to hold a referendum on May 25 to coincide with Ukraine's presidential election to replace Yanukovych. Aksyonov stated that the Crimean authorities still considered Yanukovych to be the country's legitimate president and would carry out his orders. The exact wording of the referendum question was not published. Initially the Crimean authorities said that it was not about accession to Russia, only about clarifying the republic's autonomous status.

The problem lay in the fact that Moscow had not yet decided what to do with Crimea. The liberals inside the Kremlin and the government were against bringing Crimea into Russia, pointing to the example of Abkhazia and South Ossetia, whose independence President Dmitry Medvedev had recognized in 2008 but which had not become part of Russia so as not to violate international law. Likewise, Crimea's independence should be recognized, they said. It should be a de jure independent state, although de facto under Russian control.

On February 28, the day after the announcement of the Crimean referendum, a bill was introduced in the Duma to facilitate the accession of new territories to the Russian Federation. According to the existing legislation, an entity could join Russia only if it concluded an international agreement with the government of the country from which it wanted to secede. The new law did not require such an agreement—all that was necessary was to hold a referendum and submit an application to Moscow. The draft law was submitted by Sergey Mironov, the leader of the political party A Just Russia, although behind the scenes it was penned by the Kremlin. Vladimir Putin wanted to test the waters to see how the idea would be received. It was important that the initiative be seen to come from the opposition (which was friendly), not from the Kremlin itself.

Then the hard talk began. On the night of March 1–2 Putin spoke to Obama over the phone for one and a half hours. The US president threatened to isolate Russia, saying that he would not attend the G8 summit in Sochi, scheduled for June. The next day, at a White House press conference, he said, "What cannot be done is for Russia, with impunity, to put its soldiers on the ground and violate basic principles that are recognized around the world," adding that the United States was preparing to take diplomatic steps to isolate Russia. The word "sanctions" was not mentioned.[3]

The new wording of the referendum on accession to Russia was officially approved by the Crimean Supreme Council on March 6. According to those involved in the process, the new wording was proposed around March 3 or 4.

On March 4 Putin held a press conference at which he said that Russia was not planning to annex Crimea, although he made a point of mentioning Kosovo, saying that "nobody has ruled out the right of nations to self-determination."[4] But the decision to annex Crimea had in fact already been made. Despite being under intense pressure from Obama and Merkel, Putin decided that he could not give way and in any case did not think they would impose serious sanctions. He believed that the maximum punishment would be a boycott of the G8 summit in Sochi. That in itself would have been a very strong insult, but Putin was ready to sacrifice the summit for the sake of Crimea. He was sure that the West would not dare to go any further, and if it did, then not for very long. After the war in Georgia, Russia had also been threatened with isolation, but everything had soon been forgotten.

However, Mironov's law was deemed unnecessary and was not passed. Then on the night of March 5–6 the Crimean parliament announced the change of wording to its referendum ("Are you in favor of the reunification of Crimea with Russia as a constituent entity of the Russian Federation?") and to change the date. Instead of May 25 or March 30, as had initially been suggested, it would be held even earlier, on March 16—a very small preparation window.

On March 7 a rally was held outside the Kremlin in Moscow under the banner "For our brotherly people," at which the slogan "Crimea is ours" was first sounded in public.

Crimea joined Russia on March 16. According to official figures, 96.77 percent of those voting were in favor. A similar referendum was held in Sevastopol, where the result was even more decisive, since the city was populated mostly by the Russian military and lived and breathed pro-Russian sentiment. One March 18, at a ceremony in the Kremlin, Vladimir Putin signed an agreement on the accession of Crimea and Sevastopol to the Russian Federation.

The apogee came on May 9, 2014, which was Victory Day. Putin and Shoigu arrived in Sevastopol for a triumphant victory parade. The city was buzzing with chants of "Russia, Russia!" It did indeed feel like a victory. After the parade Putin went to Yalta to the dacha of his old friend Viktor Medvedchuk to celebrate.

THE RUSSIAN SPRING

Immediately after the referendum, most of Klintsevich's "rebels" left Crimea, along with the paratroopers and FSB officers. The paratroopers returned to their permanent base, while the Russian volunteers went to eastern Ukraine to continue the implementation of Putin's idea that "Ukraine will join NATO without Crimea and the east."

The next operation was not directed by Shoigu (his man Belaventsev remained in Crimea and was appointed Russian presidential envoy to the republic). Initially the operation in the Donbass region, in the easternmost part of Ukraine, had no central decision-making body. The Kremlin gathered information and encouraged the secessionist sentiment but did not give specific instructions.

The general feeling inside the Kremlin was that Ukraine had ceased to exist as a state. The central government was no more, and the eastern regions would follow Crimea into Russia's embrace. The locals would be in favor and there would be no military resistance.

The most fervent supporter of Russia's actions in eastern Ukraine was Putin adviser Sergey Glazyev, an economist. A year earlier he had nearly been appointed the head of the central bank, but Alexei Kudrin had resisted and Putin had concurred. Back then the tone of the economic advice given to Putin was set by the liberals, and Glazyev was sidelined. Glazyev was left with little to do in Russia, so he—a native of Zaporozhye, in the southeast of Ukraine—focused all his energy on the fight for eastern Ukraine.

Glazyev supplied Putin with reports that pro-Russian sentiment in eastern Ukraine was strong and that residents of Donetsk were continuing to rally for secession from Kiev. It was Glazyev who more than anyone else promoted the concept of recreating "Novorossiya" (New Russia), a tsarist term denoting the region north of Crimea. Glazyev's vision was for Novorossiya to join Russia, as Crimea had.

But Putin did not want to take any decisive action. He repeatedly told Glazyev that the inhabitants of eastern Ukraine should be the ones to make the first move, whereupon Moscow would support them. But Putin himself did start to talk openly about Novorossiya. "What was called Novorossiya (New Russia) back in the tsarist days—Kharkov, Lugansk, Donetsk, Kherson, Nikolayev and Odessa—were not part of Ukraine back then. These territories were given to Ukraine in the 1920s by the Soviet government," Putin said on April 17.[5]

Several regions in the southeast of Ukraine (namely, Odessa, Donetsk, Luhansk, Kharkiv, and Dnipropetrovsk) were still smoldering with so-called anti-Maidan rallies. For the most part, they were genuine, not staged. People resented the fact that the Kiev authorities, both old and new, did not listen to them. The rallies, which were often well organized, were sponsored in the main by the pro-Yanukovych oligarchs, who were afraid that the new government in Kiev could make things tough for them, so they had to preempt matters by exerting their influence in the regions.

In Donetsk, for instance, the anti-Maidan protest was funded by Ukraine's richest man, Rinat Akhmetov, who had sponsored Viktor Yanukovych throughout his entire political career. Over the previous decade Akhmetov had rebuilt and upgraded Donetsk into a more European city. In 2011 the city's renovated airport was renamed Prokofiev Airport in honor of the Donetsk-born composer. A giant soccer stadium was built for Shakhtar FC, where matches were held during the 2012 European Championship. All that would be destroyed two years later, in the space of six months.

THE SHOOTER

"It was me who triggered the war," said Colonel Igor Strelkov (who was born Igor Girkin and whose chosen surname means "shooter") in an interview with the nationalist newspaper *Zavtra* in November 2014. "If our unit had not crossed the border, Kharkiv would have ended up like Odessa. There would have been dozens killed, burned alive, and arrested. And it would have been the end of it. But the flywheel of war was set in motion by our division. We reshuffled the cards."[6]

Indeed, the lightning-quick Crimean operation was not repeated in any other region. In Kharkiv and Donetsk protesters simply seized the regional administration, but nothing else happened. They did not put forward any demands.

On April 12 a group of armed men seized a police station in Slavyansk in the Donetsk region. Their leader was Igor Strelkov. That was when the armed conflict in eastern Ukraine began.

"I was an adviser to Aksyonov in Crimea," said Strelkov afterward.

> I commanded the only unit of the Crimean militia: a special-purpose company that carried out combat missions. But after the battle for the military cartography facility in which two people died (I was the commander), the company was disbanded and everyone went their separate ways. It was clear that Crimea would not be the only region affected. Crimea and Novorossiya together had been the jewels in the crown of the Russian Empire. But Crimea on its own attached to a hostile state, severed from the mainland, is not the same. As the Ukrainian government crumbled, delegates from the area of Novorossiya made frequent trips to Crimea in an effort to export the process to their own regions. They asked for help to start a rebellion. Aksyonov was working twenty hours a day, so he asked me to take charge of the northern regions. He made me his adviser on this issue. I sat down with all the delegates from Odessa, Nikolaev, Kharkiv, Luhansk, and Donetsk. All were sure that if the uprising gathered momentum, Russia would lend a hand. So I gathered together fifty-two fighters and volunteers who hadn't yet left. We went to Slavyansk because we needed an average-size city, where fifty-two people would be a force. And I was told that Slavyansk had the strongest local assets. It looked like the best option.[7]

The Slavyansk municipal administration was removed and replaced by the "home guard," as Strelkov's people called themselves. Initially the central authorities in Kiev did not respond. Russia also kept itself out of the matter; Putin was not sure of success and so gave no instructions. However, Strelkov was financed by his former employer Konstantin Malofeev, a major Russian businessman.

The Ukrainian authorities were busy preparing for the presidential elections, which were scheduled to take place on May 25. The unrest in Kharkiv was nipped in the bud when police freed the regional administration building from separatist forces. The Kiev authorities did not storm Donetsk or Luhansk for fear of bloodshed. All the while, the fighting around Slavyansk was getting worse. On one side was the "home guard," led by Strelkov, and on the other was the Ukrainian nationalist organization Right Sector, formed during the Maidan protests and headed by Dmitro Yarosh.

Pretty soon Strelkov became a public figure, giving press conferences and recording video messages. In them, he called on the Russian authorities to come to his aid and send troops into eastern Ukraine. He coordinated his actions with Moscow, above all with Glazyev. But no help arrived. Moscow was already facing sanctions over Crimea, and Putin had no intention of annexing eastern Ukraine.

"My explicit orders were not to give up Slavyansk," said Strelkov. "When I said I was planning to withdraw, I was repeatedly ordered to defend the city to the last. 'Keep defending Slavyansk. You'll be relieved,' I was told. 'How will you help?' I asked. Silence. By then I had a thousand people and thousands of their family members. I had no right to place the burden on them. So I took the decision to break through."

On July 5, 2014, when Slavyansk was nearly surrounded by Ukrainian forces, Strelkov and his people broke the encirclement and headed for Donetsk. That was the beginning of the next phase of the war.

"When we entered Donetsk, everything was serene," recalls Strelkov. "Kiev still had jurisdiction over the police. It was a typical dual-power arrangement. The city was not at all prepared to defend itself. The checkpoints were poorly manned, all the roads were open, you could go wherever you wanted. . . . It was peaceful. People were out sunbathing, swimming, jogging, drinking coffee in outdoor cafés. It was like summer in Moscow."

Within the space of a few months Donetsk, a city of one million people, was turned into a military hellhole, of which Strelkov is in fact proud. On arrival, he suggested blowing up some high-rise apartment buildings on the edge of the city to make the area easier to defend. Next, private vehicles were commandeered for military purposes. A 5 percent "war tax" was imposed on local businesses.

Rinat Akhmetov left the city in May. In August his house was burned down. He decided to move his football club, Shakhtar FC, to Lviv, in western Ukraine.

Meanwhile, in much more densely populated eastern Ukraine, the Kremlin was beginning to get involved. Sergei Glazyev teamed up with Vladislav Surkov, the plan being for Glazyev to manage the region's economy and Surkov its politics. It was Surkov who set up the government bodies of the so-called Donetsk People's Republic. The former Moscow spin doctor and publicist Alexander Borodai was appointed regional prime minister, while Strelkov became defense minister.

Glazyev initially toyed with the idea of creating a separate currency and financial system in Donetsk. But Surkov had other intentions. Putin had asked him not to build a new unrecognized state, but to maintain it as leverage over Ukraine. Surkov's mission was to integrate Donetsk and Luhansk back into the Ukrainian polity and use them to influence Ukrainian politics—for example, to prevent Ukraine's accession to NATO and other alliances.

Glazyev did not understand this objective, nor did he want to. He set about rebuilding the areas entrusted to him. As a result, he was quickly removed from the process. Surkov, meanwhile, was constantly shuttling between Kiev and Moscow, holding talks with the country's new president, Petro Poroshenko, on ways to settle the conflict in eastern Ukraine.

Surkov had long been acquainted with Poroshenko. The latter had come to the Kremlin for talks in 2004, before the Orange Revolution. Moreover, the chocolate tycoon owned a factory in Russia and assets in Crimea. Moscow could do business with him. However, Surkov's demand for either a full amnesty for all militiamen or the federalization of Ukraine and the recognition of the special status of Donetsk and Luhansk was unacceptable to Poroshenko, since his voters would accuse him of betrayal.

THE "EVIL EMPIRE" RETURNS

On the evening of July 17, 2014, Igor Strelkov posted the following comment on social media: "An An-26 aircraft has just been shot down in the region of

Torez. It's lying somewhere near the Progress coal mine. You were warned: do not fly in our sky. Here's video confirmation of the bird dropping. It fell behind a waste heap. It didn't hit a residential area. Peaceful people did not suffer. There's also news of a second downed aircraft, seems like a Su."[8] An hour later it was reported that a Boeing-777 carrying 280 passengers and 15 crew members had been shot down in the skies over Donetsk.

The downing of the Boeing shocked the world. The little-known conflict in Ukraine was suddenly headline news. Most of all, it was a shock for Putin, and a turning point. Now there could be no question of having sanctions lifted. They would only get worse.

Back in 1983 a Soviet fighter had shot down a South Korean Boeing airliner that had mistakenly entered Soviet airspace. It was a terrible blow to Moscow's image. Then US president Ronald Reagan dubbed the Soviet Union an "evil empire." Now Vladimir Putin found himself in a similar situation. The road leading back to normal relations with the West had been closed off.

The separatists did not own up to downing the plane, preferring to blame the Ukrainian side. But they were demoralized nonetheless. The Ukrainian army offensive was rapidly gaining ground. Strelkov continued to lead an active online existence, openly demanding that Putin immediately send troops to support the Donetsk militia. Ukrainian troops, meanwhile, had surrounded Donetsk on two sides and were close to cutting it off from the Russian border.

In late July the Ukrainian security forces published online a recording of an intercepted phone conversation between the prime minister of the Donetsk People's Republic (DNR), Alexander Borodai, and the militia's main sponsor, businessman Konstantin Malofeev (he was initially mistakenly identified as Surkov's aide Aleksey Chesnakov due to the fact that both had been in France when the conversation was secretly recorded—one in Biarritz, the other in Normandy). "If nothing changes in military terms, we won't last two weeks," said Borodai, confirming that the DNR forces were in trouble. He complained that he was running out of money. His sponsor promised to send some more.

Malofeev also said that he was "on a trip with Father Tikhon [Shevkunov]" and requested on behalf of the latter that Strelkov publicly declare his loyalty to Putin. "It's very important for the legendary Strelkov to openly state his loyalty," said Malofeev. "He should say on camera that even though he's operating in a different country he respects and fully supports the supreme commander [Putin], who has lifted Russia from its knees. We should look to him not in the sense of 'when can you help?' but in the sense of believing that he is our ideal and that we will comply with whatever decisions he takes because he is the all-wise leader of the Russian world."[9]

Both Father Tikhon and Putin himself were concerned about Strelkov's rising online popularity. Public opinion, which not long before had applauded Putin's takeover of Crimea, was now thirsty for new victories. Strelkov's calls for troops to be sent to Ukraine had gone over well, and people were becoming increasingly unhappy with Putin's indecision.

The situation became critical in August. It was clear that the Ukrainian army was on the cusp of strangling the separatists, cutting them off from the Russian border. If that happened, Moscow would lose its levers of influence over Ukraine. Poroshenko would win and be able to show Surkov the door. So Putin decided to deploy military personnel—in secret, just as he had in Crimea.

A CANDLE FOR THE FALLEN

To assist Strelkov, Sergei Shoigu sent the same paratroopers who a few months before had taken control of Crimea, for which they had been awarded commemorative medals. They launched an unexpected counteroffensive in the DNR. In an interview with the newspaper *Zavtra* Strelkov described the Russian troops as "vacationers," since officially they were volunteers on vacation that had gone to fight for Novorossiya.

"We'd held Donetsk for forty days before the vacationers arrived. The last days were desperate," recalled Strelkov.

The Russian troops went on the counteroffensive in the direction of the coastal city of Mariupol, the second largest urban area in the Donetsk region, where the Kiev-backed Donetsk regional administration had relocated. And they almost took it.

"It was mostly the vacationers who attacked Mariupol. The city was empty. The Ukrainian military took two days to arrive, so they could have taken it without a fight. But they were ordered not to. The order was not simply to halt the offensive. They were told *not* to occupy the city under any circumstances."[10]

The Russian offensive ended with the battle of Ilovaisk—the heaviest defeat inflicted on the Ukrainian army during the conflict, when an attempt to encircle the separatists failed and about a thousand people perished as a result.

The Russian side also suffered its first losses. Fresh graves with the bodies of paratroopers killed in eastern Ukraine were suddenly appearing at a cemetery in the Pskov region, back in Russia. It was already impossible to hide the Russian army's involvement, yet Putin continued to deny the obvious. In a telephone conversation with Angela Merkel, he claimed that the soldiers at Donetsk were indeed volunteers on vacation.

"Do Russian soldiers always go on holiday with weapons and military equipment?" exclaimed the German chancellor.

"Oh, there's so much corruption in Russia, you know. They must have stolen it from warehouses along the way," answered Putin without batting an eyelid.

Merkel hung up.

Putin did not believe that he was deceiving anyone. The soldiers, in his view, knew precisely what they were doing and fully supported the mission. On September 10, a week after the battle of Ilovaisk, he went to a church and, in his own words, "lit a candle for those who had suffered defending the people of Novorossiya."[11] It was his tribute to the memory of the participants in a war that Russia had not yet recognized. The families of the killed were paid compensation on condition that they not talk to journalists.

As for Igor Strelkov, he was sent from Donetsk to Moscow shortly after the battle of Ilovaisk commenced. His loose tongue and alleged criticism of Putin had cost him his position, and command of the operation passed to the top brass in Moscow under Sergei Shoigu. DNR prime minister Borodai also returned to Moscow, and operational control of the DNR was assumed by locals in Donetsk.

Strelkov returned to Moscow disappointed. "I thought it would be a repeat of Crimea," he said. "That would have been the best outcome. The people wanted it too. Nobody was going to defend the Luhansk and Donetsk republics. Everyone was pro-Russian. They held a referendum in support of Russia and went to fight for Russia. People wanted to join Russia. Russian flags were everywhere. There was one above my headquarters. We thought a Russian administration would be installed and one more republic would join Russia. I wasn't thinking about state-building. When I realized Russia was not going to take us in, it was a shock."[12]

DOMESTIC FOREIGN POLICY

On returning to Moscow, Strelkov began to denounce Vladislav Surkov, the Kremlin's policy maker in the Donbass region. He called him a "grand schemer" who had "pushed Novorossiya back into the arms of Ukraine in exchange for recognition of Crimea as Russian," and even accused Surkov's team of theft. "The money will be allocated, but I must emphasize that with such people in charge it will not reach the ordinary folk. . . . The system will ensure that. There'll be looting across the board, and everyone will get a cut."[13]

But this minor altercation did not affect the political process. Strelkov, a hero in Donetsk, was not even a political figure in the Russian capital, but a half-forgotten outcast. Meanwhile, Surkov continued to negotiate with Kiev and manage the unrecognized republics in eastern Ukraine. His recent failure was forgotten. Borodai is said to have once made a toast to his boss saying that only the genius Vladislav Surkov, having been transferred from domestic to foreign policy duties, could turn Russian foreign policy into a domestic issue.

It was Surkov who (together with Putin's old friend Viktor Medvedchuk) became the chief architect of the Minsk agreement, intended to halt the war. Their aim was ever the same: to secure permanent leverage over Ukraine, while maintaining complete control of the DNR.

The Russian military was also involved in a second crucial skirmish just ahead of the signing of the Minsk II agreement. Separatists took control of the city of Debaltsevo, a major transportation hub connecting Donetsk and Luhansk, whereupon more than 250 Ukrainian military personnel were killed. A few months after that, Russia restored the rail links between Donetsk and Luhansk, and passenger trains reappeared.

The war in eastern Ukraine began to resemble a frozen conflict, like the ones in Abkhazia, South Ossetia, and Transnistria. Every month 7 billion rubles (about $185 million) in cash was shipped from Russia to the Donbass (the region had no banking system), while Gazprom and InterRAO supplied free gas and electricity.

The Russian public did not object to the ongoing low-intensity conflict. On the contrary, the war was as popular as ever. The patriotic wave that had begun with the Sochi Olympics and the reunification of Crimea was still surging. Vladislav Surkov, who a decade before had simulated a war to protect Russia from a "color revolution," was now doing it for real. Russia was adamant that it was the victim, not the aggressor, in the military confrontation with Ukraine. It had been forced to defend itself against the provocations and attacks emanating from the United States and its proxies.

The symbol of Russia's newfound isolation was the seventieth anniversary of Victory Day on May 9, 2015. All G7 leaders boycotted the event (Russia had been suspended from the G8). In attendance were Chinese president Xi Jinping, Cuban leader Raul Castro, and President Robert Mugabe of Zimbabwe. But the hero was defense minister Sergey Shoigu. Viewers saw him doff his service cap and make the sign of the cross before commencing the parade. Under Putin, Communist and Orthodox traditions had merged into a new ritual.

CHAPTER 10

IN WHICH ALEXEI KUDRIN LOSES THE BATTLE FOR THE PRESIDENT'S HEART AND MIND

Alexei Kudrin is perhaps the ideal official. After leaving the government and ending up in the moderate opposition, he became the dean of the Liberal Arts and Sciences Faculty at St. Petersburg University. It suits Kudrin to a T. He has the air of a sagacious economics professor, despite spending his entire working life in the civil service. That is where he acquired his academic knowledge of economics. Back then he was nicknamed "Russia's chief accountant."

Following his resignation, those who had previously derided him now began to describe him as the most honest and professional minister in Russia. But even in his new role, Kudrin behaves like a civil servant, albeit a very liberal, educated, and intelligent one. Arranging a meeting with him is an arduous task. He postponed our interview (citing workload, unexpected meetings, urgent trips, etc.) at least ten times, on each occasion sending a polite text message.

Kudrin has a lovely office in Moscow, a kind of small, modest palace. It's located just outside the Garden Ring Road on Olympisky Prospect. It is very similar to his chambers inside the government building when he was deputy prime minister. Kudrin does not consider himself an opposition figure. He believes that he is on the "reserve bench" and that his time will come. After all, unlike the rest of the liberals, he continues to communicate with Putin and occasionally give him advice. Does he regret that he left the government over his run-in with former president Medvedev, thereby restricting his access to Putin?

In response Kudrin smiles enigmatically. "I'm often asked that question, but no, I don't regret it," he says. "I can't tell you why—not because I have any secret arrangements with Putin or anyone else in power. I have my own reasons." His tone is like that of a professor struggling to explain the essence of his research to a student.

FAREWELL, OFFICE

In March 2014 it became clear that the liberals inside the Kremlin had lost. Vladimir Putin had practically ceased to listen to them. He met roughly once a week with the new finance minister, Anton Siluanov, and heard the opinions of Siluanov's predecessor, Alexei Kudrin, about once a month. But Kudrin and Siluanov's advice pertained solely to the financial sphere. On all other aspects of policy Putin believed that he himself knew best and so did not consult the liberals.

Kudrin was still an authority, however. He took part in many meetings and often had the last word. One story relates how in late 2013 Putin summoned Kudrin to a meeting on economic issues. The talk turned to income tax changes, on which point the economics minister, the finance minister, the head of the Central Bank, and the president's economic adviser were all unanimous. Only Kudrin was against, and his status at the meeting was unclear. But after a heated debate, the president sided with Kudrin and declared the meeting ended.

Following his resignation in 2011, it took Kudrin a few months to vacate his office at the Ministry of Finance. Despite taking part in the major opposition rally on Sakharov Avenue, he kept his desk inside the old ministerial mansion on Ilyinka Street. The new minister, Anton Siluanov, did not move in right away, out of respect for his predecessor. For the first few months after his departure, Kudrin was like the ghost of Hamlet's father. He did not hold any public position, but continued to show up simply by inertia.

None of the government liberals, including Siluanov, had anything against Kudrin. He was, if not their patriarch, then at least first among equals, because in addition to his experience he had one major advantage: he was a friend of Putin's. Kudrin had direct access to "the body," as Putin was sometimes called. They had worked together since the early 1990s, and Kudrin, unlike anyone else in the present-day bureaucracy, had not been Putin's subordinate back then. They were on a par. At the St. Petersburg Mayor's Office Putin headed the international department, while Kudrin was in charge of finance and economics. Kudrin had moved to Moscow himself, without Putin's patronage, at the request of Anatoly Chubais, the architect of Yeltsin's economic reforms. Putin and Kudrin were on a first-name basis, with the president calling him "Lesha," a very familiar form of "Alexei." In short, Alexei Kudrin was perhaps the most (and last) influential liberal democrat in Russia.

In early 2014 Kudrin found himself in the strange of role of messenger, the only person in the country who dared bring the Kremlin bad news. But Putin was not listening to him anymore. The other members of his entourage told Putin that he was steering the country in the right direction, which is what the president wanted to hear.

Most significantly, Kudrin did not believe that the supposed war against Russia had been unleashed by the United States. No matter how many intelligence reports, figures, and summaries Putin presented, Kudrin did not buy it. Each time he switched the conversation to the economic consequences of what was happening, however, Putin's patience ran out. What did economics have to do with anything? The United States wanted to annihilate Russia. They were trying to overthrow Putin, as they had done in 2003 with the help of Khodorkovsky. But like then, Putin vowed, they wouldn't succeed.

In an atmosphere of war, Kudrin had no chance. Despite his bureaucratic privileges and special access, he was no longer able to convey his point of view to the president. So there was no need to burden himself with those privileges anymore. At his new office he did not even ask for a secure line to the Kremlin.

THE REVENGE OF THE SYSTEM

March 1, 2014, was a momentous day. Vladimir Putin formally asked the Federation Council, the upper house of the Russian parliament, for permission to deploy the armed forces outside the country. Although required under the constitution, such a request was a mere formality, and no president had ever approached the Federation Council for such permission before. Boris Yeltsin had not asked permission to invade Chechnya, and Dmitry Medvedev had not gone to parliament before sending tanks into Georgia. However, on both those occasions the president had described Russia's intervention as a "counterterrorism" or "peace enforcement" operation, not a war. Putin's appeal to the Federation Council was therefore symbolic. This time it was indeed war.

The world was shocked. But even more shocked was Federation Council Speaker Valentina Matviyenko, who had to convene parliament (on a Saturday) in order to unanimously approve the president's decision. The result of the vote was not in doubt—the senators always approved everything unanimously. The problem was how to get them to attend the weekend session.

When Matviyenko, a former leader of a Soviet Young Pioneers summer camp for children, found out that she had to assemble at least half the senators, she broke out into laughter. The task was ridiculously impossible. The Federation Council cannot simply be convened at the drop of a hat. Officially the upper house of the Russian parliament sits in Moscow twice a month, except during the winter and summer breaks. Although senators effectively only have fifteen to twenty working days per year, still not all of them bother to attend the parliamentary sessions. The turnout is usually about 50 percent, enough for a quorum. They receive the same salary as federal ministers, but most senators do not need it. The Federation Council is a place for billionaires in need of additional public status and former criminal bosses (also billionaires, incidentally) who need immunity from prosecution. Only in rare cases are members of the Federation Council honorable retirees from the world of politics.

The spring session had not yet begun, the Sochi Olympics had only just ended, and all the senators were on holiday: some in the Alps, others on a remote island somewhere. It was not even possible to contact some of them, let alone get them to return to Moscow. Matviyenko herself, her deputies, committee heads, and governors phoned everyone they could. Those who had private planes were ordered to go and pick up as many vacationing senators as possible.

The meeting was scheduled for six o'clock on Saturday evening. But come the appointed hour there was no quorum. Nevertheless, Matviyenko started the session, saying that a number of senators had promised to arrive a little bit later. The latecomers did indeed begin to show up, and soon ninety seats were filled.

Despite having their beach and skiing holidays interrupted, the senators were unanimously in favor of the motion, as expected. To the uninitiated, the speeches that day in the Federation Council might have sounded as if they were voting to declare war on the United States, not send troops to Ukraine.

"Barack Obama has crossed a red line. He has insulted the entire Russian people!" stormed Vice Speaker Yuri Vorobyov, the deputy and best friend of defense minister Sergey Shoigu. On vacating his post as governor of the Moscow region, Shoigu had bequeathed it to his best friend's son (and his own godson), Andrei Vorobyov. "Russia should withdraw its ambassador from Washington," the elder Vorobyov continued.

But no one was able to top eighty-four-year-old senator Nikolai Ryzhkov in the emotive stakes. His speech referred to the "coup" in Ukraine and the "brown plague" (i.e., fascism) that had infected the government as a result of the "conspiracy" of the Americans, who had already "destroyed Yugoslavia, Egypt, Libya, Iraq and so on." It was common rhetorical fare for this old Communist. But on this occasion, Ryzhkov's speech and the vote itself signified a triumphant, personal exoneration.[1]

Nikolai Ryzhkov had been the penultimate prime minister of the Soviet Union. It was he who implemented the perestroika-era economic reforms, which ended in failure. In 1990 he fell out with Gorbachev, had a heart attack, and resigned, whereupon he mercilessly criticized Gorbachev, accusing him of wrecking the great Soviet Union. In 1991 Ryzhkov tried to return to politics as Boris Yeltsin's main rival in Russia's very first, historic presidential elections. Yeltsin won convincingly in the first round, with Ryzhkov second but with only 16 percent of the vote. His political career seemed over. Everyone forgot about Ryzhkov even though he continued to hold various ceremonial posts. Then in 2003, at the age of seventy-four, he was appointed a senator.

The breakup of the Soviet Union and the collapse of the country's planned economy haunted Ryzhkov. Over the two decades that followed he castigated the Kremlin "liberals," above all Alexei Kudrin, and publicly rejoiced when Kudrin resigned.

Ryzhkov and Kudrin were polar opposites in terms of political views. The former had headed the economics section of the Central Committee of the CPSU and was a Marxist-Leninist to the core, while the latter strongly advocated a market economy. Back in the late 1980s, at the height of perestroika and the first sessions of the newly formed Congress of People's Deputies, Ryzhkov was perhaps the number one enemy of Anatoly Sobchak, the future mayor of St. Petersburg and the mentor of both Kudrin and Putin. In his memoir *Khozhdenia v vlast'* (Coming to power), Sobchak devoted an entire chapter to Ryzhkov and titled it "The Weeping Bolshevik Nikolai Ivanovich." In it, Sobchak describes the former prime minister as a cog in the Soviet machine and a member of the nomenklatura, ready to defend the Party to the last.

Ironically, twenty-three years after his political rout the "weeping Bolshevik" suddenly took revenge. The Soviet Union, of course, could not be revived, but Ryzhkov's old-school rhetoric suddenly resonated with the general mood. Moreover, the meeting of the Federation Council had been convened to sanction the introduction of Russian troops to Ukraine, and Ryzhkov was himself a native of Ukraine, having been born in the Donetsk region into a miner's family. The "weeping Bolshevik" was smiling.

Ryzhkov, it must be said, was not the only "Ukrainian" senator who voted for the deployment of troops. Speaker Valentina Matviyenko had also been born in Ukraine, although she had left to go to university in St. Petersburg, the hometown of Putin, Kudrin, and Sobchak.

In the end, every member of the Federation Council present that day voted in favor. The next day Valentina Matviyenko was reprimanded by the presidential administration (and later by Putin himself) for the low turnout at such an important sitting. Only 90 out of 168 senators had turned up.

On March 16, Crimea held a referendum on its accession to the Russian Federation. That same day the United States and the European Union published their first sanctions lists. Among the names on this list were Valentina Matviyenko and those senators who had most strongly advocated the deployment of troops to Ukraine, including Ryzhkov. Ryzhkov suddenly became a national hero. Newspaper interviews and documentary films appeared in which he was hailed as "the Empire's last prime minister." The newfound patriarch of Russian politics again branded Gorbachev and Yeltsin as "traitors" and praised Putin for reviving the country.

CONFESSION IN THE KREMLIN

On March 18, 2014, the day after the Crimean referendum, Red Square was cordoned off by riot police from Novosibirsk, who had been brought 3,000 kilometers to the capital to beef up security. The extra measures were put in place because Putin was preparing to address members of the Duma, the Federation Council, the government, and specially invited guests of honor all in one building. So extra police were shipped in from all across the country, including Siberia.

It was a cold day in Moscow as the MPs formed a long line outside the entrance to the Grand Kremlin Palace. All were dressed in very similar black coats and fur hats, like members of the Politburo. Only Duma MP Nikolai

Valuev stood out from the crowd by virtue of the fact that he was attired in gray (and also happened to be a gigantic former professional boxer). Other deputies, who came up barely to his chest, took selfies with him. Everyone was nervously joking about sanctions that the West might impose on Russia and whether or not they personally would be included on the lists. The political elite were a little jittery. They sensed that something momentous was about to happen: "I'll tell my grandchildren I was at the Kremlin on this historic day."

Putin's speech was indeed historic, and not only because he used it to declare Sevastopol and Crimea part of the Russian Federation. For half an hour he recounted the whole story of his presidency and how his worldview had changed: he had wanted to be a liberal European president but had been betrayed by his Western allies and would now never again believe in their sincerity. Never before had the Russian president uttered such heartfelt words. It was not a speech but a public confession of his personal grievances:

> Russia strived to engage in dialogue with our colleagues in the West. We are constantly proposing cooperation on all key issues; we want to strengthen our level of trust and for our relations to be equal, open and fair. But we saw no reciprocal steps.
>
> On the contrary, they have lied to us many times, made decisions behind our backs, placed before us an accomplished fact. This happened with NATO's expansion to the East, as well as the deployment of military infrastructure at our borders. They kept telling us the same thing: "Well, this does not concern you." That's easy to say.[2]

Psychoanalysts must have loved it.

Fourteen years previously, Putin's tone had been very different. Russia could become a full member of NATO "if Russia's interests are taken into account and enjoys full and equal rights," he told the BBC in March 2000, when he was a presidential candidate. It is hard to say whether he really believed those words, but he clearly wanted to please his Western counterparts.

As previously discussed, Putin soon became friends with George W. Bush. The US president famously stated that he had looked into the eyes of his "friend Vladimir" and "seen his soul." When in 2004 his friend George and his other friend, Tony Blair, accepted seven Eastern European countries into NATO, including the Baltic states, Putin took it as a personal betrayal.

"Vladimir later came to believe that the Americans did not give him his due place. Worse, he saw them as circling Russia with Western-supporting 'democracies' who were going to be hostile to Russian interests," Blair recalls in his memoirs.[3]

An even more severe blow was the decision of a London court to refuse the extradition of Zakayev and Berezovsky. Putin simply did not believe that Blair had no influence over the British judicial system. Putin considered such behavior to be hypocritical, and said as much to his audience: "Our western partners, led by the United States of America, prefer not to be guided by international law in their practical policies, but by the rule of the gun. They have come to believe in their exclusivity and exceptionalism, that they can decide the destinies of the world, that only they can ever be right."[4]

The fact that the Americans and Europeans had never recognized Russia as an equal partner had always infuriated Putin—and he admitted so with surprising candor. He had expressed his feelings in an interview with *Time* in 2007, having been selected as the magazine's person of the year: "Sometimes one gets the impression that America does not need friends. Sometimes we get the impression that you need some kind of auxiliary subjects to take command of. . . . This is the reason why everybody is made to believe like it's O.K. to pinch the Russians somewhat. They are a little bit savage still or they just climbed down from the trees, you know, and probably need to have their hair brushed and their beards trimmed. And have the dirt washed out of their beards and hair."[5] Perhaps no other world leader had ever expressed such resentment so openly.

Putin had been real partners with Hugo Chávez, whose extravagant frankness he shared. A favorite rhetorical device of both men was to use domestic speeches to lecture the United States. Once a week Chavez had hosted *Alo Presidente*, a largely unscripted TV program that lasted for hours in which he which regularly addressed the Americans, on the off chance that any were watching Venezuelan television. Putin did the same in his speech: "They are constantly trying to sweep us into a corner because we have an independent position, because we maintain it and because we call things like they are and do not engage in hypocrisy."[6] In 2006 Chávez addressed the United Nations, calling upon Americans to come to their senses and understand that Bush was the devil incarnate. In his Crimea speech Putin spoke directly to the American people, as well as the Europeans and the Ukrainians. He had never done anything like it before.

Putin's attitude toward the Soviet Union over the previous decade had not changed. In 2005, in his message to the Federal Assembly, he had described the collapse of the Soviet Union as the "greatest geopolitical catastrophe of the twentieth century" and a "supreme drama for the Russian people." Now, nine years later, he reiterated this idea, but far less formally: the Russian people were, in his words, the world's largest divided nation, and the Russian-speaking population of Crimea had been traded like a "sack of potatoes."

There was only one issue on which Putin's attitude had radically shifted. In the interview with *Time* in 2007, speaking of independent journalists, he said, "There are genuine fighters against corruption, against the criminal elements. This is something the state should pay top attention to, and where such losses have occurred, I take them as my personal losses. Such people necessarily work for the interests of consolidation of Russia internally. We do whatever it takes to protect them, to ensure their security, and to work professionally as they should."[7] The Crimea speech made no mention of dissidents, but it did feature references to "national traitors" and the "fifth column"—the latter of which, incidentally, had always been one of Chávez's favorite metaphors to describe opposition figures and liberal journalists and rob them of any semblance of sincerity and good faith.

Putin's disillusionment only deepened over time. Having decided that his Western partners had betrayed him, he would never forgive them and would only harden his position. Likewise, having branded the "liberals" and "dissidents" as "traitors," Putin was making it clear that he would never again listen to their opinion.

The Kremlin audience was in raptures. Applause erupted after every paragraph of the speech, as if an invisible hand were conducting the performance. There were twenty-seven ovations in total—the final two standing. The entire Grand Kremlin Palace arose in unison and began chanting "Russia! Russia!" and "Putin! Putin!"

Then Putin and the leaders of Crimea symbolically signed an Instrument of Accession for the peninsula to join Russia. The national anthem struck up. When it finished, the audience members headed for the exit, embracing and congratulating each other. Beaming more than most was Chechen president Ramzan Kadyrov. He strolled over to the door, singing the lines of the Russian national anthem in a full-throated baritone. On the way out he noticed an acquaintance and joked, "Right, what's next? Alaska?" Then he burst into joyful laughter.

The others too were demonstratively happy, but on the sidelines the talk was of sanctions. They told the press that inclusion in the sanctions list was "something to be proud of." "It's like being nominated for a political Oscar," said former Kremlin strategist Vladislav Surkov of his inclusion on the US sanctions list. "It's a great honor for me. I have no bank accounts abroad. In the United States I'm interested in Tupac Shakur, Allen Ginsberg, and Jackson Pollock. I don't need a visa to access their work. So I haven't lost anything." Moreover, when this intellectual and lover of European art was asked if he feared ending up on the EU sanctions list as well, Surkov exuded self-confidence: "The whole of Europe is right here in my head. That's enough."[8]

Surkov's reply demonstrated his certainty that he would indeed be on the list, making travel to Europe a physical impossibility, hence the need to store the continent in his mind. So Surkov wasted no time. The very next day (March 19) he packed his bags and took his family and friends on a valedictory trip to his beloved Stockholm. He was not wrong. On March 21 the Europeans published their own list, and Surkov's name was on it. His trip to Stockholm really was a farewell tour.

FRIENDS IN NEED

Whereas for Nikolai Ryzhkov inclusion on the sanctions lists was a moment of joy and vindication, for Surkov it was a problem. Despite having Europe in his head, he missed traveling there. And for other close allies of Putin, sanctions were a real tragedy. Some had lived abroad for many years. Their children studied there. They had properties and businesses to maintain.

But for all that, they did not try to reason with Putin. That was left to Alexei Kudrin, the disgraced former finance minister. Curiously, Kudrin was the only one to speak out. Why were the victims themselves so reticent? Why were they still lining up to praise the infallibility of Putin's policies? Why, for instance, did Putin's old friends Arkady and Boris Rotenberg (both Finnish citizens), Yuri Kovalchuk, or Gennady Timchenko (a Finnish citizen resident in Switzerland) not try to bring him around?

"Put yourself in my shoes," a friend paraphrases Yuri Kovalchuk. "If I annoy Putin like Kudrin does, telling him what he doesn't want to hear, what will happen? I'll get less access to 'the body.' I'll end up punishing myself more than the Europeans have done to me. Why would I do that?"

None of Putin's inner circle dared to argue with the president, because they knew that he was the source and guarantor of their wealth. Putin's good favor was what gave them legitimacy. Their prosperity had come not from hard work or business acumen but from their personal acquaintance with the president. Presidential opprobrium would harm their well-being. Putin's wrath was far more dangerous for them than any Western sanctions. Moreover, in a series of staged interviews Putin's oligarchs publicly boasted of their willingness to sacrifice their fortunes for the sake of their leader. "If need be, tomorrow I'll give everything to the state or to charity. Anything to help," said Gennady Timchenko in an interview with state news agency ITAR-TASS. "My wife and I have discussed the subject many times. Personally we do not need billions of dollars."

Not for nothing did Timchenko mention his wife. Elena Timchenko, an ambitious society figure, had significant influence over her husband. She lived in Switzerland at the family villa on Lake Geneva and led the life of an enlightened European benefactor. Considering herself a patron of the arts, she organized her own film festivals in Geneva attended by Russian and international film stars.

Elena Timchenko was hit hard by the sanctions. She lost access to the luxury villa and the tranquil lifestyle. As told by her husband, she had just undergone surgery and had to pay for it, but her bank account was suddenly blocked. Putin himself picked up on the story during his annual phone-in with the people in August 2014, citing it as evidence of the inhumanity of sanctions, since they affected not only those on the sanctions list but their families too.

"TWO JEWS AND A *KHOKHOL*"

The St. Petersburg International Economic Forum was one of Putin's favorite pets. In the 1990s Yeltsin's oligarchs had set up a Russian economic forum in London to attract foreign investment. Back in 2007 Putin decided that Britain was not the best place to showcase Russia's economic achievements and recommended that it be merged with the St. Petersburg forum, which had been held annually since 1997. Everyone thought 2014 was going to be a stellar year. Russia held the chairmanship of the Group of Eight, and Putin decided to combine the economic forum with that year's G8 summit. To accommodate this, the forum was moved forward from June to May.

But the annexation of Crimea and subsequent sanctions wrecked everything. Russia was suspended from the G8 (which became the G7 once again) and the summit was canceled. The St. Petersburg forum turned into a farcical wedding at which the bride failed to show up, while the groom consoled himself with the thought that he hadn't really wanted to marry her in the first place.

Almost all the heavy hitters at the forum were under sanctions, and each and every one said that, far from being a hindrance, sanctions were in fact helpful. For some, that really was the case. The head of Russian Railways, Vladimir Yakunin, for instance, was effectively saved by them. There had been storm clouds gathering over his head and rumors that he would soon be "retired," but Western sanctions put an end to all that talk. Putin could not ditch a faithful servant who had been punished by the West. So Yakunin was reappointed for a new term. (He was, however, fired a year later, in August 2015.)

At the forum Vladimir Putin was in good spirits. According to custom, he delivered a speech to business leaders and then repeated everything at a plenary session afterward and once more at a press conference. Everywhere the theme sounded that Russia had held out an olive branch to the West, but the West had rejected it. Several times he stated that Russian economic development minister Alexei Ulyukayev ("a proper liberal," said Putin with maximum disdain) had gone to negotiate with the EU, but no one—absolutely no one—had wanted to talk to him.

Putin also joked about his old friends: "Whom have they targeted with their sanctions? They've deliberately chosen two Jews and a *khokol* [a mildly offensive term for a Ukrainian]," he quipped, referring to the Rotenberg brothers and Timchenko.

On the last day of the forum Putin met foreign journalists at his out-of-town residence. For the first two hours he was relaxed and full of banter. But toward the end of the meeting, when an Associated Press reporter asked about freedom of speech in Russia, the president flew into a rage: "You Americans have no right to lecture us! Your TV stations blatantly lied about the events in Kiev. You have no moral authority to breathe a word about freedom of speech," shouted Putin, according to someone who was present.

Most of the foreign guests of the forum did not show up. And despite Putin's efforts to the contrary, the topic of sanctions dominated the event.

The only thing that remained unchanged was the entertainment. Billionaire Mikhail Prokhorov held a traditional disco reception with strippers dancing on the bar, like during the fat decade of the early 2000s.

THE FIGHT FOR PUTIN

In June 2014 President Putin was presented with an analytical report stating that the threat of losing control over a significant part of Russia's petroleum reserves was again looming large. Eleven years earlier Putin's advisers had sounded the alarm, warning that Yukos owner Mikhail Khodorkovsky, then Russia's richest man, intended to sell Russian oil assets to a US company. Putin was still grateful to them for the tip-off, and above all to Igor Sechin for preventing the sale of Russia's largest oil company to a foreign buyer.

Now the same thing was happening again, and once more it was Sechin who sounded the alarm. This time it was rumored that the Russian oil firm Bashneft could be sold off to foreigners. Such a possibility had to be forestalled, especially at a time when the United States had introduced sanctions against Russia and was making every effort to weaken the country. Despite being only the sixth-largest oil company in Russia, Bashneft was well developed and possessed excellent reserves of hydrocarbons. In September the company was due to float its shares on the London Stock Exchange, and Sechin had made it clear to Putin that such a move would remove it from the Kremlin's control.

Igor Sechin, like Alexei Kudrin, had worked with Putin since the early 1990s. But whereas Kudrin had been an equal partner, Sechin was always a subordinate. He understood Putin's mind-set like no one else. He knew that for Putin there was nothing worse than a traitor—loyalty to the president and loyalty to Russia went hand in hand. So Sechin slowly inculcated the idea into Putin's mind that Bashneft owner Vladimir Yevtushenkov was precisely that—a traitor. Afraid of sanctions, not only did Yevtushenkov want to sell the company to a foreign buyer, but he was planning to betray his comrades, fellow citizens, and the president himself.

Yevtushenkov owed his billions and status to Yuri Luzhkov, the former Moscow mayor and the informal leader of the city's business community. They were in fact in-laws: Yevtushenkov was married to the sister of Luzhkov's wife, Yelena Baturina. But when Luzhkov locked horns with President

Medvedev and was smeared by national TV shortly before being dismissed, not only did Yevtushenkov fail to stand up for his patron, but he began to distance himself, saying that he had no connection with Luzhkov whatsoever and had never even so much as had dinner with him.

Yevtushenkov was a major investor in science and IT and liked being called the "Russian Bill Gates." It was his company, AFK Sistema, that was commissioned to launch GLONASS, Russia's rival to the American GPS navigation system. The supervisor of the project was Sergey Ivanov, who in 2007 had been considered as a possible successor to Vladimir Putin but had lost the race to Dmitry Medvedev. When it became clear that Ivanov would not be the next president of Russia, Yevtushenkov's enthusiasm for the project waned. His eye was then caught by another innovation—the MTS 945, aka the "Russian iPhone," the first GLONASS-compatible smartphone. It was manufactured by China's ZTE and launched with great pomp and ceremony. But when Dmitry Medvedev moved out of the Kremlin, Yevtushenkov again lost interest in his new toy.

Sechin compiled a dossier of such episodes from Yevtushenkov's biography and showed it to Putin. He wanted to prove that Yevtushenkov was fickle and a potential traitor. The main target was, of course, Bashneft. Yevtushenkov had taken possession of it in 2009 with Medvedev's approval. Putin knew about the deal, of course, but Sechin supplied his boss with little-known details about the company's "latent shareholders."

Sechin had personal reasons for scheming against Yevtushenkov. Russia's largest oil company, Rosneft (headed by Sechin), was in serious trouble. Production was down and government subsidies were needed. The absorption of the small but prosperous Bashneft would solve Rosneft's and Sechin's problems.

Moreover, having distanced himself from Luzhkov, Yevtushenkov had become friends with the most prominent liberals in Putin's entourage, namely, Sberbank head German Gref and the architect of the Yeltsinite reforms, Anatoly Chubais. The liberals were Sechin's ideological opponents, so attacking them was a matter of principle.

There was no doubt in Sechin's mind that the debut of Bashneft's shares on the London Stock Exchange would be a blow to Russia's energy security and a stab in the back at a time when the West was waging economic and psychological warfare against Russia. So Sechin did all he could to prevent the issuance of the shares and wrest the company from Yevtushenkov's hands.

Business leaders who have dealt with Sechin say he has one particular idiosyncrasy: he immediately manages to get criminal proceedings started against any potential partner as a backup, as well to facilitate the negotiating process. Most of the time nothing comes of it and the case is simply closed. It is just a long-standing habit.

In mid-July Bashneft's shareholders suddenly learned that their shares had been seized by order of Moscow's Basmanny district court, the same body that eleven years previously had authorized the arrest of Khodorkovsky. According to the Investigative Committee, which was probing the privatization of Bashneft, the former owners had bought the company in violation of Russian law, making Yevtushenkov a dealer in stolen goods.

The seizure of the shares made the London Stock Exchange placement legally impossible. But there was more to come. Yevtushenkov informed the press that his company had been raided; two months later the same Basmanny district court put Yevtushenkov under house arrest, accused of "embezzling and laundering" Bashneft stock.

Yevtushenkov's arrest was no less a shock to Russian big business than the annexation of Crimea and the war in Ukraine. "It's far worse than any sanctions," said one billionaire, speaking for many others. "It means there are no rules anymore. Anything goes."

Indeed, from the point of view of the business community, which was well acquainted with Putin's logic, the arrest of Yevtushenkov differed crucially from the Yukos affair. Mikhail Khodorkovsky had violated the rules of the game. He had interfered in politics and was duly punished. Yevtushenkov was the polar opposite of Khodorkovsky. He was careful and circumspect, kept his ear to the ground, and never overcommitted himself or took risks. The deal to buy Bashneft had been agreed on all sides.

People rallied round Yevtushenkov, in particular his comrades Chubais and Gref. But they soon realized that their intercession was not only pointless but dangerous. The dossier on Yevtushenkov stated that both Chubais and Gref were "latent shareholders" of Bashneft, and their intervention only confirmed the assertion. Putin did not want to listen to their arguments. All the liberals inside Putin's inner circle were effectively cut off and ceased to have any influence on the president.

To get through to him, they resorted to desperate measures. Unable to get a private audience, they had to speak out in public so that Putin would hear and perhaps understand.

The first was German Gref. He made an unscheduled speech at the Russia Calling! investment forum and unexpectedly talked about the reasons behind the Soviet Union's collapse. "The Soviet leadership was remarkably incompetent. They had no grasp of the laws of economics. They lived in cloud-cuckoo-land," railed Gref. He spoke about the lack of competition and the futility of "Gulag-style motivation."[9]

Gref's speech was a bombshell, eclipsing everything else at the forum. The press wrote only about "the Gref rebellion." Putin was not present at the speech, however, and, speaking later, he did not respond to it. Instead, he joked a lot (to loud laughter from the hall) and insisted that the Russian economy was strong but needed "mobilizing," for which the state had the necessary resources. But Kremlinologists and Putin watchers noted one moment in particular. Having uttered the phrase "The devil is not as black as he is painted," the president paused, made the sign of the cross over his mouth, and said, "Lord, have mercy." Had it been the nineteenth century, no one would have batted an eyelid. But in twenty-first-century Russia, outside the cloistered world of monks, it was rather odd. Putin had been keeping company with confessors and holy fathers, concluded the liberals.

Three days later Alexei Kudrin tried to reason with him. The only way Kudrin could contact the president was through an interview on Channel One with the famous Russian TV host Vladimir Pozner. "For me, Russia's national interests are best protected by strengthening its economic might. Without that, the country cannot be a military or any other power. Our economic strength is weakening, and we cannot achieve our foreign and domestic political goals. I am becoming increasingly concerned," said Kudrin in very Putin-esque language.[10]

Kudrin hoped to remind the president of his existence and bring the old Putin back to life. Kudrin was worried that Putin's public speeches contained incorrect statistical data, among other things. The president continued to state that the economy was in order and constantly reiterated that Russia was not seeking international isolation—on the contrary, it wanted to engage in dialogue, but its Western partners were deaf.

Kudrin's colleagues opined that his resignation from the Finance Ministry had been a mistake. "Alas, the liberals have lost the fight for Putin," was the consensus among influential businesspeople. All were utterly dejected. "Nothing can be done if the train is hurtling off a cliff. You just have to try and move down to the last car," said one of Russia's largest employers. The mood was defeatist. The battle for Putin was lost.

Less than a month later, at a meeting of the Valdai Club in Sochi, the Kremlin's new policy architect, Vyacheslav Volodin, summed it up: "Russia is Putin. Russia exists only if there is Putin. There is no Russia without Putin."

CHAPTER 19

IN WHICH RAMZAN KADYROV TAKES A ROUND TRIP TO DUBAI

At the 2015 St. Petersburg International Economic Forum, Ramzan Kadyrov gave the impression of a visiting monarch. He walked imposingly through the pavilion at the head of a large retinue. Against the backdrop of ministers, governors, and deputy prime ministers (who were walking alone, sitting in cafés, or chatting with reporters), Kadyrov looked exotically oriental.

This young man, dressed in an astrakhan vest, was surrounded by two dozen gloomy-looking assistants in black. For ten years journalists had written about the practice of torture and kidnapping in his fiefdom. Some of his closest aides were wanted by Interpol. Like a medieval warlord, he was never far from rumors about how various enemies had been dispatched. The ministers quietly sitting in the forum pavilion were fearful.

It is the retinue that gives this purveyor of horrors and ruler of destinies the air of royalty. On one occasion when TV presenter Ksenia Sobchak tried to ask a question, a group of Kadyrov's assistants pushed her to one side against the glass wall of the studio. The king of Chechnya passed by without breaking stride.

Journalists who have known Kadyrov for a long time are surprised by this new image. They describe him as a young man without formal education who finds it hard to hold a conversation. He is also touchy. For example, he has never forgiven a prominent Russian publicist for once uttering the words "We've already met. Remember? I stayed with your father, and you served me tea." He in no way resembles the grizzled veterans of the Chechen wars—men who could kill a person for smiling the wrong way.

Kadyrov lost his father and elder brother at a relatively early age and appreciates the company of close friends and his father's inner circle. His favorite word is "euphoria." He applies it, for instance, to the feeling he gets from dancing the dhikr, *a Sufi dance that induces a trance. The same word is used to describe the feeling he experienced when visiting the holy Kaaba in Mecca. Kadyrov said in an interview that he once dreamed of entering the Kaaba together with all his friends.*[1] *And in 2013 he made it happen, traveling with fifteen of his closest buddies, or "brothers," as he calls them. There in the Kaaba they took selfies and posted them on Instagram. No doubt he experienced "euphoria."*

AN OPPOSITION FIGURE IS KILLED, THE PRESIDENT DISAPPEARS

During the Minsk talks in search of a settlement to the Ukraine conflict, Vladimir Putin publicly told Ukrainian president Petro Poroshenko not to repeat the mistakes that Putin himself had made. "Fill the Donbass region with money, not blood," he said.

Come 2014, the problem of Chechnya, the bugbear of Putin's first term, seemed solved. In 1999, as prime minister, he said in a television interview: "Figuratively speaking, Chechnya is everywhere. Not only in the North Caucasus." He meant that Russia had many problems: "This constant search for an external source to all our ills is wrong. . . . All our troubles are inside us. They proceed from our own carelessness and weakness. . . . Take a look at our economy—nothing but grief. And there's a gaping hole in our international relations with countries both near and far."[2]

In 2014 Putin could have repeated the phrase "Chechnya's everywhere," but with a different connotation. This time it was a symbol of nationwide stability. On December 28, 2014, the head of Chechnya, Ramzan Kadyrov, gathered all members of the Chechen police force inside a stadium and made them swear an oath of loyalty to Vladimir Putin. "It's time to make a conscious choice and tell the world that we are Vladimir Putin's foot soldiers. If the order comes, we will prove that we are so," said Kadyrov. "For fifteen years Vladimir Putin has helped our people. Now we, tens of thousands of specially trained soldiers, ask the Russian national leader and supreme commander to accept us as his voluntary special division, ready to defend Russia."[3] Twenty thousand men in camouflage answered him in chorus: "Allahu Akbar!" The somewhat menacing video from the stadium quickly spread online. It was more evidence that it was Ramzan Kadyrov who had a devoted army, not Vladimir Putin.

Yet medieval oaths by that time had become mainstream. In January 2015 groups of Afghan veterans and motorcycle gangs joined the competition for the title of Putin's most devoted servants. Franz Klintsevich, the Duma MP who the year before had led a detachment of volunteers to retake Crimea, headed the "anti-Maidan" movement, whose objective was to oppose the Euromaidan uprising of 2013–2014 and battle the pro-Western "fifth column." Another of the movement's leaders was the head of the Night Wolves biker group, former doctor Alexander Zaldostanov, who was nicknamed "the Surgeon." "The only thing that will make them [the opposition] desist is fear. They will betray and kill their sponsors for money, but they are not willing to die for money!" he said.[4]

On February 21, 2015, Moscow's main thoroughfare, Tverskaya Street, saw a pro-Kremlin, anti-Maidan rally that was widely covered by national TV. The ralliers carried portraits of their enemies—the potential organizers of a "Russian Maidan." One of them was Boris Nemtsov, a liberal opposition leader, who in the 1990s had been a deputy prime minister under Yeltsin.

A week later, on February 27, Nemtsov was gunned down on Bolshoi Moskvoretsky Bridge, right by the walls of the Kremlin. The murder shocked many, including the Kremlin itself. That night Vladimir Putin held a meeting with security officials and ordered the FSB, the Interior Ministry, and the Investigative the Committee to look into the murder, which had been committed under the windows of his official residence.

The next morning, according to official reports on the Kremlin website, Putin spoke on the phone with Jordan's King Abdullah II and Abu Dhabi crown prince Mohammed Al Nahyan. Abdullah and Al Nahyan were known in Russia for their close ties with Ramzan Kadyrov, who traveled several times a year to Jordan and the UAE. Likewise, they were frequent guests in Chechnya. Kadyrov had named an Islamic school in the Chechen town of Gudermes in honor of Prince Mohammed's father and a park in Grozny after the father of King Abdullah. And in Amman, the Jordanian capital, there is a Ramzan Kadyrov Street. Putin decided to discuss the murder of Boris Nemtsov with Kadyrov's foreign friends. After that he sent a telegram of condolence to Boris Nemtsov's mother.

At an Interior Ministry meeting on March 4, Putin demanded that the case be solved quickly: "We must rid Russia of shameful tragedies of the kind we have recently seen. I mean, of course, the brazen murder of Boris Nemtsov right in the center of our capital."

The next day he met with Italian prime minister Matteo Renzi. And after that Putin disappeared, ceasing to appear in public for a while. Perhaps no one would have noticed if the Kremlin had not started posting online reports of meetings between the president and regional governors that had actually taken place a week earlier and already been covered by the regional press. Kremlin insiders later explained that the president was suffering from a bout of flu and had gone to his residence at Valdai, outside Novgorod, to recuperate. But senior officials whispered to each other that Putin had in fact gone away to ruminate over his next move. It was even rumored that he had gone into hiding because he was afraid for his own life and wanted to let everything just blow over.

A NEW "ROOF"

As soon as the president left Moscow, the FSB got down to work. Two suspects were detained on March 7 in Ingushetia, and another died during an attempted arrest in Chechnya, allegedly blowing himself up with a grenade. The main perpetrator was named as Zaur Dadayev, a member of the Sever battalion, part of the Chechen national guard. A court sanctioned his arrest on March 8. On the same day Ramzan Kadyrov posted an Instagram message of support:

> I have known Zaur as a true patriot of Russia. . . . Zaur was one of the bravest men in the regiment. . . . He was awarded the Order of Courage and medals for bravery and for services to the Chechen Republic. I am certain that he is sincerely dedicated to Russia and prepared to give his life for the Motherland. . . . Media reports say that in court Zaur admitted his involvement in the murder of Boris Nemtsov. Anyone who knows Zaur can affirm that he is a deeply religious man and, like all Muslims, was shocked by the *Charlie Hebdo* cartoons. . . . Beslan Shavanov, who was killed while being arrested, was a brave soldier too. We hope that a thorough investigation will follow to uncover whether Dadayev is indeed guilty, and if yes, what the real reason behind his actions was.[5]

Kadyrov also tried to contact the president, but to no avail. Putin was unavailable and not shown on the news at all that day.

The next day, March 9, Kadyrov received a strange signal from Putin. The absent president awarded him the Medal of Honor, a very high level of recognition. The Chechen leader again tried to contact Putin, but once again his call was not put through. So he tried via Instagram:

> I am infinitely grateful to the Russian President and Supreme Commander of the Armed Forces of the Russian Federation Vladimir Putin for such a high award and appreciation of my modest work. I fully declare that all the credit for peace and stability in the Chechen Republic belongs to Vladimir Vladimirovich [Putin]. His wise policy, assistance, and support have achieved lasting peace and restored the republic's economy, culture, and spirituality. We are the foot soldiers of the Russian president! I will always be grateful to Vladimir Vladimirovich for everything he has done for me personally and for my people. I will always be his faithful comrade-in-arms. To give one's life for such a person is the simplest of tasks. I vow to fulfil any order and undertake any assignment for him whatever the complexity or the cost to myself. I serve Russia! I serve the people![6]

It is unlikely that Kadyrov posts his own Instagram messages, but the text was clearly his own—at that moment there was no other way to contact Putin.

Meanwhile, in Moscow's Krylatskoye district, one of the capital's most prestigious suburbs (known as "Fantasy Island"), there were some worrying developments. On the night of March 10–11 in Krylatskoye, which is home to ministers and billionaires, a skirmish took place between the bodyguards of businessman Umar Dzhabrailov, a former senator from Chechnya and former Russian presidential candidate, and bikers from the Night Wolves club—the self-declared defenders of Russia against the liberal "fifth column."

But the Night Wolves had not come to the Chechen billionaire's manor to discuss the "fifth column." Dzhabrailov's neighbors say that the bikers paid a visit to inform the entrepreneur that his protector (*krysha* in Russian, literally "roof"), Ramzan Kadyrov, was no longer the main player in town and henceforth Dzhabrailov would be under their "protection," that is, they would ensure his safety in return for money. The Surgeon and Dzhabrailov decided to settle their differences personally.

The conflict in Krylatskoye indicated that the security agencies no longer considered Kadyrov to be a mighty force, despite the fact that many businessmen in Moscow were still under the protection of the so-called Chechen mafia. There were hundreds of Chechen police operating semi-officially in Moscow under the direction of Adam Delimkhanov, Kadyrov's right-hand man and a Duma MP from Chechnya. The Chechen "police" were based at the President Hotel, a five-star establishment not far from Bolotnaya Square. Ironically, the hotel had been the headquarters of Boris Yeltsin's shadow campaign back in 1996. From there, a team of US spin doctors came up with the slogan "Vote or Lose" (copied from MTV's slogan "Choose or Lose"), which helped Yeltsin win reelection that year.

It was rumored that the Night Wolves' protection was even more powerful than that of the Chechens inside the President Hotel, since the Night Wolves were backed by the FSB. So they decided to exploit their opponent Kadyrov's momentary weakness (his lack of contact with Putin) in order to take charge of the cash flow.

On March 11 Ramzan Kadyrov was summoned to a meeting of the Security Council that was being held in the city of Pyatigorsk in the North Caucasus, chaired by Security Council secretary Nikolai Patrushev, the former head of the FSB and Russia's most influential "enforcer" or *silovik*. He told Kadyrov about the investigation into the murder of Nemtsov and about the evidence that had come to light against members of the Chechen leader's inner circle.

Returning home on March 13, Kadyrov convened an extended session of the Chechen Interior Ministry. Shortly afterward the following message appeared on Instagram:

> The US and the West are trying to undermine the situation in Russia, sap its economy and cause chaos and instability. Russia's enemies tried to use Georgia and Chechnya to ruin our country. Both times they were repelled. So they then set fire to Ukraine. It is therefore important for all the peoples of Russia to show solidarity and unite around the Russian national leader, President Vladimir Putin. The Western intelligence services are trying to strike at those who are devoted to Vladimir Vladimirovich [Putin]. Breast-fed by media and other organizations, they are using any excuse to slur the name of the head of the Chechen Republic. If there is a pedestrian struck down while crossing the road, Kadyrov is blamed. If someone is suspected of a crime, again he is guilty. A campaign is now under way in connec-

> tion with the detention of Zaur Dadayev, a former officer of the Chechen Interior Ministry. . . . I reiterate that no matter where I am or whatever I do I am selflessly devoted to Vladimir Putin and am ready to oppose the enemies of Russia. I declare that I owe my life to Vladimir Putin and am devoted to him as a person, regardless of his position. Anyone who tries to harm the president of Russia and Russia itself should be in no doubt that I will not hesitate to prevent it.[7]

Websites controlled by the Chechen underground began to write that Kadyrov was in despair over the silent treatment he was receiving from Putin. Moreover, they spread rumors suggesting that the Russian president was in talks with the rulers of Jordan and the United Arab Emirates about granting Kadyrov political asylum, which would provide a pretext for Putin to force him out of the country.

GOLDEN GUNS

"Putin and Kadyrov have a special relationship," says a Kremlin employee close to the president. "It's certainly strange. A regional leader should not consider Putin to be his sole source of authority and legitimacy. But that's how the crooked system has turned out." Likewise, Kadyrov's Instagram feed has always maintained that his political career depends entirely on Vladimir Putin.

In 2011, in an interview with Chechen television, Putin unexpectedly opened up about his relationship with the Kadyrov family. "When I first met him, my first impression was: can he actually talk? Because in response to questions he mainly snarled something unintelligible," Putin said, recalling his first encounter with Ramzan's father, Akhmad Kadyrov, the mufti of Chechnya, whom Putin had gambled on to bring order to Chechnya at the start of his presidency.

In order to stop the second Chechen war, Putin tried to "outsource" it to the local level as part of a process known as "Chechenization." The plan was to blur the insider/outsider division and to turn the Russian-Chechen conflict into an internal Chechen affair. Akhmad Kadyrov agreed to lead a pro-Russian Chechen government and generally did a good job.

"When he took charge," Putin continued in the conversation with Chechen television, "I watched in amazement at what he was saying and how he said it. He articulated the essence of what was going on and stated his opinion directly and clearly. It was a revelation for me."

Akhmad Kadyrov put in a good word for his son Ramzan, Putin said. "Akhmad said to me, 'Look, Ramzan's a good boy with bright prospects.' But he never asked or lobbied for his son to become head of the republic." Ramzan Kadyrov, who worked as the head of his father's security service, also surprised Putin: "Ramzan gets things done. I honestly didn't expect him to be so hands-on. I was in Grozny and saw the state the city was in after the fighting ended. It was like Stalingrad. I was walking among the ruins and thinking, 'When can it be rebuilt? Can it be rebuilt at all?' Ramzan took charge and got it done. I was surprised. What a guy! I thought he was only good for roaming around the mountains with a submachine gun, but no," Putin said in praise of Ramzan Kadyrov, who became the de facto leader and later president of Chechnya after his father's assassination.[8]

In 2004 Vladimir Putin and Ramzan Kadyrov effectively signed a pact. The young Chechen leader told the Russian president that he considered him his father and was ready to die for him. These words warmed Putin's soul, and in exchange for such personal loyalty he gave Kadyrov total carte blanche. First of all, Chechnya was given huge subsidies to rebuild itself (15–20 billion rubles—about $600–800 million—per year, according to official figures). However, it was stated in the "Chechen dossier" (written by former US ambassador to Russia William Burns and made public by WikiLeaks) that about a third of the money went to Kadyrov personally. Second, Kadyrov was handed the opportunity to get rid of all his political opponents, whose mistake had been not to swear personal allegiance to Putin.

Kadyrov's two most dangerous opponents were the Yamadayev brothers, though not for long. Symbolically, the elder brother, Ruslan, a former Duma MP from Chechnya, was gunned down in September 2008 in front of the government building in Moscow—that is, the offices of Putin, who at that time was Russia's prime minister. Yamadayev's car stopped at a traffic light on Smolenskaya Embankment. His killer calmly approached the vehicle and shot Yamadayev at point-blank range. The second passenger in the car survived. Several months later the killer was arrested.* Those who ordered the killing were never identified.

---

*By a strange coincidence he shared a surname with Boris Nemtsov's alleged killer seven years later—Dadayev. Just a namesake, though.

Six months later Ruslan Yamadayev's younger brother, Sulim, was assassinated in Dubai. The UAE investigative authorities proved more successful than their Russian counterparts: they arrested the hitmen (one of whom was Ramzan Kadyrov's personal stableman, caring for Kadyrov's horses) and also identified the client, Adam Delimkhanov, who was a Duma MP from Chechnya and Kadyrov's right-hand man. The killers were sentenced to life imprisonment. However, two years later the sentence was commuted to twenty-seven months, and they were then able to return from Dubai to Chechnya.

Despite the suspected involvement of Ramzan Kadyrov and his entourage, such killings had little resonance in Russia—with one exception. That was the murder of journalist Anna Politkovskaya, who was known for her investigations of torture, assassinations, and kidnappings in Kadyrov's Chechnya. She was shot dead on October 7, 2006—Putin's birthday. Only in 2014 were five people found guilty of her murder, although once again the individual or individuals who had hired them were not named. Pro-government media claimed that it was most likely a provocation by the West or the Russian opposition to discredit Putin and Kadyrov.

Although in the public consciousness Kadyrov was associated with crime, it did not affect his pact with the Kremlin. He remained loyal to Moscow and committed to keeping Chechnya under control, for which he continued to receive unlimited funding and carte blanche to enforce his own interpretation of the law.

Nemtsov's murder was the first event that did not fit into this framework. For Kadyrov's entourage, the long-standing leader of the liberal opposition was an enemy on the fringe of society. They did not associate him with power and probably knew nothing of his government past. The struggle against the liberals and supporters of a Russian "color revolution" was seen as a part of Kadyrov's obligations to Putin.

But the ruling class in Moscow, including the Kremlin, reacted to the murder quite differently. Nemtsov was more of a kindred spirit to them than Kadyrov was. Up until that moment assassinations had not concerned them, even those in Moscow, since the victims had been largely Chechen politicians, journalists, and human rights defenders. But the case of Nemtsov was another matter: the victim was a former first deputy prime minister, Putin's ex-boss, and a onetime potential successor to Boris Yeltsin.

ESCAPE TO THE EMIRATES

Meanwhile, Putin's absence continued. Even the global media began looking for him. A Russian website featured a stopwatch counting the seconds, minutes, and days that had elapsed since his last public appearance.

Members of Putin's entourage say that the president is hypersensitive about his health and does not like his press service to comment on it. Believing that the tsar should never fall ill, Putin always avoids meetings with people who might infect him with some ailment. If a senior official or minister suddenly sneezes in his presence, it might well be the end of that person's face time: "Right, out you go. I must not get sick!" says Putin in such cases. He is also obsessed with sport: every day he spends two hours swimming or working out in the gym, plus he plays ice hockey several times a week, usually at night.

During his ten-day absence, Putin not only did a lot of sports; according to insiders, but was pondering what to do with Ramzan Kadyrov. At last Putin appeared before the cameras on March 16 in St. Petersburg at a meeting with the president of Kyrgyzstan. But still he did not take Kadyrov's phone calls.

"The past few days will be remembered as a week of widespread lies," railed Kadyrov's Instagram feed.

> Perhaps never before in such a short period of time has so much gossip, hypocrisy, and blatant misinformation been poured into people's ears. The so-called political scientists, analysts, and experts spoon-fed by their Western sponsors have said that President Vladimir Putin is seriously ill and cannot run the country. Some hotheads have stated a coup is on the way. Russia's enemies have been scrambling to get the media to portray their wishful thinking as reality. Our national leader Vladimir Putin and his team are above all that! They have done the right thing by ignoring the yapping mongrels. All the doomsayers have been struck dumb by the president's appearance in St. Petersburg in the rudest of health! Russia is a great power with a strong and resolute leader. President Vladimir Putin will never allow the United States and its Western henchmen to run our country—*ever*![9]

Yet Kadyrov was still unable to talk to the president, even after the latter's public appearance. Instead, on March 26 Putin attended an FSB meeting at Lubyanka in central Moscow, timed symbolically to coincide with the fifteenth anniversary of his first election as president. Putin's entourage noticed with surprise that following his ten-day absence he had doubled his security detail.

On the same day Ramzan Kadyrov flew to the United Arab Emirates, taking with him his entire inner circle. The ostensible reason was to go to the races, where his horses were competing. But he was in no hurry to return to Chechnya. Kadyrov and his team spent ten days in the UAE. In Dubai and Abu Dhabi Kadyrov continued to swear allegiance to Putin:

> The hypocrisy of Russia's enemies knows no bounds! After reading that statement, you might think it is about the Western capitals targeting missiles at our dams and nuclear power plants. No! They understand that Russia's response will be instantaneous and so will never push the button. I'm talking about those with dual citizenship (one of them Russian) who are doing everything to undermine the country's stability from within, generously sponsored by US foundations and a handful of newspapers. Their methods are not original. They were implemented by a well-known ideologist in the 1930s–1940s, who argued that the more blatant the lie, the more readily it will be believed. . . . They are out to create the appearance of a conflict between politicians, regional heads and national leaders. Some media have even produced headlines such as, "Is the Kremlin afraid of Chechnya?" This is openly and brazenly provocative. . . . The Kremlin has nothing to fear. It is not afraid of Chechnya or Moscow or Rostov or Magadan, and it is not afraid of you. Moreover, the Kremlin is not even afraid of your beloved Londons, Washingtons, and Berlins. And the Kremlin is not afraid of your Americas and NATOs, because the Kremlin is Russia. The Kremlin is Chechnya, Moscow, Chelyabinsk, Rostov, and thousands of other towns and cities! I have always said and do so again that I am the foot soldier of Russian President and Supreme Commander Vladimir Putin![10]

Only on April 6 did Kadyrov and his team return to Grozny. That same day Putin issued a decree assigning the Chechen capital the title of "City of Military Glory"—usually reserved for cities that put up heroic resistance during the Great Patriotic War.

A day later Kadyrov went to Moscow at the invitation of deputy chief of staff Vyacheslav Volodin. The person in charge of Russian domestic policy was not an authority in Kadyrov's eyes, since the latter recognized only Vladimir Putin and Vladislav Surkov (who was half Chechen). But Volodin, sitting in Surkov's former office, reached out to the Chechen leader.

"Vyacheslav Viktorovich [Volodin], a wise and experienced statesman, has always offered important advice and supported projects to assist the Chechen Republic. It's very nice that our national leader Vladimir Putin has such dedicated comrades in his team. It gives us confidence in Russia's future!" enthusiastically reported Kadyrov's Instagram feed after their meeting.[11]

THE WOLF AND THE BEAR

"He's like a son to me," Putin said in his interview with Chechen television in 2011. "We are all human, all with our own strengths and weaknesses. He is no exception. But he is an honest person and I respect that very much."

The fact that Putin was speaking to a Chechen audience is probably what prompted him to describe Kadyrov as a son. "For him, Ramzan was always a young wolf in need of shelter," a Kremlin insider interprets Putin's feelings.

For Kadyrov, Putin had always been a role model. He adopted Putin's style of talking with foreign dignitaries, human rights activists, and business leaders, and picked up the habit of surrounding himself with Hollywood stars. In December 2010 Putin's friends arranged a "charity" evening attended by Sharon Stone, Mickey Rourke, Kevin Costner, Alain Delon, Gerard Depardieu, Monica Bellucci, Vincent Cassel, Kurt Russell, and Ornella Muti. The stars looked on as Putin gave a piano rendition of "Blueberry Hill." Ramzan Kadyrov wanted to repeat the trick. A year later he invited Hilary Swank, Jean-Claude Van Damme, Seal, and Vanessa-Mae to his thirty-fifth birthday celebration in Grozny. Their fees were not disclosed.*

When asked about where the subsidized Chechen Republic found the money for such extravagance, Kadyrov always replied, "Allah sends it." Once he got into an argument with a persistent journalist: "Prove it's not from Allah," he challenged.

According to journalists who interviewed the Chechen leader throughout his presidency, he swapped palaces several times, each one more golden and

---

*After the event was shown on Euronews, human rights organizations attacked the stars for attending, but only Hilary Swank responded, saying that she had donated everything to charity and fired her managers.

luxurious than the previous. In 2006, when he became prime minister of the republic, Kadyrov moved from the tribal village of Tsentaroy to the city of Gudermes, Chechnya's fourth-largest urban settlement, which had suffered less than Grozny during the two Chechen wars. There, Kadyrov acquired his own private zoo. Guests presented him with exotic baby animals, which Kadyrov loved to show off to journalists and demonstrate how they obeyed him. He squeezed the paws of tiger cubs and thrust his fingers into his mouth of a little bear, showing that they were tame. A couple of years later menacing howls and growls started to be heard around Gudermes at night—the sound of Kadyrov's now grown-up predators.

THE WAR CONTINUES

Just two weeks after his return from the UAE, Kadyrov was taught a lesson. On April 19, 2015, the Chechen leader was watching his favorite soccer team, Terek, in a match against Dynamo Moscow (which in Soviet times had been affiliated to the Interior Ministry). While he was away, federal police entered Grozny from the neighboring Stavropol region and killed a businessman by the name of Dadayev not far from Kadyrov's official residence.* He had apparently resisted arrest and the police had been forced to take action. The incident enraged Kadyrov. The next day he told his security forces: "The next time federal police enter your territory without your prior knowledge, whether from Moscow or Stavropol, I order you to open fire."

He received an official response from the Russian Interior Ministry: "The Russian Interior Ministry considers it unacceptable for the head of the Chechen Republic to order his forces to open fire on police officers from other regions if the local law enforcement agencies have not been informed of the operation in advance." Then Putin's press secretary, Dmitry Peskov, weighed in, saying that Kadyrov should remember the chain of command and understand that Chechnya's police answered not to him but the federal Interior Ministry in Moscow.

Interestingly, Kadyrov himself is a general in the Russian police forces. Back on December 28, 2014, when the Chechen security forces gathered inside a stadium to swear allegiance to Putin, they were forced to back up their

*Yet another namesake of Nemtsov's alleged assassin. (No, Dadayev is not an especially common Chechen name.)

verbal oath of loyalty with a written statement committing them to serve Putin, interior minister Vladimir Kolokoltsov, and Chechen leader Ramzan Kadyrov (in that order). But four months later things had changed beyond recognition.

The public spat between Kadyrov and the Interior Ministry was clear evidence that the Chechen leader had lost the ability to contact Putin directly to complain about being harassed by Moscow officialdom. But he had not lost all his political weight. A month later the Investigative Committee announced a change of personnel in the team investigating the murder of Boris Nemtsov. The inquiry would henceforth be led by the same detective who had investigated the 2008 murder of Ruslan Yamadayev and who had failed (or declined) to identity the masterminds behind it.

It turned out that after fifteen years of rule the problem that Putin had promised to tackle on taking office in 2000 was still very much unresolved. Back during the fat decade Putin had managed to make Russian society forget the horrors of Chechnya. Under the new social contract, the word "Chechnya" was taboo. The agreement suited everyone. The Caucasian republic was erased from the mass consciousness, although that did not prevent various horrific Chechnya-related events: Beslan, the *Nord-Ost* attack, and suicide bombers on planes. Through kind of mass hypnosis, Russian society adopted the axiom "let sleeping dogs lie": if we don't bother Chechnya, maybe it won't bother us.

Back then there was also a clear consensus in journalistic circles that reporting was a safe profession—as long as they didn't write about Chechnya. Anything else, fine, but Chechnya, no. The fact was that journalists who wrote about Chechnya had a tendency to end up in a body bag. The rule was understood, and virtually everyone believed that it was the one area where sacrificing the truth was for the greater good.

Chechnya made a miraculous leap from military and criminal news stories to high-society gloss. Ramzan Kadyrov began to grace the cover of magazines and give sugary interviews on television. He attended the St. Petersburg Economic Forum. Cultural and sporting figures, opinion shapers, and intellectuals of all stripes smiled for the cameras in the company of Kadyrov and Chechen politicians from his inner circle suspected of murder. Such was the social contract.

Those unfamiliar with the psychology of Russian society might suggest that it was some kind of expiation of Russian guilt for the suffering of the

Chechen people in the 1940s (when they were deported by Stalin) or the 1990s (during the two wars with Moscow)—similar to white Americans' contrition for slavery or Germans' remorse over the Holocaust. But no. In Russia the feeling is more a mixture of fear and ignorance, resulting in political apathy: "I am not interested in politics and do not know or care what is happening in Chechnya" is the general attitude.

The most curious thing about this game of peekaboo was that Vladimir Putin joined in. He too thought that all the problems with Chechnya would go away if he just kept his eyes closed long enough. In more practical terms, Putin believed that he could appease Chechnya with sacks of cash. But by 2015 the illusion was over.

Putin's entourage suddenly stopped discussing Ukraine—or rather started saying that Ukraine was not Russia's most pressing problem. Officials started spooking each other with a new phrase: "Third Chechen War."

CHAPTER 20

IN WHICH BASHAR AL-ASSAD BECOMES THE MIRROR IMAGE OF PUTIN

I met Bashar al-Assad in 2008. Although not a global pariah then, he nevertheless sensed that his prospects were grim. He was never fond of talking to journalists, but in September that year he suddenly had an urge to speak to the Russian press—that is, me in my capacity as Kommersant*'s senior international correspondent.*

Assad's sudden desire to talk was clear. He was overwhelmingly heartened by the August war in Georgia. "Some people in Russia used to think the United States could be a friend, but I don't think those people exist anymore," he told me gleefully.

Assad's overriding thought during that interview can be expressed as follows: "At long last!" He had long been waiting and hoping for Russia to stop pretending to be a Western democracy and return to the fold of Eastern despotism. Russia, he believed, should stop being ashamed of selling missiles to his country, Syria, and its ally, Iran. The war with Georgia was, in his view, a Rubicon. Having crossed it, Russia would not be forgiven by the West.

"Russia is going through the same as we did. Georgia provoked the crisis, but the West blamed Moscow," said an indignant Assad. "It's total disinformation. The facts are distorted to isolate Russia internationally. The process has been going on for years. They wanted to surround Russia with a ring of hostile

governments, then strike at the country's economy, interfere in its internal affairs and deploy a missile defense system on its borders. What we see in Georgia is the result. It's the apogee of the attempts to encircle and isolate Russia."[1]

He seemed rather naive to me: too soft and insecure for a dictator, too outspoken and talkative for an experienced politician. There was also a slight sense of facelessness. There was nothing special about his appearance, his conversation, or even the interior of his residence. The king of Jordan, for instance, who is Assad's contemporary, with whom Assad is often compared, and whom I had interviewed a year earlier, amazed me with his huge collection of toy tanks on display around his residence. By contrast, I found it hard to imagine that Assad had any kind of hobby at all.

Right after our interview he flew to Sochi, where he was scheduled to meet with Russian president Dmitry Medvedev. There he restated his case, but chose the wrong listener. Or rather he got ahead of himself. Medvedev failed to come to an agreement with Assad, and two years later he would vote with the United States in the UN for sanctions against Iran and then support the operation against Libya—the one that Putin later described as a "crusade."

Over the next seven years Russian foreign policy underwent a radical transformation. If in 2008 Assad's words seemed paranoid and delusional, come 2015 they were very much mainstream foreign policy.

OUR BASTARD

In Soviet times the Middle East had always been a zone of special interest for Moscow. No other region was covered as widely by Soviet television. No foreign leader (outside the Soviet bloc) visited the Soviet Union as often as the head of the Palestine Liberation Organization, Yasser Arafat. And no country (including the United States) was attacked by Soviet propaganda as much as the "military clique of Israel."

The Middle East had been one of the Soviet Union's "backyards," but after the Soviet collapse that came to an abrupt end. The new Russian government immediately established relations with Israel, and the new batch of Jewish oligarchs actively developed them.

Putin had never taken the Arab world seriously. He was well versed in international affairs, but not when it came to the Arabs. The region was essentially left at the mercy of opportunists. Dubious deals aplenty were struck that had nothing to do with politics, since the Arab world was—and is—no less corrupt than Russia. In the early Putin years Moscow's activity in the Middle East was limited solely to the business interests of Russian oil companies. Prewar Iraq is a case in point. Russian companies bribed Saddam Hussein for a slice of the country's oil deposits, which they subsequently lost after his overthrow in 2003.

Relations with other Arab countries, most hugely in debt to the Soviet Union, followed a similar pattern. During unsophisticated negotiations with various Arab regimes, Russian diplomats agreed to write off the amounts owed in exchange for contracts with Russian oil firms or arms manufacturers. Strictly speaking, such deals were of questionable benefit to the state budget, but very lucrative for private business.

The geographical scope gradually widened. Jordan and Algeria started buying Russian weapons. The family of Lebanese prime minister Rafic Hariri was awarded contracts for construction projects in southern Russia, and Russian Railways had plans to build a railway in Libya. Debts were forgiven, but the former Soviet Union's Arabian assets evaporated. Only Syria continued to host a Russian military base outside the post-Soviet space, but no one was interested in that. Why would they be?

The Arab Spring turned everything on its head. During the 2011 uprisings against Hosni Mubarak and Muammar Gaddafi, Vladimir Putin imagined himself in their shoes. What happened next with Bashar al-Assad prompted even more soul-searching by the Russian leader.

Putin had no particular affinity with the Syrian leader, since their backgrounds were too different. In 1991 the twenty-six-year-old ophthalmologist Bashar al-Assad left Damascus for London. Having completed an internship, he became a full-fledged member of the staff at the Western Eye Hospital in Paddington. He lived modestly in London under a pseudonym, so that no one would guess that their eye doctor was in fact the son of Syrian president Hafez al-Assad. His London sojourn ended in 1994, when a car accident killed his elder brother Bassel, who was due to inherit the presidency. Bashar was immediately recalled and dispatched to a military academy to prepare for office.

When Hafez died in 2000 and his son Bashar took over, everyone expected Syria to become a normal country, much the way the young Jordanian monarch Abdullah had restored the kingdom's dignity following his father's death in 1999. But the state machine operates according to its own laws. The numerous Hafez-era generals and relatives, all older and more experienced than Bashar, were resistant to change. The new president was nothing like a tyrant, but neither did he appear to be a reformer. The Syrian army continued to occupy Lebanon. Bashar al-Assad maintained contacts with Iran and even started selling weapons to Saddam's Iraq.

In a sense Assad was the Vladimir Putin of the Middle East: a man who accidentally became ruler of his country as the result of unforeseen circumstances, and who would probably have chosen a different fate had the choice presented itself. He did not plan to become anti-Western. More than that, he wanted *not* to be anti-Western. He simply failed to take the steps required for rapprochement with the international community and instead waited for the world to show him respect.

In many ways he was a hostage of his environment, family, and friends, as well as of a long-standing political paradigm in the region: if something goes wrong, blame the West. There was nothing devious about Assad's approach. He simply hoped that bloody-mindedness would defeat his opponents. He did not take them seriously and believed that they would eventually come round to his way of thinking.

The main difference between Assad and his fellow Arab dictators was his visceral fear of a "color revolution." With the emergence of the Arab Spring, when a wave of protests toppled the leaders in Tunisia, Libya, and Egypt, Assad decided to resist at all costs. When in January through March 2011 thousands of Syrians took to the streets, the army immediately responded with force. Several people were killed in the clashes and thousands were arrested, but the most well-known case was that of renowned Syrian political cartoonist Ali Farzat, who allegedly (and perhaps symbolically) had the bones in his hands deliberately broken during a beating.

Despite the violent crackdown by the authorities, the unrest did not abate, but escalated into a civil war. It effectively started in 2011, when the Syrian rebels began receiving aid from abroad, including Qatar, Turkey, the United States, Britain, and France. Assad stubbornly waged war despite the mounting casualties—in the first year alone 5,000 people died. Assad proved that blind, stubborn resistance can be an effective way to hold on to power whatever the cost. A lack of strategy can in fact be a strategy.

As previously mentioned in connection with Mikheil Saakashvili, Putin likes to recall a phrase attributed to US president Franklin D. Roosevelt, who allegedly said of Nicaraguan dictator Anastasio Somoza: "He may be a bastard, but he's our bastard." Putin has always cited the remark as clear proof of the Americans' double standards. For Putin, foreign policy is personal. Given that he views every event as a US-led rehearsal to remove him from power, Assad was now his bastard.

This is how a close adviser to Putin describes the president's reasoning about Syria: Bashar al-Assad was a typical Arab leader, no worse or better than the monarchs of Saudi Arabia, Morocco, and Jordan and the presidents of the UAE, Sudan, and Algeria. Why does the West look kindly on some and demonize others? Why is Saudi Arabia allowed to publicly hang and behead people without a murmur from Western human rights activists, while Syria is vilified for far less? There is only one explanation, thought Putin. Syria is an ally of Russia. It is the only country outside the post-Soviet space with a Russian military base. The Syrian regime buys Russian weapons and hires Russian military advisers.

Putin justified Assad's use of weapons against his own people as a response to the Arab Spring, which the Syrian leader alone had resisted. Putin recalled the wave of "color revolutions" in 2004–2005 across the former Soviet Union. Back then the first leader who had dared open fire on the protesters was Uzbek president Islam Karimov. Putin had immediately offered him support and promised Russian military assistance should the unrest reoccur. That put an end to the chain reaction.

When civil war broke out in Syria in 2011, Putin experienced déjà vu. Again he felt besieged, and again he had a tenacious Eastern dictator to thank for protecting him. For Putin, the Arab Spring was a rehearsal for a revolution in Russia, and Assad had effectively shielded Russia from the latest in a long line of US conspiracies.

COLD SHOULDER IN AUSTRALIA

The G20 summit was held in Brisbane on November 15–16, 2014. On the eve of the meeting, journalists tortured Western leaders with questions about what they would say to Putin and what kind of welcome he would be given after all that had happened. Australian prime minister Tony Abbott delivered the clumsiest response, promising to "shirtfront" the Russian leader. A term from Australian-rules football, it means "bump an opponent forcefully and illegally in the chest." And Abbott was the host leader, no less.

Despite his newfound pariah status, Putin made the trip. Contrary to expectations, there were no skirmishes, physical or verbal, but what happened was perhaps worse. During the traditional photo op, Putin was placed not in the center, next to US president Barack Obama and Chinese leader Xi Jinping, but on the edge, next to South African president Jacob Zuma. He had never been on the periphery before. That was followed by the pointed behavior of his colleagues during lunch. The waiter showed Putin to a table, where he effectively dined alone. Only Brazilian president Dilma Rousseff was at the same table, though she sat some distance away, at the opposite end. The other leaders were seated elsewhere.

Putin left Brisbane early the next day, November 16, without even attending the morning's working breakfast. He told journalists at the airport that his hasty departure was because he needed time to get some rest before the day's business back in the Kremlin.

Putin was humiliated by the Australian reception. It also marked the start of a new stage of Russian foreign policy. Used to being lauded abroad, Putin was now less keen to travel for fear of being treated like an outcast. Other Russian state officials, even liberal ones, followed his example, and soon contact with Western audiences was reduced to the absolute minimum. Deputy prime minister Igor Shuvalov, invited to Davos for the World Economic Forum, decided to go for just one day. He returned to Russia without attending most of the sessions.

The unpleasant feeling of international isolation continued to worsen. Another nadir was the Munich Security Conference in February 2015. Twice the hall burst into laughter during the speech of Russian foreign minister Sergey Lavrov. Russian foreign policy was greeted not with shouting or booing but chortling. Lavrov barely kept his cool, finishing his speech with the words, "You can laugh if you want. Laughter makes the world go round."

The first ripple came when Lavrov stated that the accession of Crimea had happened in accordance with the founding principle of the UN Charter—"the right of nations to self-determination." The UN Charter is famous for being contradictory and containing two mutually exclusive principles: "the right of nations to self-determination" and "the inviolability of frontiers." Crimea's "self-determination" was blatantly at variance with the second principle of the UN Charter. Ukraine was against it, and even Russia had repeatedly recognized the inviolability of its neighbor's borders; Putin had signed a treaty to that effect back in 2003.

The smirks became guffaws when Lavrov claimed that West Germany had annexed East Germany in 1989, since there had been no referendum in the latter. When Russian Duma Speaker Sergey Naryshkin had made the point in Moscow, no one had laughed. But over in the West it was greeted with howls of derision.

The fact that the conference was being held in Munich—in the occupier country, according to Lavrov—added extra spice. German chancellor Angela Merkel was a native of the former East Germany and hence a spokesperson for the illegally annexed territory. Perhaps Lavrov's comments were meant as a joke, but to most members of the audience in Munich it seemed as though he was poking fun at them. All his arguments pertained to legal norms that the West had at some point or other violated: the Adapted Conventional Armed Forces in Europe Treaty, the Treaty on Intermediate and Shorter-Range Missiles, the Anti-Ballistic Missile Treaty. What was so funny?

The reason for the audience's reaction becomes clear if one listens carefully to what was said before and after Lavrov's speech by his European and US counterparts. None of the politicians and diplomats in the Munich conference hall had any doubt that Russia was spilling blood in eastern Ukraine. When US senator Lindsay Graham asked the audience if they thought there were Russian troops in Ukraine, every hand went up.

All Lavrov's arguments seemed like ridiculous pretexts and absurd hair-splitting. "Okay, maybe someone violated something once, but you've just deployed troops in a neighboring country," said a US diplomat.

Members of the Russian delegation were struck by the fact that absolutely no one believed Russia's version of events. Every speaker in Munich openly said so. Russian officials were stunned by the undiplomatic frankness with which Russia's foreign policy was discussed in the presence of the Russian foreign minister, as if he weren't even there.

Humiliating laughter was a new phase in the evolution of Russia's relations with the West. It had also been in Munich, eight years before, in 2007, that Vladimir Putin had delivered his famous critique that left listeners shocked (rather like Hugh Grant's speech as the British prime minister in the film *Love Actually*): Putin accused the United States of almost every deadly sin, including the flouting of international law. Truth had been largely on his side, and he himself at the time was relatively guilt-free. The war in South Ossetia had yet to happen and Crimea was a long way off. Putin described the United States as the world's policeman, and his audience listened intently. They may not have trusted Putin, but they could not fail to agree with him, at least partially.

Two years later, in 2009, US vice president Joseph Biden delivered his own Munich speech. He did not say that Putin had been right in 2007, of course, but admitted that the previous US administration had been wrong. He was the first to mention the word "reset" and proposed turning over a new page in US-Russian relations.

But in 2015 things were very different, and Biden expressed his surprise in his Munich speech that year. The "reset" was dead and buried. Worse than that, Biden's words suggested that Russia did not even exist. "The Russia We Lost" could have been the title of his speech, as he referred to the country only in the past tense: "All of us, we all invested in a type of Russia we hoped—and still hope—will emerge one day: a Russia integrated into the world economy; more prosperous, more invested in the international order."[2]

Merkel in Munich spoke about Putin with the same frankness: "The problem is that I cannot imagine any situation in which improved equipment for the Ukrainian army leads to President Putin being so impressed that he believes he will lose militarily," she said, plainly asserting that it was Putin waging war in Ukraine, not some ragtag group of separatists.[3]

Moscow felt the full force of the isolation. Yet the Kremlin's response was strange and slightly irrational. It spoke of the "common grief" that had united the country. Those officials who had hoped that Russia's isolation would be short-lived began to philosophize about the conditions under which Russia and the West could be reconciled. "You'll see. There'll be something more terrible. Something so terrible we can't even imagine it. Something like a third world war," said a top Russian official in private. "It will reconcile us with the Americans."

THE BOARD OF "WORLD INC."

In May 2015 a historic event took place in Vienna—the signing of an Iranian nuclear deal, which put an end to Iran's isolation. The whole world rejoiced, except Russia. The Kremlin had an ominous feeling that this was the last negotiation process that would involve Russia as a great power.

Putin had first formulated his new concept of Russian foreign policy back in his 2007 Munich speech: the world needs a new treaty on global security. In subsequent years it became an obsession. Some Kremlin insiders dubbed the theoretical treaty "Yalta 2" (in honor of the Yalta Conference of 1945), while others referred to it as "Helsinki 2" (after the Helsinki Accords on European security in 1975, at the height of the Cold War). The agreement was intended to be proof positive of Russia's international prestige as one of the centers of the new multipolar world. The old board of directors of "World Inc."—that is, the UN Security Council—was obsolete. Putin insisted on there being a new form of global governance in which Russia would play a major part.

But almost no one paid any attention to Putin's proposal, either in 2007 or subsequently. And not due to any lack of respect. The idea of a "global board of directors" had twice proved ineffective. The League of Nations had failed in the 1930s, and its successor, the United Nations, despite outliving the Cold War, had fallen asleep in the decades that followed. It had been unable to stop the bloodletting in the Balkans and Rwanda and the operations in Afghanistan and Iraq. Even the idealists had ceased to believe that anything could be achieved through UN channels.

The Kremlin was sure that the new "board of directors" tasked with tackling the world's problems would be NATO, which is why Russian enmity for the alliance rose so markedly in the 2000s. In the early years of his presidency Vladimir Putin took every opportunity to ask George W. Bush when Russia would be invited to join, but in the end he gave up waiting for a reply and proposed his own global setup.

But no one responded to Putin's call, since the concept of a "board of directors" had been replaced by the idea of "independent arbitration." In other words, whenever a problem arose, the parties involved appealed to trusted intermediaries, which might or might not be linked to existing international organizations. For instance, the arbiters in the resolution of the Iranian nuclear issue were initially the "Eurotroika" (Britain, France, and Germany) and the International Atomic Energy Agency.

The Eurotroika achieved nothing, and the Iranian issue became more acute. So in 2006 the "Iranian dossier" was handed over to a new group of arbiters, called the P5+1: Britain, France, the United States, Russia, and China, plus Germany (the European Union played a role as well). After completing its mission in 2015, this ad hoc arbitration body was disbanded, thereby depriving Russia of a seat on one of the global "boards of directors." There was, of course, still the Minsk process—the resolution of the crisis in eastern Ukraine. But here most members of the international community saw Russia not as an arbiter but as a party to the conflict. Putin's involvement in the negotiations was a sign not of Russia's greatness but of its mounting problems.

The Kremlin racked its brain. Other than Ukraine, what else would the world be willing to discuss with Russia?

WORLD WAR III

In late summer 2015 the Kremlin press service announced that Vladimir Putin would put an end to his self-imposed moratorium on travel to Western countries and go to New York for the meeting of the UN General Assembly to present a plan to unite Russia and the United States against their common enemy, ISIS (also known as the Islamic State).

Kremlin aides had come up with the new foreign policy tactic back in May, when Russia was ceremoniously marking the seventieth anniversary of victory in the Great Patriotic War. The usual mantra sounded about how the civilized world had formed an anti-Hitler coalition in which the Soviet Union had played the decisive role. The task for the Kremlin speechwriters was to brand ISIS as the new Third Reich (in previous speeches Putin had hinted that this label belonged to the United States). By defeating Islamic terrorism, the Russians and Americans would finally succeed in creating a new world order and a new UN Security Council (the global "board of directors"), as in 1945 at Yalta. This was the concept Vladimir Putin presented in New York.

Putin was editing his speech until the last moment. And preferred to read it from his papers not using a teleprompter. His aides claim he was afraid that the Americans would change text somehow.

A week later he turned sixty-three. The celebration took place in Sochi, where he played ice hockey with a team of old Soviet Olympic champions. He scored eight goals to secure victory against a team of oligarch pals.

Next up was a celebratory birthday feast. Foreign minister Sergei Lavrov presented the president with a life-size bronze statue of Mahatma Gandhi—an allusion to an interview Putin gave back in 2005 on the eve of the G8 summit in St. Petersburg. Responding to a question from Western journalists about his democratic credentials, Putin had quipped that he was the only true democrat there was and that "after the death of Mahatma Gandhi, there was nobody left to talk to."

Back then everyone took it as a playful joke. But come 2015 the joke was cast in bronze. Putin was convinced that he was a peacemaker and a historic figure of Gandhian proportions who was trying single-handedly to save the world. And nobody was helping him. There was indeed no one left to talk to.

Putin's proposal to launch a joint war against ISIS received positive feedback, even from US diplomats. But the bonhomie did not last long. A few days later Russia began a bombing campaign in Syria. The first strikes by Russian bombers were not against ISIS but against the Syrian opposition—the enemies of Bashar al-Assad. Weeks went by, and still Russian aircraft continued to bomb the Syrian opposition. All the while Russian television asserted that Putin was inflicting damage on ISIS. But over in the US State Department, they were experiencing déjà vu. It was a repeat of Russian claims that its forces were not involved in the conflict in eastern Ukraine. No one took Putin's statements at face value anymore.

On November 15, 2015, the leaders of the G20 (the only global club of "great powers" that still had Russia as a member) gathered for a summit in Antalya, Turkey. Turkish president Recep Tayyip Erdogan was extremely disgruntled about the Russian operation in Syria, especially since his old friend Putin had not consulted with him in advance. He tried to reason with his Russian counterpart in a face-to-face meeting, but Putin was not listening.

"Vladimir, we do not like your aircraft flying in our airspace without warning," Erdogan began with faux friendliness, and requested that the Russian military coordinate its sorties with Turkey. Putin replied that Russia's central command was in contact with NATO regarding flight paths and that if Erdogan wanted to, he could request all the information from Brussels. He then said playfully, "We might pay you a visit."

"We don't like uninvited guests," retorted Erdogan angrily.

On December 1, 2015, a Russian aircraft on a mission to strike at the Syrian opposition was shot down by the Turkish air force. Kremlin insiders said sardonically that the shooting down of the Russian bomber was like the assassination of Austrian archduke Franz Ferdinand, which provoked the First World War.

Liberal economists from the government and big business, whose influence in the Kremlin was rising slightly in the wake of the growing crisis, were horrified. They had only just begun to convince Putin that power politics was damaging the Russian economy. The downed plane had wrecked all their plans.

They tried to explain to Putin that Erdogan was emotional and impulsive. The decision had been made by him alone, without consulting Washington or NATO, because he was deeply concerned about Russia's intervention in the Syrian conflict. Erdogan's "neo-Ottoman" ideology meant that the Turkish leader considered all the territories of the former Ottoman Empire to be Turkey's "backyard"—like the way Russia regarded the countries of the former Soviet Union. And just as Putin found Western intervention in Kiev unpalatable, Erdogan considered the appearance of Russian aircraft in Syria to be a hostile act. Putin's liberal courtiers told the Russian president that the risks of the Russian operation in Syria had not been properly weighed up, that it should have been discussed with Erdogan and that the Russian security forces had messed up the planning phase.

But Putin was having none of it. He was in receipt of intel from the security forces themselves. The decision to shoot down the plane had allegedly come from Brussels and Washington. It was a deliberate attempt to provoke a third world war. The Americans wanted to see if Putin would blink.

The hypothetical World War III began to acquire real contours. What had previously sounded like gibberish was now the subject of serious discussion. Foreign policy strategists suddenly started saying that a major military conflict could be an opportunity for Russia to turn the world on its head. Developments of recent years had left Russia behind, and only a sharp shock to the global system would reverse the country's fortunes, they envisioned.

Government economists began to factor World War III into their forecasts for the coming years. While the architects of Putin's reforms in the early 2000s, Alexei Kudrin and German Gref, clutched their heads in disbelief and publicly stated that Russia was on the brink of disaster, their "pupils" reinvented themselves as semi-nationalists. Economics minister Alexei Ulyukayev stated at a liberal economics conference in January 2016 that all Western economic forecasts were incorrect, the 2000s were gone for good, there would be no "business as usual" ever again, and the "new normal" was here to stay. He also recalled that as a child he had woken up every morning with the thought "How lucky I am to live in the Soviet Union!" He wanted everyone to embrace that feeling again.

Domestic policy experts from Vyacheslav Volodin's circle at the Kremlin began to (only half) joke about what repressive measures should be applied to the intelligentsia if war was to break out. The "fifth column" could be tolerated in peacetime, but wartime restrictions would soon be required—otherwise the war would be lost. Playtime was over. And by 2016 the stakes were even higher, since it was a Duma election year.

Bashar al-Assad had been warmly received in the Kremlin in October 2015—his first visit to Moscow since the start of the civil war in Syria. "Finally, you understand," he told Russian diplomats. But even he could not realize the extent to which the new Russia had fulfilled his long-cherished hopes.

CONCLUSION

PUTIN THE SAINT

On May 11, 2000, four days after Vladimir Putin's first inauguration, the film *Brat 2* (Brother 2) was released. The sequel to 1997's crime thriller *Brat*, it tells the story of a veteran of the Chechen war who travels to America to help the brother of a dead friend. There he does battle with the Ukrainian mafia ("You bastards are gonna pay for Sevastopol!" he shouts), tangles with Chicago police ("Are you gangsters?" "No, we're Russians"), and rescues compatriots in need ("In war Russians don't abandon their own"). At his most philosophical, the protagonist asks rhetorically: "Tell me, American, what is power? Is it really money? Bro said it was money. You've got a lot of money, and what of it? I think truth is power. Whoever has truth on his side is stronger."

Russian cinema at the time was in a poor state. Few films were being made, and the public was not interested. But *Brat 2* became a huge hit. In 2015 the mix of anti-Americanism and straight-talking patriotism was the political mainstream, but fifteen years earlier it had been fresh. There had been no need for state directives back then. People themselves had "ordered" *Brat 2*, which captured the mood of the crisis-ridden country.

The film made a deep impression on many viewers, including President Putin and FSB head Nikolai Patrushev. They both loved to quote the film in interviews: "Tell me, American, what is power?" The ingrained anti-Americanism epitomized by *Brat 2* dovetailed with Patrushev's worldview and his political interests.

Members of Putin's inner circle say that Nikolai Patrushev is Russia's most underestimated public figure. He has been the nerve center of most of Putin's special operations—the annexation of Crimea, for instance.

Patrushev was in no way Putin's man, even though he had been the latter's deputy at the FSB. Putin is said not to have wanted Patrushev to succeed him as head of the organization. But Patrushev dug in. It was he who went on to feed Putin stories about enemies in the woodwork, saying that the Americans were not to be trusted and that the FSB was the president's only real power base.

In the 2000s FSB chief Patrushev was one of the most non-public public figures in the Russian government. In one interview he described the FSB as Russia's "new nobility," yet in general his political views remained unexpressed.[1] He maintained a pointed silence on terrorist acts committed on Russian soil, even though his department was responsible for dealing with them.

In 2008 the newly inaugurated president, Dmitry Medvedev, dismissed Nikolai Patrushev from the post of FSB director (allegedly due to serious illness) and transferred him to the less accountable position of Security Council secretary. But Patrushev soon overcame his "ailment," and on Putin's return to the Kremlin he resumed his boisterous political activity. In the wake of the annexation of Crimea he began to comment on matters of Russian security and foreign policy, which previously had been the exclusive realm of President Putin and Foreign Minister Lavrov. He became Russia's top hawk and a cheerleader for anti-Westernism and anti-Americanism inside the Russian leadership. Only he was allowed to publicly expose the global conspiracy.

On October 15, 2014, the state-owned newspaper *Rossiyskaya Gazeta* published an interview with him—a manifesto entitled "Cold War Two." That is roughly when the rising anti-American table talk turned into an academic subject and was presented as Russia's new official ideology.

In that interview, Patrushev expounded his own version of the modern history of Russia. The Soviet Union had collapsed as a result of a plot hatched by Zbigniew Brzezinski and the CIA to weaken the Soviet economy, he said. But the collapse of the Soviet Union did not mark the end of the Cold War. The United States then set itself the objective of dismembering Russia: the West had deliberately provoked a war in Chechnya ("extremists and their adherents were supported by the US and British intelligence services, as well as allies in Europe and the Islamic world"), and Washington spent the entire post-Soviet period laying the groundwork for the crisis in Ukraine ("The upcoming generation in Ukraine was poisoned with hatred for Russia and the mythology of 'European values'"). But the West's true purpose was to strike a blow to Russia ("Even without the calamity in Ukraine, they would have found another pretext to intensify their policy of 'containing' Russia").[2]

In subsequent interviews Patrushev added to the accusations against the United States—from the creation of ISIS to the revival of Nazism in the Baltic States and Ukraine. He frequently cited former US secretary of state Madeleine Albright, who is alleged to have said that it was "unjust" that such vast and resource-rich areas as Siberia and the Russian Far East should be "under Moscow's rule."[3] There is no evidence that the former secretary of state made any such statement, however, and Albright herself denies it. In July 2015 journalists uncovered the source of the myth: a former officer in the Russian secret services alleged in 2007 that the Federal Guard Service of the Russian Federation used psychics to read the thoughts of Western politicians. One of their targets was Albright, who apparently *thought* that the riches of Siberia should not belong to Russia.

It seems that the Russian leadership was duped by its own propaganda. Petty gossip was no longer just the preserve of old ladies and the television channel RT (formerly Russia Today), which seduces viewers with conspiracy theories from around the world. Russia's top officials were now indulging in it too.

It was not the first time in Russia that a historical myth had influenced domestic policy. At the end of the nineteenth century, for example, a fake document entitled *The Protocols of the Elders of Zion* appeared in the Russian Empire, allegedly stolen from the personal files of the founder of political Zionism, Theodor Herzl, and supposedly outlining a Jewish plot for global domination. The forgery contributed to the pogroms of Jews in Russia and was reprinted in the United States and (in huge quantities) in Nazi Germany. Similarly, accounts of former CIA director Allen Dulles's plan to "morally corrupt Soviet society" made the rounds in 1990s Russia and became a tenet of post-Soviet anti-Americanism and neo-imperialism.

One prominent statesman (not a *silovik* by any means, but rather a liberal) told me a story about the 1972 treaty between the Soviet Union and the United States to ban biological weapons. Despite signing the treaty, the Soviet Union continued to produce biological weapons. At the end of perestroika Gorbachev closed down the programs and gave access to US inspectors.

At the same time Russian experts carried out checks in the United States. The Americans immediately discovered that the Soviet Union had violated the treaty, while the Russians found nothing.

What was the statesman's conclusion? "The Americans deceived us," he stated categorically. "Of course they had biological weapons. It's just that we didn't find them."

"How can you be so sure?" I asked. "Can't we just assume that the Americans were honest and kept to the agreement?"

"Of course, not," he retorted. "If we secretly violated it, they must have done so too. What, you think they're better than us?"

Perhaps the anti-Westernism of Russian politicians is not paranoia but shrewdness. They know their electorate and want to find common language. Even since the Bolotnaya protests of 2011–2012 they have become focused on the broad masses, who love conspiracy theories and dislike America. Moreover, Russian leaders know that if they do not offer television viewers a simple and plausible answer to pressing geopolitical issues, the people will draw their own (far worse) conclusions.

But such analysis is in itself a conspiracy theory. There is no evidence that Russian officials are so crafty. Most likely they really do believe in their fictions.

FRIENDS FOREVER

If this book were to be continued, the protagonist of the next chapter would be Nikolay Patrushev. And who would be after him? Vladimir Putin has many friends: Yuri Kovalchuk, Arkady Rotenberg, Gennady Timchenko, and cellist Sergey Roldugin—the last a central figure in the Panama Papers scandal of spring 2016 and the so-called secret caretaker of Putin's wealth. Each is surely waiting in the wings. But no doubt Putin's buddies had never had real political influence. They go to the sauna together, or play hockey together, or even take care of his property—but he would never ask for their advice about world policy.

There is a rumor among those who knew Putin during his first presidential term that he did not want to run for a second and wished to be rid of the burden of the presidency. It is said that Putin's inner circle spent considerable time and effort persuading him not to step down. "Volodya [Vladimir] will never harm himself" is a phrase attributed to Putin's friend Yury Kovalchuk, who, with help from others, allegedly convinced the president to stay. They explained to Putin that he had to remain, since leaving would be dangerous. Some allege that it was Nikolai Patrushev who persuaded Putin that his departure would be fraught with monstrous upheavals.

Putin's close circle of friends and colleagues became even tighter throughout Putin's presidential and prime ministerial tenures, shielding him ever more from reality—in both his and their interests. They tried to convince Putin that he was Atlas: if he walked away, the sky would come crashing to the ground.

For them, it was true. The primary source of their well-being lay in their proximity to the president. "If not Putin, then who?" was the slogan of pro-government rallies (nicknamed "Putings") in 2012. Over the past fifteen years perhaps the majority of the Russian population has come to ask the same question.

Many members of the inner circle have been hit by Western sanctions and deprived of the opportunity to travel abroad, where they have family and business interests. Nevertheless, Putin's courtiers have kept their grumbling fairly quiet.

KING FOREVER

While this book was being written, the Russian economy continued to shrink—as surely as the magic shagreen from Balzac's *La Peau de Chagrin*. All the while big business radiated nothing but calm and serenity. Hypothetically the money in Russia's coffers could last for a long time. If oil prices suddenly rise, the situation could rectify itself. If not, then welfare benefits might be cut or taxes (particularly on the oil industry) could rise. As a last resort, the proceeds of large resource-extraction companies might be seized. Business leaders generally understand that some or all of their property could at some point be expropriated in the interests of the state. They have long since come to terms with that fact. It is often said that Russia's top businesspeople are not billionaires but simply work with billions of dollars in assets. They manage what Vladimir Putin allows them to manage.

No one I interviewed sees any prospect of change. Or rather, they see the prospect of change only in one circumstance, which dare not speak its name.

Instead, they resort to euphemisms: "when the black swan flies," "when the president visits Alpha Centauri," "when the heavens fall." They all refer to the time when Putin is no longer, well, Putin.

They are wrong, of course. It is a peculiar myth that everything in Russia depends on Putin and that without him everything will change.

This book demonstrates that Putin, as we imagine him, does not actually exist. It was not Putin who brought Russia to its current state. For a long time he resisted the metamorphosis, but then he succumbed, realizing that it was simpler that way.

In the very beginning Putin did not believe that Russia is surrounded by enemies on all sides. He did not have plans to close down independent TV channels. He had no intention of supporting Viktor Yanukovych. He did not even want to hold the Olympics in Sochi. But in trying to divine the intentions of their leader, his associates effectively materialized their own wishes.

Today's image of Putin as a formidable Russian tsar was constructed by his entourage, Western partners, and journalists, often without his say. In one of the most famous photographs there is of Putin, he has the mien of a haughty ruler, the "military emperor of the world." But that is not Putin himself, merely *Time* magazine's 2007 Person of the Year staring out from the cover.

Each of us invented our own Putin. And we may yet create many more.

NOTES

CHAPTER 1

1. V. Borodulin, "15 000 000 000 долларов потеряла Россия благодаря Примакову" [$15 billion lost to Russia due to Primakov], *Kommersant*, March 24, 1999.

2. E. Tregubova, "Опера на высшем уровне: В Мариинке разыграли дипломатический" [Opera at the highest level], *Kommersant*, March 14, 2000.

3. Tony Blair, *A Journey: My Political Life* (New York: Knopf, 2010), 484.

4. Amelia Gentleman, "Putin Aims to Bridge the Gap," *The Guardian*, April 26, 2000.

5. Speaker's Advisory Group on Russia, *Russia's Road to Corruption: How the Clinton Administration Exported Government Instead of Free Enterprise and Failed the Russian People* (Washington, DC: US House of Representatives, 2000). Also available at http://fas.org/news/russia/2000/russia.

6. Peter Baker, "Blunt Political Assessments in Bill Clinton Transcripts," *New York Times*, January 7, 2016.

7. Caroline Wyatt, "Bush and Putin: Best of Friends," BBC News, June 16, 2001.

8. "Выступление министра иностранных дел Российской Федерации И. С. Иванова в программе 'Народ и Власть' радиостанции 'Маяк'" [Interview of foreign minister of the Russian Federation Igor Ivanov], Radio Mayak, March 16, 2002.

CHAPTER 2

1. "Стенограмма встречи президента России В. Путина с родственниками экипажа подводной лодки Курск 22 августа" [Transcript of the meeting of Vladimir Putin, president of Russia, with the relatives of the crew of the submarine *Kursk* on August 22], www.gazeta.ru/stenogram.shtml.

2. B. Berezovsky, "Президенту Российской Федерации Владимиру Путину: О свободе слова и акциях ОРТ" [To the president of the Russian Federation, Vladimir Putin, on freedom of speech and the actions of ORT], *Kommersant*, September 5, 2000.

3. "Десять секунд Путина" [Putin: ten seconds], posted October 19, 2012 [speech on Chekist's Day, December 1999], https://youtu.be/T76KhRl0IJw.

4. Nikolai Patrushev, "Тайна Андропова" [Andropov's mystery], *Rossiyskaya Gazeta*, June 15, 2004.

5. Independent Inquiry Committee into the United Nations Oil-for-Food Programme, *Manipulation of the Oil-for-Food Programme by the Iraqi Regime*, October 27, 2005, https://web.archive.org/web/20130823070841/http://www.iic-offp.org/documents/IIC%20Final%20Report%2027Oct2005.pdf.

6. Anna Politkovskaya, "Один Из Группы Террористов Уцелел. Мы Его Нашли" [One of a group of terrorists escaped; we found him], *Novaya Gazeta*, April 28, 2003.

7. "Мы не думали, что так скоро" [We didn't think it would happen so soon], *Kommersant*, January 20, 2003.

8. Renat Abdullin and Alexander Korzun, "Тони Блэр: столь хороших отношений у нас еще не было" [Tony Blair: We've never had such good relations], *Kommersant*, June 24, 2003.

9. "Meeting with Scientists, Public Figures and Businessmen of Scotland," June 25, 2003, http://en.kremlin.ru/events/president/transcripts/22037.

CHAPTER 3

1. John Browne, *Beyond Business: An Inspirational Memoir from a Visionary Leader* (London: Weidenfeld and Nicolson, 2010), 145.

2. Arkady Ostrovsky, "Father to the Oligarchs," *Financial Times*, November 13, 2004.

3. T. Lysova, "Ну вы понимаете, что я не буду сидеть тихо?" [Well, you know, I'm not going to sit quietly], interview with Mikhail Khodorkovsky, *Vedomosti*, September 22, 2014.

4. M. Kasyanov, Без Путина. Политические диалоги с Евгением Киселевым [Without Putin: political dialogues with Yevgeny Kiselyov] (Moscow: Novaya Gazeta, 2009).

5. National Strategy Council, "В России готовится олигархический переворот" [Russia prepares oligarchic coup], Utro.ru, May 26, 2003.

6. Gleb Pavlovsky, "О негативных последствиях 'летнего наступления' оппозиционного курсу президента РФ меньшинства" [Negative consequences of the "summer attack" of the minority that opposes the president's course], *Novaya Gazeta*, September 2, 2013.

CHAPTER 4

1. Vladimir Putin (interviewed by Nataliya Gevorkyan, Natalya Timakova, and Andrei Kolesnikov), *First Person: An Astonishingly Frank Self-Portrait by Russia's President*, trans. Catherine A. Fitzpatrick (New York: PublicAffairs, 2000), 202–203.

2. P. Netreba, "Отставка Волошина совпала с концом эпохи Ельцина" [Voloshin's resignation coincided with the end of the Yeltsin era], *Kommersant*, November 3, 2003.

3. A. Kolesnikov, "Кремлевские измельчали" [Those from the Kremlin got smaller], *Kommersant*, March 26, 2004.

4. Y. Savelyev, "Беслан: правда заложников" [Beslan: the truth of the hostages], report to the Parliamentary Commission of Inquiry, http://pravdabeslana.ru/doklad/oglavlenie.htm.

5. "Address by President Vladimir Putin," September 4, 2004, http://en.kremlin.ru/events/president/transcripts/22589.

CHAPTER 5

1. "Лужков готов пожертвовать кепкой ради Януковича" [Luzhkov is ready to sacrifice his cap for Yanukovich], RIA Novosty, November 28, 2004.

2. A. Stepanov, "Conference in Severodonetsk: A New Pereyaslav Rada?" Russkaya Liniya, November 30, 2004, http://rusk.ru/st.php?idar=102763.

CHAPTER 6

1. Mikhail Shevchuk and Dimitry Kamyshev, "Обыкновенный 'Нашизм.' Кремль создает новое молодежное движение" [Ordinary "Nashism": the Kremlin creates a new youth movement], *Kommersant*, February 21, 2005.

2. Ibid.

3. Oleg Kashin, "Знать 'Наших'" [Meet Nashi], *Kommersant*, February 28, 2005.

4. Oleg Kashin, "Отряд властоногих" [Order of the imperious], *Kommersant*, July 25, 2005.

5. Oleg Kashin, "Владимир Путин позажигал со своими" [Vladimir Putin had fun with his own], *Kommersant*, July 27, 2005.

6. "Стенограмма выступления В.Ю. Суркова на закрытом заседании Генерального совета объединения Деловая Россия" [Transcript of V. Surkov's speech at the Business Russia conference], May 17, 2005.

7. Angus Roxburgh, *The Strongman: Vladimir Putin and the Struggle for Russia* (London: I. B. Tauris, 2012), 108.

8. Ibid., 112.

9. George W. Bush, Second Inaugural Address, January 20, 2005.

10. Vladimir Putin, "Annual Address to the Federal Assembly of the Russian Federation," April 25, 2005, http://en.kremlin.ru/events/president/transcripts/22931.

CHAPTER 7

1. Igor Tomberg, "Baltic Gas Pipeline: Moscow Turns the Tables," RIA Novosti, September 15, 2005, http://sptnkne.ws/bcBq.

2. "Лукашенко назвал 'самый дурацкий проект России'" [Lukashenko named Russia's "most idiotic project to date"], Lenta.ru, January 14, 2007.

3. "Владимиру Путину вручили засекреченный подарок" [Vladimir Putin has a secret gift], VZ.ru, October 8, 2005.

4. "Interview to the Spanish Media," February 7, 2006, http://en.kremlin.ru/events/president/transcripts/23419.

CHAPTER 8

1. P. Stolyarov, "Владимир Путин выбирает преемника: пока только Владимиру Устинову" [Vladimir Putin chooses a successor for Vladimir Ustinov], *Kommersant*, June 5, 2006.

2. "Putin's Prepared Remarks at 43rd Munich Conference on Security Policy," *Washington Post*, February 12, 2007.

3. "I'm the World's Only True Democrat, Says Putin," Reuters, June 4, 2007.

4. "Speech at the Military Parade Celebrating the 62nd Anniversary of Victory in the Great Patriotic War," May 9, 2007, http://en.kremlin.ru/events/president/transcripts/24238.

5. Ekaterina Savina and Andrew Kozenko, "Эстафета поклонений: Сергей Иванов провел встречу с молодежными движениями" [Worship relay: Sergei Ivanov meets with youth movements], *Kommersant*, June 7, 2007.

CHAPTER 9

1. "Interview by Dmitry Medvedev: Dmitry Medvedev Gave an Interview to Russia Today and First Informational Caucasus Television (Kanal PIK) Channels and the Ekho Moskvy Radio Station," August 5, 2011, http://en.kremlin.ru/events/president/news/12204.

2. Condoleezza Rice, *No Higher Honor* (New York: Crown, 2011), 685.

3. Ibid., 686.

4. Ibid., 688.

5. Ibid.

6. Mikhail Zygar, "На Михаила Саакашвили накладывают вето: Москва предложит Западу сменить режим в Тбилиси" [A veto over Mikheil Saakashvili], *Kommersant*, August 12, 2008.

7. Rice, *No Higher Honor*, 688.

8. "Interview by Dmitry Medvedev."

9. "Presidential Statement on Georgia," August 11, 2008, www.c-span.org/video/?280408-1/presidental-statement-georgia.

10. Vladimir Solovyov, "Демарш-бросок. Российские танки вышли на подступы к Тбилиси" [Throw maneuver: Russian tanks reach the approaches to Tbilisi], *Kommersant*, August 12, 2008.

11. "Владимир Путин: 'Иначе придется послать доктора и зачистить проблемы'" [Vladimir Putin: "Otherwise we'll send a doctor to sort him out"], *Komsomolskaya Pravda*, July 25, 2008.

12. A. Kolesnikov, "Россия нашла стратегическую партнершу: Это Юлия Тимошенко" [Russia has found a strategic partner: Yulia Tymoshenko], *Kommersant*, October 3, 2008.

13. "Газовая проблема связана с политической борьбой на Украине—Путин" [Gas problem is related to political struggle in Ukraine: Putin], RIA Novosti, January 8, 2009.

CHAPTER 11

1. M. Chizhikov and O. Vandysheva, "Президент Венесуэлы Уго ЧАВЕС: Россия освободила нас от блокады" [President Chávez: Russia freed us from the blockade], *Komsomolskaya Pravda*, July 28, 2006.

2. M. Kvasha, "Партию для нас олицетворяет силовой блок, который возглавляет Игорь Иванович Сечин" [It is Igor Ivanovich Sechin who symbolizes a party for us], *Kommersant*, November 30, 2007.

3. Viktor Cherkesov, "Черкесов В. Нельзя допустить, чтобы воины превратились в торговцев" [We must not allow warriors to be turned into traders], *Kommersant*, October 9, 2007.

CHAPTER 12

1. Polina Romanova, "'Так проходит мирская слава': Полковник Каддафи погиб" ["Thus passes worldly glory": Colonel Gaddafi was killed], *Kommersant*, October 21, 2011.

2. "United Russia Party Congress," September 24, 2011, http://en.kremlin.ru/events/president/news/12802.

CHAPTER 13

1. "Выступление Алексея Навального на Чистых Прудах" [Speech by Alexei Navalny, Chistye Prudy], YouTube, December 5, 2011, https://youtu.be/WkgEonmQ34k.

2. M. D. Prokhorov, "Спасибо всем, кто поддержал" [Thanks to everyone who supported], LiveJournal post, December 14, 2011, http://md-prokhorov.livejournal.com/84523.html?mode=reply#add_comment.

3. E. Pismennaya, Письменная Е. Система Кудрина [Kudrin's system] (Moscow: Mann, Ivanov, and Ferber, 2013), 216.

4. Ibid.

5. Maria Tabak and Denis Voroshilov, "СК торопится, громко заявляя о злоупотреблениях в 'Сколково'—Сурков" [Investigative committee rushes to announce crimes in Skolkovo—Surkov], RIA Novosti, January 5, 2013.

6. Vladimir Markin, "Глядя из Лондона, на зеркало неча пенять" [The view from London: don't blame the mirror if your face is ugly], *Izvestia*, May 7, 2013.

CHAPTER 14

1. "РПЦ попросит за Pussy Riot" [ROC asks for Pussy Riot], interview with Tikhon Shevkunov, *Here and Now*, TV Rain, August 17, 2012.

2. Luke Harding and Owen Bowcott, "Roman Abramovich Wins Court Battle with Boris Berezovsky," *The Guardian*, August 31, 2012.

CHAPTER 15

1. "News Conference of Vladimir Putin," December 20, 2012, http://en.kremlin.ru/events/president/news/17173.

2. "A Conversation with Dmitry Medvedev: Prime Minister Dmitry Medvedev Interviewed by Five TV Channels," December 7, 2012, http://government.ru/en/news/6550.

CHAPTER 16

1. "Orthodox-Slavic Values: The Foundation of Ukraine's Civilisational Choice Conference," July 27, 2013, http://en.kremlin.ru/events/president/news/18961.

2. Sonia Koshkina, Кошкина С. Майдан. Нерассказанная история [Maidan: the untold story] (Kiev: Bright Star, 2015).

3. "Вся правда о страшном секрете Януковича расказаный Ангеле Меркель" [The whole truth about the terrible secret Yanukovych told Angela Merkel], YouTube, posted December 1, 2013, https://youtu.be/1QNFDPcPm3U.

4. "Answers to Journalists' Questions," February 17, 2014, http://en.kremlin.ru/events/president/news/20268.

5. Koshkina, [Maidan: the untold story].

6. "Interview to Channel One, Rossiya-1, NTV and RBC TV Channels," February 25, 2014, http://en.kremlin.ru/events/president/transcripts/20336.

CHAPTER 17

1. *Crimea: The Way Home*, Rossiya 1 TV film, 2015, https://russia.tv/brand/show/brand_id/59195.

2. Emma Reynolds, "Putin Is Becoming Like Tsar Nicholas and the West Is Losing Out, Warns Czech Foreign Minister," *Daily Mail*, September 27, 2012.

3. White House, Office of the Press Secretary, "Remarks by President Obama and Prime Minister Netanyahu Before Bilateral Meeting," March 3, 2014.

4. "Vladimir Putin Answered Journalists' Questions on the Situation in Ukraine," March 4, 2014, http://en.kremlin.ru/events/president/news/20366.

5. "Direct Line with Vladimir Putin," April 17, 2014, http://en.kremlin.ru/events/president/news/20796.

6. A. Prokhanov, "Кто ты, 'Стрелок'?" [Who are you, "Shooter"?], interview with the former minister of defense of the Donetsk People's Republic, *Zavtra*, November 20, 2014.

7. Ibid.

8. "Террорист Гиркин: Предупреждали же—не летайте в нашем небе" [Terrorist Girkin warned, "Don't fly in our skies"], Charter 97, July 17, 2014, https://charter97.org/ru/news/2014/7/17/107391.

9. "СБУ перехватила переговоры Пушилина,Бородая,Пургина о Стрелкове" [Ukraine's security service has tapped telephone conversations between Pushilin, Boroday, Purgin about Strelkov], YouTube, posted July 27, 2014, https://youtu.be/WbUP88finuA.

10. Prokhanov, [Who are you, “Shooter”?].

11. “Путин поставил в храме на Воробьевых горах свечку за погибших на Украине” [Putin lit a candle in the cathedral on Vorobyovy Hills for those who were killed in Ukraine], *Rossiyskaya Gazeta*, October 9, 2014.

12. Prokhanov, [Who are you, “Shooter”?].

13. Anna Samelyuk, “‘Сражаясь за Новороссию, мы сражаемся за Россию’—эксклюзивное интервью Игоря Стрелкова” [“Fighting for Novorossiya, we are fighting for Russia”: an interview with Igor Strelkov], Russkiy Vysna, September 10, 2014, http://rg.ru/2014/09/10/svechka-anons.html.

CHAPTER 18

1. Transcript of the meeting of the Federation Council, January 3, 2014.

2. “Address by President of the Russian Federation,” March 18, 2014, http://en.kremlin.ru/events/president/news/20603.

3. Tony Blair, *A Journey: My Political Life* (New York: Vintage, 2011), 484.

4. “Address by President of the Russian Federation.”

5. “Putin Q&A: Full Transcript,” Person of the Year special issue, *Time*, December 19, 2007.

6. “Address by President of the Russian Federation.”

7. “Putin Q&A: Full Transcript.”

8. “Сурков расценивает санкции США как признание своих заслуг перед РФ” [Surkov regards US sanctions as a recognition of his services to the Russian Federation], RIA Novosti, March 17, 2014.

9. Grigory Naberezhnov and Natalia Starostina, “Герман Греф призвал не мотивировать людей ГУЛАГом” [Gref proposed not to motivate people by Gulag], RBC, October 2, 2014.

10. [Interview of Alexei Kudrin by Vladimir Posner], *Posner*, Channel 1, October 7, 2014, http://www.1tv.ru/shows/pozner/vypuski/gost-aleksey-kudrin-pozner-vypusk-ot-07-10-2014.

CHAPTER 19

1. A. Nemtsova, “Ramzan Kadyrov Talks About Chechnya’s Future,” *Newsweek*, October 24, 2010.

2. “Путин: все наши беды—в нас самих (1999 г.)” [Putin: We are the reason for our problems], YouTube, posted December 21, 2015, https://youtu.be/Pc7LMbIGqb4.

3. “Клятва Кадырова. Размещено в Сообществе ‘Поговорим?!’” [Kadyrov’s oath], YouTube, posted December 28, 2014, https://youtu.be/rjLw7OEGmmc.

4. “Кадыров заявил о готовности чеченских добровольцев выполнять приказы президента России” [Kadyrov says Chechen volunteers ready to carry out Russian president’s orders], Interfax, December 28, 2014.

5. https://www.instagram.com/p/z-dKqICRua.

6. https://www.instagram.com/p/0C36UgiRh_.

7. https://www.instagram.com/p/0LN4VWCRuj.

8. "Интервью Владимира Путина чеченскому ТВ 23.08.2011 г. (Альви Каримов-пресс-секретарь Р.Кадырова)" [Interview of Vladimir Putin with Chechen TV], posted September 18, 2011, http://my.mail.ru/mail/fira70/video/8/771.html.

9. https://www.instagram.com/p/0Syp22CRi6.

10. https://www.instagram.com/p/02roHhCRly.

11. https://www.instagram.com/p/1L4_u6iRh1.

CHAPTER 20

1. Mikhail Zygar, "'Мы заранее знали, что Запад стремится блокировать Россию,'" interview with Bashar al-Assad ["We knew in advance that the West was seeking to block Russia"], *Kommersant*, August 20, 2008.

2. White House, Office of the Vice President, "Remarks by the Vice President at the Munich Security Conference," February 7, 2015, http://1.usa.gov/1RZqJKN.

3. "Merkel Says 'Weapons Won't Help' Resolve Eastern Ukraine Crisis," Deutsche Welle, February 7, 2015; Tom Parfitt and Justin Huggler, "Ukraine Crisis: Do Not Try to Scare Putin, Warns Merkel," *Telegraph*, February 7, 2015.

CONCLUSION

1. Andrei Soldatov and Irina Borogan, *The New Nobility: The Restoration of Russia's Security State and the Enduring Legacy of the KGB* (New York: PublicAffairs, 2011).

2. I. Egorov, "Вторая 'холодная': 'Отрезвление' украинцев будет жестким и болезненным—интервью с Николаем Патрушевым" [The second "cold war": an interview with Nikolai Patrushev], *Rossiyskaya Gazeta*, October 15, 2014.

3. I. Egorov, "'Кто управляет хаосом': США пытаются одолеть кризис за счет других, разрушая целые страны—интервью с Николаем Патрушевым" ["Who controls the chaos"—an interview with Nikolai Patrushev], *Rossiyskaya Gazeta*, February 10, 2015.

INDEX

Mikhail Zygar is the former editor in chief of the only independent TV station in Russia, TV Rain (Dozhd). The channel's coverage of politically sensitive issues, such as the Moscow street protests in 2011 and 2012 and the conflict in Ukraine, has been dramatically different from the official coverage by Russia's national television stations. Despite immense pressure from the government, the channel continues to operate and is the most popular Russian-language channel in many of the former USSR republics. In 2014, Zygar received an award from the ZEIT-Stiftung Ebelin und GerdBucerius fund for his work to preserve freedom of speech in Russia. The Committee to Protect Journalists in the United States also awarded him the International Press Freedom Award, and Vice news recently named him "the last journalist in Russia." Previously, Zygar worked for *Newsweek* Russia and the business daily *Kommersant*, where he covered the conflicts in Palestine, Lebanon, Iraq, Serbia, and Kosovo. He is a fluent English-speaker.

Photograph by James Hill

PublicAffairs is a publishing house founded in 1997. It is a tribute to the standards, values, and flair of three persons who have served as mentors to countless reporters, writers, editors, and book people of all kinds, including me.

I. F. STONE, proprietor of *I. F. Stone's Weekly*, combined a commitment to the First Amendment with entrepreneurial zeal and reporting skill and became one of the great independent journalists in American history. At the age of eighty, Izzy published *The Trial of Socrates*, which was a national bestseller. He wrote the book after he taught himself ancient Greek.

BENJAMIN C. BRADLEE was for nearly thirty years the charismatic editorial leader of *The Washington Post*. It was Ben who gave the *Post* the range and courage to pursue such historic issues as Watergate. He supported his reporters with a tenacity that made them fearless and it is no accident that so many became authors of influential, best-selling books.

ROBERT L. BERNSTEIN, the chief executive of Random House for more than a quarter century, guided one of the nation's premier publishing houses. Bob was personally responsible for many books of political dissent and argument that challenged tyranny around the globe. He is also the founder and longtime chair of Human Rights Watch, one of the most respected human rights organizations in the world.

• • •

For fifty years, the banner of Public Affairs Press was carried by its owner Morris B. Schnapper, who published Gandhi, Nasser, Toynbee, Truman, and about 1,500 other authors. In 1983, Schnapper was described by *The Washington Post* as "a redoubtable gadfly." His legacy will endure in the books to come.

Peter Osnos, *Founder and Editor-at-Large*

jet. More retribution to be taken, more to be earned. And then the vibration vanishes.

She pulls him toward her—or does he pull her? She cannot tell anymore to whom each movement belongs. Who grasps, who clings, who enters or is entered.

When she finally emerges, her cheeks are damp and this man she is with is wholly Goronsky in scent and shape and spirit. Marcus is gone. She knows with an inner certainty, a return of intuition, that this time it is absolute. There will be no more temporary reprieves. No journals in the mail, no hint of Marcus's voice in her ear. She feels that loss in her throat, but it is lacking the sharp edge of despair. "Cheers ciao au revoir," she says softly.

She tries to pull away. Goronsky won't let her. He is holding her palm to the light, studying the lines there. "We still have fifteen minutes," he says. "Thank God for a delayed flight."

"Goronsky." She leans on an elbow. "I'm not going."

As soon as she says it, she's relieved. And disappointed. He stares at her. He opens his mouth but doesn't speak. For a breath, his eyes are completely naked. Then he rolls on his back and stares up at the ceiling. "I knew that."

"You couldn't—" She takes a breath. "You couldn't have known." She didn't know herself until moments ago.

"You didn't bring anything except your backpack."

He's right, Caddie realizes. She's left her bag at home.

"You're more transparent than you realize," Goronsky says.

She sits up. "You've always recognized me."

He turns his back to her, his face toward the window. "The first time . . ."

"At the hospital."

He shakes his head. "Maybe a month before that. You were interviewing Palestinians at a checkpoint. You were with the photographer. I watched for a few minutes. You were serious, and then you were laughing."

"Marcus always laughed."

"You, too." He rolls on his side, facing her. "It was clear that you belonged—the way you stood, the expression on your face. That's what I wanted. That's why it stuck with me."

She takes his face between her hands.

"And so?" he asks.

She gestures with her head toward the door.

He pulls away from her. "It's a mistake," he says. "There's something between us. Something that doesn't fit into words. A tiny plant that might grow into a tree, if we water it."

"You've gone places," she says, "I don't want to go. Not anymore."

"I can come back from there, Caddie."

She sees herself reflected in his eyes. "When you get back," she whispers, "call me."

He looks away. And, looking away, he nods.

THE AIR FEELS CLAMMY as she walks down the Mount of Olives past scattered graves, stones the color of skin and blood, twisted olive trees hundreds of years old. At a distance, soaring edifices bear down on squat ones; flat rooftops press against domes. A few buildings lean apart, allowing others to be wedged between them, as messy as love triangles. The sky is brooding, but a momentary shaft of sun breaks through to illuminate the golden dome of Al Aqsa Mosque. Church bells from the Basilica of the Agony overtake the hush of Kidron Valley. The resonance brushes her face, then floats away on an indiscernible breeze, like soap bubbles.

The bells. They will be first on her list of grounds for refusing New York. Not the bells alone, but the intoxicating brew of their peals merging with the cadenced Moslem calls to prayer and the guttural allure of Hebrew. Another reason: those voices she's now ready to fully hear. The Sarahs, the Halimas. The Marcuses. A third: the flawed words themselves. The words that show how violence manipulates and corrupts and finally transforms. The words she hasn't written yet, but will. She will. Maybe even today, after she visits the mourning house.

She has, after all, a survivor's pact with this land: both are tainted now, but both will endure. That's the payback—and the revenge. She'll find a different way to explain it to Mike, though. Something cleaner, more straightforward. There are, she'll say, two types of people. There are those who leave, and those who stay.